Discretion and Public Benefit
in a Regulatory Agency

Discretion and Public Benefit in a Regulatory Agency

The Australian Authorisation Process

Vijaya Nagarajan

Australian
National
University

E PRESS

Published by ANU E Press
The Australian National University
Canberra ACT 0200, Australia
Email: anuepress@anu.edu.au
This title is also available online at http://epress.anu.edu.au

National Library of Australia Cataloguing-in-Publication entry

Author:	Nagarajan, Vijaya.
Title:	Discretion and public benefit in a regulatory agency / Vijaya Nagarajan.
ISBN:	9781922144355 (pbk.) 9781922144362 (ebook)
Notes:	Includes bibliographical references.
Subjects:	Australian Competition and Consumer Commission. Administrative agencies--Australia. Independent regulatory commissions--Australia.
Dewey Number:	351.0994

Cover design and layout by ANU E Press

Contents

Preface

The Australian process for the competition regulator to authorise anti-competitive conduct on the basis of public benefit is a distinctive one. The path followed by the regulator in its early years was significantly influenced by its chairman, who established open lines of communication with a view to avoiding litigation, while at once scolding and cajoling, using discretion innovatively, and bringing business on board to see the underlying sense of the legislation. The philosophy of dialogue and responsiveness of these early years fell away during the 1990s as the regulator took on the responsibilities of a deregulated market and a decentred regulatory environment.

Using a combination of qualitative and quantitative methodologies, including an examination of authorisation determinations over three decades and interviews with past and current staff of the Australian Competition and Consumer Commission (ACCC), this book studies the manner in which the term public benefit has been interpreted. Although the role of economic efficiency factors has always been important in these determinations, so too have the non-economic efficiency factors, including the encouragement of governance networks, equitable dealings as a means of monitoring powerful players in a decentred market, and the incorporation of a dispute resolution mechanism into codes of conduct. The meta-regulatory shift towards procedural regulation of self-regulation by the ACCC can only be explained as a triumph of practice over theory. Extemporised practice has resulted in inclusivity deficits that have grown over time. This approach, while experimental and outcome driven, remains ad hoc and under-theorised, and comes at a great cost. It is proposed that the ACCC should reassess its performance, developing overarching principles, which are founded on a discourse that is more universal than economic efficiency and with a fundamental commitment to inclusivity. With this in mind a principle-based approach consisting of nine principles is suggested.

The first principle provides a broader theoretical framework for defining public benefit by first identifying the main human rights that embody public benefits and secondly, by extracting the immanent rights that have been recognised by the regulator in practice. These two sets of rights are used to create a set of heuristics, which become principles defining public benefit, while providing sufficient flexibility to accommodate regulatory challenges. This book addresses the inclusivity deficit by developing a further eight principles for promoting responsiveness, incorporating ongoing dialogue and fostering democratic participation. This is based on finding a place for participation by designing strategies for inclusion as well as crafting the art of practice whereby participation by stakeholders is nurtured.

This book, then, brings together the principles defining public benefit and promoting responsiveness and democracy as a set of nine broad principles that can provide the basis of a shared understanding for the trade practices communities. The regulator, in collaboration with these communities, will continue to imbue these principles with inclusive practices and shape these principles to suit the regulatory considerations of our time.

Acknowledgements

There have been many people who have assisted in different ways in the completion of this book and I am grateful to have this opportunity to express my thanks to them.

I am indebted to the people interviewed for this book including Ron Bannerman, past and present staff of the ACCC and members of numerous non-government organisations. Heartfelt thanks go to John Braithwaite whose enthusiasm and generosity is second to none. I would also like to acknowledge Imelda Maher for her assistance with linking past developments in competition policy with present trajectories, and Christine Parker for her thoughtful and generous insights. I am grateful to Natalie Klein and Margaret Thornton for their encouragement and facilitations. Friends and colleagues have talked through, heard about, and read many parts of this book in seminars, over too many coffees and too long lunches. My thanks go to them all and special mention must be made of Paul Ashton, Archana Parashar, Ross Taylor and Annie Wardrop for their constant presence. I am lucky to have three wonderful women in my life for which I am grateful: my mother Nalini and my daughters Jaya and Asha. This book is dedicated to my late father, Radhakrishnan.

1. Competition Policy and the Authorisation Process

Competition law in Australia is spelt out in the *Competition and Consumer Act 2010* (Cth) and its predecessor the *Trade Practices Act 1974* (Cth). It is enforced by the competition watchdog, the Australian Competition and Consumer Commission (ACCC). The competition law provisions that are most familiar to people are those prohibiting mergers, cartel conduct and the proposed criminal penalties for cartel conduct. Much more important and much less well known, however, are the authorisation provisions within the Act. A significant part of the ACCC's work is geared to granting such authorisations. These provisions allow the ACCC to grant immunity from prosecution for a specified period of time and under certain conditions. Authorisation means that otherwise anti-competitive conduct can legally proceed, without the possibility of prosecution by the ACCC. On the one hand, anti-competitive conduct is prohibited by the Act and, on the other, it can be authorised by the regulator. A variety of conduct has been authorised in the past. Agreements between competitors, who share a vertical relationship, to set a levy on the goods they sell to customers has been authorised, as have agreements between companies, in a horizontal relationship, to fix the amount of goods supplied to another retailer, who may also be a competitor. Such agreements are anti-competitive but can be authorised.

The grounds on which authorisation can be granted are governed by the public benefit test.[1] The applicant has to satisfy the ACCC that the public benefit resulting from the proposed conduct outweighs the public detriment that is likely to result from the proposed conduct. The Act offers little guidance on how public benefit should be interpreted or who should be consulted when making the decision. The public benefit test remains vague, the meaning of the words 'public' and 'benefit' are difficult to define and the interpretation of the phrase is left in the hands of the ACCC. This discretion also carries responsibility. There are two main aspects of discretion in the context of the public benefit test that need to be noted. The first arises from the lack of clarity about the meaning of the phrase public benefit. The second aspect is the stakeholders, who should be consulted and whose views should be considered in determining the meaning of the phrase — the significance of this obligation, and how it can be fulfilled, is also unclear.

The meaning of 'public benefit' is a source of considerable debate. Some have argued benefit should refer primarily to economic efficiency factors, such as

---

1   Sections 90(6) and 90(8) *Trade Practices Act 1974* (Cth).

promotion of cost savings or improvement in administrative practices.[2] Others have argued benefits can also include non-efficiency factors such as the creation of jobs in a rural town. Still others have stated public benefits should be able to include factors such as increased personal security or improved environmental conditions.[3] It has also been contended that nothing can be regarded as a public benefit unless it flows through to the public or at the very least to the consumer.[4] These are the vexed questions that the ACCC has had to tackle when exercising its discretion.

The second aspect about discretion is that the ACCC has to decide whom to consult in making the decision about the interpretation of the phrase. The ambit of consultation will inform the meaning of the phrase. The views brought to the ACCC's attention by the applicant seeking the authorisation will be quite different to the views expressed by its competitors. It will be different again from the views of consumers or employees, who may be affected by the decision. Ideally the ACCC might engage with all the stakeholders, fostering participation in the tradition of deliberative democracy, to develop a balanced dialogue to which everyone can lay claim. But of course this ideal is not easily met. Small competitors may not have the time to raise their concerns with the ACCC. Consumers may not have the technical expertise to query the claimed public benefits the applicant may have established by relying on econometric data or expert evidence. Yet these will be the very groups affected by the decision.

This book sets out to explore some theories on how discretion is exercised and compares them to the ACCC's practice. It evaluates the way in which discretion is used by regulatory agencies and goes on to focus on the manner in which the ACCC has used its discretion in interpreting public benefit within the authorisation process.

The Empirical Study

This book relied on an empirical study of authorisation determinations over four decades from 1976 to 2010. The study of public benefit in this book is restricted to the examination of authorisation determinations involving sections 45 and 47 of the *Trade Practices Act*, whereby authorisation can be granted by the Trade

---

2   For example, see Independent Committee of Inquiry into Competition Policy in Australia, Commonwealth of Australia, *National Competition Policy* (1993) [Hilmer Report] 99.

3   See Michal Gal, *Competition Policy for Small Market Economies* (2003) 55.

4   See Rhonda Smith, 'Authorisation and the Trade Practices Act: More about Public Benefit' (2003) 11 *Competition and Consumer Law Journal* 21; John Fingleton and Ali Nikpay, 'Stimulating or Chilling Competition' Office of Fair Trading (United Kingdom) (Paper presented at Fordham Annual Conference on International Antitrust Law and Policy, New York, 25 September 2008) <http://www.oft.gov.uk/news/speeches/2008/0808> at 25 October 2008.

Practices Commission (TPC) or the ACCC under section 90(6). The study does not include mergers, which operate under a different test detailed in section 90(9). The empirical research includes both quantitative and qualitative data. While the analysis relies on ACCC authorisation determinations, court and tribunal decisions generally, it makes special use of 244 authorisation determinations made over seven years. It is also informed by 19 interviews conducted with key people involved in the authorisation process.

The seven years studied are 1976, 1984, 1998, 2003, 2006, 2008 and 2010. The choice of the years was purposive rather than random. These years represent key periods in the development of competition regulation, often reflecting important policy shifts or focus. I have collated the data after taking into account an appropriate time lag to allow for the policy effects to filter through to the authorisation process. The first set of data, from 1976, gives a good understanding of how decisions were made in the early years of the creation of the TPC. The Act was only passed in 1974 after a good deal of disquiet; the 1976 decisions illustrate the contemporary decision-making process, and they act as a basis for comparisons over time. The second set of data comes from 1984, when there was a focus by the new Labor government under Bob Hawke on creating an efficient industrial base in Australia and on economic efficiency and self-regulation. The third set of data comes from 1998 — this year was selected for empirical analysis because it was well into the implementation of national competition policy, which had a significant effect on competition policy and the authorisation process. The fourth and fifth sets of data from 2003 and 2006 examine a period following the deregulation of essential facilities and the increased scope of the Act to regulate the conduct of professionals. Finally, the data in 2008 and 2010 have been collated to closely scrutinise how the ACCC has been trying to encourage a market economy while minimising market failure. Each of the years represents a snapshot of the manner in which the ACCC made its decisions. The objective was to collate data that will allow for an assessment of the ACCC's decision-making over four decades.

There were 35 determinations examined in each of the seven years, with the exception of 2008, in which there were 34 appropriate determinations, making a total of 244 authorisation determinations. It was the year the determination was made that was considered in selecting the determinations for the study, rather than the date the application was lodged. These determinations accounted for over 80 per cent of the total determinations made in the years 1984, 1998, 2003, 2006, 2010 and 100 per cent in 2008. Due to the poor reporting of determinations in 1976, it is difficult to estimate with certainty the number of the commission's determinations.

There were 16 public benefit factors coded for each determination as part of the study and these are contained in Table 1.1. Of these public benefits, 14 were recognised by the ACCC in 1999.[5] Two other public benefits that have been recognised by the ACCC have been added to this list. The ACCC began to actively endorse environmental benefits in 2001 and this has been added to the list as PB11, Steps to protect the environment, in Table 1.1.[6] The ACCC has always recognised that such lists are non-exhaustive[7] and, accordingly, PB16, Other, has been added as a catch-all category, for benefits that do not come into one of the other 15 categories.

Table 1.1: Public benefit (PB) factors examined in the empirical study

Public benefit (PB) no	Meaning
PB1	Economic development, for example, of natural resources through encouraging exploration, research and capital investment
PB2	Industry rationalisation resulting in more efficient allocation of resources and in lower or contained unit production costs
PB3	Expansion of employment or prevention of unemployment in efficient industries
PB4	Expansion of employment in particular areas
PB5	Attainment of industry harmony
PB6	Supply of better information to consumers and businesses to permit informed choices in their dealings
PB7	Promotion of equitable dealings in the market
PB8	Promotion of industry cost savings resulting in contained or lower prices at all levels in the supply chain
PB9	Development of import replacements
PB10	Growth in export markets
PB11	Steps to protect the environment
PB12	Fostering business efficiency, especially when this results in improved international competitiveness
PB13	Assistance to efficient small business, for example guidance on costing and pricing or marketing initiatives which promote competitiveness
PB14	Enhancement of the quality and safety of goods and services and expansion of consumer choice
PB15	Promotion of competition in the industry
PB16	Other

Source: Author's research.

---

5 Australian Competition and Consumer Commission (ACCC), *Authorisations and Notifications* (May 1999) 6–7. These benefits are PB1 to PB10 and PB12 to PB15 in Table 1.1.

6 Allan Fels, 'The Public Benefit Test in the *Trade Practices Act 1974*' (Paper presented at the National Competition Policy Workshop, Melbourne, 12 July 2001) 7.

7 ACCC, (May 1999) 6, where it is stated the 'Public benefits recognised by the Commission and the Australian Competition Tribunal have included'. Also see Fels, 'The Public Benefit Test in the *Trade Practices Act 1974*' 8.

As the authorisation process involves the weighing of public benefit against the public detriment, it was important to examine the manner in which the ACCC has addressed detriments over time. Public detriment is focused on whether there has been a lessening of competition in the market and it has been acknowledged that this will include a reduction of competitors, increased conditions of entry and constraints on competitors. These three factors are coded as PD1 to PD3 in Table 1.2 below.[8] As with the public benefits, it was recognised that such lists are non-exhaustive and a fourth catch-all category, PB4 Other, was also coded for the 244 determinations.

Table 1.2: Public detriment (PD) factors examined in the empirical study

Public detriment (PD) no	Meaning
PD1	A reduction in the number of competitors
PD2	Increased conditions of entry
PD3	Constraints on competition affecting the ability of market participants to innovate effectively and to conduct their affairs efficiently and independently
PD4	Other

Source: Author's research.

Each of the 16 public benefits and 4 public detriments were coded. They were given a weight from 1 (not important) to 4 (very important) to indicate the weight attached to each of these factors by the commission in its determination. The explanation of the weights used is presented in the Appendix.

This study sought to further compare the different benefits and the importance given to them across the seven years of the empirical study. In order to do so, the weights attached to each public benefit and each public detriment were added together and the sum of these weights were used to plot a number of figures that are contained in chapters 3, 4 and 6. Where a benefit was seen to occur twice, such as cost savings in administration and cost savings in production, it was weighted twice. Other factors were also collated in the study including the type of industry that the applicant belonged to; whether conditions were imposed by the ACCC in granting authorisation; and, the type of conditions imposed as detailed in the Appendix.

---

8   Fels, 'The Public Benefit Test in the *Trade Practices Act 1974*' 9; also see the decisions of the Australian Competition Tribunal in *Victorian Newsagency* (1994) ATPR 41-357 at 42,683.

Theoretical Frameworks

There are two main frameworks that inform this book: historical institutionalism and responsive regulation.

Historical institutionalism is a diverse field, which enquires into the development and function of institutions,[9] as well as the evolution of a new institution required to operate in a multicultural and multinational environment and the challenges posed therein.[10] It is useful as it relies on historical processes to explain the present.[11] This rejects the functionalist view of institutions and, rather, sees institutions as enduring legacies of political struggles.[12] Institutions are social and cultural constructions that embody the values of the time and the emphasis is on how these institutions emerge from and are embedded in concrete temporal processes.[13] Institutions in two different jurisdictions will evolve differently depending on the cultural and social constructions they embody. Tony Freyer's work on the history of comparative antitrust regulation,[14] examines the institutional trajectories taken by different institutions in regulating antitrust in different jurisdictions.

Further historical institutionalism is *institutionalist* — it focuses on institutions. Clearly institutions provide the site for political actors to pursue their interests and it is important to understand how politics has shaped the institution. Historical institutionalists develop this line and their central theme is that institutions play a much greater role in shaping politics.[15] As Kathleen Thelen and Sven Steinmo have stated:

> institutional analysis also allows us to examine the relationship between political actors as objects and as agents of history. The institutions ... can shape and constrain political strategies in important ways, but they are themselves also the outcomes (conscious or unintended) of deliberate political strategies, of political conflict or of choice.[16]

---

9   Colleen A Dunlavy, 'Political Structure, State Policy, and Industrial Change: Early Railroad Policy in the United States and Prussia', in Sven Steinmo, Kathleen Thelen and Frank Longstreth (eds), *Structuring Politics: Historical Institutionalism in Comparative Analysis* (1992).
10   Brigid Laffan, 'Becoming a "Living Institution": The Evolution of the European Court of Auditors' 1999 37(2) *Journal of Common Market Studies* 251; Paul Pierson, 'The Path to European Integration: A Historical Institutionalist Analysis' (1996) 29(2) *Comparative Political Studies* 123.
11   Kathleen Thelen, 'Historical Institutionalism in Comparative Politics' (1999) 2 *Annual Review of Political Science* 369, 371.
12   Thelen (1999) 386.
13   ibid.
14   Tony Freyer, *Regulating Big Business: Antitrust in Great Britain and America: 1890–1990* (1992); Tony Freyer, *Antitrust and Global Capitalism 1930–2004* (2006).
15   Kathleen Thelen and Sven Steinmo, 'Historical Institutionalism in Comparative Politics', in Sven Steinmo, Kathleen Thelen and Frank Longstreth (eds), *Structuring Politics: Historical Institutionalism in Comparative Analysis* (1992).
16   ibid, 10.

The claim made by historical institutionalists is that actors may be in a strong initial position, seek to maximise their interests and, nevertheless, carry out institutional and policy reforms that fundamentally transform their own positions in ways that are unanticipated.[17] Institutions can be mediators of policy and the ways in which the policy is interpreted and applied. This is particularly relevant in an examination of the manner in which the institution, in this case the competition regulator, has shaped policy and can remake politics.[18] Historical institutionalism can help us understand how institutions can confer power on some actors while withholding power from others — in the words of Hall and Taylor historical institutionalists are explaining how institutions can be constitutive of political agency.[19] The institutions' role has a temporal quality and its priorities will change over time.[20]

Thus, an institution can shape policy, as the study by Stephen Wilks and Ian Bartle illustrates.[21] These authors examine the creation of independent agencies, which occurred at different times, to regulate competition policy in the United Kingdom, European Union and Germany. They argue that the original decision to delegate the task of competition regulation to such agencies was motivated by a need for governments to reassure citizens by appearing to act.[22] These agencies, however, each had different missions: the German mission was to defend the market economy, the European mission was market integration, and the British mission was to protect the public interest.[23] But the passing of time demonstrates that these 'agencies have become more activist and have contributed to policy through a demonstration effect, showing what can be done; as a source of technical expertise; and as an available agency of implementation to be enhanced or adapted by subsequent government.'[24] The consequences of creating agencies have been 'to populate the policy area with actors ... who have their own priorities, interpretations, and influence'.[25]

Historical institutionalism relies on critical events to explain the origins of the institution and the path it follows. Critical events, large and small, can affect the manner in which the institution evolves. However distinction must be made between the critical events that are responsible for the foundation of the institution and other critical events. The moment of institutional formation

---

17   Pierson (1996) 126.

18   See Thelen and Steinmo (1992) 10; also see Peter Hall and Rosemary Taylor, 'Political Science and the Three New Institutionalisms' (1996) 44 *Political Studies* 961.

19   Hall and Taylor (1996) 942.

20   Colin Hay and Daniel Wilcott, 'Structure, Agency and Historical Institutionalism' (1998) 44 *Political Studies* 951, 954.

21   Stephen Wilks and Ian Bartle, 'The Unanticipated Consequences of Creating Independent Competition Agencies' (2002) 25(1) *West European Politics* 153–4.

22   ibid, 149.

23   ibid, 165.

24   ibid, 149.

25   ibid.

is referred to as critical juncture. Other events that affect the institution's evolution, such as funding, political manoeuvering or global movements, are referred to as critical events.

The moment of origin or critical juncture is vital as it determines the path that the institution will follow. This critical juncture can be a lasting legacy and the institution's behavior will be shaped by its origins. But the moment of origin is not all there is. The historical development of institutions reveals that they are remade over time as a consequence of other events or actors. Wilks and Bartle's examination of independent agencies to administer law and policy in the United Kingdom, Germany and the European Union reveals that there were both expected and unexpected consequences.[26] They contend that, although the original decision to establish such agencies was motivated by a need to reassure the public, these agencies are far less independent than commonly supposed.[27] The way in which they have evolved not only differed from one jurisdiction to another, but there were also a number of unanticipated consequences, including the evolution of the agencies from a passive, symbolic defence of a competitive market economy to an aggressive promotion of market freedoms,[28] where the agencies escaped capture by business but stepped into 'the arms of lawyers and economists'[29] and where the 'old, broad, balancing public interest criteria employed by agencies' have been replaced by a 'far narrower and dogmatic focus on market efficiency'.[30]

Historical institutionalism provides a valuable lens to view the manner in which multiple political, economic and social forces came together to create the Australian competition regulator as the institution responsible for determining 'public benefit' and the manner in which that institution has mediated those forces to shape policy and apply it with existing legal culture. In order to understand the path an institution has travelled, it is useful to examine the critical juncture of its origin and the power vested in it as an independent agency to determine the public benefit within the authorisation process, and to explore the relationship between politics and the institution.

Responsive regulation and restorative justice is the second theoretical framework adopted in this study. The core idea of responsive regulation is that regulators should be responsive to the conduct of those they seek to regulate in deciding how to respond. Scholars have examined the manner in which responsive strategies can be incorporated into the competition regulators' practices, such as encouraging corporations to voluntarily include informal dispute resolution mechanisms or implement compliance programs that bring the conduct within

---

26   Wilks and Bartle (2002) 154 — for how historical institutionalism fits in to this analysis.
27   ibid, 149.
28   ibid, 170.
29   ibid.
30   ibid.

the boundaries of the law.[31] These responsive strategies can work alongside the conventional strategies of litigation and penalties. The ACCC has used a variety of responsive strategies through its history. One example of such a responsive strategy has been to grant authorisation on the basis that a complaint mechanism is adopted by the industry associations to regulate their actions. Another example is the granting of an authorisation on the condition that information about industry practices is made publicly available, thus allowing people both within and outside the industry to monitor the conduct of corporations.[32]

Criticism has been levelled at regulators adopting such approaches on the basis that they give unfettered discretion to the regulator to go beyond its grant of power. Scholarship on the manner in which regulators are constrained addresses these criticisms, arguing for the development of a new administrative law.[33] More recent scholarship has built on these contributions by providing the ideals that can guide all responsive regulators.[34] This book uses these scholarly contributions to evaluate the effectiveness of the ACCC's use of its discretion in the determination of public benefit within the authorisation process. It looks at the types of benefits that have been recognised, the processes employed and the terms on which authorisation has been granted.

Restorative justice has been more recently linked to responsive regulation in an effort consider mechanisms for allowing everyone affected by a decision the right to be included in the decision-making process.[35] An authorisation determination will affect conduct in the market and can impact on a wide cross-section of the community. Not everyone, however, can effectively participate in this process. The authorisation process makes room for submissions by interested parties and also provides, in certain instances, for the holding of a pre-decision conference, both of which are aimed at expanding the number of voices heard in the deliberations.[36] This book critically evaluates the manner in which the regulator has accommodated participation of stakeholders within its current decision-making process.

---

31 See Christine Parker, 'Restorative Justice in Business Regulation? The Australian Competition and Consumer Commission's Use of Enforceable Undertakings' (2004) 67(2) *The Modern Law Review* 209; John Braithwaite and Ian Ayres, *Responsive Regulation: Transcending the Deregulation Debate* (1992); John Braithwaite, *Restorative Justice and Responsive Regulation* (2002).

32 See *Re Allianz Australia Insurance Limited* A30217, A30218, 243 March 2004, 55 and *Medicines Australia* authorisation A90779, A90780 14 November 2003, 40.

33 See Jody Freeman, 'Private Parties, Public Functions and the New Administrative State' (2000) 52 *Administrative Law Review* 813, 854; Michael Taggart, *The Province of Administrative Law* (1997); Colin Scott, 'Accountability in a Regulatory State' (2000) 27(1) *Journal of Law and Society* 38.

34 Robert Baldwin and Julia Black, 'Really Responsive Regulation' (2008) 71(1) *Modern Law Review* 59.

35 John Braithwaite, *Regulatory Capitalism: How it Works, Ideas for Making it Work Better* (2008); John Parkinson and Declan Roche, 'Restorative Justice: Deliberative Democracy in Action?', (2004) 39(3), *Australian Journal of Political Science* 505; Christine Parker, *The Open Corporation: Effective Self-Regulation and Democracy* (2002).

36 This process, provided for by section 90A of the *Trade Practices Act*, gives applicants and interested parties the opportunity to discuss the draft determination and to put their views directly to a commissioner.

Overview

The public benefit test relies on the discretion of the regulator to interpret it, and this book explores how the ACCC has used its discretion in interpreting this phrase and evaluates ACCC performance over the last four decades.

Chapter 2 studies the history of the current authorisation process and argues that the wide discretionary powers granted for the interpretation of the public benefit test are explained by the historical developments between 1960 and 1965. This was the period when Australia settled on a distinctive approach to competition regulation, including the creation of a secret register by a regulator with wide powers who was directed to use its powers to raise awareness and gain acceptance for the legislation. It is argued that this path set the regulator on its own trajectory, which later resulted in it working responsively to create workable competition in the market.

Chapters 3 and 4 deal with the term 'public benefit'. Chapter 3 examines the interpretation of public benefit, which has been far from straightforward. There are two main questions that have been debated for four decades. The first is whether the term 'benefit' should focus primarily on economic efficiency or whether it should be open more broadly to both efficiency benefits and other benefits, such as improvement in the quality of health or environment, which may not have an efficiency focus. The second question involves the term 'public' and whether this term should be given a wide or narrow interpretation. A wide view of the term would include any section of the community, including the corporations applying for authorisation or the shareholders of those corporations. According to this view a benefit that reaches the shareholders of the corporation will be acceptable. A narrow interpretation of the term would require the benefit to reach the public or at least the consumer. The chapter explores the discourses around these two questions, concluding that, while the ACCC has been both sensitive to the different views, its responses have been constrained by the decisions of the Australian Competition Tribunal (ACT).

Chapter 4 explores the types of public benefit recognised in authorisation determinations, relying on the data set of 244 determinations. It concludes that the ACCC has been open to recognising a variety of benefits as they have become relevant. It has always recognised benefits based on economic efficiency, such as promotion of cost savings and industry rationalisations. Alongside this, it has also recognised non-efficiency benefits, such as the increasing safety and quality of goods and services as well as the promotion of equitable dealings. The ACCC has worked with a list of public benefits adding to it as new benefits were recognised. It has not, however, developed a theoretical framework for its determinations. Nevertheless, these determinations have been responsive to changing circumstances and needs. This ad hoc approach can be described as a triumph of practice over theory. The chapter concludes that the ACCC could remedy the criticism of being ad hoc by developing an overarching theoretical framework for public benefit. This would serve the applicant, all stakeholders and the regulator better than the current approach.

Chapters 5 and 6 focus on examining the use of discretion by the ACCC in applying the public benefit test. Using a multidisciplinary approach, Chapter 5 conducts a thorough examination of how the use of discretion by a regulatory agency is perceived and limited. It begins with the legal scholarship on discretion and goes on to consider the contributions of sociologists and political scientists which, it argues, better reflect the way in which regulatory agencies operate in practice. It draws on this multidisciplinary scholarship to develop a set of core values as well as a number of institutional, practical and moral factors that constrain the regulatory agency. It concludes that the operation of discretion by a regulatory agency is difficult to constrain and manage as it can exist both within strict rules or vague phrases, which remains the paradox of discretion. This discussion provides the basis for carrying out a detailed evaluation in Chapter 6 of how the ACCC has used its discretion.

Chapter 6 examines the use of discretion by the ACCC. It looks first at the regulatory scholarship that is useful to carry out such an examination and then classifies the manner in which the ACCC has exercised discretion in determining public benefit into four categories: epistemological discretion, procedural discretion, outcome-weighing discretion and immunity discretion. The chapter concludes that the ACCC has used its discretion in an experimental manner focusing on obtaining reasonable outcomes. Evidence shows, however, that not all stakeholders are engaging in the determination process. There is a need for greater consideration to be given to increasing the participation of certain groups representing non-business interests, which can include consumers and all citizens affected by decisions, by providing them with a voice in the decision-making process. It is argued that giving such groups a voice would make for a better process than the way the ACCC is currently operating.

Chapter 7 addresses the two main criticisms of the ACCC that are raised in earlier chapters: first, that the determination of public benefits would be better served by a broader theoretical framework giving greater direction to all stakeholders; and, second, that participation by non-industry groups in the deliberations should be increased. It proposes that a principles-based approach would be better able to address both these criticisms. It develops a set of heuristics based on human rights and ACCC practice to identify public benefits. This would provide an overarching theoretical framework to improve on the current ad hoc approach. This is then expressed as a principle, which is formulated as the first in the set of principles. Building on the literature on principle-based regulation and responsive regulation, a set of nine principles are then proposed. These are aimed at lowering the barriers to participation, increasing inclusiveness and making the ACCC a more genuinely responsive regulator in this area.

2. Architecture of Authorisations

This chapter looks at the origins of the authorisation process, examining the period from the early twentieth century until 2010, when the new *Competition and Consumer Act 2010* (Cth) was introduced. The design of the authorisation process within the *Trade Practices Act 1974* (Cth) can only really be understood by looking at the extended context. We should look particularly to the early 1960s to glean a better understanding of the place and architecture of the authorisation process. This was the time that the business and general community began to engage in a discourse about restrictive trade practices, setting the stage for the introduction of the 1974 Act more than a decade later.

The Regulatory Landscape: Corporations, Clubs and Cartels

The role of corporations in Australia's economic development has been influential in shaping legislation regulating restrictive trade practices. The role of corporations can be traced back to the Australian Agricultural Company, incorporated by royal charter in 1824 and conferred with the power for the cultivation and improvement of wasteland in the colony of New South Wales. The company engaged in a variety of activities, including using convict labour in gold and coal mining, and in pastoral and agricultural activities, including wool-growing. Indeed, the sudden surge in incorporation of corporations during the gold rush years of 1875 to 1888 in Victoria and New South Wales is no coincidence, merely highlighting the important role of the corporate enterprise in economic development. Big corporations were important not just for economic development, as is demonstrated by the role played by the Colonial Sugar Refinery (CSR) company, the size and location of which in northern Australia went some way to assuaging the government's concerns over security and defence. CSR had monopoly status due to government protection; it was important to the government, which had the problems of a sparsely settled continent and the resulting concerns over how these areas were going to be defended. As is illustrated by the conclusions of a 1912 royal commission, in relation to the multifaceted roles of CSR:

> [I]t follows that the supreme justification for the protection of the Sugar Industry is the part that the industry has contributed, and will, as we hope, continue to contribute to the problems of the settlement and defence of the northern portion of the Australian continent.

The recognition of the nature of this supreme justification is the first condition of a sound public policy in relation to the Sugar Industry. Relatively to it, all other issues are of minor importance.[1]

Cartels were a feature of Australian life, collusive practices were common and Australian industry was always highly concentrated.[2] It was estimated that the level of concentration of power in Australia 'is twice as great as it is in the United Kingdom and three times as great as it is in the United States'.[3] Many reasons were advanced for these levels of concentration. Particularly during the early years of Federation, governments favoured certain industries in return for support and loyalty. An example of this political dimension was illustrated by the appointment of Essington Lewis, the 'steel master' and head of the Broken Hill Proprietary Steelworks to the position of director-general of munitions in 1940 in the midst of World War II. Clearly the availability of steel was important to this position and it was remarked that, as director-general, 'Lewis controlled the production of all ordnance, explosives, ammunition, small arms, aircraft and vehicles and all materials and tools used in producing such munitions'.[4]

Prior to the introduction of statutes specifically dealing with competition, it was the common law that addressed such activity. The general rule at common law was that restraints of trade could not be enforced unless it 'is reasonable in the interests of the parties concerned and reasonable in the interests of the public and not injurious to the public'.[5] This position was established in the oft-quoted passage of Lord Macnaghten in *Nordenfelt v Maxim Nordenfelt Guns and Ammunition Co Ltd*:

> The public have an interest in every person's carrying on his trade freely: so has the individual. All interference with individual liberty of action in trading, and all restraints of trade of themselves, if there is nothing more, are contrary to public policy, and therefore void. That is the general rule. But there are exceptions: restraints of trade and interference with individual liberty of action may be justified by the special circumstances of a particular case. It is a sufficient justification, and indeed it is the only justification, if the restriction is reasonable — reasonable, that is, in reference to the interests of the parties concerned and reasonable in reference to the interests of the public, so framed and

---

1 Alan Birch and JF Blaxland, 'The Historical Background', in AG Lowndes (ed.), *South Pacific Enterprise: The Colonial Sugar Refinery Company Limited* (1956) 51.

2 For a discussion of the 14th Royal Commissions on Restrictive Trade Practices conducted in Western Australia, see Geoffrey de Q Walker, *Australian Monopoly Law: Issues of Law, Fact and Policy* (1967) 15.

3 Commonwealth, *Parliamentary Debates*, Senate, 8 December 1965, 2137, (Senator Lionel Murphy, New South Wales); Tony Freyer, *Antitrust and Global Capitalism 1930–2004* (2006) 318.

4 Geoffrey Blainey, *The Steel Master: A Life of Essington Lewis* (1981) 147.

5 Report from the Joint Committee, Parliament of Australia, *Constitutional Review* (1959) Chapter 17, para 843 116.

so guarded as to afford adequate protection to the party in whose favour it is imposed, while at the same time it is in no way injurious to the public. That, I think, is the fair result of all the authorities.[6]

This line of argument had been made to support cartel activity whereby cartel arrangements were considered reasonable and there was a public interest in avoiding cutthroat competition.[7] Even though the first statute regulating this area was introduced in the early nineteenth century, in the form of the *Australian Industries Preservation Act 1906*, it did little to alter the view that cartels may be in the public interest.[8] The main focus of the Act was the protection of Australian manufacturing industries from unfair competition from foreign companies, rather than promoting domestic competition.[9]

These public interest arguments were examined by the High Court in the *Coal Vend* case.[10] The claim was that numerous coal proprietors and shipping companies were part of a cartel engaged in price-fixing, as well as monopolising the coal trade in Newcastle and Maitland. These practices were described as conduct that was detrimental to the public because it involved the practical and persistent annihilation of competition on land and sea; excessive, arbitrary and capricious prices charged to consumers; restrictions on consumer choice; and, amongst other points, difficulties in obtaining particular classes or grades of coal.[11] The defendants claimed that the higher price could be offset by the advantages the cartel delivered to members of the community, other than consumers, in the form of the continuation of an industry.

The High Court saw the notion of public detriment as requiring the consideration of a wide cross-section of the public, including consumers as well as producers, and stated:

> It may be that the detriment, if it be one, of enhancement of price to the consumer is compensated for by other advantages to other members of the community, which may, indeed, include the establishment or continuance of an industry which otherwise would not be established or would come to an end.[12]

---

6   [1984] AC 535 at 554.

7   See David Meltz, 'Happy Birthday Mr Nordenfelt! — The Centenary of the Nordenfelt Case' (1994) 2 *Trade Practices Law Journal* 149, 153.

8   Bruce Donald and John Dyson Heydon, *Trade Practices Law* vol 1 (1978) 5.

9   David Merrett, Stephen Corones and David Round, 'The Introduction of Competition Policy in Australia: The Role of Ron Bannerman' (2007) 47(2) *Australian Economic History Review* 178; Andrew Hopkins, *Crime, Law and Business: The Sociological Sources of Australian Monopoly Law* (1978) 28.

10   *Adelaide Steamship Co Ltd v The King and the Attorney-General* (Cth) (1912) 15 CLR 65. This case rendered the *Australian Industry Preservation Act* (1906) nugatory.

11   *Attorney-General (Cth) v Associated Northern Collieries* (1911) 14 CLR 387, 399.

12   *Adelaide Steamship Co Ltd v The King and the Attorney-General* (1912) 15 CLR 65.

The court, however, did not accept that producers could be regarded as 'trustees for consumers'. The High Court found the prices had not been raised to an unreasonable amount and the conduct was not detrimental to the public. The case went to the Privy Council, which was sceptical about the value of competition, and regarded the agreement as an attempt at avoiding 'cutthroat' competition without the intention of charging unreasonable prices.[13] The efforts of the Privy Council can be contrasted to those of the American courts, which were strongly opposed to restrictive trade practices, leading to the formation of different types of business consolidation.[14]

Economic downturns, such as the depression of the 1930s, encouraged cartel activities and provided the breeding ground for trade restraints.[15] The role of trade associations in generating such practices was widely acknowledged and business did not view restrictive practices as improper; these practices were frequently termed 'orderly marketing' or, as it has been provocatively suggested, as just another consequence of Australian mateship.[16] It was stated that a club-like attitude existed and business was happy with their arrangements, which were based on a 'network of restrictive agreements'.[17] 'The rules were known to the members, but they did not want to talk about them to other people. Price agreements between competitors were common'.[18] Senator John Gorton declared that 'the growth of monopoly and restrictive trade practices has gone so far as to become a disease',[19] and it was evident any legislation overtly attempting to strike at cartels and collusions would not be supported by the business sector.

The Origins of the Authorisation Process

The postwar world introduced new issues, including industrial progress, global corporations and high levels of industrial concentration — a climate

---

13   *Attorney-General (Cth) v Adelaide SS Co* [1913] AC 781.

14   For a discussion contrasting the approaches, see Freyer, *Regulating Big Business: Antitrust in Great Britain and America: 1890–1990* (1992) 35.

15   See Report from the Joint Committee, Parliament of Australia, *Constitutional Review* (1959) 856; see also Walker (1967) 17. For the American experience during the depression years, see Eleanor Fox and Lawrence Sullivan, 'Antitrust — Retrospective and Prospective: Where are we coming from? Where are we going?' (1987) *New York University Law Review* 936, 941.

16   Maureen Brunt, 'Legislation in Search of an Objective', in John Nieuwenhuysen (ed), *Australian Trade Practices: Readings* (2nd edn, 1976) 240. See also Brunt, 'The Australian Antitrust Law After 20 Years — A Stocktake' (1994) 9 *Review of Industrial Organization* 483.

17   Interview with Ron Bannerman (Commissioner of Trade Practices Commission 1966–1974 and Chair of the Trade Practices Commission, 1974–1984) (Canberra, 27 September 2001) (Bannerman interview).

18   Ron Bannerman, 'Points from Experience 1967–84', in Trade Practices Commission, Commonwealth of Australia, *Annual Report 1983–84*, (1984) 157.

19   Commonwealth, *Parliamentary Debates*, Senate, Second Reading Speech (Trade Practices Bill 1965), 8 December 1965, 2198 (Senator John Gorton, Victoria, Minister for Works).

that encouraged cartels and anti-competitive conduct.[20] Different countries responded to these challenges in different ways.[21] The inadequacy of the common law in quelling such practices was recognised as evidenced by the report of the Western Australian honorary royal commission in February 1957, which stated that, among the trade associations studied, it had found in at least 111 of such associations there existed a standard pattern of restrictive practices, including exclusive dealing, price-fixing agreements and collusive tendering agreements.[22] Similar findings were made in the *Report of the Royal Commissioner on Prices and Restrictive Trade Practices in Tasmania* (1965), in which the commission asserted two thirds of the trade associations were involved in restrictive trade practices.[23] It was stated of this period:

> Resale price maintenance by suppliers was a way of life. The 'tied house' system in liquor retailing and petrol retailing was entrenched and thought to be essential. All these matters had been countenanced and indeed defended, by the common law and so they represented valuable 'rights'. The common law had preserved 'sanctity of contract' in the interests of the parties and largely put aside the interests of customers and the public.[24]

The growing dominance of neoclassical economics and the contributions of industrial economists who linked high levels of concentration to the firms' performance led many developed countries to introduce legislation aimed at controlling monopolies and collusive practices.[25] In Australia there had been numerous attempts at state level to regulate anti-competitive conduct.[26] These were by and large ineffective, particularly because state laws could not adequately regulate a corporation's conduct in another state.[27] The only federal statute on restrictive trade practices until this time had been the *Australian Industries Preservation Act 1906*, which had been weakened owing to the High Court

---

20 See Fox, 'The Modernization of Antitrust: A New Equilibrium' (1981) 66 *Cornell Law Review* 1141, 1149, for discussion on the increasing number of mergers in the wake of World War II; see also Freyer (1992) 269–71.

21 See Freyer (2006). See also Stephen Wilks, *In the Public Interest: Competition Policy and the Monopolies and Mergers Commission* (1999) 27; Helen Mercer, *Constructing a Competitive Order: The Hidden History of British Antitrust Policies* (1995) 3.

22 Alex Hunter, 'Restrictive Practices and Monopolies in Australia' (1961) 37 *Economic Record* 30–31.

23 Royal Commission on Prices and Restrictive Trade Practices in Tasmania, Parliament of Tasmania, *Report of the Royal Commissioner on Prices and Restrictive Trade Practices in Tasmania* (1965) 31.

24 Bannerman (1984) 157.

25 For example, Canada passed the *Combines Investigations Act 1951*; the United Kingdom passed the *Restrictive Trade Practices Act 1956*; New Zealand passed the *Trade Practices Act 1958*; six national parliaments in the European Union had ratified the Treaty of Rome, which gave some emphasis to antitrust. See also Freyer (1992) 278; John Kenneth Galbraith, 'The Development of Monopoly Theory', in Alex Hunter (ed), *Monopoly and Competition: Selected Readings* (1969) 19–23. See also Eugene V Rostow, 'British and American Experience with Legislation against Restraints of Competition' (1960) 23(4) *Modern Law Review* 477, 490.

26 See, for example, *Monopolies Act 1923* (NSW); *Fair Prices Act 1924* (SA); *Prices Act 1963* (SA); *Profiteering Prevention Act 1948* (Qld); *Unfair Trading and Profit Control Act 1956* (WA); *Trade Associations Registration Act 1959* (WA).

27 See Freyer (2006) on the efforts and effectiveness of state's attempts to regulate monopolistic practices, 318–20.

decision in *Huddart Parker* declaring parts of the Act as unconstitutional.[28] The need to have a national regulatory approach was appreciated by parliamentary committees in 1958 and 1959, which had recommended that the constitution be amended to give the federal government greater power to legislate.[29] There was a recognised need for another attempt, at the federal level, to regulate restrictive trade practices.

Two approaches to the control of restrictive trade practices, those of the United States and the United Kingdom, have informed the design of Australian competition statutes at different times. While the main US statute was a broadly worded one that relied on the courts for interpretation, the *Robinson-Patman Act 1936* allowed for administrative discretion to be exercised for protecting small business.[30] The British approach, however, relied on an administrative body, rather than the courts, to apply the legislation on a *case-by-case* analysis.[31] The first Australian statute, the *Australian Industries Preservation Act 1906*, was firmly based on the US approach, as is reflected in its language and the inclusions of treble damages.[32] The effect of this Act was severely limited by the High Court decision in the *Coal Vend* case and it fell into disuse.[33] Following this experience, the debate on the appropriate approach for Australia resurfaced. It was clear that, among both business groups and parliamentarians, there was little support for US-style legislation.

Antitrust, as a philosophy and body of law reflecting political democracy in the United States, had emerged from a tumultuous history.[34] There was much less certainty, however, about its place in Australia and it was noted by Neville Norman that the 1950s was a time when restrictive practices were rife and industry did not conceal such agreements because there was no public or political censure against them.[35] The prevailing view of the time is summarised by Maureen Brunt who was influential in the development of competition policy in Australia:[36]

---

28 (1909) 8 CLR 330.

29 Hopkins (1978) 33.

30 The main statutes were the *Sherman Act 1890* (US) and *Clayton Act 1914* (US).

31 *Monopolies and Restrictive Practices (Inquiry and Control) Act 1948* (UK); *Restrictive Trade Practices Act 1956* (UK).

32 Donald and Heydon (1978) 5.

33 See *Adelaide Steamship Co Ltd v The King and the Attorney General* (1912) 15 CLR 65. This decision denied the Commonwealth Government the power to legislate such corporate activity. See also Donald and Heydon (1978) 5.

34 Fox (1981) 1141.

35 Neville Norman 'Progress Under Pressure: The Evolution of Antitrust in Australia' (1994) 9 *Review of Industrial Organization* 527, 529; See also 'Brewery Keen to Protect Interests' *Australian Financial Review*, 22 November 1963, 4.

36 Maureen Brunt had a tremendous influence in shaping Australian competition law, sitting as part-time member of the Trade Practices on important appellant decisions, writing in scholarly journals and being an active participant in annual conferences and seminars. See Alan Fels, 'Distinguished Fellow of the Economic Society of Australia 2006: Maureen Brunt', (2006) 83, *Economic Record* 204.

In the early days, when restrictive practices were so pervasive in Australia, it was unclear to legislators how many of them might be 'justifiable' (Barwick's word) — or why. While it was thought that in the small developing Australian economy, there might well be efficiencies that were dependent upon scale or agreements, this was not the only consideration. It was thought to be unwise to be doctrinaire. At the same time, it was thought to be appropriate to give business firms the opportunity to demonstrate that their acquisitions, practices and agreements were in society's interests.[37]

It was well understood by parliamentarians and government officials that, when discussing this issue, it was best not to associate with the US approach.[38] The ties with Britain were more influential.[39] The British approach to the control of anti-competitive practices had originated in more recent times, resulting in the passing of legislation in 1956,[40] and there was the opportunity to speak with British regulators on their experiences and successes. Further, the British legislation was more palatable to business[41] and, therefore, it had a greater influence on the shape of the Australian legislation, as evidenced by the two main statutes that followed, the *Trade Practices Act 1965* and the *Trade Practices Act 1974*.

It was the notion of a 'fair go' that provided the focal point for the early discussions of regulating restrictive trade practices and competition policy. The main protagonist in these early discussions was Garfield Barwick, the attorney-general, who was responsible for beginning the discussions on regulating anti-competitive practices in Australia. After examining the American, Canadian and British approaches and speaking with many aggrieved parties, Barwick, in December 1962, presented an outline of the proposed legislation and, in November 1963, published a talking paper.[42] Barwick came to this area with the support of government, as evidenced by the governor-general's comments to parliament in 1960 pointing to the need for legislation regulating restrictive trade practices.[43]

Andrew Hopkins has argued that the decision to legislate must be seen in the context of the policies developed by the Liberal government of Robert Menzies. Hopkins asserts that the government, in its fight against inflation, wanted to

---

37 Brunt (1994) 483, 506.
38 Bannerman interview. For different views on the goals of US antitrust and UK competition law, see Wilks (1999) 27; Freyer (1992) 7–8.
39 Bannerman interview; see also Garfield Barwick, *A Radical Tory. Garfield Barwick's Reflections & Recollections* (1995) 147.
40 Freyer (1992) 295; see also *Restrictive Trade Practices Act 1956* (UK).
41 See Mercer (1995) 6. Here, Mercer argues that the British legislation was shaped fundamentally by business.
42 Barwick (1995); Hopkins (1978) 36–7, Merrett, Corones and Round (2007) 181–82.
43 Hopkins (1978) 34.

show it opposed wage rises and price increases, which were often stimulated by price agreements between competitors.[44] Thus, he argues, inflation was the main reason behind the government's decision to consider legislation in this area.

In a paper titled 'Some Aspects of Australian Proposals for Legislation for the Control of Restrictive Trade Practices and Monopolies', Barwick indicated the need for such legislation and proposed the terms of a Bill.[45] Described as the musings of a 'nineteenth century individualist, applying the techniques of the twentieth century, to bring nearer to fruition, his own ideas of individualism in society',[46] this paper was clearly directed at the predicament of small businessmen, such as storeowners who were not able to acquire goods because of the restrictive trade practices that prevented their supply to individuals outside the network. Tony Freyer has succinctly described this approach as 'the conservative idea of competition defined as free enterprise versus socialism'.[47] This unique Australian flavour , supporting small businesses and ensuring a fair go, was summarised by Barwick, when he wrote that increased efficiency from so-called economies of scale may not always be the answer to the problem of restrictive trade practices and, rather, it was necessary to consider the manner in which small- or medium-sized enterprises will be more satisfactory, both humanly and economically facilitated.[48] It was small business that was identified as deserving special attention, rather than 'consumers', the idea of which became important a decade or so later.

Barwick delivered public addresses around the country elaborating on the Bill's philosophy and harnessing support.[49] This was intended to enable interested parties to make representations and promote debate.[50] Although the Bill and Barwick's paper were much debated, it did not form part of government policy at the time and there was little available detail about the legislation. But it is clear that Barwick favoured the British approach to legislation, and David Marr has argued:

> [T]he British system of setting up a register of all agreements in restraint of trade also appealed as a clean and relatively bloodless method of collecting information on the practices he was setting out to control.[51]

---

44   ibid, 34–35.
45   Barwick, 'Some Aspects of Australian Proposals for Legislation for the Control of Restrictive Trade Practices and Monopolies', Paper presented at 13th Legal Convention, Canberra, January 1963.
46   Bannerman interview; see also Freyer (2006) 323.
47   Freyer (2006) 324.
48   Barwick (1995) 147.
49   Bannerman interview; Hopkins (1978) 36.
50   Hopkins (1978) 35.
51   David Marr, *Barwick* (2005), 188.

Barwick, however, was keen to avoid the objectionable features of the UK legislation studied.[52] From the outset Barwick identified the manner in which the Australian proposal would be different to the British counterpart. For the purposes of my discussion, I want to emphasise two features. First, unlike the open register of the British, Barwick wanted the Australian scheme to incorporate a register of agreements that may constitute restrictive practices that would be absolutely confidential[53] and, second, the decision to investigate the matters contained in the register would depend on whether the actual practice carried on was 'inimical to the public interest'.[54] The two features were innovative, departing from the British scheme and placing considerable power in the hands of officials. In later years, Barwick was equivocal about these features saying:

> The suggestion was that if the trader did not disclose that he carried on a described restrictive practice he would lose the right to assert later that the [practice was in fact harmful to the public interest.
>
> This part of the scheme was not completely understood and caused considerable opposition. In retrospect, I think it would have been better to rely on heavy penalties … on non-disclosure while retaining the trader's right to justify the practice as not harmful to the public interest.[55]

These two features were to remain as part of the legislation, which was passed many years and many drafts later. In 1963, Barwick left the Attorney-General portfolio, and passed the regulation of trade practices into the hands of the newly appointed Senator Billy Sneddon, who shaped and reshaped the idea over a period of three years, until it was eventually passed as the *Trade Practices Act 1965*.

Factors that Shaped the 1965 Act

Regulatory measures must fit with the commercial landscape and this was foremost in the minds of legislators who determined the design of the 1965 legislation. Two factors were particularly important in shaping this Act. First, there was no clear support from business for legislation controlling anti-competitive conduct and business lobbied hard, fundamentally influencing the design of the Act. Thus, the Act was a result of considerable compromise. Second, there was greater support for matters of interpretation to be dealt

---

52   Barwick, (1995) 147.
53   ibid, 148.
54   ibid; see also Merrett, Corones and Round (2007) 182, for how the legislation made further concession to business interests by softening the adjudication process used in Britain.
55   Barwick (1995) 148.

with by an administrative body, rather than being placed in the hands of the judiciary. Accordingly, the administrator was given wide powers and a tribunal created to hear trade practices matters.

Parliamentarians were more accustomed to the notion of legislation regulating trade practices during the 1960s. Business attitudes, however, were harnessed in opposition to this idea. Business was 'happy with the way things were and did not see any reason for legislation'.[56] An example is the Chamber of Manufacturers, which queried the objectives of a competitive economy, arguing the benefits derived by the manufacturing industry and its participants from anti-competitive agreements should be recognised before benefits to others.[57] This view certainly influenced the design of the 1965 legislation and the Act was described as 'one of the most ineffectual pieces of legislation ever passed by Parliament'.[58] It is clear, however, that business support and successful transition from Bill to Act status was unlikely if the legislation had been more stringent. The process from first announcement to enactment took over five years and the content of the Act changed considerably during that time.

There was support for the Act from diverse quarters. Consumer groups were in their infancy in Australia during this period and had little voice during the early 1960s. There was, however, support for the legislation from other sectors. Farmers and primary producers, who had long bought machinery and pesticides at uncompetitive high prices set by cartels, supported the legislation.[59] Likewise, small business people, who had not been able to enter the market, favoured regulation of such practices. Labour organisations and public authorities, both of which were exempted from the Bill, supported the legislation.[60] Finally the press, too, entered the fray, expressing a diversity of views.[61]

The Barwick scheme had proposed that four practices be directly banned by legislation and subject to criminal prosecution. They were: collusive bidding, collusive tendering, monopolisation, and persistent price cutting at a loss. It was proposed that these practices were per se illegal.[62] Business opposition to this was clear and loud, saying it was a 'savage application of the concept of crime'[63] and 'that no business practice could be condemned per se'.[64] As Hopkins pointed out, the reason for the success of business representations in

---

56   Bannerman interview.
57   Brunt, 'The Trade Practices Bill II: Legislation in Search of an Objective' (1965) 41 *The Economic Record* 357, 364.
58   Brunt (1994) 491.
59   Hopkins (1978) 42. It is worth noting that the Bill did not catch those activities of government marketing boards that stabilised the prices of farmers and primary producers.
60   Hopkins (1978) 42.
61   ibid.
62   ibid, 54.
63   ibid, 55.
64   ibid, 56.

opposition to the scheme was because they were based on values that were shared by government, including the non-criminal nature of businessmen, the importance of not burdening business with compliance costs and the necessity of encouraging economic growth.[65] The Liberal government of the day was sympathetic to these arguments and the Act dropped many of the Barwick proposals. The compromise was effectively to remove the per se prohibitions from the Act and make them all examinable by the regulator.

The underlying philosophy of the Act was stated by Barwick, who emphasised the public interest in controlling restrictive practices.[66] The Bill proposed a list of practices that would be unlawful, subject to a public interest defence. This list underwent numerous drafts and the provisions in the final Act were a watered-down version, evidencing the strong impact of the business lobby. The Bill that went to parliament did not attempt to control mergers and takeovers, but concentrated on price-fixing and resale price maintenance. While in some quarters it was as weak,[67] the much-redesigned Bill did, however, address the most prevalent types of restrictive trade practices. Ron Bannerman, reflecting on the Bill, stated:

> In the end the legislation wasn't much more than an introduction and its life was principally in the areas of horizontal price fixes and resale price maintenance. There were some other sections, a section that dealt with price discrimination and a section that pretended to deal with monopolisation, but they weren't real. If you are to start competition law from nowhere, you had to start with price fixing and that is what we did in Australia and we did it quite effectively under that legislation.[68]

The Act, which received Royal Assent on 18 December 1965 and came into operation on 1 September 1967, contained four practices of examinable agreements within section 36: obtaining discrimination in prices or terms of dealing,[69] forcing another person's conduct,[70] inducing refusal to deal[71] and monopolisation.[72] The Act provided for the registration of such agreements in the Register of Trade Agreements by virtue of section 40(1). This was to be a secret register, unlike the British counterpart. It has also been stated that Barwick thought this may act as an inducement for business to register.[73] Barwick had always considered confidentiality as important:

65 ibid, 65.
66 See D Stalley, 'The Commonwealth Government's Scheme for the Control of Monopoly and Restrictive Practices — A Commentary' (1963) 37 *Australian Law Journal Reports* 85, 87.
67 See Brunt (1965) 357; Merrett, Corones and Round (2007) 181; Donald and Heydon (1978) 8.
68 Bannerman interview.
69 Section 36(1)(a) *Trade Practices Act 1965*.
70 Section 36(1)(b) *Trade Practices Act 1965*.
71 Section 36(1)(c) *Trade Practices Act 1965*.
72 Section 36(2) *Trade Practices Act 1965*.
73 Bannerman interview.

> The register would be absolutely confidential, protected by severe
> penalties for disclosure. Having been registered, the disclosed practice
> could be continued without restriction or penalty until it was found by
> the appropriate tribunal to be harmful to the public interest.[74]

The proposal merely asked for the registration of practices and was hailed as
'simple and certain' as well as avoiding 'tremendous administrative costs and
harassment of business'.[75] The legality of the practice relied on whether the
requirement to register had been complied with and the legislation acknowledged
that many examinable agreements would be innocuous and should be allowed
on the basis of public interest. It was compulsory to register such agreements
and it was prosecutable if this was not complied with. The administrator had the
power to view the register and decide whether the legality of certain practices
was worth pursuing.

The Trade Practices Tribunal was to consider whether the restriction or practice
was in the public interest. This was similar to the British legislation, which had
been criticised as vague.[76] Section 50(3) provided that, in considering whether
any restriction or practices were contrary to the public interest, the tribunal
weigh the detriment against the needs and interests that may have resulted.
Section 50(2) listed the matters that were to be taken into account and these
included:

a. the needs and interests of consumers, employers, producers, distributors,
   importers, exporters, proprietors and investors

b. the needs and interest of small businesses

c. the promotion of new enterprises

d. the need to achieve the full and efficient use and distribution of labour,
   capital, materials, industrial capacity, industrial know-how and other
   resources

e. the need to achieve the production, provision, treatment and distribution,
   by efficient and economical means, of goods and services of such quality,
   quantity and price as will best meet the requirements of domestic and
   overseas markets

f. the ability of Australian producers and exporters to compete in overseas
   markets.

---

74 Barwick (1995) 148.
75 Barwick 'Administrative Features of the Legislation on Restrictive Trade Practices' (The Robert Garran
Memorial Oration, speech delivered at the Australian Regional Groups Royal Institute of Public Administration,
Canberra, 3 November, 1963) 32.
76 Wilks (1999) 36.

The definition of public interest in the legislation was imprecise. It had been much debated in Cabinet and had been 'added to and subtracted from', the final form being a compromise.[77] Ultimately, the definition was criticised on the basis that the criteria were couched in terms of benefits to sectional interests as well as competition and good performance.[78]

Brunt, one of the most longstanding scholars in trade practices regulation, wrote of this provision:

> What is the criteria of the 'public interest'? ... It is true that we have s 50 that proposes to spell out such a criteria. But examination reveals that it consists of such vague and all embracing language as to delegate to the Tribunal virtually legislative powers. In rather less mellifluous language, it seems that the Government has passed the buck.[79]

It was also pointed out that it would have been difficult to specify in advance the manner in which the interests of the different groups could have been weighed.[80] The legislation, by virtue of section 47, gave the commissioner of the Trade Practices Commission (TPC) the power to bring proceedings, on the basis that the examinable agreements were contrary to the public interest, before the tribunal which, by virtue of section 51, could determine whether the practice was illegal or unenforceable.[81] Bannerman stated of this power:

> The Commissioner ... had to decide what cases to put to the Tribunal, and had to decide personally, without the power to delegate, and couldn't do that until he had formed an opinion that what he wanted to refer to the Tribunal was against the public interest. He had to form that opinion after having conferred and consulted with the industry that was affected by it ... And I am told that this was much debated in Cabinet and reached its final form as a compromise.[82]

The second important factor in the regulatory landscape was the decision about who would be the decision-maker: which body would interpret the legislation. There was a shift away from the courts to a 'dual enforcement system': a specialist commission and tribunal.[83] Whereas the *Australian Industries Preservation Act 1906* had given the courts power to interpret the legislation, the *Trade Practices*

---

77   Bannerman interview.
78   Brunt (1965) 357, 384.
79   ibid.
80   ibid.
81   The Tribunal decision in *Re Frozen Vegetables Marketing Agreement* 18 FLR 196 was important in considering the meaning of public benefit. See John Hatch, 'The Implications of the Frozen Case for Australian Trade Practices Legislation' (1978) 48 *Economic Record* 374.
82   Bannerman interview.
83   Robert Baxt and Maureen Brunt, 'The Murphy Trade Practices Bill: Admirable Objectives, Inadequate Means' (1973–74) 1 and 2 *Australian Business Law Review* 3, 58.

Act 1965 legislated for a shift of responsibility from the courts to the newly established Trade Practices Tribunal.[84] Again, Brunt described the rationale for the creation of the tribunal, in the context of the current Act, as:

> The Trade Practices Tribunal is an Australian invention, designed to take some of the pressure off the courts, in what is largely a court-centered antitrust system, by offering a quasi-judicial resolution of some of the more economically complex trade practices matters. So in the initial design of the *Trade Practices Act* it was sought to partition subject-matter between the courts and two administrative bodies — the Commission and the Tribunal.[85]

Although here Brunt was referring to the 1974 legislation, this rationale was true of the tribunal under the 1965 legislation. And, the tribunal was empowered to consider all proceedings brought by the commissioner.[86] This shift from the courts to the tribunal was pragmatically explained on the basis that the interpretation of 'public interest' was essentially an administrative task that could not be given to the courts[87] and it was stated as follows:

> It is of course a possibility that a rule of reason such as that developed in the United States might be adopted by our Courts and other administrative authorities in their interpretation of this new law, but traditionally our Courts have taken the view that their duty is to interpret, not to make the law.[88]

This shift was criticised soundly as an attempt to avoid responsibility, and it was argued that this placed on the tribunal 'the onus of making decisions which are more appropriately the responsibility of the legislature'[89] and of 'passing the buck'.[90]

This Act established a powerful and influential regulator, and the Bill contemplated an active and nimble commissioner who would be able to seek undertakings from the regulated parties on ways to vary behaviour, and still be able to prosecute them in cases of breach.[91] The extensive powers given

---

84 Section 9 *Trade Practices Act 1965*.
85 Brunt, 'Practical Aspects of Conducting a Hearing Before the Australian Competition Tribunal', paper presented at The New Era of Competition Law in Australia Conference, Perth, July 1995, cited in Stephen Corones, *Competition Law in Australia* (2006) 38.
86 Section 47 *Trade Practices Act 1965*.
87 Commonwealth, *Parliamentary Debates*, Senate, Second Reading Speech, Trade Practices Bill 1965, 8 December 1965, 2198 (Senator John Gorton, Victoria, Minister for Works).
88 Australian Development Industries Commission, 'The Trade Practices Bill 1973 — An Analysis, with Proposals for Amendment' (February 1974) 12.
89 J Hutton and John Nieuwenhuysen, 'The Tribunal and Australian Economic Policy' (1965) 41 *Economic Record* 2387, 2389.
90 Brunt (1965) 357, 384.
91 See JE Richardson, 'The 1965 Bill: The Legal Framework', in Nieuwenhuysen (1976) 220.

to the commissioner caused much debate, with many members of parliament expressing their concern over the extent of these discretionary powers.[92] The commissioner was required to mediate between interested parties and exercise skill in deciding the order in which practices should be challenged.[93] It was noted that the commissioner needed to be a man of the world, with a good appreciation of the industrial and business scene, approachable by business without being officious and having his finger on the pulse.[94] Indeed, one example of the characteristics of the nimble commissioner was the manner in which he was expected to be able to inform the public and bring about a shift in public opinion on the need for competition.

It has been persuasively argued that Bannerman, as the First Commissioner of Trade Practices, played a pivotal role in making the Act a success.[95] David Merrett, Stephen Corones and David Round highlight the commissioner's role in raising public awareness of restrictive trade practices. The authors emphasise Bannerman's personal traits in contributing to this, including his powerful ambition for the institution,[96] being a slave of duty[97] and possessing a good deal of political nuance.[98] They point out Bannerman's recognition that, in return for statutory independence, he must remain a neutral administrator,[99] maintaining government support before building respect for the legislation among the wider community.[100] This included building an effective regulatory agency and actively developing a corporate culture with a commitment to competition principles.

One example of the importance of these personal traits was the manner in which Bannerman was able to inform the wider community about the incidence of restrictive practices in the market. Even though the Register of Trade Agreements was secret, knowledge about existing webs of restrictive trade practices was made public and the commissioner was able to bring about a shift in public opinion. As to why the secret register did not protect business, as intended, Bannerman stated:

> It [the secrecy provisions] didn't work simply because of the power and duty that the Commissioner had to present Annual Reports to the Parliament. In those Annual Reports he detailed all the information about the agreements, without disclosing names to the Parliament. The picture became clear. It became very clear across the community that there

---

92   Merrett, Corones and Round (2007) 185.
93   Barwick, 'Administrative Features of the Legislation on Restrictive Trade Practices' (1963) 43.
94   ibid.
95   Merrett Corones and Round (2007).
96   ibid, 195.
97   ibid.
98   ibid, 194–95.
99   ibid, 194.
100   ibid.

was a network of restrictive agreements, up and down and sideways all of industry. The types of them were detailed. The provisions, which were copied from one industry to another ... became known in spite of the secrecy provisions. That meant that the Commissioner's reports were much used by the press and the professions and put pressure on parliamentarians and thinkers about the adverse effects on the economy, initiative and on efficiency.[101]

Section 48 of the Act required that, prior to instituting proceedings in the tribunal, the commissioner carry out consultations with persons who would be the other parties to the proceedings, or with representatives of those persons with a view to securing some undertaking, cessation or variation of the agreement. These powers were criticised and the commissioner was called a grand inquisitor and the great bottleneck, who had been interposed between the tribunal and the object of its statutory functions.[102] These powers did, however, encourage the commissioner to engage with business and to build up a staff who could work effectively and with a shared ethos.[103]

The choice of the commission, rather than the executive department, to deal with the competition regulation was a choice being made in other jurisdictions, including the United States and United Kingdom. Marver Bernstein, in 1955, listed the advantages of relying on a commission as a regulatory tool, and they remain applicable today.[104] Bernstein pointed out that, in the nineteenth century, there was a shift in the character of economic regulation away from the judiciary to a commission that may be better resourced and better skilled in dealing with such specific areas.[105] Commissions were often seen as a means of 'taking regulation out of politics'[106] and they could engage in creative regulatory responses.[107] Further, there has always been distrust in the judiciary's ability to handle complex areas of economic regulation,[108] whereas commissions were seen as having a significant input into the determination of public policy.[109] Choosing to delegate such activity to an agency was also part of the British tradition,

---

101   Bannerman interview.

102   Commonwealth, *Parliamentary Debates*, House of Representatives, 25 November 1965, 3239 (Mr Reginald Connor, Member for Cunningham).

103   Bannerman interview. See also Merrett, Corones and Round (2007) 196.

104   Marver Bernstein, *Regulating Business by Independent Commission* (1955).

105   ibid, 26. This work is often quoted for the evolutionary lifecycle of an agency. I do not think that this is applicable today and agree with the views expressed in Michael Moran, 'Understanding the Regulatory State' (2002) 32(1) *British Journal of Political Science* 431, 433.

106   Bernstein (1955) 71.

107   For a contrary view see Paul Craig, 'The Monopolies and Mergers Commission: Competition and Administrative Rationality', in Robert Baldwin and Christopher McCrudden (eds), *Regulation and Public Law*, (1987), 197, 222, where he argues that an agency is a good way of retaining political control.

108   Bernstein (1955) 28. See also these sentiments expressed in Independent Committee of Inquiry into Competition Policy in Australia, Commonwealth of Australia, *National Competition Policy*, (1993) [Hilmer Report]. See also Craig (1987) 223.

109   Bernstein (1955) 66.

whereby such delegation was controlled in a framework of trust and the focus was on the interest of the public.[110] All these factors have been relied on from time to time in Australia and formed a part of the regulatory landscape, which resulted in the creation of the TPC as the powerful regulator.[111]

The Critical Juncture of the Authorisation Process in the *Trade Practices Act 1974*

The critical juncture for the public benefit test within the formation of the institutional support for the authorisation process, under the 1974 legislation, was the period between 1962 and 1965, before even, the passing of its predecessor, the 1965 Act. Here I use the definition of critical juncture, namely that there should be a significant change, this change took place in a distinct way, and it produced historical legacies.[112] The significant change in this case was the recognition that some attempt had to be made to control cartels, even though it may be unpopular in the electorate.

The change did indeed take place in a distinct way in Australia because of the adoption of a secret register, with wide powers granted to the independent regulator who could decide which agreements to query as being against the public interest. This choice to use a registration system handled by the independent regulator resulted in legacies that have shaped our current competition regulatory structures. It would be untrue to say these legacies were intended or, even, that Australia's current competition laws were intended or planned. This is clearly not the case. Many other factors influenced the path over the ensuing years. But the decisions to make the register secret, and to grant wide powers to the commissioner, including the power to discuss matters with business with a view to avoiding proceedings,[113] were important. Although widely regarded as weak legislation, these aspects were vital in determining the trajectory the institution took and its legacy.

The 1960s brought a change in attitude and an acknowledgement that cartels had to be controlled by legislation, as demonstrated by Barwick who stated:

> The regulation of restrictive trade practices and monopolies is a field into which most of the countries of the West who desire to maintain a

---

110   Stephen Wilks and Ian Bartle, 'The Unanticipated Consequences of Creating Independent Competition Agencies' (2002) 25(1) *West European Politics* 148, 153.

111   See John Warhurst, 'Exercising Control over Statutory Authorities: Study in Government Technique', in Patrick Weller and Dean Jaensch (eds), *Responsible Government in Australia* (1980) 151.

112   Berins Collier and David Collier, *Shaping the Political Arena: Critical Junctures, the Labor Movement, and Regime Dynamics in Latin America* (1991).

113   See Merrett, Corones and Round (2007) 182; Richardson (1976) 90.

free economy have felt themselves obliged to enter. They have entered it to varying degrees, and with varying fortunes, with quite divergent schemes.[114]

Any attempt at regulating collusive conduct, to be successful, had to be sympathetic to the existing market structure of Australian industry. It was the Liberal Country Party that had conducted the early enquiries into legislative design and proposed the legislation. The political ideology saw restrictive trade practices creating problems of both a sociological and economic nature: the sociological problems arose from activities that excluded persons from the market and limited free enterprise, while the economic problems were responsible for distorting the market and exploited consumers.[115] The proposed legislation made the link between free enterprise and competition and received bipartisan support from both the Liberal Country Party, who proposed the legislation, as well as the Labor Party, who proposed more severe legislation. Bannerman has described this Bill as providing the competition edifice that we see today.[116] Rather than being a top-down attempt to control businesses, it was recognised that, in order to survive and be successful, any regulatory approach had to be essentially a compromise that listened to and accommodated the concerns of business. This is evidenced by the comments made by Barwick addressing the Chamber of Manufacturing Industries in 1963:

> In the middle of all the harouche, we had last Monday discussions with the Industries Advisory Council. We had put to us the most balanced, sensible and impressive ideas on this matter that I have ever heard … We do not want to be doctrinaire on this matter. We, like you, want to preserve competition. We can with good sense eliminate unfairness and injustice. All I want to tell you is that what has been said to me and my colleagues in the last few days has been so helpful, and that it may well determine the future course of action.[117]

This sentiment was echoed in the long title of the *Trade Practices Act 1965*, 'An Act to preserve Competition in Australian Trade and Commerce to the extent required by the Public Interest'.[118]

The 1965 Act made similar concessions to business and the registration process was aimed at assuring business that change would not be sudden. Neither business interests nor governments wanted to rely on the courts to interpret the statute, as had been the case under the 1906 Act. Any successful attempt

---

114   Barwick 'Some Aspects of Australian Proposals for Legislation' (1963).
115   ibid.
116   Bannerman interview.
117   Marr (2005) 191.
118   For a discussion on the importance of workable competition as an important feature of Australian competition regulation and the manner in which it is consistent with the public interest, see Brunt (1994) 483.

to regulate collusive conduct had to find a distinct way, as demonstrated by Gorton's statement that 'the philosophy which runs throughout the Bill is that the agreements and practices to which it applies are lawful unless and until they have been determined by the Tribunal to be contrary to the public interest'.[119] The distinct way of embodying this philosophy was the creation of the commission to negotiate these issues, and an important feature, the sweetner, of this scheme was the secret register of anti-competitive practices.[120]

The choice of the independent regulator and the creation of the secret register produced historical legacies. A fundamental legacy of the Act was that it created an independent agency and a commissioner with the discretion to interpret the term public benefit. It recognised certain restraints of trade may be in the public interest and should be allowed — thus, what may be bad for competitors may be good for the public. This became the foundation for the authorisation process under the 1974 legislation. As time passed, this authorisation process was seen as a strength of competition regulation in Australia and it represented a recognition that there are instances in which anti-competitive conduct is of value to society.[121] This has been considered to be particularly relevant in small economies where pursuing efficiency considerations alone may not always result in optimal outcomes.[122]

Further there are three important and specific legacies. First, the creation of the secret register, which was the beginnings of the authorisation process that was to become an important aspect of the *Trade Practices Act 1974*. The authorisation process under the 1974 Act, unlike its predecessor, was not a secret process. It did, however, allow for the authorisation of certain anti-competitive processes, whereby the public benefit outweighed the public detriment. This was only possible because the business community had accepted the register under the 1965 Act with the commissioner as the referee and regulatory mechanism. The phrase 'public interest' under the 1965 Act was changed to 'public benefit' under the 1974 Act, but its meaning remains imprecise.[123] The meaning of the phrase relies considerably on the discretion of the regulator and the major discourses of the time. As stated by Bannerman:

---

119 Commonwealth, *Parliamentary Debates*, Senate, Second Reading Speech, 8 December 1965, 2133 (Senator John Gorton, Victoria, Minister for Works). For a discussion on the distinctive nature of the authorisation process, see Brunt (1994) 483.

120 Section 47 *Trade Practices Act 1965*; the commissioner only took two such cases to the tribunal. See Donald and Heydon (1978) 8.

121 See [Hilmer Report] (1993) 29; *Re 7-Eleven Stores Pty Ltd, Australian Association of Convenience Stores Incorporated and Queensland Newsagents Federation* (1994) ATPR 41-357, 42,645, 42,677.

122 Michal Gal, *Competition Policy for Small Market Economies* (2003) 55.

123 See Robert French, 'Authorisation and Public Benefit — Playing with Categories of Meaningless Reference?' (Paper presented at 4th Annual University of South Australia Trade Practices Workshop, Barossa Valley Resort, 20–21 October 2006) for a discussion of the terms public interest and public benefit, <http://www.fedcourt.gov.au/aboutct/judges_papers/speeches_frenchj21.rtf> at 1 September 2007.

Public interest can never be a precise thing that people will be able to accept or predict. It affects foreign policy, political judgment in areas of fiscal policy, tax policy and so on. It will always include anything that appears relevant and will depend on who is making the judgment.[124]

The second important legacy was the creation of the commission empowered with a wide discretion, which continues to engage in a dialogue with regulated parties and uses a diverse set of regulatory tools, and the creation of the tribunal to hear appeals on authorisations. Under the 1965 Act, Bannerman worked hard persuading parties to discontinue many anti-competitive agreements, gaining support and facilitating a gentle acceptance of the notions of competition and competitive practices. This was important in bringing about a cultural shift among the regulated groups.[125] Bannerman recounted:

The significance of the 1965 Act was that it survived and made the existence of competition law known through the community and the professions. The press became interested in it; the lawyers became interested in it; the lawyers talked about it; the Parliament has people in it who became interested in the topic. So it survived. It survived because it got bipartisan support in the Parliament and it survived because there were sufficient people within business who were prepared to use it or allow the Commissioner to use it with their support by becoming witnesses.[126]

It was successful in raising the concerns of the regulator and in beginning a dialogue between the regulator and businesses. It won acceptance from the commercial world for this type of regulation[127] and laid the groundwork for the passing of the *Trade Practices Act 1974*. As Bannerman stated, rather modestly of his role:

The role of Commissioner was important. He was an initiator, consultant who talked with industry, who in a sense corresponded with the Parliament through his Annual Report, which became a political tool in the hands of parliamentarians and the administration; his administration was able to take on many matters on legislative development and other constitutional points.[128]

---

124 Bannerman interview.
125 See Bannerman (1984).
126 Bannerman interview.
127 John Nieuwenhuysen (1976) 34–35. See also Donald and Heydon (1978) 8.
128 Bannerman interview.

Indeed, the powers of the commissioners only increased under the 1974 Act, both in an informal and formal sense. One example of such powers has been the use of undertakings in influencing industry structure.[129] On the manner in which the commission has been able to use such powers, Bannerman stated:

> The role of the Commission changed in my time and has changed very much more since ... [Under the 1974 Act] informal powers grew more and more and they are not found in the Act. Power of forbearance, for example, is very important in formalising industry structure. This is entirely non-statutory and was gathering pace in my time. Non-statutory power is now exercised by the Commission with consent and it delivers it relatively efficiently, quickly and in a semi-secret or secret manner. This is quite remarkable. This has meant that the Commission has become so important especially in the international arena. It has also become important in legislative policy because of its micro-knowledge of the industry. So the Commission has become an advisor in industry matters and does seem to hesitate to make its views known ... That would never have happened years ago. A sharp distinction was drawn between administration and policy at a government level. Now it seems to have matured to be much more a partner of government.

Certainly, the commission plays a more proactive role today, as demonstrated by the successful conclusion to its calls for amendments to legislation to provide for criminal sanctions for cartel conduct.

The third legacy of the Act was the retention of the Trade Practices Tribunal. Many saw this as the government passing the buck by delegating virtually all its legislative powers to the tribunal to interpret and give effect to the Act's vague language.[130] The tribunal, whose membership was to include a federal judge as chair and two lay persons, which in practice became a business person and an economist, fleshed out the concept of public interest in an early decision, drawing the link between competition and public interest.[131] In a set of three decisions, namely *Frozen Vegetables Processors*,[132] *Fibreboard Container Makers*[133] and the *Book Trade* decision,[134] the tribunal made a significant impact, changing forever the way in which price agreements would be viewed. Here the tribunal fleshed out the concept of public interest in an early decision drawing the link between competition and public interest and demonstrated the manner in which such a regulatory approach could work.

---

129 ibid.
130 Brunt, *Economic Essays on Australian and New Zealand Competition Law* (2003) 53.
131 See *Re Frozen Vegetables Marketing Agreement*, 18 FLR 196.
132 ibid.
133 See: *Re Agreement of the Australian Fibreboard Container Manufacturers' Association* (1973) ATPR 8377.
134 See: *Re Books*, 20 FLR 256.

The *Frozen Vegetables Processors* case involved a price-fixing agreement between frozen vegetable processors and retailers in an effort to halt the intense price cutting in the industry following excess production of peas in the 1969–70 growing season. This agreement was registered with the Commissioner of Trade Practices who decided that it was anticompetitive and was maintaining the price at a level higher than a competitive market would have allowed, and was thereby contrary to the public interest. The matter proceeded to the tribunal, where 10 public benefits were put forth by the vegetable processors. They argued that the intention behind the agreement was to prevent a price war, by providing stability to the processors and to avoid social waste. The tribunal stated that, given the structure of the industry and the change in production patterns within this industry, the agreement to fix the price at the nominated level was unreasonable and contrary to the public interest.

In the *Fibreboard Container Makers* matter, the commissioner formed the view that members of the Australian Fibreboard Container Manufacturers' Association had agreed to a number of restrictions that were contrary to the public interest. Whereas some of these restrictions were connected directly to price, such as controlling the price charged or quoted by association members, others were less direct. They dealt with the standardisation of materials and designs of corrugated and solid fibre cartons, as well as the concerted efforts of the association in relation to research and development, all of which involved agreements between competitors. Citing the *Frozen Vegetables Processors* decision as good authority, the tribunal decided that the pricing provisions were contrary to the public interest and would result in denying the benefits of price competition to consumers. As to the non-price-related agreements, the tribunal stated that these practices were likely to continue without agreement as there would be strong incentives to adhere to industry standards and continue research and development activities.

The third tribunal decision was the *Book Trade* agreement, where the major book publishers and retailers had made an agreement about the resale price of books which the commissioner argued constituted a resale price agreement contrary to the public interest. The members of the Book Trade applied to the tribunal seeking exemption from the provisions of the Act. However the Tribunal agreed with the commissioner and in doing so took a significant step, that saw Australia take a different approach to England, where a similar agreement had been exempted under their legislation.

These three decisions should be regarded as providing support for a registration process in the hands of an independent commission and tribunal as an effective way to monitor and regulate cartels. Business saw the writing on the wall and the commissioner was able to flex his muscle and a number of price agreements involving various industries were queried and practices abandoned. Agreements by bread manufacturers, concrete manufacturers, insulation manufacturers and beer breweries are some of the examples of price agreements that subsequently ceased. The tribunal decisions and subsequent actions by the commissioner laid down the groundwork for the 1974 legislation which retained a place for the tribunal. Later tribunal decisions have been able to articulate the theoretical basis of competition regulation, founded firmly on neoclassical principles while giving consideration to the context within which the conduct occurs. One example of such a decision is that in *Re Queensland Co-operative Milling Association Ltd*, which has informed all later discussion on the meaning of the term 'public benefit' within the authorisation process under the 1974 Act. The tribunal has continued to play a key role in shaping competition law developments.[135]

The critical juncture for the trajectory taken by Australian competition law was the period in the early 1960s which saw the need for a different form of regulation and which, after much compromise, settled on the *Trade Practices Act 1965*. Many events and individuals influenced this trajectory. Other key players during these early years, apart from Barwick and Bannerman, included politicians and important industry groups, and their influence led to the passing of the *Trade Practices Act 1974*, which retained an independent regulatory agency with wide powers and a registration process, albeit in a varied form.

The *Trade Practices Act 1974*

When the *Trade Practices Act 1974* was introduced, it was referred to as Austerican,[136] as it relied heavily on the British model, while also borrowing the American language and staunch belief in the importance of competitive markets.[137] The Act was introduced and passed by the Labor Party, which had won government in 1972 after 23 years in opposition. It brought with it a commitment to a host of policies on social welfare and equity, including commitment to making the consumer an important agent in the political arena. When introducing the 1974 Act, the government was set on introducing a composite package, making the link between consumer protection and restrictive trade practices.[138] It was stated that the 1974 Act was bringing together four fundamental rights: the right to be safe, the right to know, the

---

135   Some of these important decisions include *Re Media Council of Australia (No 2); Re 7-Eleven Stores; Qantas; Re Rural Traders Cooperative (WA) Ltd.*

136   Baxt and Brunt (1973–74) 6.

137   See particularly sections 1 and 2 *Sherman Act 1890* (US) and Sections 2, 3, 7 *Clayton Act 1914* (US).

138   Commonwealth, *Parliamentary Debates*, House of Representatives, Trade Practices Bill, Second Reading, 16 July 1974, 573–4; see also Commonwealth, *Parliamentary Debates*, House of Representatives, 7 November 1973, 2918 (Mr Al Grasby, Minister for Immigration); see also Commonwealth, *Parliamentary Debates*, Senate, 27 September 1973, 1013 (Senator Lionel Murphy, Attorney General).

right to choose and the right to be heard.[139] Competition policy and consumer protection was to be in the hands of the same regulator. It made sense to have both consumer protection and competition in the same regulatory hands as they were linked. Investigating a consumer complaint was likely to uncover anti-competitive practices. It has also been suggested that making the regulatory institution answerable to both consumers and business has been a key factor in preventing it being captured by any particular group.[140]

Consumer groups were encouraged to participate in the debates over trade practices and the Labor government sought to introduce consumer groups into a number of debates, including pre-Budget consultations that, in the past, had been dominated by the private sector.[141] This Act was important in making the express link between consumer protection and competition regulation and gave rise to the consumer movement as a formidable force. The role of these groups in deliberations and decisions depends on the manner in which discretion is exercised by the regulatory agency.[142]

The changing tide of economic thought and political support for neoclassical economic thought meant the secret register could not continue.[143] The *Trade Practices Act 1974* put an end to the secret register, which had been largely ineffective in controlling anti-competitiuve practices and had come to be viewed, rather, as reinforcing the 'mateship–collusion ethos'. The annual report of the TPC provided a picture of the disenchantment with the legislation and the secret register. The first report gave an indication of how widespread cartel activity among Australian industry was and subsequent reports demonstrated the limitations of the 1965 Act. The number of agreements registered rose from 5186 on 1 November 1967, to 10,841 on 30 June 1968. The 1972–73 report supplied the 'epitaph for the 1965 Act'[144] and the commissioner stated:

> The current legislation, which is clearly coming towards the end of its time, has nevertheless served a valuable role. Among other things, it provided an entry into a field substantially untouched for many years, it brought the problems to public and business attention, and it became

---

139 Commonwealth, *Parliamentary Debates*, House of Representatives, 24 July 1974, 575 (Mr William Morrison, Member for St George, Minister for Science).

140 Bannerman interview.

141 See *Australian Financial Review*, 18 June 1973, 3.

142 See Baxt, 'Consumer and Business Protection', in Frances Hanks and Philip Williams (eds), *Trade Practices Act: A Twenty-Five Year Stocktake* (2001) 172, for a discussion on the importance of consumer protection and small business unconscionability within Part V.

143 See Richard Ackland, 'Administration in public is a very fine discipline to have', *Australian Financial Review*, 8 October 1975, 5. For the support shown to the proposed Bill by the opposition Liberal Country Party, see Commonwealth, *Parliamentary Debates*, House of Representatives, Trade Practices Bill 1974, Second Reading Speech, 24 July 1974, 567 (Mr Robert Ellicott, Member for Wentworth).

144 See Bannerman (1984) 152.

a means of moving towards principle and demonstrated the need for further legislation. It was also an important vehicle for the development of constitutional law in this field and beyond it.[145]

In 1973 there were more than 14,000 restrictive agreements on the register.[146] In 1965, Senator Lionel Murphy of the opposition Labor Party pointed out some of the obvious deficiencies of a secret register and stated in the second reading speech of the 1965 legislation:

> We are entitled to clear laws against the deleterious actions of monopolies and trade conspiracies. This Bill does not give us these. It is a pretence, a smokescreen. It will set up an administrative morass. By requiring the innocent as well as the guilty to register, it will no doubt arouse opposition to any attempt to deal with commercial misconduct. The Government has done all that it can reasonably do to make the Bill ineffective.[147]

Senator Ivor Greenwood's comments on the then proposed legislation moving to an open register makes some of these inherent reservations and consequences evident:

> [T]he co-operation of business was sought by inducing companies to hand over to the Commissioner of Trade Practices agreements into which they had entered on the basis that if the agreements were with the Commissioner they would be kept secret ... But under this legislation, it appears that all those agreements will be able to be used as the basis for these quasi-criminal prosecutions which the legislation envisages. I imagine that many people would want to protest to see whether that could not be changed. These are areas in which the legislation is important and to which time for consideration ought be given.[148]

A registration process, be it via a secret or open register, was needed to gain the support of the business community, as recognised by the Minister for Manufacturing Industry, Kep Enderby, who stated:

> Special provisions are included in the Bill for no other reason than to remove uncertainty. These are the provisions for clearances and authorisations. In the great majority of cases the applicability of the provisions in this Bill will be clear. In those cases where some uncertainty

---

145   ibid, 153.
146   See Donald and Heydon (1978) 8. See also Richard Ackland, 'Trade Practices Bill Cracks Down on Business', *Australian Financial Review*, 18 September 1973, 1, 18.
147   Commonwealth, *Parliamentary Debates*, Senate, Second Reading Speech, 8 December 1965, 2137 (Senator Lionel Murphy, New South Wales).
148   Commonwealth, *Parliamentary Debates*, Senate, 24 October 1973, 1419, (Senator Ivor Greenwood, Victoria).

does arise, particularly during the early years of its administration, there will generally be opportunity for the uncertainty to be removed by seeking a clearance or an authorisation.[149]

The proposed legislation, for which considerable credit should go to Murphy, echoed the philosophy but not the design of the US antitrust legislation. This was no accident. The historical legacy of the 1965 legislation meant the commission and tribunal would deal with these matters. The determination of authorisations was to become a large part of the work of the commission as the new Act of 1974 retained the central role of the commission in determining authorisations. It also established a much clearer authorisation process, which gave the commission wide discretion to consider a range of matters, including determining authorisation decisions under a public benefit test.

The Authorisation Process and the Role of Public Benefit

Authorisations can simply be described as immunities from Australian Competition and Consumer Commission (ACCC) prosecution for breaches of the specified anti-competitive provisions in Part IV. It is described by the ACCC as:

> A process under which the ACCC can grant immunity on public benefit grounds from the application of the competition provisions of the *Trade Practices Act* except for misuse of market power. The Commission will grant an authorisation only if it concludes that the proposed conduct will result in a benefit to the public that will outweigh the detriment from any lessening of competition.[150]

Section 88 provides that the ACCC can grant authorisations in relation to the following:

i.   an anti-competitive agreement breaching section 45

ii. a secondary boycott provision breaching sections 45D, 45DA, 45DB, 45E and 45EA

iii. conduct that could constitute exclusive dealing

iv. resale price maintenance, or

v.   an acquisition that occurs outside Australia.

Regulations provide the necessary forms that the applicant is required to complete. Guidelines with checklists are also provided to applicants making such applications. Before lodging such applications, the ACCC encourages

---

149   Commonwealth, *Parliamentary Debates*, House of Representatives, Trade Practices Bill, Second Reading, 16 July 1974, 228 (Mr Kep Enderby, Minister for Secondary Industry and Minister for Supply).
150   <http://www.accc.gov.au/content/index.phtml/itemId/3663> at 21 August 2007.

applicants to have informal discussions and obtain guidance from the adjudication branch.[151] Members of staff have at times advised parties that their conduct would not attract the provisions of the Act and that authorisation would not be necessary, the officers interviewed stating that they are conscious of the need to provide information to applicants and to save them the time and expense of making an application where there are clear indications that it may not be necessary.[152] There is a fee payable for such applications.[153] Due to policies introduced in 2007, the ACCC has undertaken to consider all applications for non-mergers within a six-month period, unless the ACCC has issued a draft determination or has obtained the applicant's agreement to an extension.[154]

The Act contains two tests for authorising different types of conduct.[155]

a. The first test, contained in section 90(6), applies to proposed or existing agreements that might substantially lessen competition and proposed exclusive dealing conduct, with the exception of third line forcing.[156] This test states the ACCC can only grant authorisation if it is satisfied that this conduct is likely to result in a public benefit that outweighs the likely public detriment.

b. The second test is contained in section 90(8) and applies to proposed exclusionary provisions, secondary boycotts, third line forcing, and resale price maintenance. This test states the ACCC can only grant authorisation if it is satisfied in all the circumstances that the proposed conduct is likely to result in such a benefit that the conduct should be permitted.

The ACCC is required to keep a public register of authorisation applications as well as applications for minor variations, revocations and substitutions of authorisations by virtue of section 89. The register also includes all documents relevant to the authorisation, such as documents submitted by the applicant in relation to an authorisation application,[157] any draft determination made by the ACCC,[158] record of conferences held by the ACCC in accordance with section 90(8A),[159] and oral submissions made to the ACCC,[160] as well as the determination

---

151 Australian Competition and Consumer Commission (ACCC), *Authorisations and Notifications: A Summary* (2007) 6.

152 Interview 3. See also the discussion in Chapter 3.

153 Currently this fee is A$7500 for non-merger applications and there is provision for waivers of such fees. The ACCC will take into consideration factors such as whether the applicant is a not-for-profit organisation or whether the applicant will incur financial hardship. See ACCC, *Authorisations and Notifications* (2007) 7.

154 ibid, 8.

155 There is a separate test for the authorisation of mergers, which is outside the ambit of this discussion.

156 Third line forcing is defined as the supplying of goods or services on the condition that the purchaser acquires other goods or services from a third party.

157 Sections 89(5), 89(4)(a).

158 Section 89(4)(aa).

159 Section 89(4)(ab).

160 Section 89(4)(b).

made by the ACCC.[161] All publicly available materials are available on the ACCC website.[162] This open process is motivated by the imperative 'that claims made by those supporting an application can be tested and interested parties have the opportunity to put their views to the ACCC'.[163]

Provision is made to ensure confidential information is excluded from the register, thereby recognising the property and commercial interests in certain types of information that may be submitted as part of the authorisation process.[164] The ACCC has provided guidelines on how such requests can be made.[165] It has stated that, under the Act, the ACCC must exclude information from the public register if it contains the details of: a secret formula; the cash consideration offered for the acquisition of shares or assets; or the current costs of manufacturing, producing or marketing goods or services.[166] Where the ACCC is of the view the request to exclude material is excessive, it will discuss the matter further with a view to narrowing the claim.[167] There is also provision made for the ACCC to refuse a request to exclude information from the public register, where the request is not accompanied by sufficient supporting information or where that information is necessary to identify the conduct or arrangements for which protection is sought.[168]

The onus is on the applicant to satisfy the ACCC that the public benefit test is satisfied. The 'future with or without test' has been used by the ACCC in its recent decisions to identify and weigh the public benefit and anti-competitive detriment generated by the arrangements for which authorisation is sought.[169] This is discussed further in Chapter 3 — Discourses on Public Benefit.

While making its determination in accordance with one of the tests in section 90, the ACCC seeks the views of interested parties on the application, including: 'competitors, customers, suppliers, regulators and other relevant government bodies, industry and consumer groups, unions and independent parties with

---

161 Section 89(4)(c).

162 See website for authorisations <http://www.accc.gov.au/content/index.phtml/itemId/314462> at 10 January 2008.

163 ACCC, *Authorisations and Notifications* (2007) 9.

164 See Sections 89(5), 89(5A), 89(5D).

165 ACCC, *Authorisations and Notifications* (2007) 10.

166 See ACCC, 'Guidelines for excluding information from the public register for authorisation, merger clearance and notification processes' (2007) <http://www.accc.gov.au/content/index.phtml/itemId/776053> at 23 August 2007, 1.

167 Russell V Miller, *Miller's Annotated Trade Practices Act* (2002) 986.

168 ACCC, 'Guidelines for excluding information' (2007) 2.

169 Adopted by the tribunal in *Re John Dee (Export) Pty. Ltd* (1989) ATPR 40-938, 50206 and regularly used in authorisation decisions. In *Medicines Australia* A90779, A90780, 14 November 2003, it was stated that the 'future with and without test' was first established by the ACT in *Australian Performing Rights Association (APRA)* A90918, A90919, A90922, A90924, A90925, A90944, A90945, 8 March 2006. For examples of where the test has been used, see, for example, *The Royal Australian College of General Practitioners* A90795, 19 December 2002, paras 5.5–5.9; *NSW Department of Health* A90754, A90755, 27 June 2003, paras 6.1, 6.2; and *Mortgage Industry Association of Australia* A90880, 18 February 2004, para 5.7.

an interest or expertise in the markets and subject matter involved.'[170] The ACCC has also stated that, where appropriate, it may also seek submissions from the community through advertisements in newspapers and trade journals. In addition, the ACCC conducts its own enquiries and research.[171] Furthermore, greater reliance is now being placed on experts to provide assistance with the interpretation of complex data and econometric evidence on various aspects, including market definitions or quantification of the various benefits and costs likely to be incurred by the proposed conduct.[172] All these submissions are generally placed on the public register unless a claim of confidentiality is made. These issues are discussed in detail in Chapter 5 — Discourses on Discretion.

Section 90A requires the ACCC to prepare a draft determination. Usually the commission distributes this draft determination to the applicant and all parties who made submissions. The commission then considers any further submissions that parties may make at this stage.[173] Section 90A also provides the opportunity to interested persons to request that a pre-determination conference be held. Section 90A(7)(a) provides for the procedure to be followed at such conferences.[174] While such pre-decision conferences are generally not transcribed, a record of the parties attending and the discussions undertaken are placed on the public register. These determinations are also forwarded to the applicant and other interested parties and the decisions are also available on the internet and copies are published by commercial legal reporting services.

Section 91 allows the ACCC to grant authorisations in a number of different forms. The authorisations can be in an interim form or for a limited duration. Section 91(2) allows the commission to grant an interim authorisation in certain cases, including where a minor variation and substitution is being considered or where there is an appeal for review to the tribunal. Of particular importance is the power given under section 90(3) to grant authorisations subject to conditions; this has been actively used in the recent past.[175]

---

170 Allan Fels, 'The Public Benefit Test in the *Trade Practices Act 1974*', paper presented at the National Competition Policy Workshop, Melbourne, 12 July 2001 3; see also section 90(2) which requires the commission to take into account any submissions made.

171 For example, see the early decision of *Hardware Retailers Association* A7102, 31 March 1976, where the TPC staff surveyed approximately 10 per cent of association members in order to check on the submissions made. The TPC did not accept the applicants' submissions. Similarly in *Port Waratah* A90906-A90908, 9 July 2004.

172 For example, see the econometric evidence submitted by the parties in *Qantas Limited and Air New Zealand Limited* A30221, A 90862, A90863, 9 September 2003.

173 Fels, 'The Public Benefit Test in the *Trade Practices Act 1974*' (2001) 4.

174 The pre-decision conference was introduced by amendments to the Act in 1977. These amendments abolished public hearings for the commission, substituting the requirement for the commission to issue a draft determination on an authorisation application and to hold a pre-determination conference on the draft if any of the parties required it. Interested parties and their lawyers could attend the conferences, although they could not participate. The commissioner stated that these changes stopped the commission looking like a court and allowed direct contact with business which increased confidence in the administration. See Bannerman (1984) 170.

175 See the discussion in Chapter 6 under Outcome-based Discretion.

Minor variations can be made to the authorisations under section 91A and they can also be revoked by the ACCC under section 91B. Under section 91C the applicant can apply to the ACCC for a revocation of the authorisation and the substitution of a new authorisation for the one revoked. Any party with a sufficient interest can appeal to the Australian Competition Tribunal (ACT) against the decision of the ACCC by virtue of section 101.[176]

The inclusion of the phrase 'public benefit' was not without controversy. The Bill, which was redrafted numerous times, had initially used the term 'public interest', later changed to 'public benefit'. It has been suggested this term had the 'advantage of enabling a fresh line of interpretation by the Commission and Tribunal, unencumbered by previous judicial pronouncements on "public interest"'.[177] The phrase 'public benefit' was subject to scrutiny, much of which remains relevant. The authorisation tests were said to be 'couched in language of very high generality which will require substantial elaboration in the course of their interpretations by Courts and Commission'.[178] It was also argued the use of 'loose terms like "the public interest" invites conflict between economics and the law, by indicating government unwillingness to specify clear economic objectives for anti-monopoly policy'.[179]

The discourses that shaped competition law in the United States did not operate as clearly in Australia. Two sets of discourse have been important in the United States: the Harvard and Chicago schools. While the Harvard School's contribution is often identified as the link between Structure–Performance–Conduct, the Chicago School sees the goal of antitrust as, distinct from other public policy objectives, rather focused on the promotion of market efficiency. The authorisation process, which brings public benefit into consideration, however, demonstrates the complexity of Australian competition policy. It was clear that economics was important to understanding the new legislation and economists and their writings had provided 'reasoned intellectual foundations' for it.[180] Economists would have preferred the use of the term 'efficiency' in the Act, so that the notions of consumer welfare could be imported into the Act and the consumer welfare standard could have been adopted in determining the public benefit.[181] Following on from this were concerns about the meaning of the word 'public'. Could a benefit to a sectoral group, such as producers, constitute a public benefit or did the benefit have to apply to a wider group, such as consumers?[182] Many of these concerns remain.

---

176 For the meaning of 'sufficient interest' see *Re Telstra Corporation Ltd* [2001] ACompT 1 (7 December 2001).

177 Allan Fels and Tim Grimwade, 'Authorisation: Is it Still Relevant to Australian Competition Law?' (2003) 11 *Competition and Consumer Law Journal* 187, 200.

178 Baxt and Brunt, 'A Guide to the Act', in Nieuwenhuysen (1976) 88, 98.

179 Geraldine Gentle, 'Economic Welfare, the Public Interest and the Trade Practices Tribunal', in Nieuwenhuysen (1976) 59.

180 Bannerman (1984) 165.

181 Gentle (1976) 76, 74.

182 ibid, 73.

Shifts in the Regulatory Landscape and to the Authorisation Process

There have been many amendments to the authorisation provisions since 1974. The test as originally enacted required that, to be authorised, the conduct had to result in a substantial benefit to the public that would not otherwise be available. Recommendations of the Swanson Committee that the test be made less onerous were adopted and the Act was amended in 1977.

The importance of the market economy in regulation became central to economic policy with microeconomic reform beginning in Australia in the 1980s, reflecting the growing importance of neo-liberal philosophies across the globe. A major stage of reform came as a result of the Hilmer Committee recommendations in 1993. This resulted in Australia's current national competition policy, which emphasises the importance of attaining a uniform national competition regime; deregulating government business entities in the pursuit of competitive neutrality; and, finetuning of the Act for improved efficiency, including the extension of the authorisation provisions to all forms of conduct with the exception of monopolisation.[183] Amendments followed that extended the reach of the Act to state government businesses as well as the professions.[184] The National Competition Council was created in 1995 to act as a policy advisory body to oversee the implementation of national competition policy.[185]

Further scrutiny of the Act was undertaken through the Dawson Committee in 2003, which conducted a review of the Act. This resulted in a number of amendments to the authorisation process, primarily aimed at making it more time efficient.[186] These amendments included section 90(10), which deems that if the commission has not determined an authorisation within six months it is taken to have granted the application. Section 90(10A) provides that this may be extended by not more than six months, where the commission has prepared a draft determination and the applicant agrees to the extension. In 2007 further amendments introduced a new notification process under which small business could collectively bargain with large businesses without breaching the Act, if the total price of goods or services to be supplied is expected to be under A$3 million in a 12-month period. Further, under sections 93AA – 93AF, small businesses must notify the ACCC of the proposed collective bargaining and if the ACCC does not object within 14 days of the notification, the business which has notified the ACCC receives immunity from legal action in respect of collective bargaining for three years.

---

183   See Brunt (2003) 35.
184   Section 6(4) *Trade Practices Act*.
185   See <http://www.ncc.gov.au>
186   The amendments to the merger authorisations are not discussed herein.

3. Discourses on Public Benefit

This chapter looks at the place of 'public benefit' within Australian competition legislation, before examining each of the words 'public' and 'benefit' in the phrase and then considers the types of public benefits that the Australian Competition and Consumer Commission (ACCC) has recognised over the last four decades. Although the interpretation of both these terms has not been straightforward, the ACCC has in practice recognised a wide range of public benefits based on promoting economic efficiency as well as those concerned with social and environmental benefits. The authorisation determinations can be understood in their political and social context. Whereas the 1970s were concerned with the shape of the post-industrial economy, when economic efficiency was becoming the dominant discourse, the 1980s was a period in which concerns about market reform came to the fore. In contrast, the concerns of the 1990s revolved around becoming a competitive nation, and more recent times have brought the challenges of sustainability and climate change.

The Place of Public Benefit within the Authorisation Process

A standard introduction to the authorisation process is included at the beginning of each authorisation determination. It gives a brief outline of the test used to grant authorisation and spells out that the ACCC is able to grant businesses immunity from legal action for anti-competitive conduct where it is satisfied the public benefit from the arrangements or conduct outweighs any public detriment. The standard introduction also states that the ACCC may conduct a public consultation process, including inviting interested parties to lodge submissions outlining whether they support the application or not. After considering the submissions, the ACCC issues a draft determination proposing to either grant or deny the application. The introduction notes that, after the release of the draft determination, further written submissions on the draft determination may be lodged and the applicant or any interested party may request the ACCC hold a public conference. Following this the ACCC issues a final determination either granting or denying authorisation. In certain cases the ACCC may grant authorisation with conditions imposed, where these conditions aim either to sufficiently increase the public benefit or to reduce the public detriment.

The three main tests for granting authorisation were discussed in the last chapter and they apply to different types of conduct. All require a consideration of the public benefit that arises out of proposed conduct. There are three main tests for granting authorisation and they apply to different types of conduct. All require a consideration of the public benefit that arises out of proposed conduct. The first test in section 90(6) states the ACCC can only grant an authorisation if it is satisfied this conduct is likely to result in a public benefit that outweighs the likely public detriment. It applies to proposed or existing agreements that might substantially lessen competition and proposed exclusive dealing conduct, with the exception of third line forcing. The second test specifically relates to cartel conduct and is contained in section 90(5A) and 90(5B). This test is identical to the first and the ACCC can only grant an authorisation if it is satisfied this conduct is likely to result in a public benefit that outweighs the likely public detriment. As this was only introduced in 2009, it is of limited relevance to the study of authorisations prior to this date. The third test, contained in section 90(8), applies to proposed exclusionary provisions, secondary boycotts, third line forcing, and resale price maintenance. This test requires that the authorisation be granted only if the ACCC is satisfied in all the circumstances the proposed conduct is likely to result in such a benefit that the conduct should be permitted. The ACCC sees these tests as very similar and has stated, while applying any test it will take all public detriments likely to result from the conduct into account when assessing whether the public detriment is outweighed by the likely public benefit.[1]

Although the Australian Competition Tribunal (ACT) has stated the tests in practice are essentially the same, it has at times taken a different view.[2] In relation to the first test, the tribunal found in Re Australian Association of Pathology Practices Incorporated the test under section 90(6) limits the consideration of detriment to the public constituted by any lessening of competition resulting from the relevant conduct, whereas no such limitation is to be found in section 90(8).[3] In relation to the second test, under section 90(8), it has been suggested that because these types of conduct constitute per se offences, the test requires that public benefit be shown to exist in all the circumstances. In Re Rural Traders Cooperative (WA) Limited the tribunal stated that in this provision benefit to the public refers to a net or overall benefit after any detriment to the public resulting from the conduct has been taken into account.[4]

---

1 See Australian Competition and Consumer Commission (ACCC), *Authorisations and Notifications: A Summary* (2007) 9; see also *The South Australian Oyster Growers Association* (2010) A91229, A91230, 26–28.

2 See *Re Media Council of Australia (No2)* (1987) ATPR 40-774, 48406, 48418. For an alternative view, see *Re Australian Association of Pathology Practices Incorporated* [2004] ACompT 4 (8 April 2004) paras 92, 93.

3 *Re Australian Association of Pathology Practices* [2004] ACompT 4 (8 April 2004) para 93; see also *Re EFTPOS Interchange Fee Agreement* [2004] ACompT 7, 9, in which the ACT agreed to this limitation.

4 *Rural Traders Co-operative (WA) Ltd* (1979) ATPR 40-110, 18123.

The Meaning of the Words 'Public' and 'Benefit'

The ambit of the 'public benefit' is not defined in the Act. There has been significant discussion of this term, the manner in which it can be distinguished from the term 'public interest' contained in the 1965 legislation, and how different it is from the common law concept of public interest. It has been noted that public benefit is a nebulous concept; there is also a lack of consensus over the meaning and scope of the term public interest, and this term is difficult to translate into a workable concept.[5] The term 'public interest' under the 1965 legislation was criticised as being too vague and the term 'public benefit' was to be preferred as being more specific.[6] Further, it had been stated the term was only introduced into the statute as a result of pressure from large producer associations. This allowed the interests of investors, producers, exporters and the like to be taken into account rather than a more restricted group consisting mainly of consumers.[7]

There has not been an overt acknowledgement by the ACCC within the authorisation process of the common law concept of 'public interest', nor the manner in which this term connects to the term public interest under the 1965 legislation. The ACT has stated 'public benefit' should be given its widest possible meaning. In particular, public benefit was said to include 'anything of value to the community generally, any contribution to the aims pursued by society including ... the achievements of the economic goals of efficiency and progress.'[8]

The ACCC has compiled a list of public benefits over the years. In its Authorisations and Notifications Guide of May 1999, the ACCC stated:

Public benefits recognised by the Commission and the Australian Competition Tribunal have included:

- Fostering business efficiency, especially when this results in improved international competitiveness;
- Industry rationalisation resulting in more efficient allocation of resources and in lower or contained unit production costs;
- Expansion of employment or prevention of unemployment in efficient industries or employment growth in particular regions;

---

5   See Mike Feintuck, *The Public Interest in Regulation* (2004) 3, 12.

6   Maureen Brunt, 'The Trade Practices Bill: Legislation in Search of an Objective' (1965) 41 *Economic Record*, 357, 384; see also Geraldine Gentle, 'Economic Welfare, the Public Interest and the Trade Practices Tribunal', in John Nieuwenhuysen (ed), *Australian Trade Practices: Readings* (2nd ed, 1976) 59.

7   See Geoffrey de Q Walker, *Australian Monopoly Law: Issues of Law, Fact and Policy* (1967) 5; see also Commonwealth, *Parliamentary Debates*, Senate, Restrictive Trade Practices Bill 1971, 9 November 1971, 1745, (Senator Lionel Murphy, New South Wales, Leader of the Opposition in the Senate).

8   *Re Victorian Newsagency* (1994) ATPR 41-357.

- Promotion of industry cost savings resulting in contained or lower prices at all levels in the supply chain;

- Promotion of competition in industry;

- Promotion of equitable dealings in the market;

- Growth in export markets;

- Development of import replacements;

- Economic development, for example of natural resources through encouraging exploration, research and capital investment;

- Assistance to efficient small business, for example guidance on costing and pricing or marketing initiatives which promote competitiveness;

- Industry harmony;

- Improvement in the quality and safety of goods and services and expansion of consumer choice; and

- Supply of better information to consumers and business to permit informed choices in their dealings.'[9]

The ACCC has been consistent in referring to these factors in its decision-making. More recently, however, other factors have been discussed. In 2001, the then chairman, Allan Fels stated:

In addition, the Tribunal and the Commission have granted authorisations taking into account the following non-economic public benefits:

- the likely reduction in carbon, nitrous oxide and greenhouse gas emissions flowing from a joint venture's upgrading of a sodium cyanide plant in Gladstone, Queensland ...

- encouraging the provision of information on formula feeding from public health professionals that is accurate and balanced and not undermining the decision of women to breastfeed ...

- promoting public safety by ... ensuring the safe use of farm chemicals ...

- fostering fitness and recreation ...

- reducing the risk of conflicts of interest ...

- facilitating the transition to deregulation ...

- maintaining the viability of efficient firms. For example the Commission recognised in a recent draft decision that efficient private hospitals can provide benefits to the communities in which they operate ...[10]

---

9   ACCC, *Authorisations and Notifications, Guidelines*, (May 1999), 7; see also Trade Practices Commission, Commonwealth of Australia, *Authorisation* [pamphlet] (March 1990).

10   Allan Fels, 'The Public Benefit Test in the *Trade Practices Act 1974*' (Paper presented at the National Competition Policy Workshop, Melbourne, 12 July 2001) 7–8.

Still other benefits have been recognised in the recent past. For example, countervailing power has been an important consideration in collective bargaining authorisations,[11] while facilitating competition in deregulated industries has been raised by the applicants,[12] and meeting Australia's international treaty obligations[13] has also been discussed as public benefits.

Other factors that may have once held sway are clearly not now regarded as public benefits. One example of this is the national champions argument that assisting a business develop in the national market will assist it perform in the international market. The contribution of Michael Porter in 1990 suggested this was a flawed argument and the ACCC has clearly endorsed these views, as illustrated in the Qantas authorisation determination, where it rejected the argument by Qantas that the authorisation would assist in making Qantas increase its global competitiveness.[14]

Causal Link — The Benefit Must Flow from the Conduct

An important step in authorisation determinations is to link the claimed benefits arising from the proposed conduct to that conduct. If the claimed benefits are likely to result irrespective of the proposed conduct, there would not be a case for authorisation. The early case of Shell illustrates this point.[15] Here the Trade Practices Commission (TPC) refused a clearance application by petrol sellers to sell only their supplier's petrol — approval for exclusive dealing contracts. Shell claimed the proposed exclusive dealing arrangement would result in single brand selling, which brought with it economies of scale in supply and transportation.[16] The commission pointed out that single brand selling or solo trading is quite distinct from exclusive dealing contracts and concluded solo trading is likely to continue even if authorisation is not provided for the exclusive dealing contracts. The TPC pointed to the market structure at the time where multi-brand trading was negligible — of a total of 3636 service stations supplied by Shell, only 34 were multi branded and the remaining 3602 were solo trading. The causal link was not established and the TPC stated:

---

11 See *Australian Hotels Association* A90987, 1 March 2006; Inter-hospital agreement between *Friendly Society Private Hospital Bundaberg* A50019, 1 September 1999; *Steggles Limited and Others* A30183, 20 May 1998.

12 *National Electricity Code* A90652, A90653, A90654, 19 October 1998, and *United Energy Limited* A90665, A90666, A90670, 25 November 1998.

13 *Association of Fluorocarbon Consumers and Manufacturers Inc* A90658, 26 August 1998.

14 *Qantas and Air New Zealand* A90862, A90863, A30220, A30221, 9 September 2003, iii; *Qantas* A40107, A40108, A40109, 13 September 2006 38; Also see; Michael Porter, *The Competitive Advantage of Nations* (1990) 702; for a discussion of how Porter's work fits with Australian competition policy, see Allan Fels, Chairman, Trade Practices Commission, 'The Future of Competition Policy', (Address to the National Press Club, Canberra, 10 October 1991).

15 *Shell Company of Australia Ltd* A4540, A4543, A4544, A4665, A4666, A4668 9 December 1975, (1976) ATPR, 35.220, 16,701.

16 ibid, 16,752.

A fundamental point in the Commission's analysis is that solo trading and exclusive dealing by contract are not the same thing. The contracts secure solo trading, but it would occur in most cases without them. To accept that solo trading is efficient is not to accept the necessity of exclusive dealing contracts, removing as they do for substantial periods even the possibility of fringe movements that could have some disciplinary effect and assist the working of the market.[17]

The commission has looked carefully in other cases for this causal link. In Australian Swimmers Association Incorporated the ACCC noted the association could establish a code of conduct and make a number of representations on behalf of its representatives without raising trade practices concerns.[18] The ACCC was of the view that many of the claimed benefits would likely occur without the authorisation and, therefore, could not be overstated. Likewise in the NSW Department of Health authorisation, the NSW Department of Health sought authorisation for its policy of requiring private in-house patients in NSW public hospitals to obtain pathology services from the pathologists of NSW Department of Health.[19] One of the benefits claimed was that the proposed exclusive agreements would result in private patients receiving a higher quality of service than they would if there were multiple pathology providers. The ACCC refused to accept this argument and stated the quality of service would be largely unaffected by the proposed policy.

Similarly in the Australian Medical Association authorisation, although the ACCC allowed the authorisation it refused to accept some of the arguments put forth by the association for collective negotiation of fees.[20] The ACCC stated all of the public benefits claimed would result without recourse to the collective negotiation of fees: these benefits included the creation of a framework for dialogue between the Health Commission and medical practitioners that would prevent public hospitals extracting monopsony rents, as well as the facilitation of continuing medical education programs and increasing the availability of a skilled medical workforce to rural populations.

In the Showmen's Guild authorisation, the guild, which described itself as a trade association of showmen, applied for authorisation in relation to its code of conduct and rules of the guild, and also sought approval for collective negotiations with show societies. The ACCC stated it was not convinced the code, rules and collective bargaining arrangements greatly contributed to the development or maintenance of the circuit nor attendance at rural and regional

---

17 ibid, 16,753.
18 *Australian Swimmers Association Incorporated* A90966, 26 April 2006, 8.
19 *New South Wales Department of Health* A90754–A90755, 27 June 2003, i.
20 *Australian Medical Association Limited and South Australian Branch of the Australian Medical Association Incorporated* A90622, 31 July 1998.

shows and the circuit and current levels of attendance would be likely to exist even without these arrangements.[21] The guild successfully demonstrated such a link by making further submissions to the commission.

The BHP Billiton Iron Ore Pty Ltd[22] authorisation concerned a joint venture agreement to allow the parties to develop mining areas in the Pilbarra region with the aim of producing iron ore and delivering it to each of the parties to the joint venture. The ACCC accepted there was a necessary link between the exclusive dealing arrangement BHP had proposed and the benefits a pilot plant would bring. The ACCC asked whether there was a necessary link between the exclusive dealing agreements and the benefits BHP claimed for the pilot plant. It accepted BHP's arguments about the public benefits that the projected pilot plant might bring and accepted BHP's contention that these arrangements would be necessary before BHP could commit funds to the project. In the Qantas and Air New Zealand authorisation, however, the ACCC was not satisfied the proposed arrangements would lead to increased tourism given that the proposed arrangements were to result in higher prices and reduced capacity.[23] It had refused authorisation but its decision was later overturned by the ACT. The tribunal calculated the benefits differently, attaching different weights to benefits claimed and also on the basis that the market had altered in the time during the authorisation decision and the tribunal hearing.[24]

Benefits which accrue over the short to medium term are easier to establish than long-term benefits. The approach of the European Commission has been to discount such long-term benefits for this very reason.[25] This issue has arisen in authorisation applications dealing with deregulated industries, and the ACCC has generally accepted that industry restructuring can result in facilitation of competition in the longer term. In such cases, although benefits over the longer term are more difficult to determine, the ACCC has accepted, in numerous decisions since 1998, that deregulation of regulated industries brings longer-term public benefits, so has authorised conduct which facilitates deregulation.[26]

---

21 *Showmen's Guild of Australasia* A90729, 25 February 2003, 39.

22 *BHP Billiton Minerals Pty Ltd* A70015, A70016, A70017, 5 March 2003.

23 *Qantas and Air New Zealand* A30220, A30321, A90862, A90863, 9 September 2003, para 13.215.

24 *Re Qantas Airways Limited* [2004] ACompT 9 (12 October 2004).

25 *Official Journal of the European Union*, 'Guidelines on the Application of Article 81(3) of the Treaty' (2004) OJ C 101/08; *Official Journal of the European Union*, 'Commission Notice on Agreements of Minor Importance Which do not Appreciably Restrict Competition Under Article 81(1) of the Treaty Establishing the European Community (de minimis)' (2001) OJ C 368/13 para 70.

26 *Australian Dairy Farmers Limited* A90966, 26 April 2006; *Dairy Western Farmers* A90961, 20 February 2006; *Inghams* A90825, 22 January 2003; *Steggles Limited and Other* A30183, 20 May 1998; *Australian Wool Exchange Limited* A30185, 30 December 1998; *Australian Stock Exchange Limited* A90623, 1 April 1998.

Balancing Public Benefit and Public Detriment

Central to the authorisation process is the comparison of the public benefit and anti-competitive detriment likely to result from the proposed conduct. The tribunal in Re QCMA recognised this and stated a claimed benefit may in fact be judged to be a detriment when viewed in terms of its contribution to a socially useful competitive process.[27] Similarly, in Re 7-Eleven Stores the tribunal stated the benefits and detriments are two sides of the one coin[28] — both flow from the same conduct. Thus it is not only benefits that may be passed on to the consumer, but also detriments. It was noted in Re Coalition of Major Professional Sports that one of the results of the collective negotiations would be an increase in the costs of sports betting operators and that this increase in costs may well be passed on to consumers.[29] The 'future with or without' test, discussed below, is used for this purpose and requires an examination of the detriments likely to flow from the proposed conduct, balancing those benefits against the detriments.

Further, there is clear recognition that, while in certain instances the market may fail to take into account all the costs and benefits involved in specific actions, the ACCC has a role to consider such externalities in its decision-making. In Agsafe the ACCC acknowledged its role in addressing market failure and stated arrangements that correct market failures may constitute public benefits. Here the authorisation application sought approval for the parties to enter the drumMUSTER program, which was an agreement to give effect to an industry waste reduction scheme for agricultural and veterinary chemical containers, as well as an agreement to charge a levy in order to finance the scheme. The public benefits were associated with environmental protection; the market failure being addressed was the inability of the market to deal with the environmental impact of product packaging and disposal.[30]

ACCC staff stated in interviews that any enquiry into the public benefit of proposed conduct would also take into account the likely detriments. This was seen as part and parcel of examining public benefit. These detriments were described as negative public benefits, public dis-benefits and also as dis-efficiencies.[31] In its decisions the ACCC has paid attention to four main categories of public detriment. These categories are a non-exhaustive list and examine both structural and behavioural factors. They include: consideration of whether there has been a reduction of the number of effective competitors in the market; examination of whether the conditions of entry have increased; examination of

---

27 *Re QCMA and Defiance Holdings* (1976) 25 FLR 169, 186.
28 *Re 7-Eleven Stores Pty Ltd* (1994) ATPR 41-357, 42645, 42683.
29 *Coalition of Major Professional Sports* A91007, 13 December 2006, i.
30 *Agsafe Limited* A90871, 18 September 2003, 16.
31 Interview 8.

whether the proposed conduct places any constraints on competition by market participants, affecting their ability to innovate effectively and conduct their affairs efficiently and independently; and any other detriments.

Similar to the list of public benefits, a list of public detriments has been compiled by the ACCC consisting of four main detriments:

- A reduction in the number of competitors
- Increased conditions of entry
- Constraints on competition by market participants affecting their ability to innovate effectively and conduct their affairs efficiently and independently
- Other.[32]

The empirical study on which this book is based examined the public detriments that the ACCC found existed or were likely to exist in the determinations studied. The public detriments, which were considered to be of minor importance, important and very important, were summed and used to plot Figure 3.1, which shows the importance attached to the different categories of public detriments has varied in the different years.

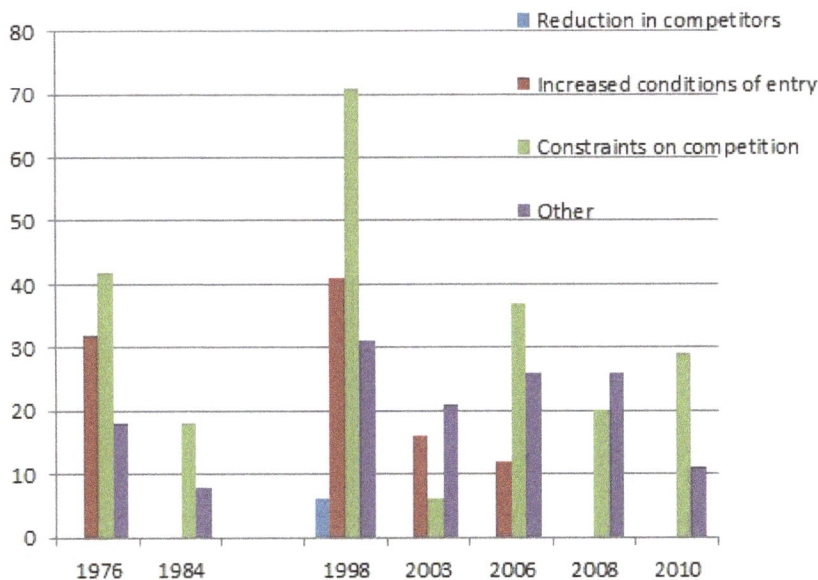

Figure 3.1: Four important categories of public detriments in ACCC authorisation determinations in the sample studied 1976–2006

Source: Author's research.

---

32   Although the wording of public detriments varies from one document to another, it covers substantially the same detriments. See Fels, 'The Public Benefit Test in the *Trade Practices Act 1974*' (2001) 9–11 and ACCC, *Authorisations and Notifications, Guidelines* (1991), 5.

The most commonly cited public detriment category in every year, except 2003 was the constraints placed on competition. For example, the United Energy authorisation was concerned with the proposed rules of a scheme that breached sections 45 and 47 of the Act. It involved agreements that had the effect of determining energy generation capacity, controlling the secondary trading of energy generation capacity and the basis for calculating seller's commission under the scheme.[33] The ACCC noted the scheme placed restrictions on participants' rights to trade in the market and this could be viewed as a public detriment. The ACCC also noted, however, that the underlying rationale was to enhance the level of confidence in the scheme, which would outweigh the public detriments.[34]

In Tasmanian Forest Contractors Association Limited, the association was seeking authorisation for collective bargaining between members, who carried out silviculture, harvesting and transport services, and a number of wood companies. The ACCC noted collective bargaining may lessen competition between forest contractors and reduce their incentive to innovate in respect of the services they provide; adversely affect the incentive to pursue more effective work practices; and also may reduce the incentive of forest contractors to differentiate themselves from their competitors.[35] The empirical study of decisions in 1984 and 2003 demonstrated that the ACCC referred to a number of the pubic detriments in its decision-making. In the NSW and ACT Newsagency System authorisation determination, the detriments cited by the ACCC included reduction in the number of competitors, increased conditions of entry, and constraints on competition by market participants.[36]

In certain instances, it is difficult to determine precisely the magnitude of the benefits and detriments and to decide whether the public benefit will clearly outweigh the detriment. In many such cases, conditions have been used to restrict the extent of the public detriment. For example, in Australian Hotels Association (NSW), which involved authorisation of collective bargaining arrangements, the ACCC was concerned about the constraints placed on competitors and granted authorisation subject to conditions that restricted the size of, and information sharing between, the negotiating committees.[37] Similarly, an appeal process within the code of conduct can be aimed at reducing the anti-competitive detriment. In Recruitment and Consulting, although the ACCC stated the code was unlikely to restrict competition in the employment services industry, the businesses being inappropriately penalised for breaching the code expressed concern about the process. The ACCC stated the existence

---

33   *United Energy Limited* A90665, A90666–A90670, 25 November 1998.
34   ibid, 13.
35   *Tasmania Forest Contractors Association Limited* A90973, A90974, 22 February 2006, 34.
36   *NSW and ACT Newsagency System* A30092, 26 April 1984.
37   *Australian Hotels Association (NSW)* A90837, 27 June 2003, i.

of a fair and transparent disciplinary process is an important means of reducing the detriment that could flow from the code of conduct.[38] It acknowledged it could not in the circumstances impose conditions because the public benefits outweighed the public detriments. The ACCC did, however, point to some ways in which the code could be improved, for example, by taking steps to bring the code to the attention of the public, including workers who might deal with its members; allowing third parties to lodge and progress complaints; and by publishing the full details of breaches of the code on the association's website. So, for example, in Agsafe, the condition imposed required information on the industry association website to be corrected in order to clearly indicate that it would be possible to procure accreditation through alternative sources.[39]

The Future With or Without Test

The 'future with or without test' is used in the process of balancing the public benefit and the public detriment. In Re John Dee (Export) Pty Ltd, the ACT discussed the place of the future with or without test and stated:

> [F]irst it is for the parties seeking authorisation to satisfy the Tribunal that benefit to the public is likely and that there will be sufficient public benefit to outweigh any likely anti-competitive detriment;

> secondly, since the likely benefits and detriments to be considered are those that would result from the proposed conduct, the Tribunal is required to consider the likely shape of the future both with and without the conduct in question; and

> thirdly, that task will generally entitle an understanding of the functioning of relevant markets with and without the conduct for which the authorisation is sought.[40]

The future with the authorisation is sometimes referred to as the factual and the future without the counterfactual.[41] Recently, the counterfactual has been used consistently in the determination of authorisations.[42] In BHP Billiton, the application was straightforward and the applicants listed the counterfactual as primarily involving economic and trade issues. They argued that if the agreement did not go ahead the result would be decreased sales, decreased trade,

---

38 *Recruitment and Consulting Services Association* A90829, 24 September 2003, 26.
39 *Agsafe* (2010) A 91234, A 91242, A91243 and A91244, 30.
40 *John Dee (Export) Pty Ltd* (1989) ATPR 40-938, 50206.
41 Stephen Corones, *Competition Law in Australia* (3rd edn, 2004) 145.
42 This is more common in the determinations after 2003. See, for example, *BHP Billiton (2003/1)*; *Association of Australian Bookmaking Companies Inc* A30243, 9 July 2006, where a standard paragraph is used to explain the counterfactual.

and decreased opportunities to expand export markets.[43] The ACCC accepted alternative arrangements to the proposed agreement in the authorisation were unlikely. In Golden Caskets Agents Association Ltd the ACCC applied the counterfactual to a collective negotiation agreement. In this case it considered whether the proposed anti-competitive agreement, which was the subject of the authorisation, is/was likely to allow the association to negotiate with the corporation and stated:

> [W]hile making no comment in relation to the extent to which the corporation engaged in a consultative process in the past, the Commission also believes that in general, parties are more likely to actively engage in effective consultation whether it is subject to a more formalised collective bargaining process rather than ad-hoc or less formal processes.[44]

Some applications are much more complex, however, raising multiple alternate counterfactuals for consideration. One example with such multi-counterfactuals was the Qantas Air New Zealand authorisation application in which five counterfactuals were considered. The counterfactual that is relied on to establish the authorisation will have a significant impact on the calculation of the net benefits.[45]

If the applicant is unable to satisfy the ACCC that the future with the authorisation is preferred, the authorisation will not be approved. In Tasmanian Forest Contractors, the ACCC denied authorisation for collective negotiations on the basis that the proposed benefits were likely to continue without authorisation approval. The ACCC asserted the likelihood of individual forest contractors continuing to engage in individual bargaining with their respective wood companies, and this would accrue the proposed benefits.[46] Similarly, in Re Australian Hotels Association, the ACCC stated that, even without the authorisation, the standard form contracts offered by service providers that allowed for limited input from the Australian Hotels Association would continue to allow for certain benefits to continue.[47] Likewise, in Re BHP Billiton the ACCC pointed out that due to other projects beginning in the area, certain benefits would occur even if the joint venture proposal was not authorised.[48]

---

43 *BHP Billiton Iron Ore Pty Ltd* A90981, A90982, A90983, 1 February 2006, 9. Also see *BHP Billiton Minerals Pty Ltd* A70015, A70016, A70017, 5 March 2003 which deal with similar issues.

44 *Golden Casket Agents Association Ltd* A90853, 4 September 2003, 18 or para 8.31.

45 *Qantas, Air New Zealand* A30220–A30222, A90862, A90863, 9 September 2003, 70-88.

46 *Tasmanian Forest Contractors Association Limited* A90973, A90974, 22 February 2006, 31–32.

47 *Australian Hotels Association* A90987, 1 March 2006, 14.

48 *BHP Billiton Minerals Pty Ltd* A70015, 5 March 2003, 28.

The Ambit of 'Public' in 'Public Benefit'

The predecessor to the Trade Practices Act contained the phrase 'public interest'. This was criticised as a key weakness of the legislation and it was stated public interest is couched in terms of benefits to sectional interests as well as competition and good economic performance.[49] An alternative approach consisting of three parts was proposed by Maureen Brunt, comprising a statement that, prima facie, the public interest is served by effective competition; an affirmation of the primacy of consumers or users; and a specification of ways in which the standard of living of the community may be raised through non-competitive organisation.[50] Much of the debate surrounding the term 'public benefit' in the 1974 legislation still involves these fundamental issues.

Since the inception of the Trade Practices Act, the meaning of the word 'public' in the phrase 'public benefit' has been widely discussed.[51] Another way of framing this issue is to ask to whom does the term 'public' refer? There are two main views on this issue and both are well represented in Australia. The first is that the public can mean any group of citizens, being producers, consumers or shareholders, with no distinction made between these sectional or sectoral interests. All that has to be established is that there is a sum benefit experienced by some sector of the public. This group would advocate the use of the total welfare standard to determine public benefit. The second view defines the public as consumers and a benefit being passed on to producers or shareholders would not constitute a public benefit. This group would prefer one of a number of other standards to be used in determining whether there is a public benefit, with most references being to the consumer welfare standard.

Private/Sectional Benefit

Some economists, including Robert Officer and Philip Williams, have argued that any benefit to a sector of the public should be recognised as a public benefit for the purposes of determining whether authorisation should be granted. This interpretation focuses on efficient resource allocation rather than optimal wealth distribution, with no distinction made between public and private benefits.[52] The proponents of this view argue the Trade Practices Act should not concern itself with specifying the group that will benefit, a process that is related more to wealth distribution. They further argue assessments about the interpersonal

---

49   Brunt (1965) 384.
50   ibid, 384–85.
51   For a discussion of the possible difficulties the interpretations may present, see, for example, Gentle, (1976) 59, 73–75.
52   Robert Officer and Philip Williams, 'The Public Benefit Test in an Authorisation Decision', in Megan Richardson and Phillip Williams (eds), *The Law and the Market* (1995) 157–66, 160–61.

comparisons of utility that consumers or producers may derive are subjective and should not be undertaken by those administering the Act.[53] Their arguments have been summarised in Pareto improvement terms:

> The essential test ... should be whether there is an improvement in the use of society's resources. If, for instance, a prospective merger would result in efficiencies, reflected in lower costs and higher profits, that is, sufficient to establish the existence of public benefit. 'Insofar as the producer is better off and the consumers are no worse off we have a Pareto improvement'.[54]

Once Pareto improvement is identified, these economists would dismiss wealth distribution or equity arguments on the basis that there would be reason to believe a benefit to a poor producer might be better than requiring the benefit to reach a rich consumer. But, because it is difficult to determine whether wealth transfers are actually taking place, it is preferable to resist using the Trade Practices Act to achieve such ends. Rather, they would suggest such ends could be met by transparently using redistributive legislation, such as tax laws, with which the Trade Practices Act does not concern itself. This school favours the use of the total welfare standard in determining authorisations, which considers the economy-wide welfare effects of an authorisation. It requires that a person may be made better off without others being made worse off. This standard is focused on efficiency.[55]

In cases where the conduct does not involve consumers, the ACCC has accepted public benefits where they accrue to a private grouping. In the Port Waratah decision, the ACCC granted authorisation to conduct that would only result in benefits to the producers of Hunter Valley coal and where the two main producers would be the recipients of the maximum savings. In this the applicants sought authorisation for a coal distribution system to be loaded onto ships with ease in order to enable export to overseas markets.[56]

Where consumers are involved, however, the ACCC has often looked for at least some of the benefits to reach consumers. In doing so the ACCC is, contrary to the view of economists discussed above, distinguishing between public and private benefits. In NSW Department of Health, authorisation was sought by NSW Health for its policy requiring private in-house patients in NSW public hospitals to obtain pathology services from the pathologists of NSW Department of Health. The ACCC concluded the transfer of five million dollars from persons with health insurance to taxpayers caused by NSW Health's pathology policy

---

53   ibid, 163.
54   Brunt (1965) 329.
55   Officer and Williams (1995) 160–61.
56   *Port Waratah Coal Services Ltd* A90906–A90908, 9 July 2004.

was not a public benefit for the purposes of this authorisation.[57] Authorisation was granted on other grounds, however, subject to conditions. In Re Australian Hotels Association (NSW) the ACCC considered the transfer of benefits from one group to another may not constitute a public benefit. In this case the ACCC noted that gains transferred between businesses may not in themselves constitute a public benefit and stated: 'a mere transfer between businesses (that is a transfer of money from wagering and broadcasting service providers to hotels) is not itself a public benefit'.[58] A similar decision was reached in Re Australian Association of Pathology Practices Incorporated, although the ACT did not agree, and focused its attention on the analysis of anti-competitive conduct generating financial benefits and on economic efficiency considerations.[59]

There have been a number of cases where the private benefit occurs alongside other benefits to a wider section of society. One such example is the Australian Medical Association Limited and South Australian Branch of the Australian Medical Association Incorporated authorisation, which related to a fee-for-service agreement between the association and public hospitals in South Australia.[60] Here, although the authorisation was granted, the ACCC refused to accept some of the benefits claimed on the grounds that 'the public benefits claimed would result in private benefits that would enhance the welfare or bargaining position of the applicants, but would not result in broader public benefits'.[61]

The ACCC has stated it does not consider a sectoral interest to necessarily constitute a public interest and it is looking for something more comprehensive in application. The TPC in its first annual report addressed whether a private benefit could be considered to fall within the definition of public benefit. Here it stated that the test would require benefits to the public and not merely to the applicant or some other limited group.[62] The ACCC, and the TPC before it, has been consistent in requiring that there be some benefit beyond that accruing to the members of an association.[63] In the Hardware Retailers Association of WA authorisation, the members of the association applied for authorisation to circulate price lists to its members. The TPC denied this authorisation application on the basis the 'applicant's submissions ... emphasise benefits to the Association

---

57 *NSW Health* A90754, A90755, 27 June 2003, para 7.69, 28.

58 *Australian Hotels Association* A90837, 27 June 2003, 55.

59 *Re Australian Association of Pathology Practices Incorporated* [2004] ACompT 4 (8 April 2004).

60 *Australian Medical Association Limited and South Australian Branch of the Australian Medical Association Incorporated* A90622, 31 July 1998.

61 ibid, 50. The authorisation was granted, however, on the grounds that it would facilitate the profession's full compliance with the Act.

62 See *Re QCMA* (1976) 25 FLR 169, 182.

63 See, for example, *National Automatic Laundry and Cleaning Council* (1976) ATPR (Com) 35-200, 16533; *ACI Operations Pty Ltd* (1991) ATPR (Com) 50-108; *BMW Australia Limited* (1998) ATPR (Com) 50-001; see also *Qantas/New Zealand* A30221, 9 September 2003.

member retailers themselves rather than the public as a whole'.[64] In the Qantas and Air New Zealand authorisation the applicants sought authorisation for arrangements which coordinated activities related to scheduling and pricing for all passenger and freight services on all Air New Zealand and Qantas flights within and departing from New Zealand. The applicants argued the public benefits included increased tourism and cost efficiencies. The ACCC refused to accept the benefits as claimed on the basis that 'the benefits accrue to the Applicants and their shareholders rather than consumers in an environment where there is reduced competition'.[65]

Thus, the general rule is that the ACCC has expected evidence of a benefit to a group that is wider than a small sectoral group. In a number of instances, however, the ACCC has granted authorisation to cases where only a private benefit is evident; in Medicines Australia, the ACCC stated the code of conduct that was the subject of the authorisation generated a public benefit, but the size of the public was not clear.[66] Similarly, in the Australian Tobacco Leaf Corporation authorisation, the ACCC was sympathetic to the tobacco growers who were moving from a highly protected industry to a competitive environment and who were the main beneficiaries of the authorisation.[67] In Pareto improvement terms, as long as there is a net benefit the conduct would be authorisable. In the Qantas and Air New Zealand authorisation application, the ACCC was not willing to accept that the claimed benefit, which would go primarily to shareholders, constituted a public benefit.[68] On appeal to the tribunal, the applicants to the authorisation argued benefits flowing to every member of the community, including both final consumers and producers, should be treated alike.[69] The ACCC argued that unless benefits were shared with consumers it was inappropriate to characterise such benefits as 'public' benefits, except in exceptional circumstances. The ACCC submitted that the tribunal should treat the cost savings that would accrue to the applicants and their shareholders as deserving little or no weight.[70] In allowing the appeal, the tribunal rejected the ACCC's argument, saying the 'public verses private' dichotomy in relation to cost savings claimed by the applicants 'is of fairly limited assistance when examining public benefits' and proposed:

---

64 *Hardware Retailers Association* A7102, 31 March 1976; (1976) ATPR 35-200, 16540.
65 *Qantas, Air New Zealand and Air Pacific Limited* A30220–A30222, A90862, A90863, 9 September 2003. Note this decision was overturned on appeal by the ACT [2004] ACompT 9 (12 October 2004).
66 *Medicines Australia Ltd* A90779–A90780, 14 November 2003, para 5.52.
67 *Australian Tobacco Lead Corporation Pty Ltd A90532*, (1992) ATPR 50-124.
68 *Re Qantas Airways Ltd* [2004] ACompT 9 (12 October 2004) para 8.
69 ibid, para 168.
70 ibid, para 169.

Does it fall in to the category of 'anything of value to the community generally'? If it does, what weight should be given to that benefit, having regard to its nature, characterisation and the identity of the beneficiaries of it?[71]

Benefit to a Wider Group

Perhaps the widest group to whom the public benefit would flow is the world at large. This issue was discussed in the Association of Fluorocarbon Consumers and Manufacturers Inc.[72] Here the commission accepted benefits would flow from the agreement between association members to limit the imports of hydrochlorofluorocarbon gases and to cease the importation and/or manufacture of disposable containers of hydrochlorofluorocarbon and hydrofluorocarbon gases. The commission stated a scheme or arrangement that contributed to limiting the risk to human health and the improvement of the environment would benefit the Australian public and may also benefit the total world population and environment. It is worth noting, however, that the Trade Practices Act deals only with conduct within Australia. This also applies to the recognition of public benefit as reflected by the ACT decision in Qantas, in which the benefits flowing to foreign shareholders were not considered to benefit the public.[73]

A narrower notion of the public was canvassed in Re Coalition of Major Professional Sports. The applicants claimed that members of the professional sports groups bargaining collectively would result in benefits to the wider community, including the development of sport at a grassroots and amateur level, increasing Australia's profile in the international community through publicity generated by the sports, as well as focusing on the ongoing promotion of sports.[74] The ACCC accepted these public benefits and granted the authorisation.

Usually economists espousing a flow through of benefits are not looking at such a wide definition of the public. Rather, they concentrate on the consumer when discussing the 'public'. They have argued that any saving of resources must be a public benefit. Brunt, however, stated that cases where the benefit is not passed on to the consumer may raise other concerns about market conduct and market structure:

It is not the immediate distribution of benefits that is important but their durability. If a merger, for example, gives rise to rationalisation

---

71 ibid, para 188.
72 *Association of Fluorocarbon Consumers and Manufacturers Inc* A90658, 26 August 1998. Further, there was considerable government support for this authorisation.
73 *Re Qantas Airways Limited* [2004] T 9 (12 October 2004), paras 770.
74 *Coalition of Major Professional Sports* A91007, 13 December 2006, 10.

economies and higher profits that are not 'passed on to the Consumer', one needs to ask why this is so. It may well reflect enhanced market power which would need to enter the benefit-cost equation; and there may well be a question of whether the lack of competitive pressure will allow productivity gains to be lost — 'benefit' to be dissipated — in slackness and rent-seeking activities.[75]

The consumer welfare standard is the most popular standard advocated by those who require that for something to constitute a public benefit the beneficiaries must be the consumer.[76] The consumer welfare standard is the sum of the individual benefits derived from the consumption of goods and services.[77] This standard looks at the effect of a proposed authorisation on the consumer. It disregards the benefits experienced by producers or shareholders and would require the benefit to be passed on to consumers.

Although a clear adherence to either the consumer welfare standard or the total welfare standard is not evident in the authorisation determinations, the ACCC has required at least some of the public benefits be passed on to the consumer in a number of determinations.[78] For example, in Re Showmen's Guild, the guild argued that the code for which it sought authorisation resulted in providing assistance to small businesses as well as providing greater bargaining power to such businesses. The ACCC stated it would be more likely to recognise the transfer of bargaining power as a public benefit if such benefits were felt by consumers, for example, in the form of lower prices to consumers or the reduced prospect of unconscionable conduct.[79]

The Role of 'Pass-through'

Strict adherence to the consumer welfare standard has been proposed as appropriate for determining public benefit. Rhonda Smith has recalled Brunt's comments, discussed above, on consideration of market structure and proposed the following rationale:

---

75   Brunt (1965) 330.

76   The other standard is the balancing weights standard and further discussion of the alternative standards is contained in Chapter 6.

77   Rhonda Smith, 'Authorisation and the Trade Practices Act: More about Public Benefit' (2003) 11 *Competition and Consumer Law Journal* 21, 23. See also John Fingleton and Ali Nikpay, 'Stimulating or Chilling Competition', Office of Fair Trading (United Kingdom), (Paper presented at Competition Enforcement Conference, 25 September 2008) <http://www.oft.gov.uk/news/speeches/2008/0808> at 25 October 2008.

78   See *Qantas* A90962, A90963, A30220, A30221, 9 September 2003.

79   *Showmen's Guild* A90729, 25 February 2003, 41.

Failure to pass-through some of the savings indicates that the firm/s concerned is/are not subject to much competitive pressure. Consequently, the efficiency gains anticipated from the conduct may not eventuate or may be dissipated subsequently.[80]

Pass through occurs when there is evidence to show that the public benefit can be passed on to a consumer or a group of consumers. The empirical work in this book indicates that both the concept and the term 'pass-through' have become more accepted in ACCC determinations since 1998. The decisions since this time deal with the extent to which the claimed benefits may flow through to the consumer. In the decisions studied, the term and concept are used in the determinations from 1998,[81] whereas they are not referred to at all in the commission decisions of 1976 and 1984.[82]

Pass-through will be easier to show in cases of economic efficiency that can result in cost savings, as illustrated in Southern Sydney Regional Organisation of Councils. The ACCC acknowledged that there were a number of public benefits that could arise from the proposed conduct although it was clear that it was easier to quantify the pass-through where there were cost savings involved. The ACCC noted: 'improvements in business efficiency and the reduction of operational and transaction costs to councils are likely to result in lower prices to ratepayers'.[83] The ACCC also noted, however, the other benefits of the proposed conduct were environmental in nature, reducing the amount of waste diverted to landfill, but this was not clearly connected to pass-through in the decision.

The reported decisions at times clearly refer to the term pass-through and at other times the reference is oblique. For example, in Australian Hotels Association, pass-through was an important factor in the commission's decision, stating it was of the view that 'any increase in PubTAB commissions or reduction in SKY Channel fees is unlikely to result in a significant pass-through to consumers'.[84] The ACCC in its determinations has not required all the benefits to reach the consumer, as illustrated in the Australian Society of Anaesthetists, where the ACCC accepted that improved efficiency represents a public benefit even where the full extent of the benefit is not passed on to the final consumer.[85]

---

80 Smith (2003) 28.
81 For example see: *Job Futures Market* A90625, 8 April 1998; *Australian Medical Association Limited* A90622, 31 July 1998; *Qantas* A90962, A90963, A30220, A30221, 9 September 2003; *Inghams* A90825, 22 January 2003; *Australian Direct Marketing Association* A90876, 29 June 2006; *Coalition of Major Professional Sports* A91007, 13 December 2006; *Australian Performing Rights Association (APRA)*, A90918, A90919, A90922, A90924, A90925, A90944, A90945, 8 March 2006.
82 Some reference to the concept is made in *Real Estate Institute of Australia* A90396, 25 June 1984; *International Air Transport Association* A3485, 31 October 1984.
83 *Southern Sydney Regional Organisation of Councils* A90980, 25 January 2006.
84 *Australian Hotels Association* A90987, 1 March 2006, 58.
85 *Australian Society of Anaesthetists* (2000) ATPR 50-278, 53412.

The empirical study collates the instances where pass-through was referred to in either the authorisation application or determination. Figure 3.2 shows that the discussion of pass-through has increased over time by charting the times the concept of pass through is raised in the ACCC determinations included in the sample study. It also illustrates the number of cases where the authorisation was granted when pass-through was raised — which means that the authorisation was successful. Figure 3.2 also shows the number of cases where the concept of pass through was raised although the authorisation was not granted. This figure shows that, in 1976, the concept of pass-through was discussed in five cases although the authorisation was not granted. In 2006 and 2010 pass-through was raised in 23 and 24 decisions respectively and authorisation was granted in all these cases. This may point to an improvement in the types of guidelines being issued to the authorisation applicants as well as growing familiarity with the concept itself.

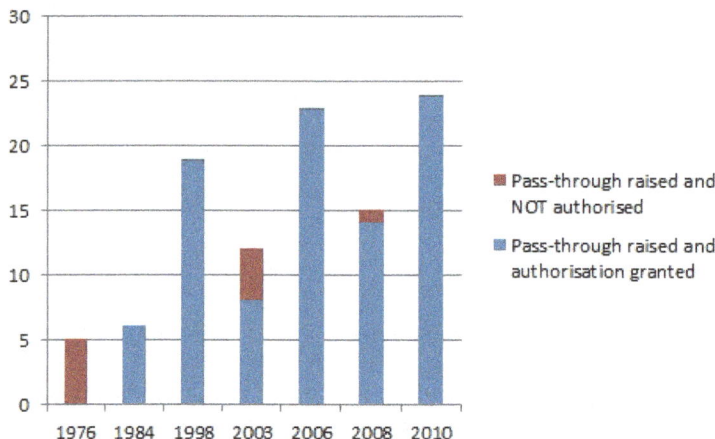

Figure 3.2: Evidence of pass-through in ACCC authorisation determinations in the sample studied 1976–2010[86]

Source: Author's research.

In the Qantas and Air New Zealand authorisation, the ACCC looked at whether the benefits were going to be passed through to the consumer and stated it was of the view that benefits to a particularly small group or segment of the community may be regarded as benefits to the public. The ACCC expressed reservations about the extent of public benefit claimed and stated any cost savings were likely to accrue to shareholders rather than consumers in an environment of reduced competition.[87] These reservations were rejected by the ACT on appeal, where it rejected the consumer welfare standard.[88] As discussed earlier, the ACT

---

86 Evidence of pass-through was noted by the ACCC as present in these decisions.
87 *Qantas* A90962, A90963, A30220, A30221, 9 September 2003.
88 *Re Qantas Airways Limited* [2004] ACompT 9 (12 October 2004), paras 190, 191.

clearly did not require the consumer welfare standard to be satisfied for public benefit to be established. There was no need for the benefits to directly accrue to the consumers and the tribunal stated efficiencies need not 'necessarily be passed on to consumers', although 'gains that flow through only to a limited number of members of the community will carry less weight.'[89] In the later decision the ACCC clearly stated that not all of the efficiency benefits accrued from the proposed arrangements would be benefits to Australians.[90]

Following the tribunal decision in Qantas and Air New Zealand, the ACCC demonstrated a clearer approach to the consideration of public benefit. For example, in the Australian Performing Rights Association (APRA) authorisation, the ACCC recognised that the cost savings generated by the proposed arrangements would be passed on to APRA's members who were also composers, many of whom were overseas composers. Nevertheless the ACCC, referring to the Tribunal's decision in Qantas and Air New Zealand, accepted that 'while carrying less weight than if they were passed through, significant weight should be accorded to those cost savings the benefits of which accrue primarily to APRA's members'.[91]

The need for some of the benefits to reach the consumer was acknowledged in Australian Hotels Association. Here it was argued that allowing the collective bargaining process to be authorised would mean more favourable terms of trading for members and this would result in reduced costs, which would be passed on to the consumers in the form of enhanced service standards and facilities.[92] It was pointed out that in this case the benefit that reached the consumer was likely to be low. The ACCC, however, accepted this as a public benefit, stating the revenue gains to the hoteliers, who were the association members, would likely be passed through in the form of lower prices and improved quality to consumers as a result of the collective bargaining process and that this would constitute a public benefit.[93] In Australian Brick and Blocklaying Training Foundation Limited, the ACCC recognised that authorising the implementation of a levy on the sale of bricks intended to fund a national training program to alleviate shortages of skilled bricklayers would have a number of benefits. It would result in increases in efficiency in an industry that is 'the engine room of the Australian economy' and would contribute to increases in the gross domestic product, which would provide public benefits that spread across the economy.[94] Thus the benefits would be to a wider cross-section of the public.

---

89 ibid, 50.
90 *Qantas* A40107, A40108, A40109, 13 September 2006, 35.
91 *APRA* A90918, A90919, A90922, A90924, A90925, A90944, A90945, 8 March 2006, 689.
92 *Australian Hotels Association* A90987, 1 March 2006, 19.
93 *Australian Hotels Association (NSW)*, A90837, 27 June 2003, 58, para 11.63.
94 *Australian Brick and Blocklaying Training Foundation Limited* A90993, 26 April 2006, 30.

At times, pass-through may be an easy issue to resolve, as illustrated by the Myer authorisation where the ACCC stated: 'given the large number of Myer stores ... this is likely to result in significant discounts across a range of retail goods being offered to consumers across Australia'.[95] Smith, however, pointed out pass-through can be difficult to determine and stated the 'problem for the ACCC in assessing the claimed efficiency gains from conduct is that it cannot know whether the benefits will be enduring'.[96] Such information can only be gained by monitoring the conduct after the authorisation has been given.

This was discussed by both the ACCC and the ACT in the EFTPOS decision. This application concerned the use of Electronic Funds Transfer at Point of Sale (EFTPOS) transactions. Such transactions are facilitated by a debit card that is issued by the cardholder's financial institution and linked to a transaction account. The cardholder is able to use this card to purchase goods and withdraw cash at various merchants. The cardholder is able to use the merchants' electronic network to instruct the merchant's financial institution to transfer the funds and this information is communicated via the merchant's financial institution to the customer's financial institution. In 2003 there were approximately 63.8 million EFTPOS transactions processed at a value of A\$4 billion. The proposed authorisation application was an agreement among card-issuing financial institutions and merchant-acquiring financial institutions to set the interchange or wholesale fees for EFTPOS transactions to zero. As such an agreement was likely to attract the price-fixing provisions under section 45A, the authorisation application was necessary. Both the ACCC and the ACT pointed out that pass-through was not easy to identify. In the draft determination, the ACCC was concerned competition between card-issuing institutions may not be sufficient to ensure a lasting pass-through of the savings by card issuers to cardholders, and that the barriers to entry erected from this agreement may inhibit potential new entrants that may also adversely affect the benefits that could be passed on to the wider community.[97] Following the draft determination, the Australian Payments Clearing Association, among other interested parties, made submissions to the ACCC. The ACCC reassured the association that access reform would be introduced and this would reduce the barriers to entry for new entrants. Further, the submissions made by the applicants on ways in the authorisation would enhance disclosure and the details of the information campaign it proposed to implement also reassured the ACCC that the benefits may be passed on to the consumers. Following these submissions the ACCC granted authorisation.

---

95 *Myer Stores Limited* A400082, 4 June 2003, 17. See also reauthorisation of the same conduct in 2008: *Myer* A91091, 3 September 2008, 13.
96 Smith (2003) 28.
97 *Re EFTPOS Interchange Fee Agreement* [2004] ACompT 7 30.

The ACT, however, did not agree with the ACCC's decision stating the 'Proposed Agreement is likely to have the effect of passing on to the general body of consumers an annual cost of $170 million, or a substantial part thereof'.[98] The ACT queried the evidence on pass-through from the banks, stating: 'while all economists who gave evidence agreed with the general proposition that the proposed change in interchange fees is likely to be passed on (at least to some extent) to cardholders, the evidence presented leaves us quite unable to make any worthwhile finding as to the quantification'.[99] The tribunal also pointed out there was unlikely to be any audit of the claim so pass-through to consumers would be guaranteed.[100] This again raised the issue of how all types of public benefit claims can be monitored. In the Cuscal[101] and Suncorp Metway[102] applications, authorisation was granted for an agreement not to charge cardholders for ATM transactions operated by network members, which was an attempt to reduce the competitive disadvantage that smaller financial institutions faced when competing with larger financial institutions with broad networks.

There are other reasons that make the pass-through requirement difficult to establish in all cases. This includes cases where the conduct is at an intermediate stage of production, which does not necessarily translate to consumer savings. In the Agsafe authorisation, which dealt with a code of ethics among distributors of veterinary and agricultural chemicals, the commission noted that the distributors' additional costs of compliance with the code were likely to be passed on to retailers and, in turn, consumers, as well as the benefits of having more information and safer handling processes.[103] In other cases, however, the effect on the consumer is more difficult to establish, as illustrated in the Port Waratah and Newcastle Port Corporation authorisation decisions. The applicants in Port Waratah were granted authorisation for a capacity distribution system. This system aimed to match the amount of coal that was marked for export by Hunter Valley coal producers to the capacity of the rail and port systems to transport coal onto vessels in the port of Newcastle. The commission granted authorisation on the basis of benefits that would accrue to the producers of coal in the Hunter Valley. There was no evidence, however, that these benefits would be passed on to the consumer and the ACCC stated the difficulties in requiring such evidence:

---

98   ibid, 41.
99   ibid, 30–31.
100   ibid, 31.
101   *Cuscal Limited & Ors* (2010) A91175–A91177.
102   *Suncorp Metway Limited & Bendigo & Adelaide Bank Limited* (2010) A91232–A91233.
103   Agsafe (2010) p 24, 28.

It does not seem practical to attempt to measure exactly how much of the benefit and detriment flows through to the Australian community. The Commission therefore proposes to discount both the benefit and detriment equally.[104]

Furthermore there may be cases where the effect on the consumer is difficult to determine or where no consumer is affected. This occurs in deregulated markets such as primary producers of chickens or milk. These parties have sought to gain authorisation for collective bargaining to work as a group in entering contracts with wholesale purchasers of their product. In such instances, the end consumer is absent and pass-through may be difficult to gauge. In the Victorian Farmers Federation[105] the chicken-meat growers sought authorisation for collective bargaining with nominated processors of the produce. Here the effect on the consumer was not at issue. Rather it was the ability of the small growers to bargain that was important and pass-through was not directly relevant.[106]

In the Surgeons authorisation, the proposed conduct involved processes within the Royal Australasian College of Surgeons, which provides for the training of surgeons and the provision of continuing training programs. The benefits to the consumer from having qualified surgeons were recognised, although the issue of pass-through did not receive extensive attention.[107] Similarly in Refrigerant Reclaim Australia Ltd, the public benefit in the form of improvement to the environment was acknowledged, although the actual pass-through, however obvious, was not discussed.[108] And, in Central Queensland Local Government Association, the applicant argued that authorisation would benefit the ratepayers through a streamlined and consistent waste and recyclables collection service,[109] and the ACCC stated that it was reasonable to expect that the benefits would be passed on to the taxpayer,[110] although there was little discussion of how this might happen.

Many professional groups, including lawyers, accountants and architects, have submitted applications dealing with codes of conduct and the incorporation of ethical practices or fixed fees. These have been authorised in the past by the ACCC on the basis that, even though such conduct may be anti-competitive, there are overall benefits in promoting ethical practices via self-regulation

---

104   *Port Waratah* A90906–A90908, 9 July 2004, 62. See also *Newcastle Port Corporation* A91072–A91073, 23 April 2008.

105   *Victorian Farmers Federation* (2010) A91214.

106   See also *Tasmania Farmers & Graziers Association* (2010) and *Premium Milk* (2010) A91236 22 in which pass-through was examined.

107   *Royal Australasian College of Surgeons* A90765, 30 June 2003.

108   *Refrigerant Reclaim Australia Ltd* A90854, 7 May 2003. See also *The South Australian Oyster Growers Association* (2010).

109   *Central Queensland Local Government Association* (2008) A91087 13 August 2008, 22.

110   See also *Council of the Municipality of Ashfield* (2008) 24.

mechanisms.[111] In the example of the Australian Medical Association Limited and South Australian Branch of the Australian Medical Association Incorporated authorisation, the ACCC accepted the main public benefit was facilitation of the application of the Act to the medical profession. Although it is clear there would be a long-term benefit from the wider application of the Act and the creation of a more competitive marketplace, a pass-through of the benefit to the consumer within a specific time frame may be difficult to achieve. Price agreements between health practitioners in one workplace has also been authorised on the basis that consistency of fees, continuity of patient care and predictability of cost is a benefit to consumers.[112] Similarly, authorising a code of conduct that gives improved information and complaints avenues to consumers is working at empowering different stakeholders in the marketplace, although it may be difficult to assess whether the information or complaints procedures will be more frequently accessed by consumers.[113]

The European Commission has recognised some of these problems and noted such qualitative efficiencies may be harder to pass-through to the consumer in the short term and, where these consumer gains may occur sometime in the future, the value of future gains must be discounted.[114] It also stated it would consider allowing agreements on research and development that may result in the creation of a safer product to proceed because the safety effects are greater than the anti-competitive effects. It acknowledged that any such assessment necessarily requires value judgment/s and it is difficult to assign precise values.[115]

The above discussion illustrates the many complexities involved in interpreting the term 'public'. Much discussion has turned on who the public is that benefits from the proposed practices. Can it mean one slice, section or part of the community or does the benefit have to flow to a wider group, requiring evidence of pass-through? Decisions of the ACCC after 1998 show a greater awareness of the concept, and reference to the concept in deliberations is common. The approach has become even more consistent in the 2006 deliberations included in the empirical study, following from the tribunal's decision in Qantas, where the ACCC indicated its acceptance of benefits accruing to both sectoral groups as well as the wider public.

---

111 See Fels, 'Regulation, Competition and the Professions' (Paper presented at the Industry Economics Conference, Melbourne, 13 July 2001).

112 *Australian Dental Association* A91094, A91095, 10 December 2008, 20, 22. See also *CALMS Ltd* A91092, 30 June 2008.

113 See *Generic Medicines Industry Association Pty Ltd* A91218 & 91219, 3 November 2010; see *Vision Group Holdings Limited* (2010) A91217.

114 ACCC, *Authorisations and Notifications, Guidelines* (1991) 88.

115 ibid, 16, para 103.

The Meaning of 'Benefit' in 'Public Benefit'

The starting point for any examination of the word 'benefit' within the phrase public benefit is the seminal decision in Re QCMA, where the tribunal opted for the widest possible conception of public benefit and stated:

> This we see as anything of value to the community generally, any contribution to the aims pursued by the society including as one of its principal elements (in the context of trade practices legislation) the achievement of the economic goals of efficiency and progress. If this conception is adopted, it is clear that it could be possible to argue in some cases that a benefit to the members or employees of the corporations involved served some acknowledged end of public policy even though no immediate or direct benefit to others was demonstrable.[116]

This issue was discussed in the Re 7-Eleven Stores Pty Ltd decision, where the ACT agreed that it would be a public benefit to encourage small businesses as long as they were efficient.[117] Here the applicants were seeking a review of the commission decision that refused authorisation. The facts concerned the system of distributing newspapers in Victoria: a system that granted territorial monopoly rights to newsagents. This system had been authorised previously. The tribunal's decision clearly emphasised the economic goals of efficiency and progress. The tribunal returned to the QCMA decision and the phrase 'efficiency and progress'. It stated:

> The assessment of efficiency and progress must be from the perspective of society as a whole: the best use of society's resources. We bear in mind that (in the language of economics today) efficiency is a concept that is usually taken to encompass 'progress': and that commonly efficiency is said to encompass allocative efficiency, productive efficiency and dynamic efficiency.[118]

The emphasis is on economic efficiency, which is viewed as the ultimate goal of competition policy.[119] The ACT was of the view that the distribution system was protecting inefficient business (the newsagent and the subagent) and preventing other small business (convenience stores) from entering this market.[120] In

---

116 Re QCMA (1976) 25 FLR 169, 182–83.
117 Re 7-Eleven Stores Pty Ltd, Australian Association of Convenience Stores Incorporated and Queensland Newsagents Federation (1994) ATPR 41-357, 42645, 42681.
118 ibid, 42677.
119 Allan Fels and Tim Grimwade, 'Authorisation: Is It Still Relevant to Australian Competition Law?' (2003) 11 Competition and Consumer Law Journal 187, 200. See also Re Qantas Airways Limited [2004] A Comp T 9 (12 October 2004) para 157, in which the tribunal stated that it is necessary to consider the significance of allocative, dynamic and productive efficiency.
120 Re 7-Eleven Stores Pty Ltd (1994) ATPR 41-357, 42645, 42681.

considering the arrangements, the tribunal stated that they had resulted in 'past losses to the community incurred through suppression of competition [that] can never be recovered'.[121] The tribunal also stated the proposed arrangements resulted in 'efficiency losses through the non-achievement of available scale economies, and lost consumer choice'.[122] It stated these losses could be lessened by hastening the advent of fully competitive market forces. The tribunal proposed different transition periods to a deregulated market for the different types of arrangements under consideration.

In the Re Australian Wool Growers Association Ltd decision, the tribunal was asked to review a decision by the ACCC granting authorisation to the Business Rules, which included rules providing for quality control procedures, market reporting, and research and development activities of the Australian Wool Exchange Limited. The tribunal was satisfied that the rules of the marketplace provided a properly supervised and controlled facility for the offering of wool for sale in a competitive environment. The tribunal pointed out:

> It is a benefit to the public that there be administered, as part of the process of offering of wool for sale, a system of quality control and quality assurance whereby quality standards can be propounded, supervised and controlled by an entity such as the Wool Exchange whose standards and controls are recognised throughout the industry.[123]

It is clear that the term benefit has been construed widely.

The Role of Economic Efficiency in Examining Public Benefit

At various times throughout history, antitrust policy has had different objectives.[124] This is no less true of Australia than elsewhere.[125] Today the primary objective of competition law and policy is the attainment of economic efficiency. The importance of economic theory is largely unquestioned. This is attributable partly to the failure of previous regulatory regimes to deliver results, partly to the soured relationship between business and the regulators, and partly because it promises a value-free, objective way to allocate resources. Dominance of economic theory in regulation is unlikely to fade.

---

121 ibid.
122 ibid.
123 *Re Australian Wool Growers Association Ltd* [1999] ACompT 4 (3 September 1999), para 72.
124 See Eleanor Fox and Lawrence Sullivan, 'Antitrust — Retrospective and Prospective: Where Are We Coming From? Where Are We Going?' (1987) 62 *New York University Law Review* 936, 942–47.
125 See Vijaya Nagarajan, 'The Accommodating Act: Reflections on Competition Policy and the Trade Practices Act' (2002) 20(1) *Law in Context* 34.

Economic efficiency arguments have been important in the assessment of public benefit since the inception of the Act.[126] Both the commission and the tribunal have emphasised the importance of economic efficiency, while recognising that there is room for other matters to be considered.[127] The Hilmer Committee, which reported on Australia's national competition policy in 1993, heard a number of submissions calling for a change in the authorisation process whereby economic efficiency would become the sole objective of the Act. Although the committee saw a place for both economic efficiency and other considerations, it recommended the legislation be amended to confirm that, in determining questions of public benefit, primary emphasis should be placed on economic efficiency considerations.[128]

Table 3.1 divides the commonly claimed public benefits into three categories: economic efficiency benefits, non-economic efficiency benefits and those benefits that could fall into either category.

Table 3.1: Public benefits claimed in authorisation determinations

Clearly efficiency-based benefits	Benefits which may overlap efficiency and non-efficiency	Benefits not justified on efficiency grounds
Economic development	Facilitating competition through deregulation	Promotion of equitable dealings in the market
Industry rationalisation	Enhancement of safety and quality of goods and services	Promotion of certain types of conduct* (usually in the Other category)
Expansion of employment in efficient industries	Steps to protect the environment	Professional ethics
Promotion of cost savings resulting in lower prices at all levels in the supply chain	Attainment of industry harmony	Access to dispute resolution
Growth in export markets	Supply of better information to customers and suppliers to permit informed choices	Enforcement of codes
Benefits flowing from import substitution	Promotion of employment in particular areas	National security
Promotion of competition in the industry	Development of import replacements Providing countervailing power	Meeting Australia's treaty obligations

* See, for example, ACT Law Society (1977) ATPR (Com) 16615 where the then TPC considered the potential risks of conflicts of interest arising from solicitors acting for both the vendor and purchaser in land sales. See also the recognition of self-regulation schemes and codes of conduct that are recognised as public benefits: Australian Tyre Dealers and Retreaders Association (1994) ATPR (Com) 50–162.

Source: Author's research.

---

126   See Joseph Griffin and Leeanne Sharp, 'Efficiency Issues in Competition Analysis in Australia, the European Union and the United States' (1996) 64 *Antitrust Law Journal* 649, 649.
127   See Fels and Grimwade (2003) 200–01; see also Independent Committee of Inquiry into Competition Policy in Australia, Commonwealth of Australia, *National Competition Policy* [Hilmer Report] (1993) 97.
128   [Hilmer Report] (1993) 99.

It has been generally accepted that non-efficiency benefits have a place in the consideration of public benefit.[129] Fels commented that a broader range of social benefits are recognised by the ACCC under Australian law than under its European Union counterpart.[130] It is unclear, however, how much weight should be given to non-efficiency factors or these factors alone could become the basis of a successful authorisation application. Emphasising allocative efficiency and couching public benefits in the language of economics has made it difficult to develop a thorough approach to such non-efficiency benefits.

Furthermore, the important autonomous and active role attributed to the consumer in the market, and idea about consumer rationality have been criticised as too simplistic and not reflecting real market behaviour. Behavioural economists have queried the proposition that market failures result only from information failure and have proposed that market failures are caused by consistent biases in consumer behaviour.[131] There are numerous biases that have been recognised; the most relevant to this discussion is the 'endowment effect'. This is an attempt to explain the observed phenomenon that, irrespective of price, some consumers will be loyal to a particular supplier. Behavioural economists suggest that, rather than approaching the market with a firm shopping list, consumers' behaviour can be influenced by the environment in which the market transaction is taking place, where issues, such as stress of changing suppliers, may determine the decision.[132]

All these contributions query the underlying assumptions of neoclassical economics and the uncritical acceptance of economic efficiency as the central focus. They advocate a move away from a 'one size fits all' policy to one that allows for greater scrutiny and assessment.

Economists have also queried the viability of one competition policy for all economies. Early on, in the mid eighties, Richard Caves identified the connection between small economies and concentrated markets,[133] while Porter discussed the varieties of institutions and environments that can shape the competitiveness of a nation.[134] More recently, Michal Gal suggested that the competition policy of large economies may not necessarily suit small economies.

---

129 See ACCC, 'Submission to the Commission of Inquiry: Review of the Competition Provisions of the *Trade Practices Act 1974* (Dawson Review)' (June 2002) 247; for an alternative view on the decline of non-efficiency factors, see Organisation for Economic Co-operation and Development (OECD), 'The Goal of Competition Law and Policy and the Design of Competition Law and Policy Institutions', (2004) 6 (1 and 2), *Organisation for Economic Co-operation and Development Journal of Competition Law and Policy* 78, 79.

130 Fels, 'The Public Benefit Test in the *Trade Practices Act 1974*' (2001) 3.

131 OECD (2004) 13. Also see: Department of Treasury, 'Consumer Policy in Australia: A companion to the OECD Consumer Policy Toolkit', <http://www.consumerlaw.gov.au/content/consumer_policy/downloads/Companion_to_OECD_Toolkit.pdf>

132 See OECD (2004) 14.

133 Richard Caves, 'Scale, Openness and Productivity in Manufacturing Industries', in Richard Caves and Lawrence Krause (eds), *The Australian Economy: A View from the North* (1984) 313.

134 See Porter (1990).

She identified Australia as a small economy because most of its industries are characterised by concentrated market structures.[135] Gal argued small economies have key characteristics that should be taken into account before determining the design of competition policy. Three of these key characteristics are worth noting in relation to Australia. First, unlike large economies, a firm's ability to realise economies of scale and adopt efficient technologies is limited in small economies.[136] Second, high levels of industrial concentration are likely to affect the contestability of local or regional markets in small economies. Third, high barriers to entry, such as Australia's tyranny of distance, may create supply constraints on factors of production or inhibit institutional and technological change, whereas in large economies this may result in new and better products.[137]

Gal argued that these key factors place a handicap on economic performance. Market forces alone cannot achieve efficiency in such cases, and 'competition policy in a small economy is thus a critical instrument with respect to determining domestic market structure and conduct and the intensity of competition.'[138] For Gal, it is important that competition policy in small economies has clear goals, namely economic efficiency goals that should not be sacrificed for broader policy objectives.[139] She identified small business protection for special mention and stated such protection would be to the detriment of consumers. Gal argued that, even if small business protection were a chosen goal, competition law should not be the method employed to achieve this.[140] Many economists would agree with this view. Officer and Williams argued that, whereas Part V of the Trade Practices Act addresses the wealth distribution issue, Part IV is directed at the promotion of efficient or optimal resource allocation.[141] They emphasised the need for Part IV of the Act to focus clearly on economic efficiency.

So, what does Gal propose as the appropriate design for competition policy in Australia? She argued small economies should reject per se rules and opt for 'a rule that balances possible efficiency enhancements against the anti-competitive effects of cooperative conduct and allow arrangements in which the benefits offset the restrictions on competition.'[142] On this basis it would appear that the design of Australia's authorisation process, which allows for such examination, is appropriate.

---

135 Michal Gal, *Competition Policy for Small Market Economies* (2003) 55, 2. See also Fels and Grimwade (2003) 196–98, for a discussion of size and competition policy in Australia.
136 ibid, 45.
137 ibid, 20–21.
138 ibid, 21, 45.
139 See ibid 50–51. Gal examines the multiplicity of goals in the competition statutes of Israel and Canada.
140 ibid, 48.
141 Officer and Williams (1995) 157–66.
142 Gal (2003) 174.

Gal, however, would focus more on efficiency benefits than other benefits. Gal accepts that, in certain circumstances, non-economic considerations may be relevant and cited as an example for the need to produce a particular product within jurisdictional borders for security reasons. An Australian instance that falls into this category The Council of Textile and Fashion Industries Limited authorisation decision, where the parties sought an authorisation of the arrangements in the Homeworkers Code of Practice.[143] Here the ACCC accepted many non-efficiency benefits, such as social and health benefits, as public benefits. They included: lessening the risk of exploiting a less advantaged group; the provision of information to homeworkers to understand their entitlements; and the provision of improved working conditions for such workers and their families. Another, earlier authorisation decision that raised interesting issues was the Tasmanian Farmers and Graziers Association decision.[144] Here, the 600 growers of poppies used in the production of opiate alkaloids, which are in turn used in the manufacture of pharmaceutical products, sought authorisation for collectively negotiating with the purchasing companies. The growing and production of the poppies, in accordance with the Single Convention of Narcotic Drugs 1961, is required to be closely controlled and supervised and Tasmania is the only state where the growing of poppies is permitted. The TPC approved the authorisation, recognising that it was important for the international market to perceive Australia as a secure and reliable source of supply.[145]

Environmental concerns were the reasons for the authorisation of the Australian Retailers Association Code of Practice for the Management of Plastic Bags, which was a voluntary code for the managed reduction and recycling of lightweight plastic bags.[146]

There have been many who have emphasised the need for public benefits to be efficiency-based. Frances Hanks and Philip Williams discuss the different approaches of the commission and the tribunal in determining vertical restraint cases, and express similar views.[147] Their preference is for greater emphasis to be placed on current economics literature. Reviewing the decisions in the area, they point to the number of benefits that may result from vertical restraints, including the provision of cost-minimising dealership services in the case of franchises; the prevention of free riding on services of the manufacturer in the case of exclusive supply contracts; and, the existence of an optimal number of

---

143   *The Textile, Clothing and Footwear Union of Australia and The Council of Textile and Fashion Industries Limited* A90722–A90725, 31 July 2000; *The Textile, Clothing and Footwear Union of Australia and The Council of Textile and Fashion Industries Limited* (2000) ATPR (Com) 50-282, 53,544.

144   *Tasmanian Farmers and Graziers Association* A80001 (86) ATPR (Com) 50127, 55447.

145   ibid, 50127, 55447, 55453.

146   *Australian National Retailers Assn Limited* (2008) determination.

147   Frances Hanks and Philip Williams, 'The Treatment of Vertical Restraints Under the Australian Trade Practices Act' (1987) 147 *Australian Business Law Review* 147 165–67.

dealerships in the case of resale maintenance agreements.[148] They are critical of the commission for not giving adequate consideration to these factors and conclude that, while 'the authorities are generally well-informed when analysing anticompetitive detriment, their analysis of offsetting benefit to the public would be enhanced if arguments were presented along the lines of the contemporary economics literature.'[149] Such an approach would add transparency to decision-making. There are, however, no straightforward definitions of efficiencies as David Round stated:

> Efficiencies come in all shapes and sizes. Real ones and pecuniary ones; scale and scope economies; technical and allocative efficiencies; dynamic efficiencies and x-efficiencies; short run and long run efficiencies; and production, management, distribution, buying and retailing efficiencies. Some are harder to achieve than others … Some are easier to measure, others are not. Some are mere wealth transfers. Some are of more lasting value to society than others. Do we count them all equally? Should we? Are they all of equal value to society?[150]

Clearly, adopting a limited view of efficiencies would make recognition of non-efficiency-based benefits difficult, as quantifying benefits, such as environmental protection or the facilitation of collective bargaining, is a fraught task (discussed below). Alternatively, there is no justification for ignoring efficiency benefits without a considered coherent analysis capable of withstanding close scrutiny.

Benefits Recognised in the Commissions' Determinations

There has been a good deal of emphasis placed on economic efficiency arguments in interpreting the phrase 'public benefit'. Economic discourse, however, can only partly explain a nation's competition law. For example, Peter Hall and David Soskice emphasise the role of informal rules and understandings that lead actors to coordinate on one outcome rather than another, when both are feasible in the presence of a specific set of formal institutions.[151] The manner in which firms coordinate their activities are different in a liberal market economy

---

148 See ibid, 167–68.
149 ibid, 168.
150 David Round, 'W(h)ither Efficiencies: What is in the Public Interest? A Commentary on "The Great Efficiencies Debate in Canadian Merger Policy: A Challenge to Economic Foundations of Canadian Competition Law or a Storm in a Teacup?" by Michael Trebilcock' (Paper presented at the Fifteenth Annual Workshop of the Competition and Policy Institute of New Zealand, Auckland, 13–15 August 2004) 2–3.
151 Peter Hall and David Soskice, 'An Introduction to Varieties of Capitalism', in Hall and Soskice (eds), *Varieties of Capitalism: The International Foundations of Comparative Advantage* (2001), 13.

from a coordinated market economy.[152] Likewise, efficient antitrust principles in a liberal market economy will be different from those in a coordinated market economy in the context of institutions, such as intellectual property rules or industrial policy, which regulate the activities of firms. Michael Porter, Hirotaka Takeuchi and Mariko Sakakibara further illustrate this in their study of how Japan could increase its competitiveness, in which they argue that, rather than becoming a clone of American capitalism, the answer may lie with developing a distinctly Japanese conception of competition.[153] Joseph Stiglitz added that a free market cannot solve all problems and argued 'one-size-fits-all' economic policies can damage rather than help countries with unique financial, government and social institutions. He argued that the answer for public institutions may be for them to become more responsive to their constituents.[154] Thus, reliance on economic efficiency alone may not be appropriate, and the context in which the conduct is occurring needs careful attention.

Reliance on economic discourse is also fraught for other reasons. Maher referred us to the difficulties faced by an enforcement agency in adopting one particular theoretical perspective, when alternatives are available.[155] Experts can present lucid, well-honed arguments for either side. Furthermore, although it is best for legislation to be focused towards clear goals, such as efficiency, there is always a contest between what is thought to be more manageable and what is thought to be more important. The Trade Practices Act 1974 has tried to do many things in the past and, even today, it is concerned with the protection of small business in ways that may be at odds with the goal of economic efficiency.[156] The question as to whether it should do so is, however, unresolved.

Interviews with ACCC staff indicate that, whereas staff in the past relied more on experience in determining public benefits, there had been a greater focus on efficiency benefits in the recent past. Two past staff members were critical of relying solely on economic evidence, one saying that, in many instances, economic evidence can be flawed and cited the Australian Meat Holding case as an example.[157] In this case, several economists proposed different definitions of the market, which prompted the court to state: 'economics is a study of human behaviour and to determine the boundary of a market, one has to consider what people do and what they are likely to do in the market — in fact and not merely

---

152   Hall and Soskice classify the United States, the United Kingdom, Australia, Canada, New Zealand and Ireland as liberal market economies, whereas Germany, Japan, Switzerland, the Netherlands, Belgium and Sweden among others are classified as coordinated market economies. See ibid, 19.
153   See Michael Porter, Hirotaka Takeuchi and Mariko Sakakibara, *Can Japan Compete?* (2000).
154   Joseph Stiglitz, *Globalization and its Discontents* (2000).
155   Imelda Maher, 'Regulating Competition' (Paper presented at the Regulating Law Conference, Canberra, 21 March 2003) 3.
156   See Nagarajan (2002) 52–56; see also Senate Economics References Committee, Parliament of Australia, *The Effectiveness of the* Trade Practices Act 1974 *in Protecting Small Business* (2004).
157   Interview 9.

in economic theory'.[158] Another current staff member stated that efficiency arguments of mainstream economists have begun to dominate the authorisation process, excluding issues of vulnerability of consumers.[159] Yet another current staff member stated that the diversity in economic thought, particularly that of behavioural economics, was not a large part of the deliberation of the ACT and rarely considered by the parties involved in the authorisation application or parties making submissions in relation to the application.[160]

Seven figures have been plotted to illustrate the changing emphasis given to the 16 public benefits considered by the ACCC in determining authorisations.[161] In each of these figures (Figure 3.3 to Figure 3.9), the public benefits are plotted in order of their importance, except for the category of 'Other', which appears below all of the named public benefits. The number in brackets on the vertical axis, next to each of the public benefits, refers to the number of determinations in which authorisation was granted out of the number where it was accepted as present by the commission. On the horizontal axis, each public benefit is coded and the summed weights are plotted. The figures in this section collate the public benefits which were weighed as important and very important in compiling the data. A number of different benefits may have been considered in the same determination.

Figure 3.3 deals with 1976, when only nine out of the 35 determinations studied were successful in gaining authorisation, which may say much about the operation of a regulatory agency in it neophyte stage than is possible to discuss in this article. This period was also a time when domestic policy was being shaped by postwar economic growth and increasing global business. The need to dismantle a protectionist regime, reconsider the cost of high tariff protection[162] and restrictive trade practices in terms of competitiveness could no longer be ignored.[163] All these factors are reflected in the shape of the Trade Practices Act, which contained far-reaching anti-competitive measures.

---

158 *Australian Meat Holdings Pty Ltd v Trade Practices Commission* (1989) ATPR 40-932, 51105.

159 Interview 8.

160 Interview 10.

161 Benefits that are 'very important' in the determination are given a weighting of 4 and those that are 'important' are given a weighting of 3, 'minor importance' a weighting of 2, 'minimal importance' a weighting of 1. Where a benefit is seen as occurring twice, such as cost savings in administration and production, it is weighed twice. These weights are added together and the sum of these weights is used to plot Figures 3.3 to 3.7. Further discussion of the weighting used is discussed in Chapter 1 and the Appendix.

162 The Vernon Report of 1965 was instrumental in this shift in thinking, recommending several changes to the Tariff Board to place a greater emphasis on the broader economic consequences of the protection of particular industries.

163 John Warhurst and Jenny Stewart, 'Manufacturing Industry Policies', in Brian Head and Allan Patience (eds), *From Fraser to Hawke: Australian Public Policy in the 1980s* (1989) 160; Fred Brenchley, *Allan Fels: A Portrait of Power* (2003) 24; Margot Hone, *From Industry Assistance to Productivity: 30 Years of 'the Commission'* (2003) <www.pc.gov.au/about-us/history 2, 10–11>.

1976

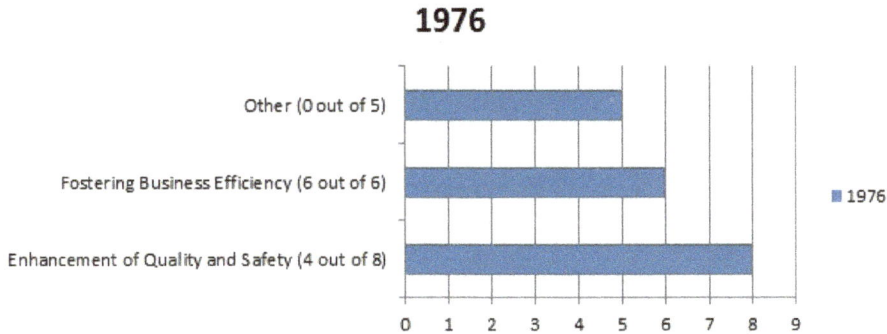

Figure 3.3: Summed weights of important public benefits and the number of cases in which authorisation was granted by the TPC in the sample studied in 1976 (9 out of 35 determinations were successful)

Source: Author's research.

Nevertheless it was, in many respects, these provisions that were incompatible with the structure and operation of the Australian national economy where protectionism was the result of the long-standing tradition of state intervention to both improve the efficiency of capitalism and temper its adverse impacts. Protection of the manufacturing sector to maintain local industry and labour-market regulation in the form of the industrial arbitration system which guaranteed a minimum wage had historically formed the basis of what is described as the 'Australian Settlement', where an accommodation between capital and labour had become the settled policy of the Australian state.[164] The Trade Practices Act was the culmination of a growing recognition of this, marking the end of bipartisan support for high levels of protection.[165] Figure 3.3 reflects the concerns with promoting efficient business as a means of increasing competition, where 'fostering business efficiency' was successfully argued in six determinations.[166]

The 1980s saw a continuing shift from interventionist policies towards a greater emphasis on market forces.[167] The Liberal government under Malcolm Fraser (1975–83) had introduced economic rationalism into policy debate, raising awareness of the need for economic reform. It began deregulation of the financial system and, in January 1983 foreign banks were permitted to apply for an

---

164   See: Jenny Stewart, 'Industry Policy', in Brian Galligan and Winsome Roberts (eds), *The Oxford Companion to Australian Politics* (2007) 275 and Geoffrey Stokes, 'Australian Settlement', Galligan and Roberts (2007), 56–57.

165   See: Ray Steinwall, 'The Legislative Basis of the Act', in Steinwall (co-ordinator), *Butterworths Australian Competition Law* (2000) 9. See also Brenchley (2003) 28.

166   See, *Permanent Building Societies* A5077, A21277, A21289, A21290, A21291, (1976) 17/11/1976.

167   Within the Liberal Party, the 'new right' emerged in the 1970s, and included those who subscribed to what became known in Australia as 'economic rationalism', a reworking of classical laissez-faire economics. They were the Australian equivalent to the Thatcherites in Britain and the Reaganites in the United States (www.primeministers.naa.gov.au/primeministers/fraser/in-office.aspx at 26 January 2012).

Australian license. The Hawke government was elected in 1983 and continued with deregulation of the financial system and with the floating of the Australian dollar, which saw economic reform firmly placed on the agenda.

1984

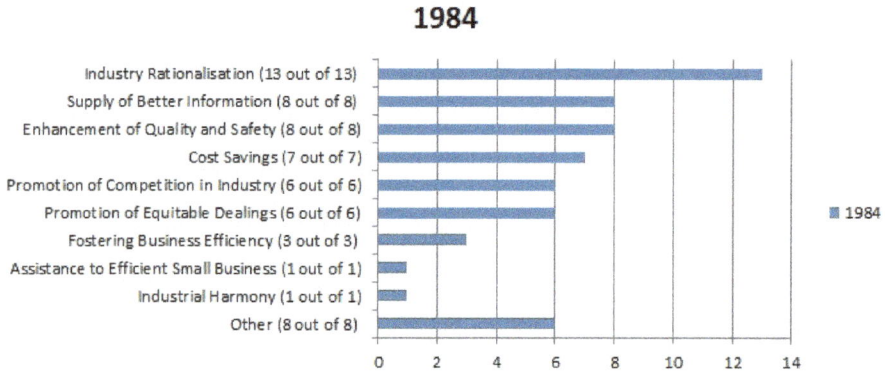

Figure 3.4: Summed weights of the important public benefits and the number of cases where authorisation was granted by the TPC in the sample studied in 1984 (33 out of 35 determinations applications were successful)

Source: Author's research.

Of the nine categories of public benefit featured as important in 1984, Figure 3.4 illustrates that 'industry rationalisation' was most prominent having been argued successfully as an important public benefit in all 13 determinations. Cost savings was accepted as an important public benefit in seven determinations while the promotion of competition in industry was accepted in six determinations, and fostering business efficiency in three determinations. This reflects the stronger focus on economic efficiency factors in the commission's decision-making. This is offset by the recognition of the promotion of equitable dealings as an important public benefit in six determinations, all of which dealt with ethical conduct within professional codes of conduct.[168] For some time, professional ethics provisions had been acknowledged as an important regulatory tool by the commission. It recognised the value of industry codes and stated that codes are an effective and market-sensitive mechanism for delivering the detail of consumer protection rules, provided they are appropriately framed, administered and monitored.[169] The importance of consumer protection was not forgotten, with eight determinations accepting supply of better information as an important public benefit and, likewise, eight accepting the enhancement of quality and safety.

---

168 For example, see *Real Estate Institute of Qld* (1984) A90396 and A30397, 1984; *Society of Auctioneers and Appraisers Inc* A60009; *Canberra/Queanbeyan Panel Beaters Group* A90371; *Stock and Station Agents Association of NSW* A90400.

169 ACCC, 'Submission to the Financial System Inquiry (Wallis Inquiry)', September 1986.

By the 1990s, microeconomic reform had come to dominate the economic and political agenda and the associated policies included the removal of tariff protection, corporatisation of government utilities and business enterprises, the deregulation of industries including the airline industry and the abolition of the two-airline policy and introduction of competition to the telecommunications sector, all of which fostered competition. The governments' focus was on promoting economic growth in a global market.[170] The national competition policy (NCP) of 1995, an outcome of the Hilmer Report, involved the application of the principles of competition policy to the states and territories[171] and resulted in amendments to the legislation extending the application of competition to include the professions, public utilities and government enterprises.[172] By the mid 1990s, competition policy had 'reached right into the bowels' of the Australian economy[173] and forged a cultural change in Australian business.[174] An important tool of this reform was the Productivity Commission, established in 1998 to operate as the government's principal advisory body on all aspects of microeconomic reform. Not only did this body replace the Industry Commission, but its broader charter gave greater emphasis on productivity performance of industry.[175] Its primary role was to identify obstacles to improved productivity in particular sectors, having 'due regard to the important relationships between improved use of resources in one sector and the rest of the economy'.[176]

Figure 3.5 illustrates the importance to the various public benefit factors in 1998 where 29 out of 35 determinations were authorised. The bar graphs reflect the continuing concern with the promotion of competition in industry, fostering business efficiency and cost savings. Promotion of competition and fostering business efficiency were important factors alongside the non-economic efficiency public benefit of enhancement of quality and safety. Wider application of competition laws across all sectors saw the commission faced with authorisation applications from bodies that were previously exempt. Although promotion

---

170   For a discussion of the Labor party's changing economic agenda, see Kevin Davis, 'Managing the Economy', in Brian W Head and Allan Patience (eds), *From Fraser to Hawke: Australian Public Policy in the 1980s* (1989) 66–109, 68.

171   Against the backdrop of major microeconomic reforms, in October 1992, Prime Minister Paul Keating commissioned an independent inquiry into national competition policy, chaired by Professor Frederick Hilmer, which reviewed the structural inefficiencies that limited the effectiveness of competition law and prevented development of a competition regime across all sectors.

172   Among the reasons identified in favour of developing a national competition policy was that Australia was now 'for all practical purposes a single integrated market as the economic significance of state and territory boundaries diminished', Hilmer Report (1993) xvii–xviii.

173   Brenchley (2003) 18.

174   ibid, 8.

175   Hone (2003) 87, 94.

176   Commonwealth, *Parliamentary Debates*, 7720, cited in Hone (2003) 93.

of competition was advocated as a public benefit in many applications, it was not always accepted, as demonstrated by the Australian Performing Rights Association determination.[177]

1998

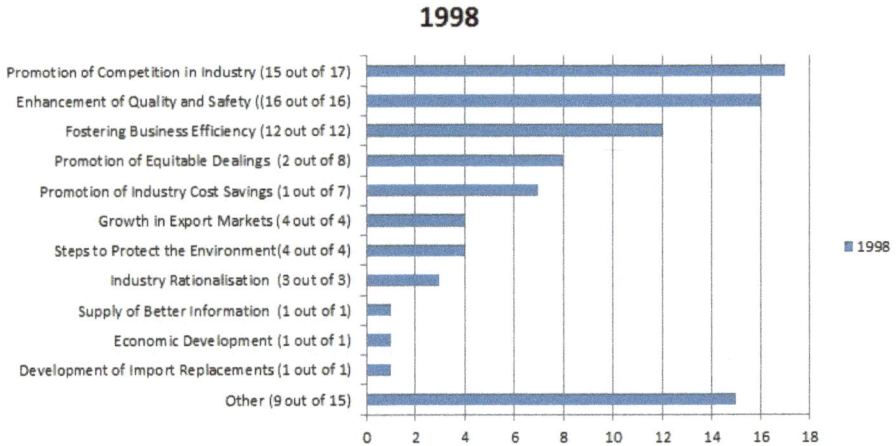

Figure 3.5: Summed weights of the important public benefits and the number of cases where authorisation was granted by the ACCC in the sample studied in 1998 (29 out of 35 were successful in 1998)

Source: Author's research.

The focused efforts described in the last section to build a competitive market economy remained a priority in the first half of the last decade. The Productivity Commission had been asked to assess the impact of the NCP reforms and, in 2005, it reported that productivity and price changes would be likely to raise Australia's GDP by around 2.5 per cent.[178] The increasing use of modelling and quantification in order to enable assessment of policy was being promoted by government and used by regulators.[179]

---

177   *Australian Performing Rights Association* (1998), A30192 and A30193.
178   See Productivity Commission, *Review of National Competition Policy Reforms*, Inquiry Report No 33, Canberra, February 2005.
179   Interview 2; see also Department of Finance and Deregulation, Commonwealth of Australia, Office of Best Practice Regulation (OBPR), 'Cost Benefit Analysis', which emphasises cost benefit analysis. <http://www.finance.gov.au/obpr/cost-benefit-analysis.html> at 15 October 2008.

2003

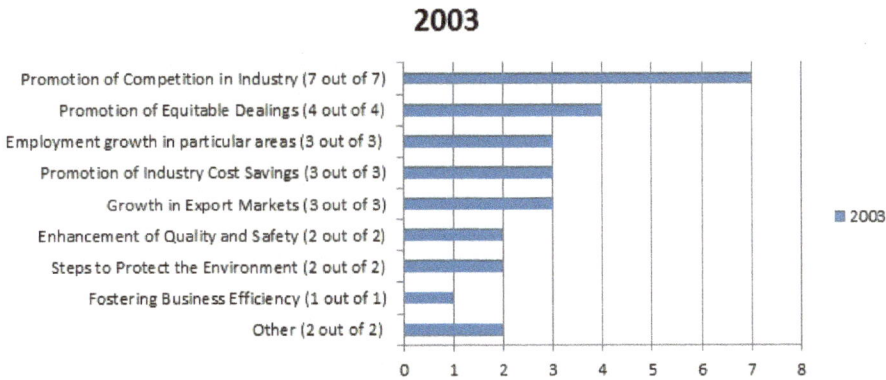

Figure 3.6: Summed weights of the important public benefits and the number of cases where authorisation was granted by the ACCC in the sample studied in 2003 (31 out of 35 were successful in 2003)

Source: Author's research.

2006

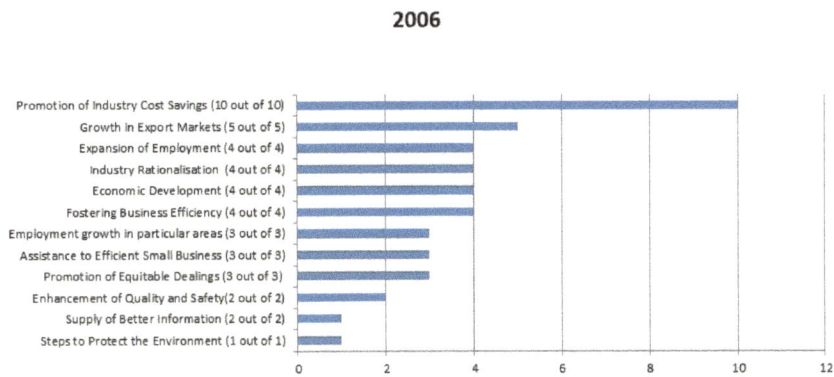

Figure 3.7: Summed weights of the important public benefits and the number of cases where authorisation was granted by the ACCC in the sample studied in 2006 (32 out of 35 applications were successful in 2006)

Source: Author's research.

This is reflected in the 2006 determinations in Figure 6 where the promotion of industry costs savings was more commonly cited in these ACCC determinations, featuring in 10 out of 35 determinations in that year. This factor is linked to economic efficiency and has the advantage of being open to quantification, which was steadily increasing in Australia following the necessity for government departments and regulators to improve transparency of decision-making. Unlike all the years studied previously, the category of 'Other' was not referred to, perhaps indicating a preference for identifying specific public benefits. Fostering business efficiency and growth in export markets were often cited and this year also saw the return of expansion of employment as a criterion, which had not had a showing since 1976. Steps to protect the environment appeared in one determination, which was lower than in 1998 and 2003.

2008

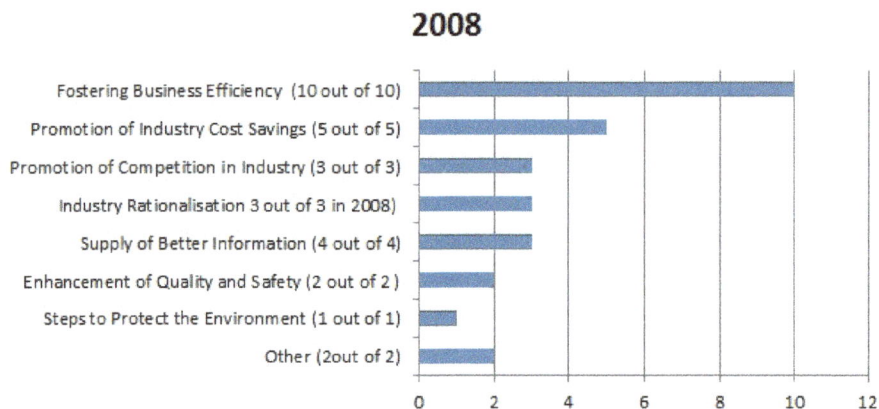

Figure 3.8: Summed weights of the important public benefits and the number of cases where authorisation was granted by the ACCC in the sample studied in 2008 (33 out of 34 were successful in 2008)

Source: Author's research.

The focus on competition and economic growth was shaken by the recognition that the rollout of competition policy into all sectors may not be straightforward. This focus was also shaken, perhaps more indirectly, by the challenges posed by the global financial crisis and climate change. These factors have impacted on competition policy in two main ways that are relevant to the discussion on authorisation determinations: first the complexities inherent in introducing competition to infrastructure and technology industries such as the health care sector and deregulated sector was recognised and a number of authorisations dealing with these industries came before the commission; second the need to promote business-driven initiatives aimed at market stability and environmental sustainability also played out in the determinations made in 2008 and 2010.

By 2006, all the main NCP reforms had been implemented and the impediments to achieving productivity in certain sectors, particularly health care, were acknowledged.[180] Regulating the health industry via competition laws has been controversial. This was partly explained by the tribunal when it stated that the health industry is unique in way that result in market failure and, in such circumstances, more competition is not necessarily a good thing for efficiency.[181] The application of the competition law to the medical profession

---

180   See Paul Gretton, 'Assessing the importance of national economic reform — Australian Productivity Commission experience' in Conference on the Micro Foundations of Economic Policy Performance in Asia, (New Delhi, 2008).
181   *Australian Association of Pathology Practices Incorporated* [2004] ACompT 4 (8 April 2004), paras 144, 158.

and related health industries has caused confusion among the profession,[182] as illustrated by the Australian Medical Association determination[183] in which the association stated that the reason for making the application was to provide it with certainty and legal protection in its dealings with state and territory health departments.[184] Similarly, in Australian Dental Association,[185] the commission agreed that the accepted norm of having consistency of fees within a medical or dental practice, although constituting exclusionary conduct, would ensure a shared responsibility for the continuity and quality of patient care within a shared practice.[186] In 2008 there were six authorisations dealing with the medical and dental sectors and they were all authorised.[187]

2010

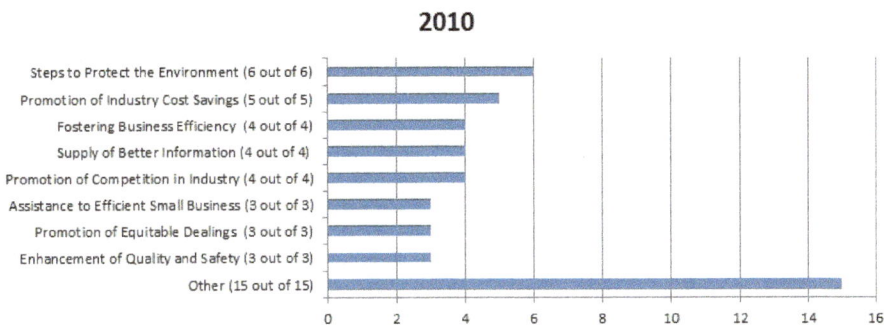

Figure 3.9: Summed weights of the important public benefits and the number of cases where authorisation was granted by the ACCC in the sample studied in 2010 (34 out of 35 were successful in 2010)

Source: Author's research.

The position was similar in 2010. Environmental concerns were raised in 6 determinations successfully in 2010, including the Agsafe and Refrigerant Reclaim authorisations. Cost savings and fostering business efficiency still remained as important public benefits, although the number of determinations where other public benefits (outside those in the list in Table 1.1) was increasing.

---

182 See Stephen G Corones (2005), 'The uncertain application of competition law in health care markets' (2005) 33(6) *Australian Business Law Review* 407–28.

183 *Australian Medical Association Limited & Ors* (2008) A91100.

184 ibid, 14, 33.

185 *Australian Dental Association Inc* (2008) A91094 & A91095.

186 *Australian Dental Association Inc* A91094 and A91095, 20; see also *Vision Group Holdings Limited* (2010) A91217, 8.

187 *Australian Dental Association* (2008) A91094 and A91095; *Australian Medical Association* (2008) A91100, A91088; *CALMS Ltd* (2008) A91092; and *Rural Doctors Association of Australia Limited* (2008) A91078.

In Summary ...

It is clear from this survey of benefits recognised in the seven years under scrutiny that the ACCC's determinations reveal a continuing acceptance of both economic efficiency benefits and other benefits, such as the enhancement of safety and the promotion of professional ethics. The manner in which the term public should be interpreted has, however, been less clear. Earlier authorisation deliberations do not make reference to the concepts of pass-through, or the consumer welfare standard, and often deal with authorisation applications from which there was little likely impact on consumers, such as approval for agreements between professional groups or associations. As the economic discourse has gained widespread acceptance in government policy, there have been attempts by the ACCC to give effect to these discourses by seeking evidence of some benefits finding their way to consumers. Following the tribunal's decision in Qantas and Air New Zealand, however, the ACCC's deliberations have been more circumspect. More recent deliberations are specifically located within the principles expressed by the ACT and plainly refer to the decision, demonstrating the importance of the economics discourse in shaping the meaning of this phrase.

4. Types of Public Benefit

This chapter builds on the discussion in the last chapter by examining in detail the types of public benefits that have been recognised in Australian Competition and Consumer Commission (ACCC) determinations. The discussion is divided into three main sections. The first part deals with economic efficiency benefits, the second examines non-economic efficiency benefits, and the third part looks at specific areas where public benefit analysis is more complex, defying easy categorisation. It is clear from this that ACCC authorisation determinations have become more myopically focused on efficiency. Although economic efficiency concerns have always focused the regulator's attention, reflecting the rise of economic rationalism by Australian governments and indeed globally, a number of varying non-economic efficiency benefits, such as environmental benefits or increasing safety of goods, have been emphasised at different times during the last 30 years. The study reveals that the ACCC has recognised these benefits in its determinations and has been able to work with the changing regulatory state by varying its use of regulatory strategies, most interestingly by being able to enlist others in the regulation game, such as professional associations, in incorporating ethical practices and appeals procedures into their codes of conduct.

Role of Efficiency-based Public Benefits

Competition is usually linked to efficiency and it is generally acknowledged that competition is valued for what it can deliver in terms of allocative, productive and dynamic efficiency.[1] Interviews with ACCC staff, including members of the Australian Competition Tribunal (ACT), suggest that any authorisation decision-making process begins with economic efficiency factors before moving to non-efficiency factors.[2] It has been stated that the ACCC's primary emphasis is on those detriments that affect competition and economic efficiency, although other factors have been recognised.[3]

The public benefits used by the commission are listed in Table 1.1 and, of the 16 public benefits in this table, only 14 are classified as economic efficiency

---

1 *Re Australian Association of Pathology Practices Incorporated* [2004] ACompT 4 (8 April 2004) 32.

2 Interview 2 and Interview 10.

3 Allan Fels and Tim Grimwade, 'Authorisation: Is it Still Relevant to Australian Competition Law?' (2003) 11 *Competition and Consumer Law Journal* 187, 2003; see also Dawson Report Committee of Inquiry, Commonwealth of Australia, *Review of the Competition Provisions of the Trade Practices Act* [Dawson Review] (2003) 32; Productivity Commission, Commonwealth of Australia, *The Growth and Revenue Implications of Hilmer and Related Reforms: A Report of the Industry Commission to the Council of Australian Governments* (1995) 385 <http://www.pc.gov.au/ic/research/independent/hilmer/finalreport> at 1 November 2007.

related, with PB11 (environment) and PB16 (other) not dealing with economic efficiency. Many of the factors overlap with each other and, for example, in the deregulated sector the public benefits of industry rationalisation and the promotion of competition go hand in hand. Likewise, the promotion of cost savings is usually coupled with the facilitation of business efficiency. These factors are often cited and discussed together in ACCC determinations.

The three most important public benefit factors based on economic efficiency are plotted in Figure 4.1. The public benefits that are considered to be of minor importance, important and very important were summed for the compilation of these figures. Of a total of 244 determinations studied across the 36-year span, cost savings was considered to be of importance on 73 determinations, fostering business efficiency was considered important in 56 determinations, and the promotion of competition was considered important in 68 determinations.

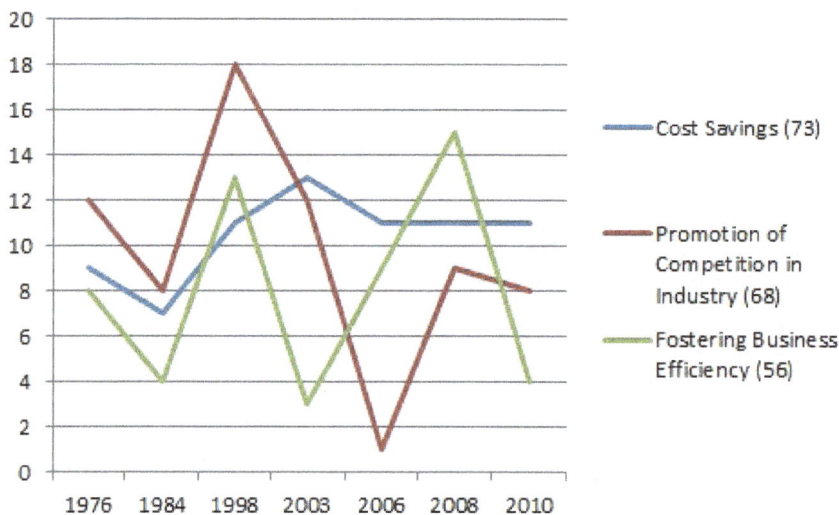

Figure 4.1: Top three public benefits based on economic efficiency across seven years

Source: Author's research.

The role of cost savings has been constant across all the years studied, with it becoming the most important factor in 2006 and again in 2010. The ability to increase efficiency via reduced costs has been consistently argued in applications stemming from a variety of industries, including the milk, liquor and iron ore industries.[4] It was the most consistently considered factor across time, despite spikes in arguments based on fostering of business efficiency and promotion

---

4   See: *Liquor Stax Australia Pty Ltd* (2010) A91237; *Premium Milk Ltd* (2010) A91236; *Tasmanian Farmers and Graziers Association* (2010) A91197; *North West Iron Ore Alliance* (2010) A91212.

of competition in 1998, this year having been selected for the study in order to examine the effect of the implementation of the national competition policy (NCP) on authorisation determinations. This factor has levelled out, being raised consistently in 11 determinations in each of 2006, 2008 and 2010, which should be read against the increasing use of modelling and quantification being promoted among regulators in the assessment of policy.[5]

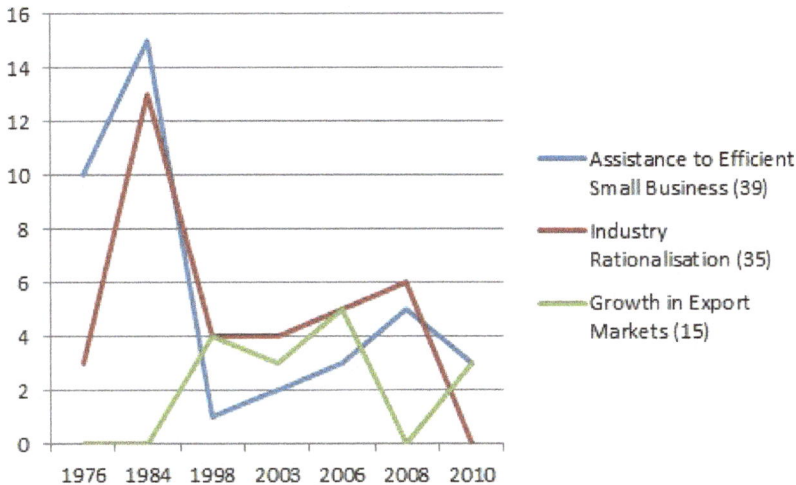

Figure 4.2: Less important public benefits related to economic efficiency across seven years

Source: Author's research.

That promotion of competition and fostering business efficiency peaked in 1998 can be understood against the backdrop of the microeconomic reform programs in the late 1980s when the Labor government under Bob Hawke and Paul Keating (1983–96) deregulated financial markets, floated the dollar, cut tariffs and privatised and corporatised government businesses, like many other European counterparts.[6] This is reflected in the Organisation for Economic Co-operation and Development reports that pointed to Australia having less interventionist strategies than other countries after the United States, United Kingdom and Ireland.[7] As discussed in Chapter 3, another obvious explanation for this spike is that it reflects the deregulation strategies that were implemented following the

5   Interview 2; see also Department of Finance and Deregulation, Commonwealth of Australia, Office of Best Practice Regulation (OBPR) 'Cost Benefit Analysis', which emphasises cost benefit analysis. <http://www.finance.gov.au/obpr/cost-benefit-analysis.html> at 15 October 2008.
6   Some of the corporatised and privatised businesses included the Commonwealth Bank, Qantas Airlines, Telecom Australia and the Commonwealth Serum Laboratories. See also Vijaya Nagarajan, 'Reform of Public Utilities: What About Consumers?' (1994) *Competition & Consumer Law Journal* 155.
7   Organisation for Economic Co-operation and Development, *Economic Surveys: Australia*, (August 2001) 118.

NCP. The authorisation determinations in 1998 included the wool,[8] electricity[9] and gas[10] industries as well as *Stock Exchange*.[11] The expanded application of the Act in 1995 also meant previously unregulated conduct of professionals could now be regulated: this accounts for the *Australian Medical Association*[12] and the *Australian Performing Rights Association (APRA)* decisions.[13]

In 2003, while the promotion of competition and cost savings continued to be important, numerous other factors also rated mention, providing a more even spread across the public benefits factors dealing with economic efficiency. This can be partially explained by the determinations in 2003 covering a variety of conduct, with nine of the 35 decisions involving the aviation industry.[14] Further, in 2003, there was a greater reliance on non-efficiency factors, illustrated by the *CSR Limited* authorisation as well as the *Golden Casket Agents Association Ltd* determinations in which the ACCC found that one of the public benefit grounds was the promotion of equitable dealings and, in *Refrigerant Reclaim* and *Agsafe*, in which the commission found that environmental benefits would be delivered by the proposed practices.[15] The 2006 figures mimic the 2003 data, although the role of exports increased. Consideration of a wide range of public benefits during these years is interesting and refutes the claim of a rigid regulator, strictly adhering to the book.

In interviews, representatives of consumer groups stated that the ACCC emphasised economic efficiency considerations in its determinations: 'economic efficiency is paramount and social environmental considerations don't get an airing'.[16] Another representative of a consumer group stated that concerns about an association's standard contracts were dismissed by the ACCC on the grounds that such contracts were economically efficient.[17] These comments are consistent with the views expressed by Stephen Wilks and Ian Bartle of the English competition regulators, which they argue 'steadily developed a stronger economic input and used economic analysis, and economic doctrine, to build

---

8   *Australian Wool Exchange Limited* A30185, 30 December 1998.
9   *National Electricity Code* A90652, A90653, A90654, 19 October 1998.
10 *Gas Services Business Pty Ltd* A90630, 19 August 1998.
11 *Australian Stock Exchange Limited* A90623, 1 April 1998.
12 *Australian Medical Association Limited* A90622, A90622, 31 August 1998.
13 *Australian Performing Rights Association Limited* (APRA) A30186–A30193, 14 January 1998. See also Honourable JJ Spigelman AC, 'Are Lawyers Lemons? Competition Principles and Professional Regulation' (The 2002 Lawyers Lecture, St James Ethics Centre, 29 October 2002).
14 *Air New Zealand on behalf of all members of the Star Alliance* A30209–A30213, 4 September 2003; *Qantas and Air New Zealand* A90862, A90863, A30220, A30221, 9 September 2003.
15 Golden Casket Agents Association Ltd A 90853, 4 September 2003; CSR Limited A90808, 10 June 2003; *Refrigerant Reclaim Australia Ltd* A90854, 7 May 2003; *Agsafe Ltd* A30194, 2 September 1998; see also *Medicines Australia Inc* A90880, 18 February 2004; these factors are discussed later in this chapter.
16 Interview 14.
17 Interview 13.

their credibility'[18] and point to the prominence of economists in the relevant agencies. They contend that this approach has 'moved the agencies towards a narrower and less critical judgment of market behavior.'[19]

ACCC staff expressed mixed views, with one past staff member stating the ACCC appeared to place greater emphasis on efficiency-related factors than previously in its history.[20] Another staff member pointed out that distributive justice issues cannot be ignored in decision-making, but should not drive the decision.[21] Simply recognising diverse factors, however, may not be enough. It was stated by another ACCC staff member that 'bad economic analysis can occur with both efficiency factors and non-efficiency factors'.[22]

By 2008, all the main NCP reforms had been implemented and the impediments to achieving productivity in certain sectors, particularly health care, were acknowledged.[23] In 2008 there were six authorisations dealing with the medical and dental sectors and they were all authorised.[24] These relied on the a combination of efficiency related and non-efficiency related benefits in their applications and, for example, in *Australian Dental Association*, the public benefits that were accepted as important were cost savings and enhancement of quality of services, with assistance to small business being seen to be of minor importance.[25] The importance of the environment, which had featured in the determinations since 1998, was the most important benefit in the 2010 determinations studied, with six determinations successfully raising it as an important factor. For example, in the *Agsafe*[26] and *Refrigerant Reclaim*[27] authorisations, environmental benefits were accepted as important in granting authorisation, reflecting once again the manner in which regulatory decision-making has to deal with the economic and social concerns of the day.

Of the three less-considered factors (Figure 4.2), assistance to small business spiked in 1984, rising again in 2008, which reflects the political emphasis on a micro-economic reform program which began in the 1980s and was again raised after the widening scope of the Act to include deregulated industries

---

18   StephenWilks and Ian Bartle, 'The Unanticipated Consequences of Creating Independent Competition Agencies' (2002) 25(1) *West European Politics* 148, 167.

19   ibid, 170. See Bronwen Morgan, 'The Economization of Politics: Meta-Regulation as a Form of Nonjudicial Legality' (2003) 12(4) *Social & Legal Studies* 489.

20   Interview 5.

21   Interview 4.

22   Interview 10.

23   See: Paul Gretton, 'Assessing the importance of national economic reform — Australian Productivity Commission experience' in Conference on the Micro Foundations of Economic Policy Performance in Asia, (New Delhi, 2008).

24   *Australian Dental Association* (2008) A91094, A91095; *Australian Medical Association* (2008) A91100, A91088; CALMS Ltd (2008) A91092; and *Rural Doctors Association of Australia* (2008) A91078.

25   *Australian Dental Association Inc* A91094, A91095, 10 December 2008.

26   *Agsafe* A91234, A91242–A91244, 27 October 2010.

27   *Refrigerant Reclaim Australia Ltd* A91079, 14 May 2008.

and the professions. Industry rationalisation was the fifth-most-cited economic efficiency public benefit, and it spiked up in 1984. This spike can be partly explained by the fact that a significant number of decisions dealt with industry associations, including the *Master Locksmiths Association*,[28] the *Real Estate Institute of Australia*[29] as well as those in Queensland,[30] Australian Capital Territory[31] and Victoria,[32] the *Stock and Station Agents Association*,[33] *Queensland Motor Industry Association*,[34] groups within the newsagency industry[35] and the *Society of Auctioneers and Appraisers*.[36] The other factor in Figure 4.2 is growth in export markets, which was at its highest in 2006 and 1998. This factor was not present in 1976 or 1984 and was only recognised in 1998 reflecting the importance of globalisation and competition among nations.

Types of Efficiency Benefits

The following discussion examines the main types of efficiency benefits that have been recognised in the commission's authorisation decisions. Figures 4.2 to 4.6 and Figures 4.8 to 4.13 show each of the public benefits, as they were raised in the authorisation application or determination, and the weighting given to them in the discussions,[37] across seven years.

Industry Cost Savings

By providing evidence about cost savings, the applicant would be in a better position to satisfy the 'future with or without test' used by the ACCC, as well as provide the necessary casual link between the proposed conduct and claimed benefit that the ACCC seeks, improving the chances of a successful authorisation application.[38] This factor has been consistently cited over the time studied (Figure 4.3), as is reflected by the 1976 determination in *United Permanent Building Society* in which the commission accepted there would be administrative cost savings that were 'difficult

---

28 *Master Locksmiths Association of Australia Ltd* A90377, A90388, 15 March 1984.
29 *Real Estate Institute of Australia* A90393, 12 January 1984.
30 *Real Estate Institute of Qld* A90393, A90397, 25 June 1984.
31 *Real Estate Institute of ACT* A97, A98, 30 November 1984.
32 *Real Estate and Stock Institute of Victoria* A4432, A4433, 10 October 1984.
33 *Stock and Station Agents Association of NSW* A90404, 11 September 1984.
34 *Queensland Motor Industry Association Ltd* A40009, 24 October 1984.
35 *NSW and ACT Newsagency System* 26 April 1984; *Mercury Newsagency System* 9 May 1984.
36 *Society of Auctioneers and Appraisers Inc* A60009, 6 September 1984.
37 A determination could raise more than one benefit and it could be given a weighting of very important (4), important (3), minor importance (2) or minimal importance (1).
38 For a discussion of the future with or without test and for discussion on the causal link see Chapter 3.

to quantify but of some magnitude' brought by the proposed authorisation.[39] Similarly, in the *Port Waratah* determination in 1998, the ACCC accepted that there would be significant cost savings in the form of reduced demurrage costs.[40]

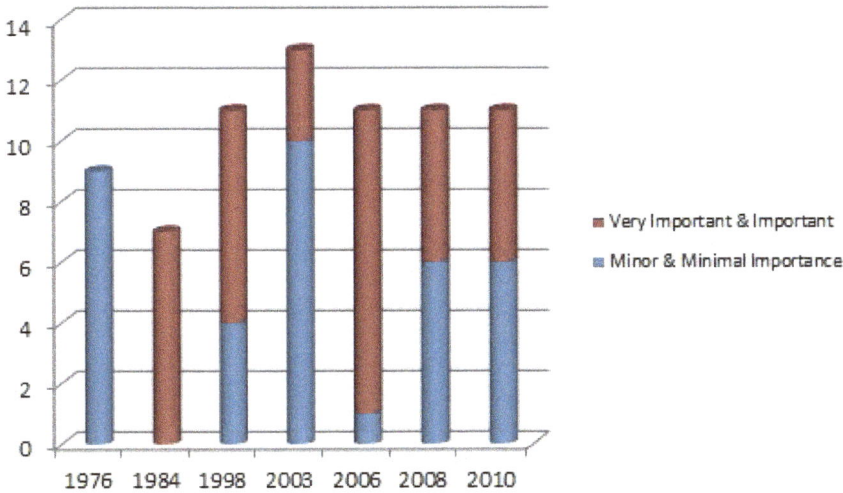

Figure 4.3: Promotion of industry cost savings in ACCC authorisation determinations in the sample studied across seven years

Source: Author's research.

This factor is essentially linked to economic efficiency and has the advantage of being open to quantification. In *Qantas Airways and New Zealand*, the tribunal was satisfied the proposed alliance would result in significant cost savings that the applicants could pass on to travellers by way of lower fares, depending on the competitive pressure it faced from other airlines in the industry. Cost savings would result from integrating technology and networks, management as well as crewing and maintenance.[41] The tribunal was critical of the quantification methods used by certain experts to calculate tourism benefits.[42] One interviewee, a senior staff member of the ACCC, stated that certain groups were 'strong on quantification', requiring staff to have 'expertise in econometrics and statistical analysis' and 'it would be up to consumer groups to bring awareness of these issues that cannot be quantified, to the ACCC's attention'.[43] This factor was consistently referred to in 11 determinations in 2006, 2008 and 2010.

---

39 *United Permanent Building Society* (1976) ATPR 35-220, 16789, 16877.
40 *Port Waratah* A90650, 25 March 1998, 18.
41 *Qantas Airways Limited* [2004] ACompT 9 (12 October 2004), para 648.
42 ibid, para 645.
43 Interview 10.

Fostering Business Efficiency

The ability to increase efficiency via reduced costs has been consistently argued by applicants. Although it might be reasonable to expect that the promotion of competition and fostering business efficiency apply to the same set of facts, this is not necessarily the case, as is reflected in this empirical study and plotted in Figures 4.3 and 4.4. These diverse figures reveal that both these factors have not been given the same emphasis in the determinations by the ACCC. Promotion of competition and fostering business efficiency spiked in 1998: fostering business efficiency was important or very important in 16 out of the 35 determinations for that year whereas promotion of competition was important or very important in 18 of the 35 determinations.

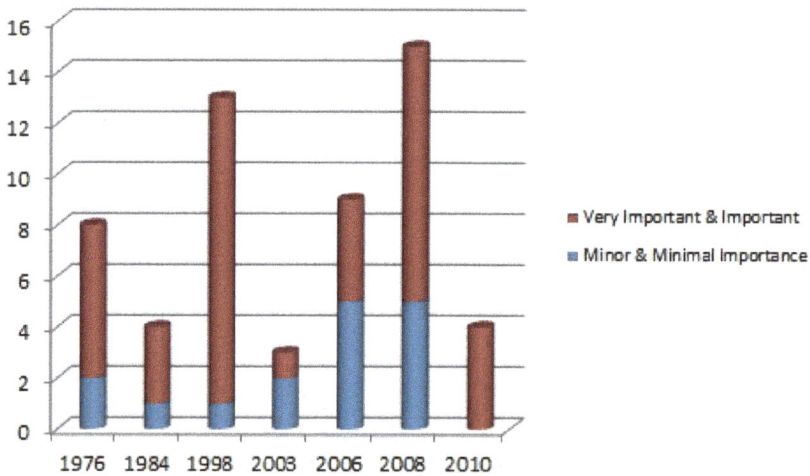

Figure 4.4: Fostering business efficiency in ACCC authorisation determinations in the sample studied across seven years

Source: Author's research.

Both featured as 'important' or 'very important', however, in only two decisions that year — *Vencorp*[44] and *United Energy*,[45] which together accounted for six of the 35 decisions. Both these factors were only considered to be of 'minor importance' in the *Australian Medical Association* authorisation.[46]

Fostering business efficiency was endorsed in the *United Energy* authorisation, where the applicant sought approval to enter a scheme for the provision of hedging cover to electricity retailers and generators during periods when the

---

44   *Victorian Energy Networks Corporation (Vencorp)* A90646, A90647, A90648, 19 August 1998.
45   *United Energy Limited* A90665, A90666, A90670, 25 November 1998.
46   *Australian Medical Association* A90622, 31 August 1998.

spot price for electricity was very high. The ACCC was satisfied the scheme provided a risk management tool that would provide for lower risk-management costs, that may translate to a benefit to the public through increased allocative efficiency.[47] In the *Victorian Energy Networks Corporation* authorisation, the ACCC stated that, even without the proposed arrangement, competition would evolve over time. It was satisfied, however, that the proposed arrangement would promote economic efficiency and introduce competition in a sector of the deregulated energy market. Likewise, in the *Australian Payments Clearing Association Limited* authorisation, the commission accepted that a move from cheques to the High Value Clearing System would yield cost efficiencies.[48]

Fostering business efficiency through structural reform was successfully argued in cases involving the deregulated sectors in 1998.[49] It was the second-most important public benefit criterion among the authorisation decisions involving the deregulated sector, after the promotion of competition, across all the years studied. This is reflected in the *Australian Medical Association* authorisation, where the ACCC stated that 'there is some public benefit in facilitating the transition to full compliance'[50] with the Act and the authorisation would provide a transition phase to allow industry participants to adjust to a different system of negotiation, which would presumably lead to greater efficiency.[51]

Figure 4.4 shows that fostering business efficiency was again an important factor in 2008 with 10 determinations considering it to be an important public benefit. These authorisations allowed corporations to reach agreement on specific types of conduct with competitors. There were several determinations dealing with the authorisation of an interim system to manage demand for coal-loading services, which were aimed at reducing the queuing of ships waiting to be loaded[52] and the authorisation of agreements between competitors for betting products.[53]

Promotion of Competition in the Industry

There has been a gradual recognition of the necessity for Australian industry to compete internationally. This is evident from the manner in which promotion of competition increased in importance from 1976 to 1998, before dropping back again (Figure 4.4). The spike for 1998 could be explained by the emphasis

---

47   *United Energy* A90665, A90666, A90670, 25 November 1998, 15.

48   *Australian Payments Clearing Association Limited* A90617–A90619, 1 April 1998, 32.

49   See *Australian Communications Access Forum* A90613, 22 April 1998; *Australian Performing Rights Association Limited* A30186–A30193, 14 January 1998.

50   *Australian Medical Association* A90622, 31 July 1998, 51.

51   ibid.

52   These accounted for six of the 10 determinations. See: *Dalrymple Bay Coal Terminal Pty Ltd* (2008), A91060–A91062; *Donaldson Coal Pty Limited* (2008) A91075–A91077.

53   *Tabcorp Manager Pty Ltd* (2008) A91065 – A91067.

placed on deregulation, with the deputy commissioner pointing out that the 'Commission has been given a significant regulatory role in relation to communication, energy and transport'.[54]

In 1998, over a third of the decisions dealt with deregulatory industries, including *Vencorp*,[55] the *National Electricity Code*[56] and *United Energy*.[57] For example, in the *Gas Services Business* authorisation, the commission accepted that the proposed arrangements were significant in bringing about an orderly transition to a restructured gas market.[58] In *Vencorp* it was noted that the 'development of a truly competitive gas market on both the demand side and supply side is of vital concern to the Commission' and it was recognised that 'the achievement of a more competitive market structure in the upstream gas production sector will be a difficult task'.[59]

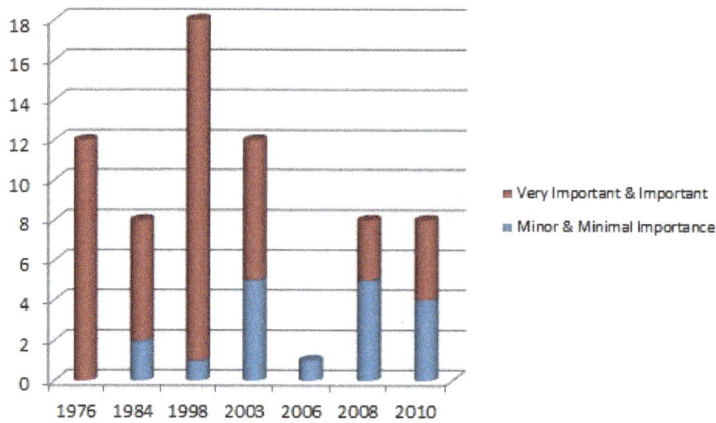

Figure 4.5: Promotion of competition in ACCC authorisation determinations in the sample studied across seven years

Source: Author's research.

The spike in the 1998 determinations cannot be overestimated, as it can also be explained by the inclusion of the APRA determination in the study, which accounted for eight of the 18 decisions where this factor was rated, and a total of 35 studied in 1998. The promotion of competition in the industry was a 'very important' factor here, which means that it has been summed for eight cases leading to the spike in 1998 in Figure 4.5. As seen from this figure, this factor was

54   Allan Asher, 'Regulatory Risks', (Committee for Economic Development of Australia — Infrastructure Deficiencies: The Strategic Imperatives Conference, 3 December 1998) 2.
55   *Vencorp* A90646, A90647, A90648, 19 August 1998.
56   *National Electricity Code* A90652, A90653, A90655, 19 October 1998.
57   *United Energy* A90665, A90666, A90670, 25 November 1998.
58   *Gas Services Business Pty Ltd* A90630–A90631, 19 August 1998, 16.
59   *Vencorp* A90646, 19 August 1998, 35.

only raised in four decisions in 2006, but only accepted as of minor importance by the ACCC in one determination.[60] In 2008 it was accepted as important in one determination and, in 2010, it was accepted as important or very important in four decisions. The *Cuscal Limited & Ors* authorisation accounted for three of the four decisions in 2010, and it dealt with an agreement between network members to not directly charge each other's cardholders for ATM transactions.[61]

Benefits Flowing from Import Substitution and Growth in Export Markets

These are usually listed as two separate public benefits and addressed separately in the determinations. Although these two factors are likely to be related, import substitution was only cited as a public benefit in 1998 for all the determinations examined from 1976–2010. In the *North West Shelf Project*, both these factors were considered to be 'very important' by the ACCC. The applicants sought authorisation to discuss the terms, conditions and price at which gas was to be marketed. The ACCC noted that the applicants estimated an increase in Australia's GDP by A$1.5 billion per annum as arising from the agreement.[62] This could be viewed as contrary to the predominant theory of the time. By the 1980s import substitution was discredited as a doctrine of manufacturing policy left over from the conservative era under Prime Minister Robert Menzies. This was a period of economic reform that included the floating of the currency, deregulating the financial markets and systematically reducing trade barriers to produce a 'more flexible and outward looking economy'.[63] As one interviewee stated, this could be viewed as a 'triumph of practice over theory'.[64] This is supported by the release of the white paper on the manufacturing industry in 1977, which endorsed the government's commitment to reducing tariff protection and promoting competition in international markets, reinforced by the Commonwealth government's economic statement in 1988.[65]

Growth in export markets is more frequently cited than import replacements (Figure 4.6). It has become more important, reflecting the greater emphasis on global business and trade. In the 1998 *Ansett* authorisation, the commission accepted that an expansion of services in the longer term would result

---

60 It was raised in *Qantas Airways and Air New Zealand* A90862, A90863, A30220, A30221, 9 September 2003 by the applicants but not accepted by the ACCC and it was raised and accepted as a public benefit by the ACCC in *Australian Dairy Farmers Limited* A90966, 24 April 2006 as being of minor importance.

61 A91175, A91176 and A91177, 27 January 2010.

62 *North West Shelf Project* A90624, 29 July 1998, 21.

63 See National Competition Council, 'What is National Competition Policy and How Did It Come to Be?', <http://www.ncc.gov.au/articleZone.asp?articleZoneID=16> at 20 October 2008.

64 Interview 6.

65 See Productivity Commission, Commonwealth of Australia, *Setting the Scene: Monitoring Micro Reform*, Report 95/1 (1996) <http://www.pc.gov.au/bie/report/96-0> at 20 March 2008.

in increased freight capacity being available to Australian exporters and, accordingly, was a trade benefit.[66] In 2006, this was a 'very important' factor in the *BHP Billiton* authorisation, where the commission identified numerous public benefits including security of supply for Australian users, the prospect of substantial export earnings, and job opportunities, as well as the introduction of new technology and promotion of economic development.[67] Growth in export markets was cited as being of minor importance, for much the same reason, in the *Rio Tinto Aluminium* authorisation in 2010.[68]

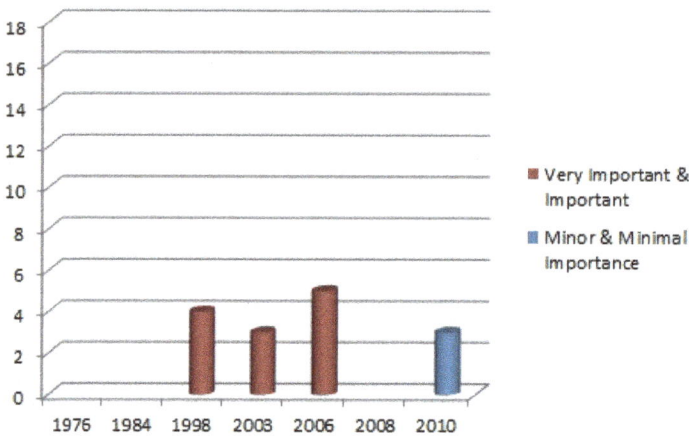

Figure 4.6: The summed weights of growth in export markets and the number of cases in ACCC authorisation determinations in the sample studied across five years

Source: Author's research.

In *Re Australian Wool Growers Association Ltd*, the applicants submitted that 95 per cent of the wool produced by association members was exported, and so they successfully sought authorisation for imposing a levy to fund an advertising campaign in the United States. The tribunal agreed with the ACCC finding and stated the provision of a properly supervised marketplace for the sale of wool in a competitive environment was a benefit to the public in the form of a significant contribution to Australia's export earnings and a source of income for many persons in Australia.[69]

---

66   *Ansett Australia, Ansett International, Air New Zealand and Singapore Airlines* A90649, A90655, 22 July 1998, 74.

67   *BHP Billiton Iron Ore* A90982, A90983, 1 February 2006.

68   *Rio Tinto Aluminium Limited & Ors* A91205–A91207, 2 June 2010.

69   *Australian Wool Growers Association Ltd* [1999] ACompT 4 (3 September 1999], para 71–72.

Expansion of Employment in Efficient Industries

This issue is usually seen as a consequence of economic efficiency. It is generally linked to other issues, such as economic development, as acknowledged by the ACCC in the *Australian Wool Growers Association*[70] and *United Energy Limited*[71] authorisations discussed above. The data suggest, however, that in practice this is not an important issue, with only 1976 and 2006 having employment expansion in efficient industries as important issues. In 1976 only one decision noted this, namely *Australian Chamber of Shipping*;[72] in 2006 four decisions noted this factor, namely *Southern Sydney Regional Organisation of Councils*[73] and *BHP Billiton*,[74] which accounted for three of the determinations. While it was raised in *BHP Billiton*[75] as an important factor, alongside numerous other factors, including export earnings and promotion of competition, it has never been the single most significant criterion in the decision-making process. A discussed below, where the employment is in regional areas, it is not necessarily linked to efficiency.

Industry Rationalisation

This factor has not been very important in authorisation determinations (Figure 4.6), and is more frequently cited in 1984 than in any other year studied.

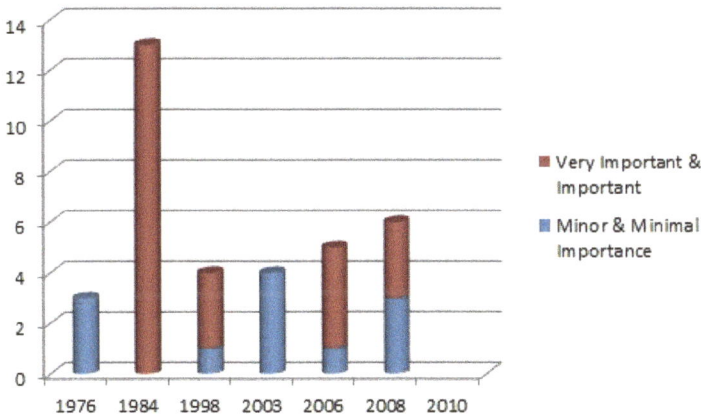

Figure 4.7: The summed weights of growth in industry rationalisation and the number of cases in ACCC authorisation determinations in the sample studied across five years

Source: Author's research.

---

70   ibid.
71   *United Energy Limited*.
72   *Australian Chamber of Shipping* A3193, 21 June 1976.
73   *Southern Sydney Regional Organisation of Councils* A90980, 25 January 2006.
74   *BHP Billiton* A90981, A90982, A90983, 1 February 2006.
75   *BHP Billiton* A90982, A90983, 1 February 2006.

The spike in 1984 can be explained by the *Re Australian Associated Stock Exchanges* authorisation,[76] in which this factor was considered 'important' in six of the total 35 determinations examined for 1984, and one of 14 determinations in which it featured as a factor in that year.[77]

It was also in this year that the Button Car Plan was implemented by John Button as minister of trade in the Labor government. Prior to this plan, the local motor industry had been protected with a 57.5 per cent tariff, which left the consumer with a limited choice of 13 different models of cars from five manufacturers. Many saw this plan as the start of market reform in Australia.[78] The relatively high reading in 2006 was because industry rationalisation was raised in two decisions, the *Queensland Turf* and the *Federation of Australian Wool* authorisations, both of which accounted for four of the 35 authorisations studied for that year. In *Queensland Turf*, two turf clubs sought authorisation for a joint venture agreement to provide for the development of thoroughbred horse racing facilities among other activities, with the longer-term aim of developing a merger between the two clubs within five to seven years. The ACCC accepted these arrangements would allow the applicants to 'centrally co-ordinate and finance certain of their operations, allowing them to take advantage of operational synergies and other cost savings' and assist 'in the efficient co-ordination and funding of capital works'.[79]

In *Federation of Australian Wool* three applicants sought authorisation for the imposition of a levy per bale of wool sold in order to raise approximately US$2.8 million which was to be used to partly fund a test marketing campaign for promotion of Australian wool in the United States. The ACCC noted that the levy would assist in funding the promotion campaign resulting in increasing consumer demand for Australian wool over the long-term and consequently also increase production of wool.[80] Another example is in the *International Air Transport Association* decision, in which the commission accepted that the association's tariff coordination, which provided the industry with the underlying basis for determining fares, was a public benefit.[81]

Economic Development

In the *BHP Petroleum Pty Ltd* authorisation, BHP had applied for authorisation to enter into exclusive dealing arrangements with two consumers of methanol.

---

76 *Re Australian Associated Stock Exchanges* A90409, A30102, A30095, A30096, A30097, A30098, 4 October 1984.
77 ibid.
78 Peter Robinson, 'The Man with the Plan', *Wheels Magazine*, 15 April 2008, <http://www.wheelsmag. com.au/wheels/site/articleIDs/9C2C51C8E6517ACDCA25742D0018FE70> at 20 April 2008.
79 *Queensland Turf Club Limited & Brisbane Turf Club Limited* A91000, 31 May 2006, iii.
80 *Federation of Australian Wool Organisations* A90984, A90985, 11 January 2006, 18–20.
81 *International Air Transport Association* (1984) ATPR (Com) 50-083, 55531.

This arrangement was intended to allow BHP to build a pilot plant to test the viability of new technology. The commission accepted this contention and stated that the pilot plant was likely to have a beneficial impact on the Australian economy in terms of introducing a new technology that would allow value to be added to a resource that Australia has in plentiful supply, natural gas.[82]

Economic development has not been cited often in the determinations studied, being referred to in one determination in 1976, three determinations in 1998 and four determinations in 2006. The slight increase in the 2006 figures is attributed to the fact that the *BHP Billiton* decision accounted for three of the four decisions in which it was raised that year. Here, the ACCC authorised the joint venture agreement and cited economic development as important because this joint venture for mining, processing and sale of iron ore was likely to prove the viability of Lower Channel Iron Deposits ore and, with the aid of the shared technology, was going to be used in the manufacturing of steel. This was likely to establish a market for Lower Channel Iron Deposits ore and consequently bring a number of other benefits in the form of investment and employment.[83]

Role of Non-efficiency-based Public Benefits

There are many reasons for recognising non-efficiency-based benefits. All are examples of market failure, be it because the good is a public good or because of externalities.[84] Non-efficiency benefits have always featured in ACCC determinations, although the ones that have been relied on have changed. One instance of market failure is where the market may not be able to regulate certain activity, especially where it cannot be reflected in price. This is true of providing safe work practices, which is often associated with higher production costs. Another instance is where the good has the characteristics of a public good, such as security, or an improved environment. The market in such cases may not be ideally suited to rewarding individuals for producing such goods. Another example involves the undertaking of research and development in public hospitals. These benefits can be used by all parties in the industry (unless protected by intellectual property rights) and the parties carrying out the research may not be rewarded by the market.

A third instance where market failure can occur is in situations where there may be certain types of conduct that are considered worthwhile but which may not be facilitated by the market because it does not necessarily yield high returns. For

---

82 *BHP Petroleum Pty Ltd* (1992) ATPR 50-116, 56212, 56223.
83 *BHP Billiton Minerals Pty Ltd* A70015–A70017, 5 March 2003.
84 Economists have identified four main causes of market failure, first, the abuse of market power; second, externalities; third, where the good is a public good and fourth, where there is incomplete or asymmetric information. See <http://www.economist.com/research/Economics> at 31 October 2008.

example, promoting ethical practices may not be reflected by lower production costs or a higher product price. Indeed, this can also be said about deregulation of public enterprises, or the encouragement of self-regulation measures.

Allan Fels and Tim Grimwade recognised multiple situations where non-efficiency-related benefits equate to public benefits in the commission's decision-making and stated:

> Less tangible benefits than economic efficiency gains may still be regarded as public benefits, such as gains to the environment or public health, which are of course valued by the community. That is, authorisation can be granted not only where there is market failure in the technical sense, but also where there is some wider inadequacy of market functioning in the specific case to address broader social values.[85]

It is clear that these less tangible benefits are generally much harder to measure and quantify. Another interviewee from the ACCC stated the process of assessing public benefit begins with economic efficiency factors and then moves to the non-efficiency factors.[86] The *Clay Brick and Paver Association of Victoria* authorisation was used to illustrate the manner in which non-efficiency factors can have a role in the application of the public benefit test. In this decision the association lodged an application involving association members related to an arrangement to fund an industry-based training initiative for apprentice and trainee bricklayers, and to charge a common fee for the initiative. The aim of the scheme was to address the problem of the cyclical shortage of skilled bricklayers in Victoria. The commission accepted that the arrangements would have public benefits, which would result in improvements to project completion times.[87]

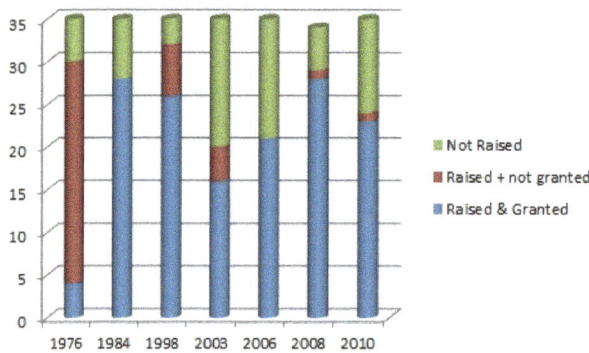

Figure 4.8: Count of non-economic efficiency public benefits in 35 authorisation determinations from the sample studied across five years

Source: Author's research.

---

85   Fels and Grimwade (2003) 201.
86   Interview 4.
87   *Clay Brick and Paver Association of Victoria* A90738, 12 December 2000, 10.

Figure 4.8 gives an overall picture of the place of non-efficiency benefits in the determinations studied. Whereas such arguments were raised in 30 determinations in 1976, of which four were granted (13 per cent success), this ratio changed rapidly. In 1984 and 2006, all the determinations in which such benefits were raised were sucessful (100 per cent success). In 1998, it was successful in 26 of 32 determinations (81 per cent success) rising to 28 out of 29 in 2008 (97 per cent success) and 23 out of 24 in 2010 (96 per cent success). Clearly the place for non-efficiency public benefits is increasing.

Types of Non-efficiency-based Public Benefits

The ACCC has consistently referred to non-efficiency-based benefits in its determinations (Figure 4.8). Assistance to small business and the safety and quality of goods and services were the main non-efficiency benefits cited in 1976. These factors continued alongside the related benefit of supplying better information to consumers and businesses in 1984. A new factor also began to be commonly cited — promotion of equitable dealings; this has continued to be an important non-efficiency determinant in the subsequent years of the empirical study. It is interesting to note that this factor includes the authorisation of ethical dealings,[88] which is a challenge facing regulators in the post Global Financial Crisis environment — how to use light handed regulatory techniques to promote ethical governance in a market-centred economy.

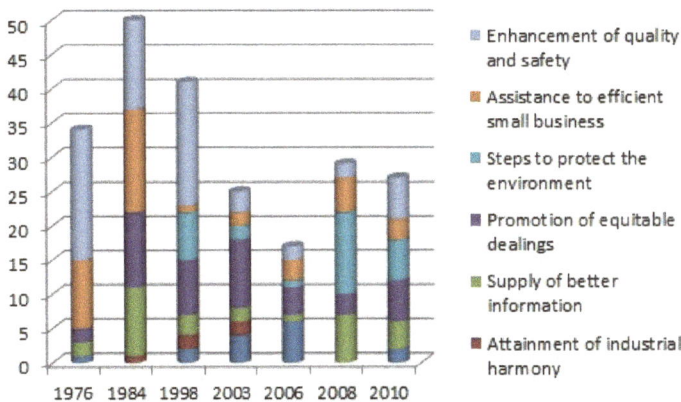

Figure 4.9: The summed weights of each of the non-economic efficiency public benefits in ACCC authorisation determinations in the sample studied across five years

Source: Author's research.

---

88   For example see: *Real Estate Institute of Australia* 12 January 1984, *NSW and ACT Newsagency System* 26 April 1984, *Stock and Station Agents Association of NSW* 11 September 1984 where it was weighted as very important (4) or important (3).

By 1998 safety of goods and services was again the most cited factor and the importance of climate change was finding its place, reflected in the increasing number of authorisations related to industry-driven arrangements for reducing environmental damage. In 2008, the environment was cited in one determination as an important factor and in 11 as of minor importance.

Again, industry was being co-opted effectively in the job of self-regulation, as reflected by Commissioner David Lieberman's statement that many of the codes of conduct in place in 1998 were dated, 'formulated in an environment of close government regulation of the industry in every jurisdiction'[89] and needed to be reviewed to bring them in line with the changing forms of regulation, including the introduction of a code of ethics that could do more than promote honest behavior by reflecting 'a greater recognition of the operating environment, a greater customer/client focus and focus on the industry's relationship with the community in general'.[90] The place of each of these non-efficiency benefits is discussed below.

Safety and Improving Quality of Products and Services

At different times, the safety of employees, consumers and the wider public have been taken into account as constituting public benefits. The safety issue was important in the 1998 determinations (Figure 4.9). The *Agsafe Limited* authorisation[91] is one such illustration where two companies sought authorisation for an accreditation scheme for the transport, storage and handling of farm chemicals, which could have attracted the application of third line forcing provisions and exclusionary conduct provisions. Here, the commission recognised that improved safety measures would benefit employees and users of the chemicals and noted the crossover between the anti-competitive conduct and the safety issues involved:

> Under ACCC authorisation Agsafe trains industry participants in the understanding of relevant safety and regulatory requirements. Agsafe also inspects premises where agvet chemicals are stored to ensure that they comply with all relevant state and federal safety regulations. Where premises are found to be in breach of these regulations Agsafe is able to, as a last resort, impose trading sanctions ... The ACCC would generally be concerned with arrangements whereby an organisation can impose trading sanctions on other businesses. However, the ACCC

---

89   David Lieberman, Commissioner, ACCC, 'Aspects of National Competition Policy', (Speech presented at the Real Estate Institute of Australia, Annual Policy Conference, Hyatt Hotel, Canberra, 15 October 1998) 9.
90   ibid, 10.
91   *Agsafe Limited* A90680, A90681, 21 May 2003. See also *Avcare Limited* A30194, 2 September 1998.

has examined the Agsafe program and is satisfied that it is an effective means of ensuring compliance with relevant safety requirements for the transport, handling, and storage of agvet chemicals.[92]

Authorisation for this conduct was granted in 2010 on the basis that Agsafe clarify on its website that it is not the only body offering such an accreditation scheme.[93]

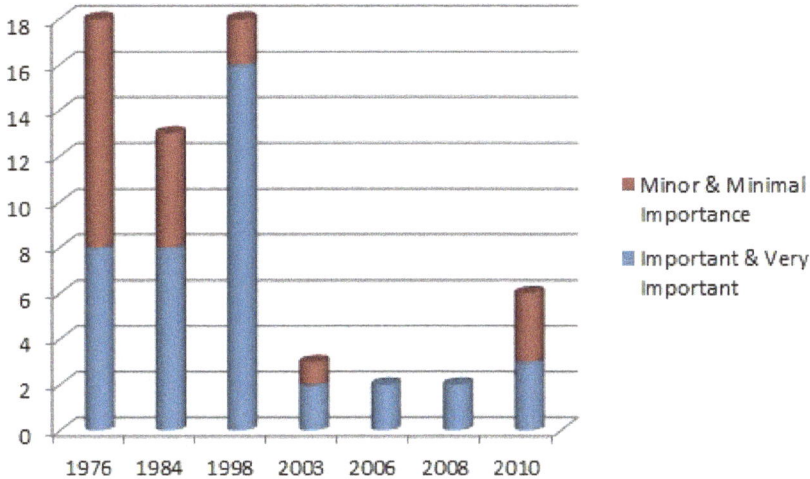

Figure 4.10: The weights of enhancement of quality and safety of goods and services in ACCC authorisation determinations in the sample studied across seven years

Source: Author's research.

International standards have been considered by the commission, as illustrated in *Association of Fluorocarbon Consumers and Manufacturers Inc.*[94] This application related to the industry participants reaching an agreement to reduce the production of ozone-depleting substances. The ozone layer protects human health and the environment from damaging ultraviolet B radiation and the term ozone-depletion refers to a thinning of the ozone layer in the earth's atmosphere resulting from released depleting gases. The commission noted that international standards, established under the Montreal Protocol 1987, dealt with the introduction of quota systems for the phasing out of ozone-depleting substances.[95] It pointed out, however, that there were no specific regulatory controls under Australian regulation.[96] In this instance, industry were

---

92   See ACCC, 'ACCC Authorises Agvet Chemical Safety Program' (Press Release MR 131/02, 28 May 2002).
93   *Agsafe Limited* A91234, A91242–A91244, 27 October 2010.
94   *Association of Fluorocarbon Consumers and Manufacturers Inc* A90658, 26 August 1998.
95   ibid, 2.
96   ibid.

cooperating with the Australian Government under the 'National Greenhouse Response Strategy' to set the cap at less than half of the level set under the Montreal Protocol for ozone-depleting substances.[97] The commission accepted the public benefits proposed by the applicants to the authorisation, stating the proposal would contribute to limiting risk to human health:

> The Commission holds the view that a scheme or arrangement which contributes to limiting the risk to human health and the improvement of the environment would benefit the Australian public, and may also benefit the total world population and environment.[98]

Industry and professional groups may seek to improve the quality of the products or services supplied by engaging in improved training facilities or investing in research and development. The benefits of such investment are often classified as a public good, as other parties, who are not investing in such training or research and development expenditure, can use them. Further the benefits of such investment are often not realised over the short-term and may not be reflected in the price of the products or services. The community, however, generally benefits from such measures and the commission has recognised them as constituting public benefits. In *South Australian Oysters Growers Association* authorisation, the commission renewed the authorisation, first granted in 1999, to charge a levy which could be directed to research and development.[99]

Industry groups seeking to monitor the quality of their products and the skills of the persons supplying services may enter into accreditation schemes and apply for authorisation. One such example was *Quilted Products Manufacturers Association of Australia*,[100] where the commission granted authorisation for a self-regulation scheme intended to cover 70 per cent of the market. The self-regulation scheme aimed at improved labelling of products and monitoring of industry participants, all of which were intended to ensure the quality of the product supplied to the consumer. In the *Australian Association of Pathology Practices* decision, the tribunal examined the value provided by the larger teaching hospitals as natural locations for research, which they called a public good issue because the private sector and its customers also benefit from the research carried out in these hospitals. Although there were no exact figures, the tribunal accepted that research from the public hospitals would benefit the wider community and should be recognised in assessing public benefit.[101]

---

97   ibid.

98   ibid, 9.

99   *The South Australian Oyster Growers Association Inc (SAOGA)* (2010), A91229, 17 May 2010 and A91230, 20 May 2010.

100 *Quilted Products Manufacturers Association of Australia* (1993) ATPR (Com) 50-130.

101 *Australian Association of Pathology Practices Incorporated* [2004] ACompT 4 (8 April 2004) paras 192, 193. Similar concerns were expressed by the ACCC. See *NSW Department of Health* A90754–A90755, 27 June 2003, 27.

In the *Australian Tyre Dealers and Retreaders Association*,[102] the association applied for authorisation to enter into a voluntary program for organisations operating tyre-retreading processes. The commission recognised the public safety issue here and acknowledged there was no legislation specifically covering the retreading industry[103] and that the proposed program went beyond the current standards and therefore delivered public benefits:

> The ability of the ... program to generate higher operational standards in participating factories goes beyond current legislation which only covers the production standard. The Commission accepts that such procedures may have the potential to contribute to efficiency gains in the factories' operations, but considers that the procedures will lean towards the delivery of personal benefit to the factories rather than benefit consumers.[104]

Supply of Better Information to Consumers and Businesses

A certain degree of information is important for efficient markets. It has long been acknowledged that this may not be automatically provided by market forces. It may have to be mandated in order to enable informed choice by consumers; one example is found in the product safety provisions in the Act.[105]

Supply of information was an important criterion in the 1984 determinations (Figure 4.11) and in the *Royal Australian Institute of Architects* authorisation, the institute successfully sought authorisation of a professional code of conduct that included documents specifying the services provided and the bases of payment and fee guidance.[106] Similar arguments were successfully made in *Society of Auctioneers and Appraisers*[107] and *International Air Transport Association*.[108] Later determinations, until 2008, however, do not have supply of information as a prominent criterion (Figure 4.11), probably reflecting the fact that such information disclosure is dealt with under different regulatory regimes, such as the *Corporations Act 2001* (Cth) or *Credit Act 1984* (NSW).

---

102 *Australian Tyre Dealers and Retreaders Association* (1994) ATPR (Com) 50-162.
103 Note, however, that the parties were required to comply with the processing standard AS1973–1993 as well as other general occupational and safety standards.
104 ibid. See also the earlier decision *Australian Tyre Dealers and Retreaders Association* (1991) ATPR (Com), 50115.
105 Schedule 3 of the *Trade Practices Act 1974*.
106 *Royal Australian Institute of Architects* A58, 7 September 1984.
107 *Society of Auctioneers and Appraisers* A60009, 6 September 1984.
108 *International Air Transport Association* A3485, 31 October 1984.

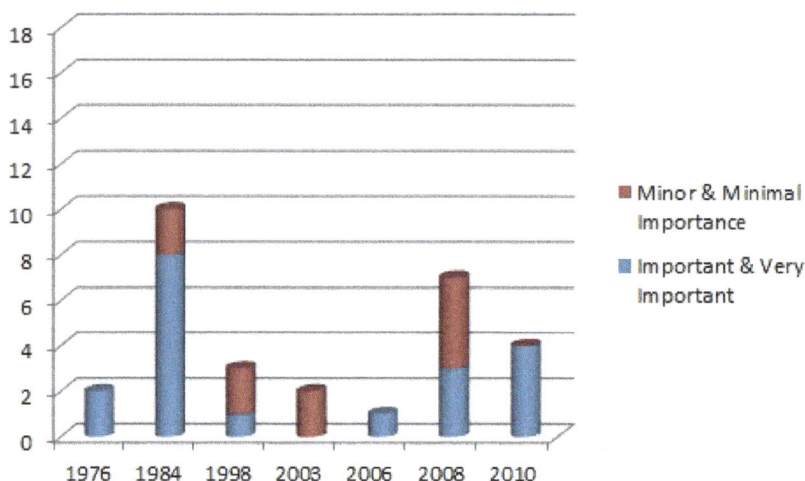

Figure 4.11: The summed weights of the supply of information in ACCC authorisation determinations in the sample studied across five years

Source: Author's research.

The increase in the number of authorisations in which supply of information was an important factor, rose in 2008 to three and, in 2010, to four. In *Generic Medicines Industry Association*, the ACCC stated that it is 'important for consumers to have information available which helps to ensure that the dispensing decisions by pharmacists, acting in their capacity as health care professionals, have not been unduly influenced'.[109]

Improved Environmental Practices

The environment can be viewed as a public good and the market may not necessarily be responsive to environmentally sound practices. This has only become an important factor for granting authorisation since 1998 (Figure 4.12), where seven of the authorisation applications raised this factor, reflecting the growing community concern and awareness of environment issues. In the *Agsafe* decision the ACCC recognised that there is a public benefit in correcting such market failure:

> The Commission is of the view, that where the market fails to take into account negative externalities of industry conduct, for example, the sorts associated with environmental protection, there may exist a public benefit in correcting such failure. In this case, the Commission accepts that absent the proposed arrangements, the pricing of the relevant chemicals fails to take into account the negative externalities

---

109   *Generic Medicines Industry Association Pty Ltd* (2010) 37; see also SAOGA (2010).

associated with the disposal or environmental impact of the packaging of those products. The Commission therefore believes arrangements which correct, or correct to a certain extent, these failures are likely to constitute public benefits.[110]

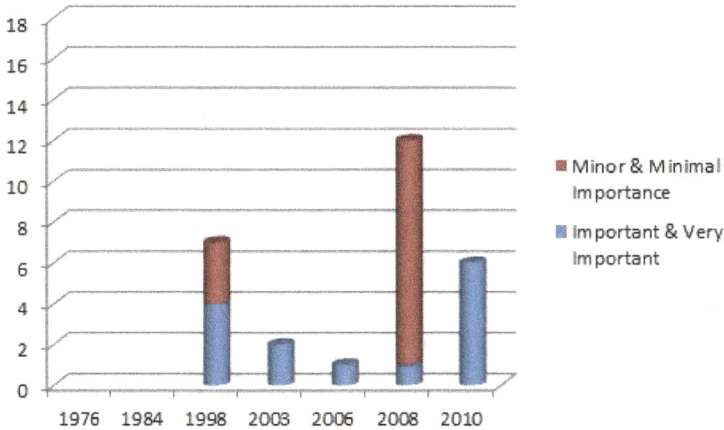

Figure 4.12: The summed weights of improved environmental practices in ACCC authorisation determinations in the sample studied across five years

Source: Author's research.

In *Association of Fluorocarbon Consumers and Manufacturers*,[111] the environmental benefits resulting from the proposed agreement between industry participants was acknowledged by the commission: 'a scheme which contributes to human health and the improvement of the environment would benefit the Australian public, and may also benefit the total world population and environment'.[112] In *Refrigerant Reclaim*,[113] the commission allowed authorisation of a scheme for a refrigerant-gas recovery program to cover synthetic greenhouse gases. It was also stated that the scheme would add only a negligible amount, of about $0.20c to the price paid by the consumer.[114]

In the *VENCORP* decision[115] the commission accepted the environmental benefits of using gas and stated: 'the use of gas has environmental benefits when

---

110   *Agsafe Ltd* A30194, 2 September 1998, 4. Also see: *Agsafe Limited* A90871, 18 September 2003, 16, para 6.5.

111   *Association of Fluorocarbon Consumers and Manufacturers Inc* A90658, 26 August 1998.

112   ibid, 9.

113   *Refrigerant Reclaim Australia Ltd* A90854, 7 May 2003; for an earlier authorisation covering the same agreement see A90548, 29 July 1994. See also *Australian National Retailers Association Limited* A910939, 13 August 2008.

114   ACCC, 'ACCC Draft Decision Proposes to Allow Greenhouse Gas, Ozone Recovery Program' (Press Release MR 042/03, 27 February 2003).

115   *Victorian Energy Networks Corporation* A90646–A90648, 19 August 1998.

compared with other carbon based forms of energy'.[116] The weight attached to this public benefit was not significant, however, and the main public benefit was considered to be economic efficiency and facilitating structural reform.

It is interesting to note that this factor has been more relevant over the recent past with 11 decisions referring to it as a minor factor in 2008 and six considering it to be a major benefit in 2010. The *Refrigerant* determination in 2008 and the *Agsafe* determinations in 2010 raised this issue again, and the ACCC considered it to be of importance and the *DP World Australia Limited & Patrick Stevedores* determination prompted the ACCC to comment that the reduction of truck movement would lower carbon emissions and bring environmental benefits.[117]

Equitable Dealings and Empowering Small Business

Small business protection has been one of the concerns of Part IVA of the *Trade Practices Act*.[118] There are a number of provisions in the Act, which directly or indirectly deal with small business interests.[119] The authorisation process too has been used for the purpose of protecting small business interests. In 1976, such authorisations for collective negotiations were granted on the basis that it was of assistance to efficient small businesses. Collective bargaining is defined as an arrangement whereby multiple competitors in an industry come together, either directly or through the appointment of a representative to negotiate on their behalf, to negotiate the terms and conditions of supply with another, usually larger, business.[120]

The authorisation applications on collective negotiations fall into two groups.[121] The first group of authorisations relates to the negotiation of fees for service. An example of this is the *Australian Medical Association Limited* authorisation.[122] Here, the South Australian and federal Australian medical associations jointly applied to the ACCC for authorisation for its members to negotiate and give effect to a common service agreement for the remuneration of visiting medical officers practicing in 65 SA rural public hospitals. The main issue in the SA medical system was the difficulties in attracting doctors to rural areas. This application

---

116 ibid, 26.

117 *DP World Australia Limited & Patrick Stevedores Operations Pty Limited* (2010), 25.

118 Efforts made to provide greater protection to small businesses can be found in s 51AC in Part IVA of the *Trade Practices Act*. See Nagarajan, 'The Accommodating Act: Reflections on Competition Policy and the Trade Practices Act' (2002) 20(1) *Law in Context* 34, for a discussion of this point.

119 See Graeme Samuel, 'Big Business v Small Business' (Speech delivered at the Australian Graduate Management School Dinner, Sydney, 4 November 2004). See also Business Council of Australia, 'Submission to the Committee of Inquiry: Review of the Competition Provisions of the *Trade Practices Act 1974*', 9 July 2002, 25.

120 ACCC, 'Authorising and Notifying Collective Bargaining and Collective Boycott: Issues Paper' (July 2004) 2.

121 Rhonda Smith, 'Authorisation and the Trade Practices Act: More about Public Benefit' (2003) 11 *Competition and Consumer Law Journal* 21, 34.

122 *Australian Medical Association Limited A90622*, 31 July 1998.

was successful.[123] The second group is the authorisation applications by small business to jointly negotiate in order to increase their bargaining power. Such businesses are usually negotiating with large corporations to sell or buy goods and services. An example of this form of conduct is the recent authorisation of *Tasmanian Vegetable Growers*, which allowed these growers to collectively bargain with Tasmania's two vegetable processors.[124]

Collective bargaining increases the bargaining power of small businesses because it makes possible a credible threat of a collective boycott.[125] The Dawson Committee noted:

> Collective bargaining at one level may lessen competition but, at another level, provided that the countervailing power is not excessive, it may be in the public interest to enable small business to negotiate more effectively with big business.[126]

Such conduct may bring about a wealth distribution from big business to small businesses. It does not necessarily increase efficiency or pass on the savings to the consumer. The ACCC has considered that certain public benefits may flow from collective bargaining. These include improved bargaining power, transaction cost savings, redistribution of monopoly profits and easing the transition to industry deregulation.[127] These benefits, however, come at certain costs and the public detriment recognised by the ACCC includes lost efficiencies resulting from collusion, effect on competitors outside the bargaining group, reduced scope for new market entry, and increased potential for collective activity beyond that authorised.[128] Figure 4.13 illustrates the importance of this factor in ACCC determinations from 1984 to 2003, where it has accounted for more than a quarter of the determinations in each of these years.

After considering concerns expressed to it, the Dawson Committee recommended a notification process for collective bargaining, which was introduced in 2006 (discussed in Chapter 2). Notification of collective bargaining reinforces the recognition of non-efficiency-based benefits by the ACCC, and this amendment to the Act represents a step in strengthening the power to recognise such benefits. The new streamlined process was actively promoted by the ACCC. It is

---

123 Other examples include: *St Vincent's Private Hospital* (2001) ATPR (Com); *St Vincent's Private Hospital and Others* A90679, 28 June 2000.

124 See *Tasmanian Farmers and Graziers Association* A90914, 17 November 2004.

125 Smith (2003) 35. See also A Hood, 'The Confused Case of Countervailing Power in Australian Competition Law' (2000) 8(1) *Competition and Consumer Law Journal* 1.

126 [Dawson Review] (2003) 3.

127 ACCC, *Guide to Collective Bargaining Notifications* (March 2008) 28–32. Other public benefits include continuing viability of small business, opening up marketing opportunities, reduced risk of unconscionable conduct, improved industrial harmony and promotion of industry associations.

128 ibid, 34–34.

likely that the fall in 2006 in this criterion being cited in determinations (Figure 4.13) can be explained by applicants preparing to shift from the authorisation process to the notification process.[129]

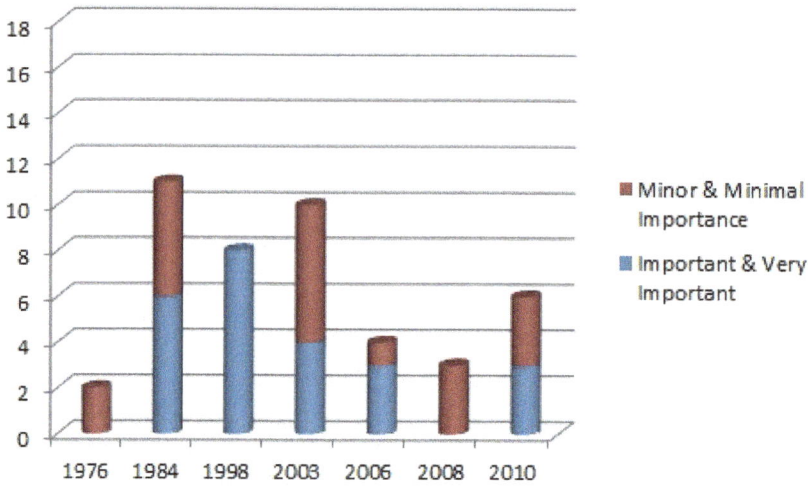

Figure 4.13: The summed weights of the promotion of equitable dealings in ACCC authorisation determinations in the sample studied across five years

Source: Author's research.

These notification determinations were conducted on similar lines to the authorisation process in 2007 and there were four such notifications.[130] Although it was referred to as being of minor importance in 2008, it is in 2010 that this factor was relied on again in three cases dealing with applications to collectively negotiate.[131]

---

129   John Martin, 'The ACCC & Small Business', (Speech delivered at the Swan Chamber of Commerce Conference, Perth, 27 October 2005) <http://www.accc.gov.au/content/index.phtml/itemId/713033> at 31 October 2008. See also Martin, 'Trade Practices Issues for Small and Medium Enterprises', (Speech delivered at the Law Institute of Victoria Commercial Law Conference, Melbourne, 18th November 2005) <http://www. accc.gov.au/content/index.phtml/itemId/715317> at 31 October 2008; Martin, 'Racing, Sports Betting and the ACCC', (Speech delivered at the Racing and Sports Betting Forum, Sydney, 12 December 2006) <http:// www.accc.gov.au/content/item.phtml?itemId=776979&nodeId=a8da0e38e9e32a4aabae7582da16ae9a&fn=R acing,%20sports%20betting%20and%20the%20ACCC.pdf> at 31 October 2008.
130   See Graeme Samuel, 'Taking a Holistic Approach to Assisting Small Business' (Speech delivered to the National Small Business Summit, 11 June 2008) 5, where it was stated that this process is still underutilised. For examples of collective boycott notifications see *Nelson Enterprises Pty Ltd & Ors* CB00001 & CB00002 (23 August 2007); *The Wangaratta Anaesthetic Group* CB00006 (17 December 2007); *Australian Newsagents' Federation Limited* CB00003 (13 September 2007).
131   See: *Liquor Stax Australia Pty Ltd* (2010) A91237; *Premium Milk Ltd* (2010) A91236.

Increased Employment in Particular Areas

Employment is sometimes addressed under two separate headings of public benefits, one referring to employment in efficient industries and the second referring to employment in particular geographic areas. Figure 4.14 deals with employment as one category. In the *Ansett* authorisation,[132] it was claimed that the proposed conduct would result in increased employment. The ACCC concluded that it was unable to determine whether this was likely to occur on the available evidence (even though authorisation was granted on other grounds). Employment in particular areas was a 'very important' criterion in 2006 with BHP Billiton, as employment was likely to increase within the Pilbara region. The commission also stated that the royalties paid to the Western Australian Government were likely to be applied towards investment projects and infrastructure across Western Australia, resulting in short- and longer-term employment and investment.[133] This factor was also cited as being of minor importance in the *Federation of Australian Wool Organisations* and *Southern Sydney Regional Organisation of Councils* authorisations.[134]

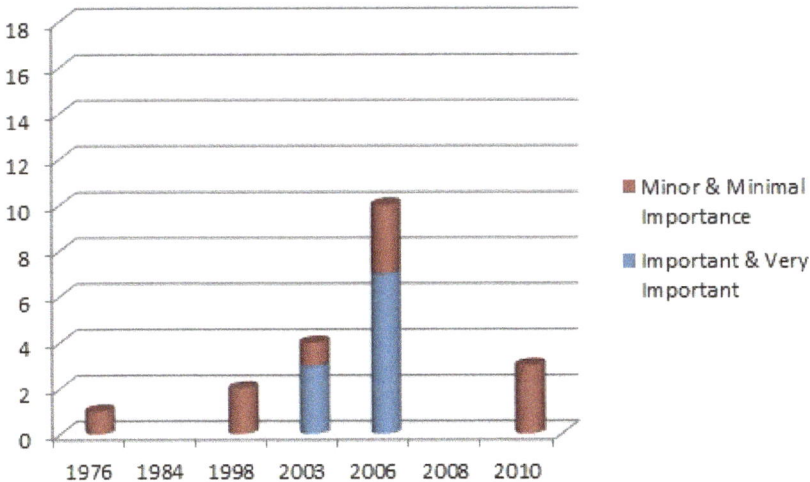

Figure 4.14: The summed weights of the expansion of employment and employment growth in efficient industries in ACCC authorisation determinations in the sample studied across five years

Source: Author's research.

---

132   *Ansett Australia, Ansett International, Air New Zealand and Singapore Airlines* A90649, A90655, 22 July 1998.
133   *BHP Billiton Iron Ore Pty Ltd* A90981, A90982, A90983, 1 February 2006, 22.
134   *Federation of Australian Wool Organisations* A90984, A90985, 11 January 2006; *Southern Sydney Regional Organisation of Councils* A90980, 25 January 2006.

In the *Federation of Australian Wool Organisations* authorisation, submissions by numerous bodies, including the Australian Superfine Wool Growers' Association Incorporated, the New South Farmers Association and Australian Wool Exchange Ltd claimed the employment of wool classers, shearing and shed-hand contractors, as well as those employed in the brokerage and handling sectors, would increase if the proposed conduct was authorised.[135] It was accepted by the ACCC only as a minor benefit, the major benefits being industry rationalisation, discussed above.[136] Once again this benefit was considered in 2010 in two determinations, namely *Santos Queensland* and *Brisbane Marine*. In the former, the ACCC accepted that the joint marketing arrangements would assist to maintain employment in the region,[137] and, in the latter, the ACCC accepted that the authorisation of an exclusive agreement would guarantee, among other factors, the employment of pilots.[138]

Increasing Industrial Harmony

This benefit has not been a significant feature of the determinations, only being considered 'very important' in the *Australian Rail Transport Federation* authorisation in 1984,[139] which accounts for its high rating as a summed weight in the graph (Figure 4.15). This authorisation was lodged by the federation, a registered organisation of employers for agreements made with the Transport Workers Union of Australia. The agreements were about the terms and conditions in long-distance road transportation and freight contracts of owners/drivers in the road transport industry. The federation had successfully submitted an earlier application and this application, which was also successful, sought to broaden the ambit of authorisation.[140] In all the other determinations, including the 1984 *Australian Road Transport Federation* authorisation,[141] the 1998 Steggles[142] and the *Australian Medical Association Limited* authorisations,[143] as well as the 2003 *Australian Hotels Association* authorisation[144] and the *CSR* authorisation,[145] this public benefit was only classed as being of 'minor importance'.

---

135   ibid, 20–1.

136   See earlier discussion in this chapter.

137   *Santos QNT Pty Ltd* (2010) A91215–A91216, 2 June 2010, 12.

138   *Brisbane Marine Pilots Pty Ltd* (2010) A91235, 28.

139   A30103, 1 November 1984.

140   *Re Australian Road Transport Federation* A30103, 1 November 1984; for earlier application see *Re Australian Road Transport Federation* A90346, 4 March 1982, ATPR (Com) 50-031, 55355.

141   *Australian Road Transport Federation* A30103, 1 November 1984.

142   *Steggles Limited* A30183, 20 May 1998.

143   *Australian Medical Association Limited* A90622, 31 July 1998.

144   *Australian Hotels Association (NSW)* A90837, 27 July 2003.

145   *CSR Limited* A90808, 10 June 2003.

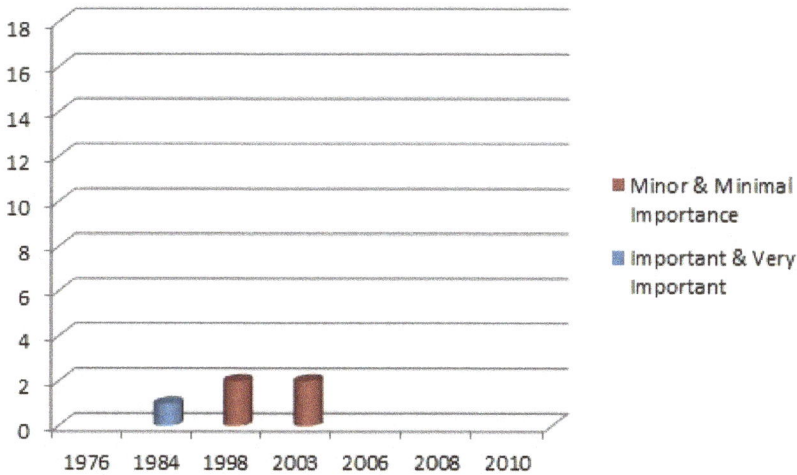

Figure 4.15: The summed weights of increasing industrial harmony in ACCC authorisation determinations in the sample studied across five years

Source: Author's research.

Regulation of Illegal Activity

The ACCC has stated that attempts to control illegal activity would be viewed as a public benefit. Graeme Samuel acknowledged the importance of industry codes to 'address the growing problem of the backyard manufacture of speed using commonly available over the counter cold and flu decongestants'.[146] This was the main reason for the authorisation of a code aimed at preventing common cold and cough medicines being obtained by backyard laboratories for the manufacture of amphetamines.[147]

Complex Sites of Public Benefit Analysis

Although many authorisation decisions can be straightforward, such as the *BHP Billiton* authorisation, which concentrated on efficiency benefits, other decisions are more complex and call for a detailed analysis. This section discusses six such sites, which have raised a myriad of issues that have, at times, been difficult to identify and prioritise.

---

146   ACCC, 'ACCC Authorises Industry Code to Restrict Manufacture of Illegal Amphetamines' (Press Release MR 229/03, 27 October 2003).

147   *Australian Self-Medication Industry* A30223, 22 October 2003. Also see *Tasmanian Farmers and Graziers Association* A80001 (86) ATPR (Com) 50127.

Health of Patients, Consumers and Workers

Regulating the health industry via competition laws has been controversial. This was partly explained by the tribunal when it stated that there are several things special about the health industry that results in market failure and, in such circumstances, more competition is not necessarily a good thing for efficiency.[148]

One reason for the health industry needing special consideration is its delivery of a service that is considered to be an important right of persons in the community. The tribunal has termed this a 'merit good', where community values override consumer sovereignty and income is redistributed in part through the provision of merit goods on a free or subsidised basis.[149] In *The Royal Australian College of General Practitioners* authorisation, the College sought authorisation for general practitioners to agree on the fees they charged their patients. One of the benefits cited by the college was that such an agreement would provide continuity of patient care, as patients would be aware of the fees charged by all the general practitioners in the practice and would face no barriers to seeing another general practitioner when their preferred general practitioners was not available. The commission accepted that this benefit was likely to contribute to maintaining the quality of care provided by general practitioners.[150] The ACCC recognised the importance of high quality health care and stated:

> The Commission recognises that the Australian community expects that high quality healthcare will be widely available. Successive Commonwealth governments have responded to this by subsidising the provision of healthcare in Australia, particularly by GPs through Medicare. This highlights the fact that GPs are a key foundation of the Australian health system. Consequently, the Commission recognised that maintaining or improving the quality of healthcare provided by GPs is an important public benefit.[151]

Further, the instances of market failure are common in many areas of the health industry. The tribunal examined the provision of services by pathologists for examples of market failure. Three main causes of market failure were discussed. These reasons are applicable to many services provided by the health industry. First, the provision of pathology services is characterised by the 'moral hazard' associated with the existence of insurance, since the existence of insurance cover

---

148 *Australian Association of Pathology Practices Incorporated* [2004] ACompT 4 (8 April 2004), paras 144, 158.
149 ibid, para 38.
150 *Royal Australian College of General Practitioners* A90795, 19 December 2002, para 5.32. The ACCC stated that this benefit was likely to be minimal because, even where general practitioners in the same practice begin by charging different fees, within a short period of time competition among general practitioners in a practice is likely to result in a common fee being charged.
151 ibid, para 5.24.

tends to make patients relatively insensitive to the price of medical services and hence consume too much.[152] Price insensitivity is likely to be valid for all types of medical services.

A second reason for market failure is classified as the principal-agent problem. The tribunal pointed out that the patient goes to the doctor and the doctor orders pathology tests. It is not the doctor who pays for these services and hence will not generally consider the marginal costs and benefits of them. Such a problem is likely to be common to all medical specialist services, as well as to general practitioners who may prescribe drugs, but usually do not inform the patient of the costs and alternative drugs available.

Third, the tribunal pointed out that pathology services also have some characteristics of a public good, which is defined from an economic perspective as one in which there is no rivalry in consumption and everyone can consume the total output.[153] The tribunal pointed out that there are a number of benefits derived from such a service, including the improved health of the population and productivity of the workforce. Further, the training of pathology registrars is a costly exercise that is usually borne by the public hospital system, involving the payments to registrars and their supervisors and the provision of materials and equipment. Once trained, the pathologists leave the hospitals where they have received their training and work for another laboratory, which receives the benefit of their training without paying for it.[154] All these benefits were recognised as public benefits by the tribunal and the ACCC for the purposes of the authorisation decision.

The commission considered the health of the general public, consumers as well as employees, in its decisions.[155] In 1998 Deputy Commissioner Allan Asher stated that the authorisation of collective bargaining agreements between doctors in rural South Australia and the SA Health Commission would benefit the consumer through access to professional health services at a lower cost than would otherwise have been available.[156] In *Tasmanian Oyster Research Council*,[157] the authorisation application related to the imposition of a levy to fund scientific research aimed at producing disease-free oysters. The commission granted the authorisation stating that the maintenance of health and safety measures was a public benefit.[158]

---

152   *Australian Association of Pathology Practices* [2004] ACompT 4 (8 April 2004) para 33.
153   ibid, para 35.
154   ibid, para 39.
155   See, for example, *Australian Meat and Livestock Corporation* (1987) ATPR (Com) 50-061; *Commonwealth Serum Laboratories Commission Novo Industries A/S and Novo Laboratories Pty Ltd* (1985) ATPR 50-088.
156   Allan Asher, 'Sustainable Economic Growth for Regional Australia', (Speech delivered at the Competition Issues and the Regions, National Conference, Beaudesert, 3 November 1998) <http://www.accc. gov.au/content/index.phtml/itemId/96907> at 1 November 2004.
157   *Tasmanian Oyster Research Council* (1991) ATPR (Com) 50-106.
158   ibid, 56-054.

In the *Abbott Australasia Pty Ltd and Nestle Australia* authorisation,[159] the application related to an arrangement to adopt a code of marketing between manufacturers and importers of infant formula, which could have breached the exclusionary provisions of the Act. Here the commission noted that the main benefits included the availability of information to health care professionals and consumers, particularly women who were determining whether or not to breastfeed.

In the *Homeworkers*[160] authorisation, a code of practice was authorised by the ACCC on the basis that it would bring a number of societal and health benefits to the workers involved. The code regulated the employment entitlements of homeworkers and sought to assist them by promoting improved working conditions for workers and their families. These included lessening the risk of exploiting a less advantaged group, provision of information to homeworkers to assist them to understand their entitlements, and the provision of improved working conditions for homeworkers and their families.

The application of the competition law to the medical profession and related health industries has caused confusion among the profession,[161] as illustrated by the *Australian Medical Association* determination[162] in which the association stated that the reason for making the application was to provide it with certainty and legal protection in its dealings with state and territory health departments.[163] Similarly, in *Australian Dental Association*,[164] the commission agreed that the accepted norm of having consistency of fees within a medical or dental surgery, although constituting exclusionary conduct, would ensure a shared responsibility for the continuity and quality of patient care to be maintained within a shared practice.[165] In 2008 there were six applications dealing with the medical and dental sectors, all of which were authorised.[166] In 2010 there were three such determinations authorised.[167]

---

159   *Abbott Australasia Pty Ltd and Nestle Australia Limited* (1992) ATPR (Com) 50-123.

160   *The Textile, Clothing and Footwear Union of Australia and the Council of Textile and Fashion Industries Limited* (2000) ATPR (Com) 50-282.

161   See: Stephen G Corones (2005) 'The uncertain application of competition law in health care markets' 33(6) *Australian Business Law Review*, 407–28.

162   *Australian Medical Association Limited & Ors* (2008) A91100.

163   ibid, 14, 33.

164   *Australian Dental Association* (2008) A91094 & A91095.

165   ibid, 20, see also *Vision Group Holdings Limited* (2010) A91217, 8.

166   *Australian Dental Association* (2008) A91094 & A91095; *Australian Medical Association* (2008) A91100, A91088; *CALMS Ltd* (2008) A91092 and *Rural Doctors Association of Australia Limited* (2008) A91078.

167   *Generic Medicines Industry Association* (2010), *Vision Group Holdings* (2010).

Right to Due Process/Right to Justice

The right to access appeal mechanisms and have a fair hearing has been considered a public benefit. This issue has not presented itself to the commission in a direct manner, as access to due process is not the main point of authorisation applications. They are repeatedly encountered indirectly, however, in those applications dealing with the adoption of a code of conduct. The commission has often sought to strengthen governance processes, such as the access to appeal mechanisms, by using its conditions power under section 90(3).

One reason for the imposition of such conditions is to curb any misuse of market power and increased market concentration, conditions that are addressing long-term efficiency in the market. Another equally important reason is that the ACCC is facilitating the decentring of regulation. Doing so allows private enforcement by the participants in the scheme. When dealing with authorisations involving deregulated industries, the commission has imposed conditions primarily dealing with governance issues, such as incorporating the right to appeal against decisions made by associations. In 1998, out of the 36 decisions studied, the ACCC granted authorisation on the basis of conditions in 16 instances.

In the *Steggles* application,[168] the ACCC reviewed a proposed arrangement between Steggles Limited, a purchaser of chickens, and a number of small chicken farmers, who were the sellers of the chickens. The arrangement would allow Steggles Limited to negotiate with the growers collectively concerning the rates and conditions for the raising of broiler chickens. The commission was satisfied that the proposed arrangements would assist in a smooth transition to deregulation for the SA chicken-meat industry.[169] Other public benefits that the commission considered were likely to result from the arrangement included: addressing the inequality in the negotiating process for growers who would benefit from being able to negotiate collectively and a reduction in costs for both Steggles and the growers. The commission, however, expressed concern about a dispute resolution provision in the proposed agreement and granted authorisation subject to a condition that required this provision to be amended. The proposed dispute resolution provision allowed for the SA Steggles Consultative Committee to bind parties in dispute to a decision made unanimously by that committee. The commission considered the proposed dispute resolution to be insufficiently independent or fair and stated:

> The Commission considers that the constitution of the committee would not always be sufficiently independent such that fairness of a decision made by the committee could be guaranteed. Consequently,

---

168 *Steggles*, A30183, 20 May 1998.
169 ibid, para 8.32; see also para 8.15.

the Commission considers that in order for Rule 13 not to contain a provision for conduct that may be likely to contravene provisions of the Act. Rule 13(b) should be amended to include provision for appeal to independent arbitration by a party mutually agreed to by the parties in dispute.[170]

The ACCC asked for the rule to be amended to include provision for appeal to independent arbitration by a party mutually agreed to by the parties in the dispute. Similarly, in *Real Estate Institute of Australia Limited*, the ACCC was asked to authorise a code of conduct. The ACCC agreed to the authorisation only if adequate provision was made for consumer access to the complaint-handling mechanism and for appeals to be made to an independent arbitrator. The ACCC stated:

> The establishment of a complaint handling mechanism that provides for an avenue of appeal to an independent arbitrator and the making of decisions in accordance with the principles of procedural fairness as well as public reporting is important, therefore, not only to ensure that the Code is likely to result in a benefit to the public but also to act as a check against any attempt to use the complaint handling procedures in an anticompetitive manner.[171]

Again, in the *Agsafe* determination, the commission asked for the code to be varied to ensure 'independence and allow for natural justice and procedural fairness'.[172] In *Victorian Energy Networks Corporation*,[173] the application was made by a statutory gas company established by legislation and it sought approval for the terms and conditions on which access to transmission pipeline services would be made available to third parties. Here, the commission granted authorisation on the basis that the corporation report to the market on a prompt basis in order to make information available in a timely and transparent manner.

Another example can be found in *Australasian Performing Rights Association (APRA)*, in which authorisation was granted on the basis of a number of conditions, one of which required APRA to set up a new dispute-resolution mechanism to handle complaints between it and its users. The conditions required that disputes be heard before a panel of three adjudicators to determine the outcome and also required APRA to bear the cost of the dispute-resolution process. APRA contested this on the basis of the cost involved and proposed another model that saw APRA paying the cost of the mediator in the dispute-

---

170   ibid, para 8.14.
171   *Real Estate Institute of Australia Limited* (2000) ATPR (Com) 50-279, 53453.
172   *Agsafe* (1994) ATPR (Com) 50-150, 55261; see also *Australian Communications Access Forum Inc* (1998) ATPR (Com) 50-262, 55246; *Australian Hotels Association (NSW)* A90837, 27 June 2003, where the applicants agreed to develop a dispute resolution mechanism as a condition of the authorisation being granted.
173   *Victorian Energy Networks Corporation* A90646–A90648, 19 August 1998.

resolution process, but proposing that the remaining administrative costs, such as the costs of the stenographers and room hire, should be shared between the parties. The ACT in its decision found a middle ground and commented that such a process was an essential avenue for dissatisfied members to air their grievances against APRA, which retained a monopoly position in the market.[174] The decision recognises that adequate dispute resolution mechanisms may be one way of monitoring the activities of monopolies.

At times, these dispute-resolution processes are in addition to those available under the law. They offer, however, cheaper, quicker and less formal alternatives with more flexible remedies. In the *Australian Amalgamated Terminals Pty Ltd* (AAT) authorisation the ACCC required the incorporation of a dispute-resolution process, with provision for mediation and, ultimately, expert determination accessible by end users of AAT's terminals.[175] This was in addition to other dispute-resolution process in operation and was not intended to compromise the operation of these existing processes.[176] Likewise, in the *Victorian Egg Industry Cooperative* authorisation, the conditions provided an independent appeal mechanism for producers in addition to the procedures provided under the *Commercial Arbitration Act 1984* (Vic).[177] Similarly, in the *Australian College of Cosmetic Surgery* authorisation, the ACCC required the inclusion of a condition in the college's code requiring that the member of the external appeals committee not be a member of the college.[178] In the *College of Surgeons* authorisation, the conditions imposed required that a number of the members of the appeals committee had to be nominated by the Australian health ministers, reflecting the public interest issues involved in the determination.[179]

Facilitation of Deregulated Industries

The commission dealt with an increasing number of authorisation applications from the deregulated sectors of the economy that came within the ambit of the Act after the amendments made to it in 1995. Accordingly, only the authorisation decisions studied in 1998 include applications from deregulated industries. Of the decisions studied, the largest number of applications were from previously state-owned enterprises, including electricity, water and gas industries. Others included industries that had received protection from statute, such as the Wool Board or the Egg Marketing Board, as well as the professions, including the medical profession, which has been subject to competition law since 1995.

---

174 *Australian Performing Rights Association Ltd* A30186–A30193, 14 January 1998, para 330.
175 *Australian Amalgamated Terminals Pty Limited* (2009) A91141, A91142, A91181, A91181.
176 ibid, 36–37.
177 *The Victorian Egg Industry Co-operative* (1995) A40072 29. This authorisation determination is not part of the empirical study.
178 *Australasian College of Cosmetic Surgery* (2009) A91106, 56.
179 *Royal Australasian College of Surgeons* (2003) A91106, 217.

Both efficiency and non-efficiency arguments were advanced and accepted by the commission in many of these cases. The most commonly accepted efficiency criteria were fostering business efficiency and the promotion of competition in the industry. Equally important were the non-economic benefits. The two most important were the promotion of equitable dealings in the market and the enhancement of the quality and safety of goods and services. Evidence of these benefits being passed on to the public is not always present. The need to allow time for deregulated industries to operate within a competitive market was acknowledged by the commission:

> The Commission is of the opinion that there is some public benefit in facilitating the transition to full compliance with the *Trade Practices Act* in certain circumstances. This will help minimise the adjustment costs that could result from too precipitous a change from the previous exemption. A public benefit arises because a transition phase may help to allow industry participants to adjust to new negotiation systems.[180]

This flexible approach is necessary in a time of transition and it would be difficult to bring about structural change and allow such industries to function in a competitive market with hard and fast rules. Further, the ACCC intends that, by adopting such an approach, it is building commitment to long-term compliance to the Act, which would be viewed as a public benefit. The most important non-efficiency benefits that featured prominently in 12 out of the 19 decisions examined was the enhancement of quality and safety of goods and services.

Encouraging Compliance and Self-regulation

Often, self-regulation, compliance and the encouragement of ethical practices are interrelated. For example, in the *Medicines Australia Limited* authorisation[181] the applicant was a national association representing the prescription medicines industry in Australia. It was seeking authorisation for its code of conduct, which had the likely effect of breaching section 45 of the Act. The applicant successfully argued that the code would encourage compliance and self-regulation via, among other things, the inclusion of ethical practices.[182]

---

180 *Australian Medical Association and South Australian Branch of the Australian Medical Association Incorporated* A90622, 31 July 1998, 51.
181 *Medicines Australia Limited* A90779, A90780, 14 November 2003.
182 In other cases, facilitating compliance with legislation has been considered to be a minor benefit. See ibid, para 5.32.

John Braithwaite and Christine Parker discussed the new regulatory state's move from command and control toward indirect governance.[183] One way in which such governance can occur is by facilitating self-regulation, and the commission has played an active role in doing just that. Since the mid 1980s, self-regulation in the form of codes of conduct has been viewed as an efficient regulatory tool by the commission.[184] The then Commissioner, Ron Bannerman, identified three broad influences which affect the pursuit of efficiency: market forces; rationalisation, meaning the efficient reorganisation of resources and the methods of using them so as to reduce the cost of production and distribution; and, self-regulation, which can be a lower-cost method than government regulation and can thus contribute to efficiency.[185] Bannerman, however, voiced the main concerns expressed about self-regulation by saying: 'a point sometimes overlooked is that particular sorts of self-regulation prevent the operation of market forces and may thereby actually reduce efficiency'.[186]

Clearly, proposed self-regulation schemes can bring both benefits and detriments, and consideration of such proposals is usually complex. The importance of self-regulation has been recently reinforced by Samuel, when he announced that the ACCC would introduce a system of endorsement for high quality industry codes of conduct because it 'has the potential to provide effective industry codes that deliver real benefits to businesses and consumers with the least possible compliance costs placed on either'.[187] This statement demonstrates the recognition that self-regulation can be more efficient and less costly than regulation, which relies on command and control strategies.

In *Media Council of Australia (No. 2)*, the tribunal considered an appeal by the Australian Consumers Association about a commission decision to authorise four applications relating to a number of codes of conduct and asked the council to consider a number of variations. The tribunal acknowledged that such self-regulatory strategies were achieving government policy. It recognised that there were some efficiencies of both a procedural and enforcement kind that would result from the proposed conduct. In refusing to grant the authorisation, however, the tribunal found, among other things, that the proposed codes were not reflective of community standards and values, and that the rights of appeal under the codes were inadequate. The tribunal went beyond economic

---

183   John Braithwaite and Christine Parker, 'Conclusion', in Christine Parker, Colin Scott, Nicola Lacey and John Braithwaite (eds), *Regulating Law* (2004).
184   See, for example, *Royal Australian Institute of Architects* A58, 7 September 1984; *NSW and ACT Newsagency System* A30093, A30093, 26 April 1984; *Mercury Newsagency System* A4782, A4937, 9 May 1984; *Master Locksmiths Association of Australia Ltd* A90387, A90388, 15 March 1984. See also *Homeworkers* (2000) ATPR (Com) 50-282.
185   Ron Bannerman, 'Points from Experience 1967–84', in Trade Practices Commission, Commonwealth of Australia, *Annual Report 1983–84* (1984) 157, 191.
186   ibid, 192.
187   See ACCC, 'ACCC to Endorse High Standard Voluntary Industry Codes of Conduct' (Press Release MR 168/03, 11 August 2003). As far as the author is aware, this has not been fully implemented.

efficiency matters to examine the best way to give effect to community values and stated the current proposals had inbuilt design faults that allowed biased conduct against the new entrant, the small advertiser and the novel product.[188]

In *Australian Communications Access Forum Inc*, the forum's primary role was the generation of recommendations on declared services and submitting such draft access codes for approval by the ACCC. This application dealt with the constitution and rules of governance of the forum. One of the primary benefits recognised by the commission was the facilitation of self-regulation, and authorisation was granted.[189]

Chief concerns about self-regulation schemes are that they may encourage anti-competitive conduct, or that they may allow members to be unfairly treated without any avenue to obtain relief. The ACCC has used conditions to address such concerns. Once again, the importance of an appeals process and the costs implementing one have also been explored in the determinations. In the *Australian Institute of Mining and Metallurgy* authorisation the ACCC recommended that 'the introduction of an appeals process for applicants denied admission to the Institute and the enhancement of procedural fairness through the introduction of a requirement for the Board to give reasons for its decisions'.[190] While the first of these two issues were dealt with by the institute following the draft determination, the second was dealt with by the ACCC through the imposition of a condition to the grant of the authorisation. Another concern has been the need to have external oversight of compliance and, in the *North West Shelf* authorisation, the condition required an ACCC approved independent compliance auditor to review compliance with the terms of the authorisation and the agreed protocol. The conditions also required the applicants to implement all of the auditor's recommendations. The auditor was required to report annually on the finding of the review as well as reporting on any non compliance with recommendations of the review.[191]

In *Medicines Australia Inc*, the ACCC considered that the Medicines code of conduct may not have the deterrent impact it promised and granted authorisation on the basis of a number of conditions.[192] These included increased reporting and monitoring of specific activities and that any amendments to the guidelines in the code were supplied to the ACCC. In the *College of Surgeons* authorisation the ACCC was concerned with the exclusive role of the college in setting the standards for accrediting hospitals and training positions within hospitals. The

---

188 *Media Council of Australia* (No 2) (1987) ATPR 40-774, 48451. See also John Duns, 'Competition Law and Public Benefits' (1994) 16 *Adelaide Law Review* 245, 265.
189 *Australian Communications Access Forum Inc* A90613, 22 April 1998, 15.
190 *Australian Institute of Mining and Metallurgy* (2004) A90824, 20.
191 *North West Shelf* (1998) A90220, A91221, A91222 & A91223, 90.
192 *Medicines Australia* A90779–A90780, 14 November 2003, 37, para 5.58.

conditions imposed included a requirement that the college establish a public, independent review of the criteria for accrediting hospitals for the provision of various surgical training positions.[193] This condition was supplemented by others involving the participation of the state health ministers in the nomination of hospitals for accreditation[194] and another condition required the college to establish an independent chaired committee to publicly review the tests that medical colleges use to assess overseas-trained surgeons.[195] In *Agsafe* the condition required the independent monitor to report on the progress that the company is making in complying with the conditions imposed by the ACCC in the authorisation annually.[196]

Promoting Ethical Conduct

For some time, professional ethics provisions have been acknowledged as an important regulatory tool by the commission. It has recognised the value of industry codes and has stated that it considers codes to be an extremely effective and market-sensitive mechanism for delivering the detail of consumer protection rules, provided they are appropriately framed, administered and monitored.[197] The commission examines codes to ensure that they contain rules encouraging appropriate conduct and internal and external dispute resolution procedures to monitor such conduct.

Professional ethics arise in authorisations as a subsidiary issue where a code of conduct is being considered for authorisation. In *The Mortgage Industry Association of Australia* authorisation, concerns about unethical conduct in the form of fraudulent conduct engaged in by some brokers in the mortgage industry had been commented on in a number of reports, including those undertaken by the Australian Prudential Regulation Authority and the Consumer Credit Legal Centre.[198]

Ethical conduct has at times arisen in the context of conditions subject to which authorisation has been granted. In *Real Estate Institute of Australia Limited*,[199] the ACCC granted authorisation to a real estate agents' code of conduct on a number of conditions. One of these conditions required changing a clause in the code that required a member not to engage in conduct that was detrimental

---

193   *College of Surgeons* (2003) A90765, 166.

194   ibid, 167–68.

195   ibid, 172.

196   *Agsafe* (2002) A90680 and A9068, 61.

197   ACCC, 'Submission to the Financial System Inquiry (Wallis Inquiry)', September 1986.

198   *Mortgage Industry Association of Australia* A90880, 18 February 2004, 10–1, paras 2.16, 2.18.

199   *Real Estate Insitute of Australia Ltd* (2000) ATPR (Com) 50-279. See also *Real Estate Institute of Australia* (1981) ATPR (Com) 50-013 for an earlier decision on the code of ethics.

to the reputation or interests of the profession, the institute or its members. The ACCC saw such a clause as being at odds with the promotion of ethical standards and stated:

> In the Commission's view, clause 1.3(b) may lead to the Code being interpreted in a manner that is focussed on the interests of the REIA [Real Estate Institute of Australia], its affiliated institutes and the real estate profession rather than being interpreted in a manner that is primarily focussed on promoting ethical standards or real estate practice in the public interest.[200]

In the *Mortgage Industry Association of Australia* decision the ACCC did not impose any conditions on the basis that the proposed arrangements met the authorisation test. It did, however, suggest that the association consider adopting proposals made by interested parties, including Consumer Affairs of Victoria, on how the code could be improved and thereby enhance the standing of mortgage brokers.[201] In *Australasian College of Cosmetic Surgery* a condition required the code to be amended so as to provide for an independent auditor to be appointed to report findings of checks on the manner in which the complaints panel of the college dealt with complaints made to it. The results of these audits are to be reported to the ACCC, as well as the college's code administration committee.[202]

Protecting Certain Sectors of the Community

At different times the commission has viewed protection of specific sectors of the community as a public benefit. In the *Homeworkers* authorisation, lessening the risk of exploitation of a less advantaged group was seen as a public benefit.[203] In the *Agsafe* authorisation the benefits flowing to the rural sector were considered important and the chairman stated in a press release:

> The ACCC considers that the Agsafe program is of particular benefit to rural and regional Australia where agvet chemicals are predominantly used. Through its accreditation and training scheme, the Agsafe program has significantly increased knowledge and understanding of existing regulatory requirements for the safe transport, handling, and storage of agvet chemicals.[204]

In *Job Futures*, the ACCC recognised that a public benefit resulted from assisting people with physical or intellectual impairment to gain employment. The ACCC

---

200   ibid, 50-279, 53455.
201   *Mortgage Industry Association* A90880, 18 February 2004, 27, para 6.32.
202   *Australasian College of Cosmetic Surgery* (2009) A91106, 57, 79.
203   *The Textile, Clothing and Footwear Union of Australia and the Council of Textile and Fashion Industries* (2000) ATPR (Com) 50-282, 53550.
204   ACCC, 'ACCC authorises Agvet chemical safety program' (2002).

stated that the statement of values adopted by Job Futures reflected a focus upon the delivery of services to people who are most disadvantaged in relation to employment as a consequence of long-term unemployment or physical and intellectual disabilities.[205] The commissioner stated:

> The ACCC also recognises the public benefit in having smaller community based organisations participating in the Job Network, particularly as a result of their diversity in approach and local focus in delivering these services. These smaller non-profit organisations often provide employment services to disadvantaged people in places where larger for-profit organisations do not operate.[206]

In the Distilled Spirits Industry Council of Australia authorisation, conditions imposed required an independent review to be conducted of the effectiveness of the Retailer Alert Scheme, which was a system for regulating inappropriately named or packaged alcohol products from the market. The ACCC noted that this scheme was weak as it did not contain a mechanism to enforce compliance and required the association to report to it on the findings of the review.[207]

In Summary …

This chapter has categorised public benefits from ACCC determinations across four decades. The determinations themselves have become more detailed, longer and transparent with the public benefits being much more clearly emphasised. The commonly held view that the ACCC's decisions have become focused on economic efficiency is not supported by the empirical study, which shows that both efficiency and non-efficiency benefits have always had a place in the determinations. It also shows that non-efficiency benefits are more often and more successfully argued today than in 1976 or 1984. The study also shows that varying benefits have been emphasised at different times.

The place of non-efficiency benefits is even more intriguing. Although some of these benefits, such as safety and quality, had long been acknowledged, others have become more important over time, and environmental benefits is one such example of this. The advantages of self-regulation had been recognised since

---

205 *Job Futures* A90625, 8 April 1998, 12. This was again authorised in 2008. See Job Futures Limited A91084, A91085 (18 September 2008). See also *Australian Medical Association Limited and South Australian Branch of the Australian Medical Association* A90622, 31 July 1998, where the ACCC recognised the importance of attracting doctors to rural sectors. It should be noted that this reason came within Industry Rationalisation because it resulted in a more efficient allocation of resources.

206 ACCC, 'ACCC proposes to authorise employment services collective tendering arrangements', (Press Release MR 183/08, 26 June 2008) <http://www.accc.gov.au/content/index.phtml/itemId/833255> at 30 September 2008.

207 A91054 & A91055, 31 October 2007, 34–35, 48.

the 1980s, with the commission encouraging it by approving codes of conduct that were, in effect, self-governance systems. Promotion of equitable dealings has become more important and has often been used as a way of monitoring powerful players in the deregulated market. This was also the explanation for the increasing incorporation of dispute-resolution mechanisms and appeal processes, which the commission sought to incorporate using the conditions power in granting authorisations. We might conceive this as a meta-regulatory shift towards procedural regulation of self-regulation by the ACCC.[208]

---

208   Christine Parker, *The Open Corporation: Effective Self-Regulation and Democracy* (2002).

5. Discourses on Discretion and the Regulatory Agency

The authorisation process is a complex one that relies on the exercise of discretion. Those of the epistemic trade practices and competition policy community will understand how this discretion may be used and the outcomes it can deliver. But for others, the process is opaque. While legal and institutional factors can limit the exercise of discretion, so too can the regulatory strategies relied on. The Australian Competition and Consumer Commission's (ACCC) strategies have embraced many of the principles of responsive regulation, which rest on wide discretionary powers, and which, although difficult to contain, deliver many positive outcomes.

Discretion as a 'Tube of Toothpaste'

Discretion here is considered from an interdisciplinary perspective.[1] The degree of discretion granted to regulatory agencies has increased significantly over the last century.[2] As the work of government extended in the second half of the twentieth century, so too did the work undertaken by government departments and agencies that relied on administrative discretion. The growth of discretionary powers in Australia has been largely a product of increased state regulation, which was direct during the 1960s and 1970s, and more indirect in the last three decades.[3] Discretion has been examined in different ways and the two groups of significance in this discourse have been legal philosophers and sociologists. Legal philosophers, while focusing primarily on the manner in which judges use discretion, have looked at the manner in which discretion can be curtailed. Sociologists, on the other hand, see discretion as all pervasive and are more sceptical about controlling its use.

Discretion can be simply defined as allowing the decision maker or official to choose from a number of legally permissible options. Discretion can be viewed both positively and negatively. Where an official uses discretion to pursue commonly acknowledged goals, it can be viewed positively and where the official's discretion is for the most part strictly determined by rules, discretion

---

1   DJ Galligan, *Discretionary Powers: A Legal Study of Official Discretion* (1986); Keith Hawkins (ed), *The Uses of Discretion* (1992); M Adler and S Asquith (eds), *Discretion and Welfare* (1981); Carol Harlow, 'Law and Public Administration: Convergence and Symbiosis' (2005) 79(2) *International Review of Administrative Sciences* 279.
2   Harlow (2005) 284.
3   Margaret Allars, *Introduction to Australian Administrative Law* (1990) 9. See also Allars, 'Public Administration in Private Hands' (2005) 12 *Australian Journal of Administrative Law* 126, 126; Harlow (2005).

is a residual concept and can be viewed negatively as a 'lacuna in a system of rules'.[4] Both these views have coloured the way in which discretion is viewed and controlled. Nielsen has pointed to the Danish regulatory inspectors whose work is characterised by a high level of dialogue and where discretion is likely to deliver positive outcomes.[5] Alternatively discretion can be used negatively and Elaine Campbell has cited studies that examined the power of the police to stop and search.[6] The circumstances where this power is used is open to interpretation and Campbell pointed out that the power can only be exercised where police have reasonable suspicion before doing so. Simply being known to the police, however, or fitting a stereotype of suspicions through appearance or lack of conformity can also be sufficient to attract police attention.

Discretion has been described by Kenneth Culp Davis, the American legal academic, in the context of a public official within an administrative agency, as 'a public official [having] discretion whenever the effective limits of his power leave him free to make a choice among possible courses of action or inaction'.[7] Davis was concerned with the arbitrary use of discretion and favoured rule-making, so forcing administrators to work inside a framework of rules. 'Rule-making, Davis hoped, 'could fill the gap by moving discretion up the hierarchy and containing the line bureaucracy inside a framework of "tick-this-box" type of rule.'[8] Davis's contribution has been criticised as an over-legalistic approach and the ability of rules to constrain discretion has been queried.[9] Robert Goodin pointed out that discretionary power can exist within rules, and that some kinds of discretion are not eliminable and the problems with discretion are insurmountable.[10] Facts can be interpreted differently by officials and different legitimate outcomes can result, indicating the presence of discretion. Different outcomes can arise because different weights are attached to the relevant factors or because different facts are emphasised, again pointing to the importance of discretion.[11] It has long been acknowledged that all rules require interpretation and all interpretative work involves discretion.[12]

The argument that the more vague a rule the greater the discretion, and the more specific and compelling the rule the less room there may be for discretion,

---

4   Robert Goodin, 'Welfare Rights and Discretion' (1986) 6 *Oxford Journal of Legal Studies* 232, 233, 234.

5   Vibeke Nielsen, 'Are Regulators Responsive?' (2006) 28(3) *Law and Policy* 396, 401.

6   Elaine Campbell, 'Towards a Sociological Theory of Discretion' (1999) 27(2) *International Journal of the Sociology of Law* 79, 86.

7   Kenneth Culp Davis, *Discretionary Justice: A Preliminary Inquiry* (1969).

8   See Harlow (2005) 285.

9   See Robert Baldwin, *Rules and Government* (1995) 21; Goodin (1986) 232.

10   Goodin (1986) 233.

11   Administrative Review Council, Parliament of Australia, *Automated Assistance in Administrative Decision Making*, Report No 46, (2004) 12.

12   Galligan (1986) 260, See Baldwin, 'Why Rules Don't Work' (1990) 53(3) *Modern Law Review* 321.

has been discounted by many.[13] It has been contended that discretion and rules are not 'in a zero sum relationship such that the more rules there are the less the discretion there is and visa versa.'[14] A mass of detailed rules can in fact increase discretion rather than reduce it and may be too complex to facilitate compliance.[15] Julia Black has stated the presence of rules alone is not sufficient to limit discretion and the exercise of discretion will be governed by bureaucratic and organisational norms, as well as broader political and economic pressures and moral and social norms.[16] It is generally agreed that both rules and discretion have a place in regulation and 'it is not a choice between discretion and rules, but rather a choice between different mixes of discretion and rules'.[17] Discretion can be regulated procedurally as well as by rules, for example, by requirements to render the exercise of discretion accountable to others by reporting requirements and transparency that enables the appealability of discretion.

The notion that discretion can be managed in order to confine its exercise to certain actors and to limit the way in which those actors use it, has been widely discredited. Discretion is always present.[18] John Braithwaite, Toni Makkai and Valerie Braithwaite, in their study on regulating aged care, looked at the relationship between rules and discretion. They examined the historical shift in the United States from broad, vaguely defined standards to specific ones, which resulted in the Illinois code for nursing homes having over 5000 quality-of-care regulations in the 1980s.[19] This shift from broad-based standards to specific ones was intended to improve reliability, which the authors, using empirical studies, found did not eventuate. Having an impossible number of standards has meant inspectors tend to concentrate on some issues while neglecting others for a variety of reasons, including the institution's enforcement history or the inspector's professional background; this causes endemic unreliability.[20] The authors argued that, hand in hand with a paradox of reliability, is a paradox of discretion and stated:

> More and more specific standards are written by lawmakers in the misplaced belief that this narrows the discretion of inspectors. The

---

13   Julia Black, 'Managing Discretion' (Paper presented at the Australian Law Reform Commission Conference, Penalties: Policy, Principles and Practice in Government Regulation, Sydney, June 2001) 2; see also Goodin (1986) 232–34, Baldwin (1990) 16; Lorraine Gelsthorpe and Nicola Padfield (eds), *Exercising Discretion: Decision-making in the Criminal Justice System and Beyond* (2003) 5–16.

14   Black (2001) 2.

15   ibid, 7; see also Julia Black, Martyn Hopper and Christa Band, 'Making a Success of Principles-based Regulation' (2007) 1(3) *Law and Financial Markets Review* 191.

16   Black (2001) 2; see also Robert Baldwin and Julia Black, 'Really Responsive Regulation' (2008) 71(1) *Modern Law Review* 59, 70.

17   Carl Schneider, 'Discretion and Rules: A Lawyers' View', in Hawkins (1992) 49; Black, *Rules and Regulators* (1997) 20; Carol Harlow and Richard Rawlings, *Law and Administration* (1984) 105.

18   Black (2001) 2; see also Goodin (1986) 238.

19   John Braithwaite, Toni Makkai and Valerie Braithwaite, *Regulating Aged Care: Ritualism and the New Pyramid* (2007) 222–23.

20   ibid, 224–25.

opposite is true: the larger the smorgasbord of standards, the greater the discretion of regulators to pick and choose an enforcement cocktail tailored to meet their own objective. A proliferation of more specific laws is a resource to expand discretion, not a limitation upon it.[21]

Sociologists have argued that an officer's own sense of discretion can shape the way it is exercised, and also that discretion is shaped by various external social, economic and political factors.[22] Sociologists see discretion as existing at every stage of administration: policy creation, policy implementation, and problem identification.[23] Even the manner in which evidence is gathered may be based on discretion.[24] Discretion is not just attached to rules and 'can be a property of rules, a property of behaviour, or a sense the people have of their freedom to act.'[25] Nicola Lacey has argued the sociologists' contribution will inevitably shape the strict legal construction of discretion today.

Anthony Giddens proposed a link between action and structure. The law as a structure can be enabling and permissive; it can provide a language of communication and signification of legally relevant incidents and it can establish norms for officers.[26] Giddens proposed that day-to-day life is a continuous flow of intentional action and many acts have unintended consequences which may also become conditions of action.[27] Christine Parker's study on cartels provides an example of the intended and unintended consequences of exercising discretion. Here Parker examines the effect that media attention, which accompanies a win in a cartel case, can have on the industry. The ACCC had been able to use this attention to inform and motivate business to comply with the Act, to shame business convincing them to rehabilitate and also as a dialogue for persuasion.[28] Publicity for the ACCC's actions was relied on heavily during the years when Allan Fels was chairman and it has been stated that 'In effect this became the shield for Fels' ACCC, creating an aura of power and public support that protected the agency from attacks by politicians and business.'[29] This is much like the approach of open dialogue combined with censure in the annual reports adopted

---

21 ibid, 226.

22 Hawkins (1992) 20; Nicola Lacey, 'The Jurisprudence of Discretion: Escaping the Legal Paradigm', in Hawkins (1992) 360, 364; Campbell (1999).

23 Lacey, ibid, 364.

24 See Administrative Review Council (2004) 14 where the Social Security Appeals Tribunal noted that decisions ultimately rest on assessing the evidence and making a judgment.

25 Richard Lempert, 'Discretion in a Behavioural Perspective', in DJ Galligan (ed), A Reader on Administrative Law (1996) 393.

26 Anthony Giddens, Profiles and Critiques in Legal Theory (1982) 30–31; see also discussion in Campbell (1999) 81–84.

27 Giddens (1982) 30–31.

28 Parker, Christine, Ainsworth, Paul and Stepanenko, Natalie, 'ACCC Compliance and Enforcement Project: The Impact of ACCC Enforcement Activity on Cartel Cases' (Working Paper, Centre of Competition and Consumer Policy, Australian National University, May 2004) 96–97.

29 Fred Brenchley, Allan Fels: A Portrait of Power (2003) 279.

by Chairman Ron Bannerman, discussed in Chapter 2, which was successful in motivating a culture of compliance, as has been evident through the ACCC's history. There could, however, be unintended consequences flowing from such actions, as Parker illustrates of the Fels period — the adverse media attention given to one alleged price-fixing investigation involving oil companies resulted in many lawyers and compliance officers losing faith in the ACCC; this led to the development of attitudes of resistance, defiance or disengagement towards the regulator.[30] These events shaped the agency future trajectory — it made sectors of the trade practices community critical of the ACCC; many, including Fels, did not expect to be reappointed which created an atmosphere of uncertainty and undermined the assuredness of the ACCC and the officials within it; and the regulator faced review of its powers, including its use of discretion in the Dawson reviews that followed. Clearly, the manner in which the ACCC exercised its discretion in this area, before the raids on the oil companies which alleged had breached the law, by the regulator to gain evidence and adverse media coverage, was quite different to the manner in which it exercised its discretion after the raids.

Any examination of discretion must acknowledge Ronald Dworkin's categorisation of discretion. Dworkin characterised discretion as the 'hole in the doughnut' — discretion does not exist except as an area left open by a surrounding belt of restrictions.[31] Dworkin distinguished three senses of discretion, two 'weak' and one 'strong'. Strong discretion occurs where a person is not bound by the standards set by the authority in question.[32] For Dworkin, discretion in this sense does not exist as there are always existing principles, such as rationality and fairness, that govern any such decision.[33] Weak discretion is said to exist in two forms, the first where discretion requires some form of choice or judgment to be exercised by the decision-maker, even though standards exist; the second where the official has final authority for making a decision, which thereafter cannot be altered. For my purposes, strong discretion would not usually apply to regulatory agencies because their decisions are generally governed by principles in the form of internal guidelines and internal review mechanisms. This is the case with the ACCC and its interpretation of public benefit, governed by principles developed both by the ACCC in its guidelines and the Australian Competition Tribunal (ACT) in its decisions. The second type of weak discretion would not apply to most regulatory agencies because the decisions of such agencies are reviewable. The decisions of the ACCC in the authorisations area

---

30 Parker, Ainsworth and Stepanenko, (2004) 98. Also see Valerie Braithwaite (ed), 'Responsive Regulation and Taxation' (2007) Special Issue *Law and Policy* 3; Valerie Braithwaite, Kristina Murphy and Monika Reinhart, 'Taxation. Threat, Motivational Postures and Responsive Regulation' (2007) 29(1) *Law and Policy* 137.

31 Ronald Dworkin, *Taking Rights Seriously* (2005) 31.

32 ibid, 31–33.

33 Galligan (1986) 20.

are reviewable by the ACT. It is the first type of weak discretion that would apply — that the officials in the ACCC have to interpret the standard of 'public benefit'.

Denis Galligan has been critical of Dworkin categories of discretion arguing 'discretion occurs at a variety of points within any exercise of power'[34] and it is shaped by other factors. Galligan argued discretion is a way of characterising power in respect of a certain course of action. In the case of discretion by officials in a regulatory agency, it begins with the official being aware of the purpose of the discretionary power and then determines the manner in which the purpose will be exercised. It can include the process of creating standards; settling what can come within existing standards; individualising and interpreting loose standards and assessing the relative importance of conflicting standards. It can also include choosing the policies, strategies, standards or procedures that may suit a particular situation.

Galligan proposed that discretionary power is based around two variables. The first is the scope that the official has for the assessment and judgement of the issues. In connection to this, Galligan stated there is discretionary power when there is a relative absence of guiding standards, accompanied by the inference that it is for the authority to establish its own.[35] Further, Galligan pointed out that, even where there are standards, they may require further exercise of discretion in the creation of more specific, individualised standards. This is clearly applicable to the ACCC's determination on the meaning of public benefit. The phrase itself is not defined, nor are there any guiding standards in the legislation, leaving it for the regulator to determine its meaning. The choice of the term itself caused considerable controversy and its inclusion was criticised (discussed in Chapter 3). Jeffrey Jowell stated that the use of standards, such as 'public interest' or 'fair and reasonable', usually give decision-makers a high degree of discretion.[36] In the case of the ACCC, this is certainly true and it is left to the regulator to decide whether non-efficiency-based benefits, such as sustainability or improved safety conditions, will be recognised as public benefits. The discussion in this chapter demonstrates that many efficiency-based, as well as non-efficiency-based benefits have been recognised at various times. One controversial example is the empowering of small businesses; something ACCC officials have been recognising as a public benefit for some time has now been codified by virtue of the collective bargaining provisions.[37]

The second variable is the surrounding attitudes of officials as to how the issues are to be resolved. The regulatory institution itself may provide incentives and

---

34   ibid.
35   ibid, 23.
36   Jowell (1973).
37   See Sections 91AA–91AF *Trade Practices Act 1974* (Cth).

disincentives for people to make decisions in particular ways.[38] Here it is the institutional arrangements and the attitudes they engender that are important.[39] The mere existence of discretion does not necessarily mean that it is used. As Galligan has pointed out, 'what may be discretionary from an external, legal point of view, may be anything but discretionary from the internal point of view of officials within the system'.[40] Other institutional arrangements likely to influence the manner in which the decision will be exercised come from both within and outside the agency. Galligan stated that the official's own attitude to his powers, to the institutional framework, are important considerations in understanding how powers are exercised and reflexively shape the nature of the institution.[41]

All these factors apply to the ACCC. At different times, the officials within the organisation have focused on raising awareness and encouraging compliance rather than simply falling back to rule ritualism.[42] The regulator itself has, by and large, engaged in a dialogue with business, leading one study in 1987 to classify it as a 'modest enforcer' that used its discretion responsively to incorporate prosecution, fines and compliance.[43] External scrutiny has always been important to regulators and this comes in different forms, the most obvious form being the appeals to the ACT.[44] For example, in the *Qantas* decision, the ACCC did not approve the authorisation on the basis that the benefits were primarily going to the applicant and were not passed on to consumers. This decision was overturned by the ACT, which did not require that the benefit be passed on to the consumer.[45] Although ACCC staff indicated their concern at the decision of the ACT, they nevertheless accepted that all further decisions would be governed by the ACT's interpretation of public benefit.[46] Another form of scrutiny, usually regarded as particularly demanding, is the Senate Committee Hearings, at which senior officials of a regulatory agency are subject to strenuous questioning on the conduct of the agency by members of the committee. All these factors will shape the manner in which officials within the regulator exercise their discretion. These limits and constraints on discretion are discussed in greater detail in the following section.

---

38   Hawkins (1992) 6.
39   Galligan (1986) 13.
40   ibid.
41   ibid, 12.
42   Christine Parker and Vibeke Lehmann Nielsen, 'Do Businesses take Compliance Systems Seriously? An Empirical Study of the Implementation of Trade Practices Compliance Systems in Australia' (2006) 30(2) *Melbourne University Law Review* 441.
43   John Braithwaite, Peter Grabovsky and John Walker, 'An Enforcement Taxonomy of Regulatory Agencies' (1987) 9 *Law and Policy* 323.
44   See Karen Yeung, 'Does the ACCC Engage in "Trial By Media"?' (2005) 27(4) *Law and Policy* 549.
45   See *Re Qantas Airways Limited* [2004] ACompT 9 (12 October 2004).
46   Interview 2.

The metaphor of a 'tube of toothpaste' has been used to describe discretion — squeezing it from one area does not remove discretion; it merely moves the bulge to another area. The example of the use of conditions by the ACCC illustrates this point. An authorisation is determined on the basis that public benefit outweighs public detriment. In numerous cases, however, authorisation is granted on the basis of conditions that commonly address anticompetitive practices.[47] This illustrates that the ACCC's use of discretion is moving from the area of identifying and balancing public benefit and public detriment to imposing conditions to restrict public detriment and is aimed at gaining positive outcomes. In other words, it is difficult to control the amount of discretion and the direction in which that discretion may move.

The Constraints to Discretion

The traditional constraints on administrative power were expounded by AV Dicey in the late nineteenth century as part of his analysis of the rule of law. Dicey's view on the rule of law clearly recognised the need to make agencies accountable, and one of the key features of the rule of law is the need to curb conferral of discretionary power to government officials in the interests of certainty and predictability. This approach views officials as being accountable to the courts.

The shortcomings of this construction of the rule of law have been discussed by many scholars.[48] Dicey's main concern was the arbitrary exercise of discretionary powers and his emphasis upon those areas of personal liberties concerning arrest, search, seizure and detention.[49] The Diceyan view was to rely on the courts as the protectors of a person's liberty against the arbitrary exercise of power by officials.[50] This approach, categorised as the red light theory of administrative law,[51] can be contrasted with the 'green light' theory of administrative law, which relies on the 'realist' and 'functionalist' jurisprudence that developed in the United States in the late nineteenth century. Rather than relying on judicial control of executive power, green light theorists rely on the political process. Whereas red light theorists are focused on external controls, the green light theorists would see the control of administrative activity as both internal, such as hierarchical supervisory measures, and external, such as being responsible to parliament. For red light theorists, the control is retrospective, green light theorists favour prospective control achieved through decision-making with administrative bodies, articulation and revision of policy, participation by

---

47   Examples of such authorisations include: *Mercury Newsagency System*, 9 May 1984, *NSW and ACT Newsagency System*, 26 April 1984. See Chapter 6 for further discussion.
48   Allars (1990) 9–10; Harlow and Rawlings (1984) 38–40; Galligan (1986) 199–202.
49   Galligan (1986) 201.
50   Allars (1990) 9.
51   Harlow and Rawlings (1984) 29–66.

interest groups in policy formulation, and establishing internal review/s.[52] In Australia, as a result of the statutory reforms, compendiously referred to as 'the new administrative law',[53] there was a shift away from the Diceyan approach in the 1970s. Today a combination of factors, including legal, practical and moral constraints, influences the exercise of discretion.[54]

Although the notion of discretion carries connotations of the freedom to choose how to act, it also has a negative characterisation directed at constraining the exercise of discretion.[55] Much of the research concentrates on the manner in which discretion is constrained, the most fundamental being that the use of discretion must be for the purpose for which it is granted — it must constitute a lawful exercise of power. Discretion, however, may be constrained by non-legal factors, which include the amount of available resources, time, professional norms, and the political pressures to which the decision-maker perceives it to be subject.[56]

There have been numerous attempts to categorise the range of limits imposed on the exercise of discretion. I have distilled the main arguments on constraints on discretion in Table 5.1 which instills both the legally recognised constraints as well as the institutional constraints. The first three factors can be grouped together as legal constraints, widely accepted as necessary for a democratic society, governed by the rule of law, namely: authorised by law, procedural fairness, accountability, and rationality. The remaining six factors can be grouped together as institutional constraints, namely: nature of the task, efficiency and effectiveness, organisational issues, political and economic considerations, the overall attitudes of officials and, finally, a catch-all category titled 'other factors'.

Table 5.1: Constraints to discretion

Authorised by law Procedural fairness Accountability	Legal constraints
Nature of the task Efficiency Organisational issues Political considerations Overall attitudes Other factors	Institutional constraints

Source: Author's research.

---

52 Allars (1990) 10.
53 ibid.
54 Galligan (1986) 30.
55 Goodin (1986) 232; Dworkin (2005) 31.
56 See Jeffrey Jowell, 'The Legal Control of Administrative Discretion' (1973) *Public Law* 180; see also Imelda Maher 'The Rule of Law and Agency: The Case for Competition Policy' (Working Paper No 06/01, International Economics Program 2006) 8; Black (1997) 246.

Discretion in the authorisation arena is framed by the legal limits. The institutional factors are, however, equally important — for example, a regulator and its officials who are receptive to the concerns of all stakeholders and able to negotiate with business will be more successful in gaining overall support and commitment for its actions from the wider community, including government, the trade practices community and consumers. Such a regulator will be much more successful in harnessing support than a regulator who goes by the book and whose officials are simply timekeepers.

Legal Factors Constraining Discretion

Authorised by Law

Clearly an officer exercises discretion over thousands of matters in a working day, including when to work and when not to work and what pictures to hang on the office walls. The discretion that concerns us in this discussion is that attached to giving effect to a rule. The exercise of discretion in this sense has the goal of advancing the purposes for which the powers have been granted.[57] Much of the delegation of discretion to an agency is through legislation, for example, the discretion given to the ACCC to determine the manner in which the term 'public benefit' may be interpreted. But discretion can also be called upon in other circumstances.

The discretion of police officers is an example of some of these other circumstances. An individual officer's discretion can dictate how they will respond to complaints of crimes, who they decide to release and who they decide to prosecute, and how they will intervene in conflicts between members of families, employees or landlords.[58] All these circumstances are ways of interpreting the objects of the law. This may include determining how specific powers, for example, the power to investigate a robbery, can be used. Sometimes determining the objects of the law may not be a simple matter. Where the objects and/or purpose are a matter of conjecture, discretion must be exercised in determining the objects of the legislation. In effect, determining the objects and/or purpose becomes part of the discretionary assessment that has to be made.[59]

Matters which have become important to officials over a course of decisions or over a period of time may also be important in deciding the way in which the objects and purposes of the legislation should be determined. For example, information that officials in the immigration department have about the

---

57 Galligan (1986) 30; Yeung, Karen, *Securing Compliance: A Principled Approach* (2004) 37; Baldwin and McCrudden, *Regulation and Public Law* (1987) 33; Administrative Review Council, above, n 14.
58 Schneider in Hawkins (1992) 53; Campbell (1999) 81–84.
59 Galligan (1986) 31; Campbell (1999) 81–84.

political condition of various countries will necessarily be taken into account in determining an application by an individual seeking refugee status. Likewise, the kinds of matters that may be taken into account by courts empowered to hear appeals will also be important in deciding the way in which the objects and purposes of the legislation should be determined.

Social scientists have pointed out the shortcomings of concentrating on whether discretion is authorised rather than the manner in which it is used. They argue discretion cannot always be identified in terms of explicit or implicit legal grants of discretionary power. While officials may be seen to have discretion, they may not in fact exercise it.[60] Studies indicate that officials probably behave in a more routine way than is generally acknowledged. The study by John Braithwaite, Peter Grabosky and John Walker pointed to some Australian regulators as being token enforcers. Conversely, it has also been noted that officials who appear to have little discretion may in fact exercise considerable power. Goodin's description of manipulation of discretionary powers by the gentry in connection with the penal sanction in eighteenth century England points to the misuse of these powers.[61] It is not uncommon for the receptionist of an organisation to play an important role in directing callers and, subsequently, on whether the complaints proceed and the manner in which such complaints are resolved. The first port of call in deciding whether to apply for authorisations is to approach the officials within the ACCC informally to discuss the potential anticompetitive effects of the conduct being proposed. This is often an informal telephone conversation, but it may be crucial in determining whether an authorisation application has to be made or whether immunity is going to be effectively granted.

In deciding authorisation applications, officers are required to determine the kind and the amount of public benefit in the context of section 90.[62] The object and purpose of the legislation was introduced via an amendment into the Act in 1995 in the form of section 2:

> The object of this Act is to enhance the welfare of Australians through the promotion of competition and fair trading and provision for consumer protection.

On the matter of statutory interpretation, McHugh J in *Visy Paper Pty Ltd v ACCC* stated: 'Questions of construction are notorious for generating opposing answers, none of which can be said to be either clearly right or clearly Wrong. Frequently, there is simply no "right" answer to a question of construction'.[63]

---

60   Baldwin and McCrudden (1987); Goodin (1986) 239–40.
61   Goodin (1986) 239–40.
62   See discussion in Chapter 3.
63   *Visy Paper Pty Ltd v ACCC* (2003) 216 CLR 1.

The ACCC has addressed the issue of the scope of its discretion to the ACT in the *Medicines* authorisation and stated:

1. A factor which does not constitute an anti-competitive or public detriment because it is not causally related to the proposed conduct but is relevant in all the circumstances of the application. So a Voluntary Industry Code may regulate some, but not all, aspects of a certain area. Insofar as the Tribunal considered that a detriment arose from failure to regulate the remaining aspects of that area, it might consider that omission a reason not to exercise its residual discretion or to do so conditionally notwithstanding that the reason would not be causally related to the proposed conduct.

2. A factor which constitutes a public detriment which is neither an anti-competitive detriment nor a detriment entailed by a purported benefit (leading to the discount of that benefit) which is or is not causally related to the proposed conduct but which is relevant in all the circumstances of the application. This could include a morally offensive provision in an otherwise net beneficial code of ethics such as a provision that involved inappropriate discrimination.[64]

In stating the above, the ACCC is emphasising the need to show a causal connection between the proposed conduct and the public benefit or detriment. It is also acknowledging the power to grant authorisations based on conditions by virtue of section 91(3).[65] Regarding the scope of this discretion, the ACT stated:

> The discretion conferred on the ACCC and on the Tribunal by s 88(1) is enlivened upon satisfaction of the necessary conditions as to public benefit set out in s 90. It is not in terms limited other than by the subject matter, scope and purpose of the TPA [Trade Practices Act] and the statutory context in which it appears: Water Conservation and Irrigation Commission (NSW) v Browning [1947] HCA 21; (1947) 74 CLR 492 at 505; Oshlack v Richmond River Council [1998] HCA 11; (1998) 193 CLR 72 at 84. The discretion is not narrowly confined given the enormous variety of circumstances to which it may have to be applied. It is neither necessary nor desirable to try to define its outer limits. It is sufficient to say that considerations relevant to the objectives of the Act may play a part in the exercise of the discretion even where the public benefit test has been satisfied.[66]

---

64 See *Medicines Australian Inc (2007) ACT*.
65 See discussion in Chapters 2 and 6.
66 See *Medicines Australian Inc (2007) ACT*.

The importance of translating such objects and purposes into specific policies is clearly recognised by the regulator, which has issued policy guidelines on the types of benefits that will be considered and the process that will be employed. My analysis shows that the types of benefits recognised during the different decades is more a reflection of the political, social and economic concerns that permeate the regulator and its officials' actions, rather than the guidelines themselves. For example, although the role of the public benefit 'enhancement of quality safety' has never been high on the regulator's lists, it has featured as important in the empirical study. Out of a list of 16 public benefits analysed for importance, it ranked top of the list in 1976 (Figure 3.3), third in 1984 (Figure 3.4), second in 1998 (Figure 3.5), sixth in 2003 (Figure 3.6), tenth in 2006 (Figure 3.7), sixth in 2008 and eighth in 2010 (Figures 3.8 and 3.9). Further the consideration given to both the non-economic efficiency benefits in authorisation applications reflect a flexible approach aimed at providing time to bring about structural change and proceduralisation of self-regulation.[67] This flexibility is not clearly expressed in the guidelines and indeed may be very difficult to achieve when the event has not yet occurred. This illustrates the importance of practice over lists and guidelines.

Manuals that list the types of authorisation decisions made have been maintained. In the 1970s and 1980s, some of these manuals categorised the decisions into types of industry, bringing together the historic knowledge of the market structure within which such industries operated. The ACCC regularly uses the conditions power under section 91(3) to grant authorisations under specific conditions. The most commonly imposed conditions are aimed at enhancing compliance and incorporating appeal processes with codes of conduct.[68] Today, this is process is specialised and there are officers dealing with specific types of authorisations; for example, officers develop an expertise in merger authorisations or in the aviation industry or collective bargaining applications within the dairy industry.

Procedural Fairness

The concept of procedural fairness is recognised as a guiding principle by most lawyers and is connected to the notion of natural justice. It has been translated into two main principles, usually in the context of judicial decision-making. The first principle is that the parties to a dispute should be given a fair hearing, the second that they should be heard by an impartial adjudicator.[69] Likewise

---

67   See Chapter 6 for discussion on the manner in which conditions are used for this purpose.
68   See Vijaya Nagarajan, 'Co-Opting for Governance: The Use of the Conditions Power by the ACCC in Authorisations' (2011) 34(3) *University of New South Wales Law Journal* 785.
69   Galligan (1986) 32; Administrative Review Council (2004); Baldwin and McCrudden, (1987), 45.

an official's exercise of discretion is constrained by these principles because officials are required to act in an unbiased manner and allow those affected by decisions the opportunity to be heard.[70]

Studies undertaken by social scientists support the proposition that, whereas this notion may be well entrenched in judicial decision-making, it may not be applied with the same degree of consistency by officials deciding matters in independent statutory authorities.[71] Others have also argued the notion of procedural fairness is too broad and requires further clarification. Guiding principles that explain who should participate in the decision-making process and the manner in which they should do so have been called for.[72]

Black's contribution on regulatory conversations is useful here. She has painted a picture of some regulatory processes where communicative interactions are actively pursued, stating that this is more likely where 'regulators are given broadly defined and conflicting objectives to fulfil or principles to follow, where they operate in a dynamic context in which problem definitions are complex and the consequences of regulatory action uncertain'.[73] All of this appears to query the notion that procedural fairness can only be seen to operate where there are standard procedures and set guidelines. Rather Black saw regulatory conversations as vehicles through which new interpretive communities could grow with a view to ultimately changing behaviour.

Parker's work on the ACCC and compliance gives a clear example of the manner in which interpretative communities may be developed. Moving away from the strict concept of procedural fairness, the ACCC has utilised a range of strategies, including nurturing compliance professionals in the industry,[74] and coaxing the courts to go further in ordering companies to rectify the damage done and to put in place systems to prevent it happening again.[75] It was also able to use the undertakings power in section 87B to incorporate compliance procedures into corporate governance. For example, in the AMP case discussed by Parker, the company undertook to change its own standard contracts to incorporate provisions aimed at resolving future disputes.[76] Indeed the comments of the first chairman of the competition regulator are supportive of the notion of creating interpretative communities:

---

70   Yeung (2004) 41.

71   Sainsbury in Hawkins (1992) 305.

72   Baldwin and McCrudden (1987), 45.

73   Black (1997) 172, Nielsen (2006).

74   Christine Parker, 'Compliance Professionalism and Regulatory Community: The Australian Trade Practices Regime' (1999) 26 *Journal of Law and Society* 215, 227.

75   ibid, 221.

76   ibid, 222; see also John Braithwaite, *Restorative Justice and Responsive Regulation* (2002) 22.

Business groups and professional groups or institutes, particularly umbrella bodies, are a good means of reaching their members, whether companies or individuals, in an attempt to achieve compliance with the law by consultation and education instead of having to rely disproportionately on compulsion through courts. I have always engaged a lot in this process of open discussion, and so have my colleagues and the senior staff. I acknowledge at once that the TPC is not so much teaching as engaging in two-way contact from which it also is learning.[77]

Procedural fairness has been recognised as important by regulatory agencies and the ACCC clearly emphasises these notions in all its notices.[78] The procedures for authorisations are clearly spelt out in the *Guide to Authorisations* and the steps to be followed are available both in soft and hard copies.[79] Interviews with current staff and lawyers indicate that most authorisations involve legal or professional advice and these advisers are well versed with the procedures and processes in place. The processes and documentation related to authorisation are all available online and include formal as well as informal procedures. The formal processes include: applications for authorisations, submissions by interested parties and responses by the applicants, draft determinations by the regulator, provision for further submissions, and the opportunity to seek a public hearing. The informal processes include: the preliminary discussions that the applicants and their advisers, including lawyers and compliance officers in the trade practices community with experience on how the ACCC has used its discretion in the past, and with the officials in the ACCC; the manner in which officials may verify the assertions made in the submissions, which may include the hiring of consultants to study the particular industry or scenario, or by calling for the quantification of the alleged benefits that are likely to result for the proposed conduct; and, the advice that officials may seek from experts in the field that may include other members of the trade practices community or from consumer groups with whom the official has developed a relationship.

Accountability

Accountability, in its simplest conception, means being required to give an account of one's actions — it can also be viewed as the ability to give account. The most commonly cited form of accountability is political accountability, where voters make elected representatives accountable for their actions and legislators make regulatory agencies accountable for their activities. Richard Mulgan has argued that this type of political accountability has been extended beyond its external focus. It has been applied to internal aspects of

---

77   Trade Practices Commission, Commonwealth of Australia, *Annual Report 1982–83* (1983) 166.
78   See Australian Competition and Consumer Commission (ACCC), *Annual Report 2004–05* for a discussion on accountability.
79   ACCC, Guide to Authorisation (2002); ACCC, Authorisations and Notifications: A Summary (2007).

official behaviour, including controlling the activities of officials within an organisation, making officials responsive to public wishes beyond simply being called to account and to democratic dialogue between citizens, in which no-one is being called to account.[80] Accountability is relevant to both the public and private sectors. In the public sector, it is important within the activities of public sector departments, as well as public sector commercial activities. In the private sector, accountability is relevant to commercial activities as well as non-profit activities.[81]

Accountability is a central tenet of administrative law scholarship, inquiring into the manner in which a public body and the officials within it, who have been given a good deal of discretion, can be held responsible for the manner in which the discretion is applied. The dominant view comes from Dicey's concept of the rule of law. It is geared to protect the rights of the citizen and requires the state and regulatory institutions within the state to be responsible for its exercise of power. It recognises the need to make regulators accountable and one of the key features of the rule of law is the need to curb the conferral of discretionary power of government officials in the interests of certainty and predictability.[82] As Jody Freeman has stated, this is usually done by rendering agencies indirectly accountable to the electorate via legislative or executive oversight and judicial review.[83]

Many have been critical of this model of accountability, arguing that it is not a true representation of agency decision-making.[84] Colin Scott proposed traditional accountability can involve both 'upwards' as well as 'horizontal' mechanisms.[85] Before proceeding any further, it is also worth bearing in mind the two key accountability questions in relation to this study: to whom is the accountability owed,[86] and for what is the ACCC accountable? Both these questions are addressed in Table 5.1.

Upward mechanisms of accountability are widely accepted (Table 5.1). It makes agencies such as the ACCC accountable to a variety of bodies. First the ACCC

---

80   Richard Mulgan, '"Accountability": An ever-expanding concept?' (2000) 78 *Public Administration* 555, 555–56.

81   See Neil Carter, Rudolf Klien and Patricia Day, *How Organisations Measure Success: The Use of Performance in Government* (1995); see also James Cutt and Victor Murray, *Accountability and Effectiveness Evaluation in Non Profit Organizations* (2000).

82   The other two key features are the ability to seek a remedy in courts should the government act illegally and the importance of equality before the law.

83   See Jody Freeman, 'The Private Role in Public Governance' (2000) 75(3) *New York University Law Review* 543, 546; see also Harlow and Rawlings (1984); Anthony Ogus, *Regulation: Legal Form and Economic Theory* (1994) 115.

84   Colin Scott, 'Accountability in a Regulatory State' (2000) 27(1) *Journal of Law and Society* 38; see also Colin Scott, 'Spontaneous Accountability', in Tony Prosser et al (eds), 'Law, Economic Incentives and Public Service Culture' (Working Paper Series No 05/129, Centre for Market and Public Organisation, University of Bristol 2005); see also Freeman 'The Private Role in Public Governance' (2000).

85   Scott (2000) 42.

86   These questions along with 'Who is accountable?' are referred to by Scott (2000) 38.

is accountable to the courts in a number of ways. Judicial review proceeds in the Federal Court, as can matters involving defamation,[87] breach of confidence, abuse of process,[88] or contempt of court proceedings.[89] Second, the ACCC is also accountable to parliament and is required to submit an annual report to the Commonwealth parliament. It is also required to appear each year before parliamentary committees, such as the House of Representatives Standing Committee on Financial Institutions and Public Administration and, on an irregular basis, before other committees, such as the Dawson Committee.[90] Third, and most important for this study, the ACCC is accountable to the ACT, which repeatedly reviews its decisions involving authorisations and regulated industries.

Horizontal mechanisms of accountability also impact on the ACCC's actions (Table 5.2). Many of these horizontal mechanisms developed in the 1980s in Australia, reflecting the dissatisfaction with the 'upward' mechanisms of accountability. The dissatisfactions stemmed from these systems becoming overloaded, being inordinately costly, and being too formal. By comparison, the horizontal mechanisms were informal, cost-free alternatives that possessed the advantage of allowing the freedom to access or scrutinise information closely, to arbitrate or negotiate an outcome and to settle on a range of non-adversarial alternative remedies.[91]

Horizontal mechanisms include complaints to the Commonwealth ombudsman by persons who believe the commission has treated them unfairly or unreasonably. The ACCC is subject to the *Freedom of Information Act* that allows parties to seek access to documents about investigations or complaints. External audits are another accountability mechanism, and these have been undertaken by the auditor-general, the Department of Finance and Administration in the past.[92]

Today, lawyers widely acknowledge the inadequacy of these traditional accountability measures. First, it has been pointed out that those traditional administrative law principles, with their gaze firmly on the public arena, are inadequate to fulfil a public interest mission in mixed economies where governments and private capital play shared productive roles.[93] Second, it has been noted that deregulation has resulted in regulators being given wider discretion to make determinations and negotiate compliance,[94] while little

---

87 See *Giraffe World Australia Pty Ltd v ACCC* (1999) ATPR 41-178.

88 See *Gardiner v Walton* (1991) 25 NSWLR 190.

89 See ACCC, *Annual Report 2004–05* (2005) 172.

90 ibid, 167.

91 See generally Harlow and Rawlings (1984) 401–04.

92 ibid, 172.

93 Mark Aronson, 'A Public Lawyer's Responses to Privatisation and Outsourcing', in Michael Taggart (ed), *The Province of Administrative Law* (1997) 40, 63, 69.

94 For example, see *Royal Australasian College of Surgeons* A90765 30 June 2003 and *The Victorian Egg Industry Co-operative* (1995) A40072.

attention is being given to the accountability process that may be necessary in these circumstances.[95] Third, the regulators have been criticised as not making their decisions in a totally transparent manner because they operate on the basis of vague criteria responding more to overall economic objectives, where there may be confusing division of responsibilities between regulators and other government agencies.[96]

Table 5.2: Traditional accountability mechanisms

	To whom is the ACCC accountable?	For what is the ACCC accountable?
Upward mechanisms	Internal review	Manner in which each officer has dealt with the investigation
	Courts	Manner in which ACCC exercises its powers
	Tribunals	Authorisation decisions can be reviewed
	Parliamentary committees	ACCC could be accountable for specific or general activities
Horizontal mechanisms	Ombudsman	Decision where complaints are made
	External audit	Manner in which it has been carrying out its functions
	Freedom of information	Decisions made and the relevant information considered
	National Competition Council	Introduction of national competition policy

Source: Author's research.

Scott argued that such regulatory institutions have long been subject to less transparent accountability mechanisms than merely formal ones, such as parliamentary accountability. These may have included being accountable to Treasury, which controls the purse strings, or being accountable to consumer committees, which have an important say in decision-making.[97] Scott's contention that a regulatory institution is accountable to many other parties beyond those suggested by the traditional accountability mechanisms is undoubtedly true. Freeman pointed out that formal legal procedures and agency oversight may provide the appearance of adequate accountability, but informal mechanisms can play an important and undervalued role in the process.[98]

---

95   Cosmo Graham, 'Is There a Crisis in Regulatory Accountability?', in Robert Baldwin, Colin Scott and Christopher Hood (eds), *A Reader on Regulation* (1998) 471.

96   Christine Parker, 'Restorative Justice in Business Regulation? The Australian Competition and Consumer Commission's Use of Enforceable Undertakings' (2004) 67(2) *The Modern Law Review* 209.

97   Scott (2000).

98   Jody Freeman, 'Private Parties, Public Functions and the New Administrative State' (2000) 52 *Administrative Law Review* 813, 854. For a different view proposing that self-regulation mechanisms could clash with the rule of law in France and Germany, see Jan Freigang, 'Is Responsive Regulation Compatible with the Rule of Law' (2002) 8(4) *European Public Law* 463.

Unlike those who advocate the development of a new administrative law to apply to these changing times,[99] Scott suggested extended accountability will develop in different ways depending on each policy domain.[100] I wish to explore one of the models developed by Scott — the interdependence model. This model identifies and maps out the manner in which actors are dependent upon each other in their actions. Scott argued this interdependence is a result of the dispersal of key resources of authority, information, expertise and capacity to bestow legitimacy, such that each of the principal actors has to constantly account to others for some of its actions within the space as a precondition of action. Scott applied this model to the telecommunications sector in the United Kingdom and examined the relationship between British Telecom (BT), the privatised telco, and OFTEL, a semi-independent regulator created in 1984. Interdependency explains why OFTEL is being constantly scrutinised by a number of players and is itself daily scrutinising these same players. Scott stated:

> The accountability of BT to the regulator, OFTEL, is also more focused, in the sense that OFTEL has a considerable stake in getting its regulatory scrutiny right, being itself scrutinised closely by BT, by other licensees, and by the ministers, in additional to the more traditional scrutiny by the courts and by public audit institutions. OFTEL's quest for legitimacy has caused it to develop novel consultative procedures, and to publish a very wide range of documents on such matters as competition investigations and enforcement practices.[101]

In Scott's view, OFTEL's accountability under the interdependency model would include both traditional and extended accountability measures. Traditional accountability measures would see OFTEL being accountable to parliament, the courts, the ombudsman, and the Auditor as well as to BT. The interdependency model would mean that OFTEL is dependent on and affected by the actions of a much wider group, including: the minister for an annual report; the Mergers and Monopolies Commission which has the power to scrutinise some of OFTEL's actions; other licensees; the European Court of Justice; and consumers via the Telecommunications Consumer Council.

Applying this model to the ACCC gives a different picture of accountability (see Table 5.2). The ACCC is accountable to other industry participants in order to ensure that competition in the long-term either remains unchanged or is enhanced. Other industry participants are active in the authorisation process, either submitting individual comments or comments via an industry association on the proposed application. The names of all those parties are

---

99   See Taggart (1997).
100   Scott (2000) 50.
101   ibid.

usually listed in the determinations. The interests of consumers, employees and the community are represented in many authorisation decisions over the recent past, particularly in the wake of deregulation. In the *Gas Services* authorisation decision,[102] it was the Victorian Council of Social Services that challenged the application querying the contention that major benefits have resulted from the Victorian gas reform process.[103] The ACCC was careful in handling this claim, stating that it shared the concerns expressed and allowing the authorisation on other grounds.[104]

The actions of one regulator may impact on the activities of other regulators, and this is particularly likely where there is an overlap in their regulatory functions. One such example appeared in the decision involving the Australian Stock Exchange, which was seeking authorisation of its business rules because it could have breached section 45 of the *Trade Practices Act 1974*.[105] The Australian Securities Commission, as it was then known, made its concerns known to the ACCC. It stated that it was necessary for the proposed rules, which were the subject of the authorisation application, to meet the tests of market efficiency and investor protection required under the corporations law.[106]

The ACCC addressed these concerns via the imposition of conditions that it stated 'are likely to limit the anticompetitive use of such subjective and undefined rules.'[107] Another case involved the EFTPOS authorisation,[108] dealing with the regulation of payment systems, including interchange systems, which was eventually taken over by the Reserve Bank of Australia, which saw itself as the regulator of this space.[109]

102　*Gas Services Business Pty Ltd* A90630–A90631, 19 August 1998.
103　ibid, 8–9.
104　ibid, 14.
105　*Australian Stock Exchange Limited* A90623, 1 April 1998.
106　ibid, 26.
107　ibid, 37.
108　*EFTPOS interchange fees* A30224, A30225, 11 December 2003, *Re EFTPOS Interchange Fee Agreement* [2004] ACompT 7 30.
109　The Reserve Bank of Australia, *Reforms of Australia's Payment Systems: Conclusions of the 2007/08 Review* (September 2008).

Table 5.3: Extended accountability mechanisms

To whom is the ACCC accountable?	For what is ACCC accountable?
Parties directly affected by the proposed conduct (eg other industry members)	For its decision, as it may affect the level of competition in the market
Parties indirectly affected by the proposed conduct (eg consumers)	To all parties who may be affected by the availability, price or quality of the product or for employment in an industry
Courts	Accountable for its actions, which may be in breach of legislation and common law
Australian regulators (eg Australian Securities Commission, Australian Prudential Authority and Reserve Bank of Australia)	Certain decisions may affect the way in which other regulators operate and the ACCC may be accountable to these regulators
Ministers	Particularly relevant where the minister may have discretion, eg access regime
Parliament	For actions to parliament and specific parliamentary committees
Overseas regulators (eg New Zealand)	Where the ACCC's actions may impact directly or indirectly on the competition elsewhere
Governments and governmental bodies (eg state governments)	Authorisation decisions may have ramifications for other sectors of the economy which are managed by separate government departments
Private regulatory bodies (eg Standards Australia)	Decisions may have serious consequences for the activities of the association which is regulating the conduct of its members
International regulatory bodies (eg UNCTAD, Standard and Poor's)	Increasingly accountable for regulation of global regulation of business activity
Trade practices professionals (eg lawyers, compliance officers, economists and other experts)	To comply with the objectives of the legislation and the spirit of the law as well as to show a loyalty to the regulator
Non-government organisations (eg Australian Consumers Association	To ensure that the groups represented by such non-government organisations and a range of public interest issues are taken into account in deliberations
Media	Accountable to the media which disseminates information and evaluates the performance of the ACCC's decision

Source: Author's research.

The ACCC is aware of the impact that its decisions may have on the deliberations and actions of both state and federal governments as well as on the functions of government departments. This is illustrated by the *Steggles* authorisation, which involved an application in relation to the collective negotiation of chicken growers' contracts, where submissions were received from the SA Department of Primary Industries, and the Queensland Department of Primary Industries as well as the SA minister for primary industry.[110] The interdependency model is useful in understanding the relationship between the ACCC and governments. Not only is the ACCC listening with care to these bodies, but governments are also dependent on the ACCC. This was explained by the commission in its decision regarding the SA Government's moves to deregulate its poultry industry:

> The Commission understands that debate of the Bill in the Upper House had been adjourned until the receipt of the Commission's determination on application for authorisation A90595 lodged by Inghams Enterprises Pty Ltd ... The Commission has now been informed that since elections in late 1997, the SA Government is reviewing its priorities, and that in all likelihood the Bill would be reconsidered by the SA Lower House in late 1998.[111]

Whereas references to other regulators have been infrequent in the past, with the ACCC referring on occasion to New Zealand, such references have become more common in the age of global competition.[112] Links between different competition agencies are growing and there is a recognition that, without concerted international effort, the attempt at regulation will not be effective.[113]

With the increase in privatisation and greater reliance on self-regulation, professional associations have been playing an increasingly important role in regulation.[114] The ACCC has been facilitating this by closely examining the manner in which these bodies have governance mechanisms in place and by requiring certain safeguards to be incorporated. This is well illustrated by the number of instances in which the ACCC has incorporated dispute resolutions into the constitutions of associations, thereby ensuring that any member is able to have its/their grievances heard.[115] Although it may not be accountable to such bodies under the traditional accountability mechanisms, it is clear that they

---

110   *Steggles* A30183, 20 May 1998, 15.

111   ibid, 3.

112   See, for example, *Ansett Australia, Ansett International Limited, Air New Zealand and Singapore Airlines Limited* A 90649, A90655, 22 July 1998; *Australian Performing Rights Association Limited* A30186–A30193, 14 January 1998. A further example of the greater notice being paid to the manner in which other competition agencies function is illustrated by the recent ACCC, *Cracking Cartels: International and Australian Developments* (Paper presented at the Law Enforcement Conference, Sydney, 24 November 2004), which involved overseas representations including presentations by Canadian, US and Japanese authorities.

113   For example, this was emphasised at the ACCC 'Cracking Cartels' Conference, 2004.

114   This has been happening since the 1980s in Australia. See Parker (1999) on self-regulation and compliance.

115   See *New South Wales and Australian Capital Territory Newsagency System* (1984) ATPR (Com) 50-070, A30092–A30093, 26 April 1984; *Royal Australian Institute of Architects* (1984) ATPR (Com) 50-077, 7 September 1984.

are an important consideration in the decision-making process. By ensuring such mechanisms are in place, the ACCC is reducing the possibility of misuse of market power[116] and is facilitating the decentralisation of regulation.[117]

Non-government organisations (NGOs) have always been an important force in holding the competition regulator accountable. The private action launched by the Australian Federation of Consumers Organisation (AFCO) and Action on Smoking Health in the Federal Court against the Tobacco Institute Australia (TIA) is a vivid example of their influence. These NGOs successfully argued that a remedial advertisement, negotiated by the TPC and the TIA was misleading.[118] Justice Morling held in this case that the remedial advertisement was misleading and deceptive, breaching section 52 of the *Trade Practices Act* as nonsmokers were likely to be misled into believing that passive smoking is not harmful to health. Similar examples of the role of NGOs in holding the competition regulator accountable can be seen from the appointment of Allan Asher from the Australian Consumers Association to the TPC and the subsequent appointment of Louise Sylvan as deputy chairman of the ACCC.[119]

The role of the epistemic community has always been important, and more so with shifts in self-regulation. Compliance officers, competition lawyers, experts in aviation or shipping, all types of economists — including behavioural economists — are all part of this community and are responsible for giving effect to the law and working with the regulator to do so. So, for example, if an ACCC officer is criticised for how she has exercised discretion in the presence of many or most of the kinds of actors in Table 5.2 at a meeting of the Australian Compliance Institute, then this may be a powerful form of accountability because of its very multiplexity.

The role of the media in providing a positive spin has long been appreciated,[120] and the ACCC has been actively using the media for a number of purposes, including the dissemination of information and gaining positive publicity for itself.[121] The manner in which the ACCC has used the media in the past has been the subject of debate, including discussion in the Dawson Report.[122]

116   See Black (1997).
117   ibid, 165.
118   *Australian Federation of Consumers Organisation v Tobacco Institute of Australia* [1991] FCA 137. See also John Braithwaite, 'Thinking Laterally: Restorative and Responsive Regulation of OHS' (Working Paper No. 13, Regulatory Institutions Network (RegNet), ANU, August 2003) 4.
119   See Tony Freyer, *Antitrust and Global Capitalism 1930–2004* (2006) 356.
120   See Michael Schudson, 'The News Media as Political Institutions' (2002) 5 *Annual Review of Political Science* 249; see also Jonathan Moses, 'Legal Spin Control: Ethics and Advocacy in the Court of Public Opinion' (1995) 95(7) *Columbia Law Review*, 1811.
121   For criticisms on the manner in which the ACCC has used the media, see *Electricity Supply Association of Australia v ACCC* (2001) ATPR 41-838 [Dawson Review].
122   Dawson Report Committee of Inquiry, Commonwealth of Australia, *Review of the Competition Provisions of the* Trade Practices Act [Dawson Review] (2003) [Dawson Review]; see also Brenchley (2003) 249–51.

In relation to authorisations, however, the ACCC has made use of the media in less controversial ways. It has issued media releases in relation to authorisation decisions, particularly in areas that are either politically sensitive, such as collective negotiations[123] and medical services,[124] or areas of community concern, such as protection of the environment.[125]

Traditional accountability mechanisms do not acknowledge the manner in which the ACCC is influenced by and accountable to the diverse range of interests contained in Table 5.2. In a sense, it is possible to summarise the disparate accountabilities by describing the ACCC as accountable to a competition and consumer policy epistemic community.[126] The community constitutes a diffused and pluralised networking of accountability. This should be the first step in rethinking the process by which the ACCC determines an authorisation decision.

Rationality

Rationality requires that decisions are based on reason and can be fully explained. Economic rationality is just one kind of rationality against which the ACCC is evaluated. Legal rationality is another master narrative against which ACCC discretion is recurrently evaluated. Four reasons for requiring officials to exercise their discretion rationally have been identified within that more legal discourse.[127]

- It is intended to reduce biased, capricious or arbitrary decision-making.
- The reasons for the decision must be capable of being explained in connection with the purpose for which the discretion is granted.
- It ensures that the official acts impartially.
- It ensures that there is consistency in the decision-making.

The ACCC, as with all administrative agencies, is scrutinised by a range of interested parties. It emphasises the logical and transparent manner in which it makes decisions, as set out in its guides and website.

---

123   The ACCC authorised Inghams to continue collective negotiations with SA Chicken Growers, see ACCC, 'ACCC Proposes to Allow Inghams to Continue Collective Negotiations with SA Chicken Growers' (Press Release MR 312/02, 9 December 2002); see also 'ACCC Allows Tasmanian Vegetable Growers to Collectively Bargain' (Press Release MR 257/04, 18 November 2004).

124   See ACCC, 'ACCC Proposes Surgical College Reform to Help Address Surgeons Shortage', (Press Release MR 016/03, 6 February 2003).

125   See ACCC, 'ACCC Draft Decision Proposes to Allow Greenhouse Gas, Ozone Recovery Program' (Press Release MR 042/03, 27 February 2003).

126   Peter M Haas, 'Epistemic Communities and International Policy Coordination' (1992) 46(1) *International Organization* 1.

127   Galligan (1986) 140; Yeung (2004) xx; Goodin (1986) 244–46.

Factors Influencing Discretion

The Nature of the Task

Galligan has drawn attention to the exercise of discretionary powers and the kinds of tasks undertaken in using them. Tasks that are complex, involving many interests, may be suited to an approach that allows consideration of various possibilities and ensures the maximum representations of interests. On the other hand, decisions of a complex kind that are made regularly may be better governed by relatively settled, if oversimplified standards. In such cases, complexity is compromised in order to gain in efficiency and consistency. Galligan illustrated this proposition with two examples. Where the regulator is using its discretion to determine the site of an airport, it would be necessary to adopt an approach that allows for the maximum representation of interests. On the other hand, the decision on granting licenses to conduct public houses, which are being made regularly, could be determined by straightforward standards.[128] This issue has been examined by the Administrative Review Council, which concluded that full automation of decision-making is not appropriate where the decision-maker is required to exercise discretion once the facts are established.

In the authorisations area, the decisions are varied, and some are much more complex than others. The ACCC has adopted different strategies depending on the matter lodged. Preliminary enquiries are often directed to officials to determine whether an authorisation application may be necessary. Other officials develop expertise in specific areas and deal with those authorisation applications. Where the matters are complex, such as aviation or mergers, they may be handled by a group of officials who have developed expertise in the area. Where matters require further scrutiny, the power to call a pre-determination conference can be utilised to canvass the complex issues that may arise and benefit from open discussion.[129] There are, however, benign matters which raise the same issues and benefits, such as collective bargaining, which is now dealt with via a new and more efficient process.[130]

Clearly, the allocation of funds to the agency will affect its operations.[131] It will determine the types of strategies the agency will adopt — lesser funds will mean that the agency will have to be selective in deciding the cases it may enforce. Although a limited budget may not bar an agency from developing its role, it can impede effective enforcement, in particular when there are insufficient

---

128 Galligan (1986) 137; Yeung (2004); Nielsen (2006) 402–03.

129 Section 90A of the *Trade Practices Act 1974* (Cth).

130 Allan Fels and Tim Grimwade, 'Authorisation: Is it still Relevant to Australian Competition Law?' (2003) 11 *Competition and Consumer Law Journal* 187, 200.

131 Galligan (1986) 290; Goodin (1986) 241; see also Richard Grant Politics and Public Administration Section, Department of Parliament Services, *Australia's Corporate Regulators — the ACCC, ASIC and APRA* (Research Brief No 16, 14 June 2005) 23.

resources to deal with the number of cases.[132] The manner in which an agency can seek to deal with a limited budget is illustrated by the manner in which the European Union has sought to deal with its equivalent to authorisations. The exemptions process was abandoned in May 2004 mainly because of the cost burden placed by the system on the regulator. Now the regulator can challenge an agreement in court and the onus would be on the parties to the agreement to show that their agreement is not in breach of Article 81(3).[133] This amendment is moving away from a regulator-centred, prospective-approval-based regulatory approach to a court-based adversarial approach.

Efficiency

Efficiency is often defined as the ability to accomplish a job with a minimum expenditure of time and effort. It refers to the relationship between resources and results.[134] More specifically there are two aspects of efficiency — productive efficiency and allocative efficiency. Productive efficiency refers to producing a good or service at the lowest cost. Allocative efficiency refers to resources being allocated in a way that maximises the net benefit gained through their use. Thus it refers to a situation in which the limited resources of a country are allocated in accordance with the wishes of consumers.

Whereas business organisations have acknowledged efficiency as an important goal, since the 1970s in the United Kingdom and the 1990s in Australia this has become more important in the context of government agencies.[135] Efficiency became the rationale for outsourcing and deregulating many government activities. The term New Public Management was coined to describe the shift in the way government agencies functioned,[136] with many scholars evaluating the consequences this shift has brought for administrative law.[137] It has meant that public administration is monitored by reference to the overriding criteria of value for money, illustrated by the establishment of the Office of Best Practice Regulation, which has a central role in assisting departments and agencies to meet the Australian Government's regulatory impact analysis requirements, and in monitoring and reporting on their performance, with an emphasis on quantification and cost benefit analysis.[138]

---

132   Maher (2006).

133   *Official Journal of the European Communities*, 'Introduction', Council Regulation (EC) No 1/2003, (16 December 2002) para 3.

134   Galligan (1986) 129; Yeung (2004) 30.

135   Independent Committee of Inquiry into Competition Policy in Australia, Commonwealth of Australia, *National Competition Policy* [Hilmer Report] (1993); [Dawson Review] (2003).

136   Christopher Hood, 'A Public Management for all Seasons' (1991) 69 *Public Administration* 3.

137   Harlow and Rawlings (1984) 141.

138   Department of Finance and Deregulation, Commonwealth of Australia, Office of Best Practice Regulation (OBPR) 'Cost Benefit Analysis', which emphasises cost benefit analysis. <http://www.finance.gov.au/obpr/cost-benefit-analysis.html> at 15 October 2008.

Organisational Issues

The design of the organisation, the ethos of the agency as well as its leader will have an influence on discretion. The organisational design of the regulator will determine the discretionary power granted to officials within it, as well as the manner in which the discretion is used. Detailed guidelines on how discretion should be exercised may do away with discretion completely and has been discussed in the context of automated expert systems.[139] For example, the Department of Veterans' Affairs has an automated expert system that guides the officer's decisions and ability to exercise discretion. The officers' ability to override the ultimate result of the expert system is limited, reducing the manner in which the officer could ultimately act.[140] Another example is the office of National Legal Aid which had a different take on its officers' use of discretion. Because the guidelines for legal aid are flexible and the range of circumstances that individuals find themselves in are not easily reduced to business rules, the officer's role becomes important and such decisions are not easily made by automated decision-making format.[141] Further, it may be possible for the guidelines to limit discretion. For example, the guidelines may prescribe certain modes of communication or certain language to be used for the communication and this might be difficult for some groups to engage with. Whereas in some agencies the guidelines may allow the officers to adopt a conciliatory stance, in others they could force officers to 'go by the book'.[142] Similarly, requiring all submissions to be made by lawyers or economists may reduce participation by groups without access to resources to employ professionals.

The ethos of the organisation, although difficult to define, is crucial to the manner in which the regulator functions. Here the dominant language and knowledge of discourse within the organisation will influence the exercise of discretion. This point has been illustrated by the manner in which doctors use discretion. Rather than using the term discretion, doctors use terms such as professional judgment and the exercise of clinical freedom.[143] Scientific knowledge is used by the profession to assert its position and the manner in which such information is regarded by the community. Likewise, the ACCC's emphasis on compliance rather than enforcement reflects its current ethos.[144] Similarly, emphasis by the ACCC on economic efficiency and its quantification has been a way to assert the rationality of decision-making. This is further driven by the need for such

---

139   G Smith, 'Discretionary Decision-making in Social Work', in Adler and Asquith (1981) 47, 48.
140   Administrative Review Council (2004) 13.
141   ibid.
142   Black (2001) 13.
143   T McGlew and A Robertson, 'Social change and the shifting boundaries of discretion in medicine', in Adler and Asquith (1981) 200, 201.
144   Parker and Nielsen (2006); Nielsen (2006).

agencies to be accountable for their actions and expenditures. This may, however, have the impact of ignoring non-efficiency benefits, such as improvements in health or promotion of healthy lifestyles.

The manner in which this discretionary power is communicated within the agency is important. Some regulatory agencies have broad guidelines aimed at increasing awareness and compliance. In a study on nursing homes, John Braithwaite and Toni Makkai looked at whether trust nurtures compliance — if treating regulated groups as worthy of trust would be repaid with voluntary compliance.[145] The study found that, although there was a correlation between trust and compliance, regulatory institutions should be able to deal both with cases where trust is respected and where trust is abused. Such practices, where implemented, would give officials within the regulatory institution wide discretion.

Where there are comprehensive standards and strict guidelines as matters of policy, strategy as well as procedure, the officials themselves may have little discretion. The study by Richard Lempert on the adjudicative discretion that Hawaiian state law provided to a public housing eviction board showed changes in the eviction process from 1969 to 1987. Lempert identified a number of behavioural factors that affected the exercise of discretion by the board. These included training sessions for board members in order to promote legalistic decision-making; not reappointing members with views regarded as too pro-tenant and new appointments to the board. Changes to the board size and the hearing process to allow more eviction action to be heard, use of lawyers in presenting the views of the Hawaiian Housing Authority, amendments to the legislation which provided further grounds on which appeals could be made could also affect discretion.[146]

Braithwaite, Grabosky and Walker conducted a study on enforcement approaches in enforcement agencies, which illustrates that many factors determine enforcement practices, including regulatory policy, enforcement practices and the attitudes of officials. Thus officers' use of discretion is a determinant of enforcement practices. The authors examined 101 Australian regulatory agencies and identified seven dominant enforcement types: conciliators, benign big guns, diagnostic inspectors, detached token enforcers, detached modest enforcers, token enforcers, and modest enforcers. The authors found most Australian enforcement agencies to be token enforcers that performed

---

145   John Braithwaite and Toni Makkai, *'Trust and Compliance Administration'* (Working Paper No. 9, Compliance and Governability Program, February 1993) 11.
146   Lempert (1996) 373–76.

perfunctory rulebook inspections.[147] The TPC in this study was classified as a modest enforcer, which made use of a variety of enforcement methods including prosecution, fines, injunctions and adverse publicity.[148]

Christine Parker and Vibeke Nielsen examined business' opinions of the ACCC, which is of interest here. They used three indices to measure this: a strategic sophistication index, the procedural and substantive justice index and the flexibility index. The authors reported that opinions of businesses tended to be neither extremely negative nor extremely positive. Businesses saw the ACCC most positively in relation to its strategic sophistication. They also viewed the ACCC as an effective regulator, whose activities were beneficial to the Australian economy, but they were critical of the ACCC's use of the media.[149]

The leadership within the organisation will influence its operations as well as the operations of the officials within it. In discussing the enforcement style adopted by regulatory officials, leadership has been pointed to as an important factor.[150] Leadership style can determine the approach to regulation, the intra-agency commitment and competence, the networks that may be actively used, and the relationship that may develop with other agencies. The ACCC has had leaders with diverse personal styles, who have shaped the organisation. For example, the operational style of Bannerman was based on dialogue, as demonstrated by the following statement:

> The TPA has always been a very public body, and I hope it remains so. It must often talk softly, sometimes talk firmly, and reach for the third alternative rather rarely. It needs to earn and retain respect in order to do its work effectively. The Commissioners have to be publicly known. They have to go onto platforms and into groups. They have to respond to urgent calls for conferences. While avoiding the risk of being remote, they have to avoid the opposite risk of being thought to identify with those whose conduct they must scrutinize.[151]

The leadership style will be important in defining the organisation in the public eye. This was an issue that was brought to the fore by Fels, whose use of the media kept the chairman and the regulator in focus. Explaining/defending his use of the media, Fels stated:

> I have sought and maintained a high media profile because I believe my statements and media interviews help build a general culture of understanding and support for competition law. Accusations from some

---

147   Braithwaite, Grabovsky and Walker (1987) 323.
148   ibid, 340.
149   Parker and Nielsen (2006) 160.
150   Yeung (2004) 188.
151   Trade Practices Commission, (1983) [211].

quarters of being a media tart are a small price to pay for raising business and consumer confidence in competition law. The more people who realise their obligations and rights, the greater the degree of genuine competition within the economy.[152]

The background of the leader is also important, as demonstrated by the discontent among four of the state governments that refused to support the appointment of Graeme Samuel to the position of commissioner in 2003.[153] Samuel's track record was described as having been 'forged more in the boardrooms of corporate Australia than with the tens of thousands of small businesses who look to the ACCC as a buffer against the bigger players'.[154] There was, however, bipartisan support for the appointment of Ron Sims, an experienced regulator, to this position in 2011.

Political Considerations

Institutional design can give politics an important role and can have an influence on discretion. Reliance on discretion, rather than rules, could provide an escape route for governments seeking to avoid difficult decisions.[155] This is certainly true of the Australian *Trade Practices Act*, which has relied on the granting of discretion to the regulator and left appeals in the hands of the tribunal rather than the courts.

Tony Freyer's analysis of antitrust regulation in Britain and the United States shows the different considerations faced by policy makers in the two countries that shaped the manner in which restrictive practices were regulated.[156] Paul Craig pointed out that the structure of the British antitrust legislation during the 1980s gave ultimate control to the political arm of government. He argued the important role played by the secretary of state in the initiation of monopoly and merger references, the preference given for public enforcement of competition policy rather than private enforcement, and the limited role provided to the judiciary all resulted in giving the government of the day an important role.[157]

---

152   Allan Fels, ACCC Update, 13 June 2003, <http://www.accc.gov.au/content/item.phtml?itemId=349239 &nodeId=34326161a1928dde07b97cf4878b8390&fn=Update_13.doc> at 10 December 2007; see also Parker, Ainsworth and Stepanenko, (2004).

153   See ABC Radio, 'States block ACCC appointment', *The World Today* 13 November 2002 <http://www. abc.net.au/worldtoday/stories/s726027.htm> at 8 February 2008.

154   ABC Television, 'Controversy surrounds ACCC appointment', *The 7.30 Report* 29 May 2003 <http:// www.abc.net.au/7.30/content/2003/s867709.htm> at 6 January 2008.

155   Tony Prosser, 'The Politics of Discretion: Aspects of Discretionary Power in the Supplementary Benefits. Service', in Adler and Asquith (1981) 148, 149.

156   See Tony Freyer, *Regulating Big Business: Antitrust in Great Britain and America 1880–1990* (1992).

157   Paul Craig, 'The Monopolies and Mergers Commission: Competition and Administrative Rationality', in Baldwin and McCrudden (1987) 197, 217.

The role of politics can be overt but is commonly more indirect or subtle. An example of direct influence can be by virtue of the legislative design. This is illustrated by the access regime that provides for ministerial approval of certain access applications on the grounds of public interest.[158] Today, federal and state governments make submissions to the ACCC in relevant authorisation deliberations.

The Attitudes of Officials

The outlook of officials working within the agency will shape the exercise of discretion. Braithwaite, Makkai and Braithwaite pointed to the manner in which the professional background of the inspection team can frame which standards they choose to enforce. In their study on aged care, they reported that if a nurse is inspecting the aged care premises it will be nursing deficiencies in the survey report, if a pharmacist, pharmacy deficiencies are the focus; a sanitarian, sanitary deficiencies; a lawyer, patient rights.[159]

Galligan pointed out that the manner in which officials apply their moral policy is complex. Here, there may well be defining national and institutional characteristics which shape this discretion. For example, it has been pointed out that in the American regulatory tradition businesses are treated with distrust whereas, by contrast in Japan, business executives are treated as honourable citizens.[160] This may well affect the way officials operate in making decisions. But it is likely to affect the official's perceptions of statutory purposes and to influence the interpretation put on them, as well as the formation of the subsidiary goals that are set in achieving overall purposes. It may also influence the agency's approach to enforcement. Galligan cited the example of pollution control. His study suggested that wilful or negligent rule breaking will influence whether the officer decides to take enforcement action. Enforcement in this study depends on the officer's moral judgement.[161] A study by David McCallum on the 1890s policy of removing Aboriginal children from their homes again demonstrates the important role of the official. In this case the manager of each mission station was empowered to make representations about whether the child could stay with the family or be removed by the Office of the Board for Protection of Aborigines. The author reported that 'some managers were more pressing than others in ensuring that children who were sickly were able to remain on the mission with their families'.[162] Interviews with ACCC staff support

---

158   See Nagarajan, 'The Accommodating Act: Reflections on Competition Policy and the Trade Practices Act' (2002) 20(1) *Law in Context* 34.
159   Braithwaite, Makkai and Braithwaite (2007) 224.
160   Braithwaite and Makkai (1993).
161   Galligan (1986); Black (2001) 15.
162   David McCallum, 'Informal Powers and the Removal of Aboriginal Children: Consequences for Health and Social Order' (2007) 35 *International Journal of the Sociology of Law* 29.

the proposition that the officer's own attitudes influence the manner in which authorisations are conducted. For instance, officers from a consumer advocacy background asserted the need for giving attention to consumer's interest in the deliberations.[163]

The manner in which the decisions of officials are scrutinised shapes discretion. Of particular significance to lawyers is the manner in which decision-making can be constrained to ensure that discretion is exercised in accordance with the rules and for the overall proper legal purpose.[164] In this context, Galligan paid particular attention to the role of the courts, which, in many such instances, hear appeals to determine the amount of discretion that the decision maker possesses and whether this discretion has been exceeded. Clearly, over-emphasising such appeal decisions by courts, or other equivalent bodies, can give a distorted view of the activities in such regulatory agencies. It focuses more on their pathology rather than their day-to-day activities.[165] It does, however, ensure that there is outside scrutiny of the agency and allows an enquiry into whether the agency's activities are legal, whether the agency is competent, and whether it is exercising its powers in a proper manner.

Interviews with ACCC officers indicate that they have guidelines on the types of public benefits to be considered. Staff have specialties and are allocated tasks in specific areas, for example, mergers, electricity, or aviation. Flexibility exists on the manner in which staff go about gathering further information. Existing relationships with groups, such as consumer groups or expert witnesses, and advice obtained on submissions made by applicants will depend on the particular official.[166]

Other Factors

Numerous other factors can also shape discretion, including the customs and norms in the nation and within the agency. The importance attached to the specific regulatory area will be reflected in the position that the agency occupies. Imelda Maher pointed out that the status of competition law varies from nation to nation in the European Union. While competition law has a high constitutional status in Germany, this has not historically been the case in the United Kingdom and reflects on the status and legitimacy of the agency. Further, the constraints can be cultural. Maher gave the example of a farmers' association where the association ignored the injunction secured under competition law

---

163   Interview 8.
164   Allars (1990) 9; see also Allars, 'The Rights of Citizens and the Limits of Administration Discretion: The Contribution of Sir Anthony Mason to Administrative Law' (2000) 28 *Federal Law Review* 197; Schneider in Hawkins (1992) 47, 53.
165   Baldwin and McCrudden (1987) 55.
166   Interview 6.

and chose instead to pay a fine, and continue its prohibited boycotts.[167] These constraints are not necessarily fixed and can change as demonstrated by the cultural shifts experienced during the Bannerman years (discussed in Chapter 2).[168] Similarly the importance attached to competition law, clearly articulated by the adoption of the competition principles, has also been significant for the ACCC in giving it the status it had previously lacked.[169]

Relational distance has also been discussed as a relevant factor in regulation as 'the quantity of law will vary directly with relational distance, the more law will be used in cases of disputes and visa versa'.[170] It has been argued that relational distance is important in offences affected by the relationship that the regulatory agency has with the offender. In cases where the conduct is continuing and offences are a result of a set of circumstances, such as cartel conduct, the relational distance is likely to be important. In cases, however, where the conduct is a one-off, discrete and relying on specific facts that can be communicated with ease, relational distance is likely to be less important.[171] In the case of the ACCC and authorisations where the public benefits claimed are quantifiable with ease, relational distance is likely to be of minor importance. Where the public benefits are not easily quantifiable, however, such as improved working conditions or increased work safety, relational distance may become more important.

Discretion and Regulatory Strategies

Determining an authorisation application is a complex issue that can have long-term consequences. The ACCC, as with many other large regulatory agencies, faces many challenges in responding to the demands of governments, business, competitors, consumers, and other regulators. Regulatory theory has addressed the issue of how regulators can rise to these challenges. It may be trite to say that law is not static, but neither are the regulatory theories and regulatory approaches adopted by regulators. Carol Harlow's description of the changing nature of administration, law and regulatory scholarship provides a lucid, 'big picture' explanation of these changes and it is far from trite.[172] It is relevant to an examination of regulatory agencies and regulatory scholars. Harlow pointed out the law's contribution to public administration varies according to time and place. As the role of government has changed, so too has the direction

---

167 Maher (2006) 8–9.
168 See Chapter 2.
169 Bronwen Morgan, *Social Citizenship in the Shadow of Competition: The Bureaucratic Politics of Regulatory Justification* (2003).
170 Black (2001) 11.
171 ibid, 5, 11.
172 Harlow (2005) 279.

of administrative law, which is concerned with making administrators and regulators accountable. Regulatory scholars tend to be from a multidisciplinary background, which has added to the diversity and richness of the scholarship.

Harlow suggested that the dominance of administrators in the twentieth century saw regulatory scholars seeking to develop strategies of controlling the manner in which regulatory agencies used their discretion.[173] Considerable scholarship was devoted to the manner in which rules could be used and whether they constrained discretion or, rather, whether discretion flourished within such rules.[174] The rise of New Public Management in the 1970s in the United States and Europe, and a decade or so later, in Australia, with its emphasis on output oriented values, saw regulatory scholars beginning to push the case for procedural fairness and accountability. Regulators were asked to identify their objectives and look at different ways of achieving them. Responsive regulation and the development of 'soft law' were particularly influential, favouring informal dispute resolution.[175] The importance of human rights as a discourse has also influenced public administration, which is required to deliver services economically, efficiently and without violating human rights.[176] The final episode Harlow discussed is global governance, referred to by regulatory scholars as global administrative space, where international organisations, such as the World Bank and the Organisation for Economic Co-operation and Development (OECD), have a pivotal role in governance. They rely on national or international enforcement machinery, such as the European Commission, for enforcement and implementation.[177] Many of these discourses described by Harlow are evident in the ACCC's determination of authorisations. This change in the regulatory environment is illustrated by the role played by state and federal governments, which now make submissions and comment on authorisation applications just like any other private party. Likewise, the accountability push has witnessed much documentation providing maps of processes and a proliferation of specific rules.[178]

---

173   ibid, 284–85.

174   ibid, 282–83. Also see the discussion on Discretion and its Meaning in Chapter 5 of this thesis.

175   Harlow (2005) 291; see also Ian Ayres and John Braithwaite, *Responsive Regulation: Transcending the Deregulation Debate* (1992).

176   Harlow (2005) 287; see also Bronwen Morgan (ed), *The Intersection of Rights and Regulation — New Directions in Sociolegal Scholarship* (2007).

177   Harlow (2005) 288–91: John Braithwaite and Peter Drahos, *Global Business Regulation* (2000); Imelda Maher, 'Competition Law in the International Domain: Networks as a New Form of Governance' (2002) 29(1) *Journal of Law and Society* 112; Imelda Maher, 'Networking Competition Authorities in the European Union: Diversity and Change', in Claus Dieter Ehlermann and Isabela Atanasiu (eds), *European Competition Law Annual 2002: Constructing the EU Network of Competition Authorities 2002* (2005) 223.

178   See the lists on public benefit Trade Practices Commission, Commonwealth of Australia, *Authorisation* [pamphlet] (March 1990); ACCC, *Authorisations and Notifications, Guidelines* (May 1999) 7. See also Braithwaite, Makkai and Braithwaite (2007) 226.

There are a number of contributions by regulatory scholars that are particularly relevant to the process of authorisation determinations by the ACCC. Responsive regulation has influenced the manner in which the ACCC has directed much of its regulatory activity. A core idea of responsive regulation is that regulators should be responsive to the conduct of those they seek to regulate in deciding whether a more or less interventionist response is needed; they should be responsive to how effectively citizens or corporations are regulating themselves before deciding whether to escalate intervention.[179] Scholars have proposed a variety of regulatory strategies in the form of a regulatory pyramid developed by Ian Ayres and John Braithwaite (reproduced in Figure 6.1). The amount of space at each layer reflects the amount of enforcement activity at that level.

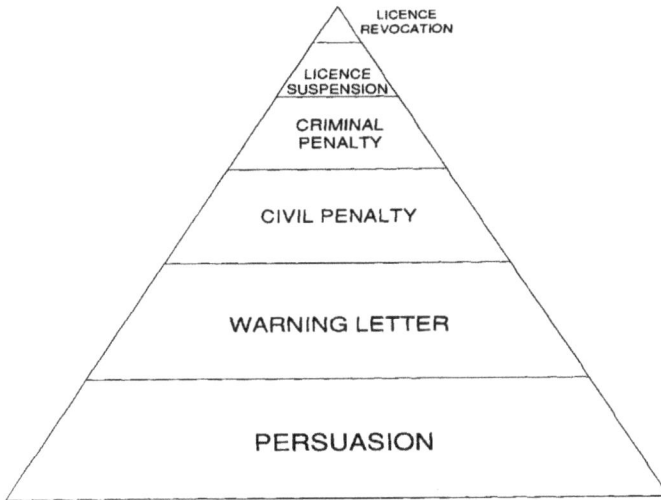

Figure 5.1: Example of the regulatory pyramid and regulatory strategies

Source: Modified from Ian Ayres and John Braithwaite, *Responsive Regulation: Transcending the Deregulation Debate* (1992).

The base of the pyramid is persuasion — a responsive, dialogue-based approach. This includes encouraging compliance and relying on self-regulation. Moving up the pyramid are more demanding and punitive approaches, including warnings, civil and criminal penalties, and licence suspensions. The model is a dynamic one that does not specify the types of matters needing consideration or the point in time when the regulator sees fit to move up the pyramid away from persuasion to penalties.

---

179   Ayres and Braithwaite (1992); Braithwaite *Restorative Justice* (2002) 231; Valerie Braithwaite (2007) 3.

This model has been criticised on many levels.[180] Some studies have found that, although persuasion may be a cheaper regulatory strategy, it is also more often subject to failure.[181] Many of these criticisms have been taken on board and the model has been reworked considerably given changing contexts, specifically the changing role of the state in regulation.[182]

Robert Baldwin and Julia Black sought to develop some of these ideas in their article 'Really Responsive Regulation'.[183] To be really responsive, it is not only the regulators' point of view but also the regulatee's points of view that matter and this is a continually reflexive process. They argued that to be really responsive, 'regulators have to [be] responsive not only to the compliance of the regulatee, but in five further ways'[184] — the firms' own operational and cognitive frameworks (their attitudinal setting); the broader institutional environment of the regulatory regime; the different logics of regulatory tools and strategies; the regime's own performance; and, the changes in each of these elements.[185] Baldwin and Black also argued this approach needed to be applied across all the different tasks involved in the regulatory activity. They proposed five elements for this approach: detecting undesirable or non-compliant behaviour; developing tools and strategies for responding to that behaviour; enforcing those tools and strategies on the ground; assessing their success or failures; and modifying approaches accordingly.[186] This holistic approach is challenging for the regulator, requiring it to have clear objectives, to know all there is to know about the regulatee and its changing environment, to be fully equipped to develop the necessary rules and tools, to be sensitive to all changes and be continuously reflexive. It is a big call and perhaps represents an ideal that regulators should always aim for while accepting that it may be difficult to attain.

The responsive regulation model has been further developed by linking it to restorative justice. Here, John Braithwaite sought to examine the changing regulatory landscape and integrate three theories of a justice system: restorative justice, deterrence, and incapacitation. It is recognised that all of these three theories are flawed and the weakness of one is addressed by the strength of the others. The greatest emphasis, however, should be placed on restorative justice, reflected by its position at the base of the pyramid with the largest space devoted to it. Stepping up the pyramid are deterrence strategies, including litigation and revocation of licences. These may be used by the regulatory institution

---

180   Two examples of these critiques can be found in Parker (1999) 223–25; and Baldwin and Black (2007) 59.
181   See Fiona Haines, *Corporate Regulation: Beyond 'Punish or Persuade'* (1997) 15–16.
182   See John Braithwaite, *Regulatory Capitalism: How it works, Ideas for Making it Work Better* (2008) 94–100.
183   Baldwin and Black (2007).
184   ibid, 61.
185   ibid.
186   ibid, 76.

where restorative practices are not effective. At the top of the pyramid are punitive sanctions, including criminal penalties and imprisonment (Figure 6.2). The middle level consists of deterrence strategies including enforceable undertakings, formal settlements and restricted licenses which have been important to the ACCC's approach and which it has described as 'an integrated approach'.[187]

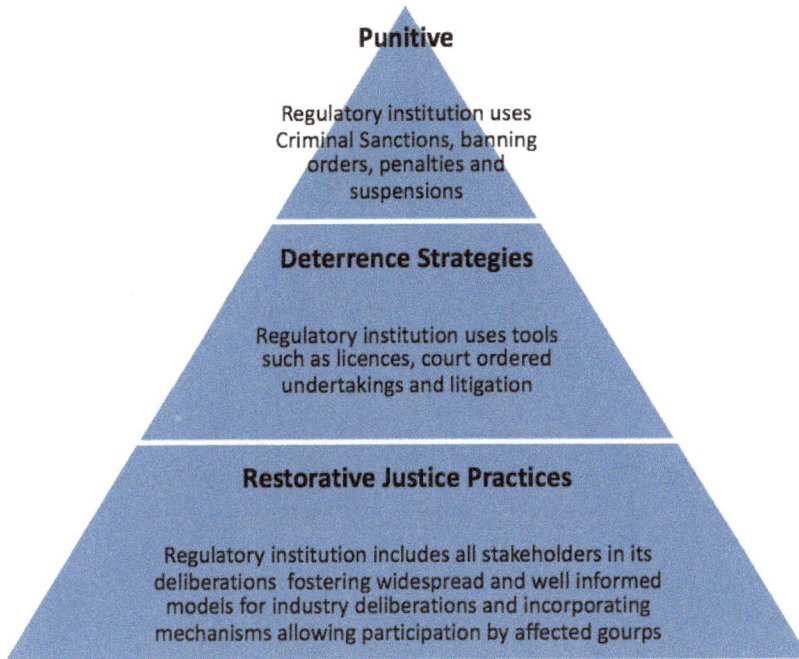

Punitive

Regulatory institution uses Criminal Sanctions, banning orders, penalties and suspensions

Deterrence Strategies

Regulatory institution uses tools such as licences, court ordered undertakings and litigation

Restorative Justice Practices

Regulatory institution includes all stakeholders in its deliberations fostering widespread and well informed models for industry deliberations and incorporating mechanisms allowing participation by affected gourps

Figure 5.2: Strategies available to the regulatory institution

Source: Modified from John Braithwaite, *Restorative Justice and Responsive Regulation* (2002) 231.

Restorative justice is described as an approach where all the stakeholders affected by an injustice have an opportunity to discuss how it has hurt them, to discuss their needs and what might be done to repair the harm. Its greatest attribute is that it is an approach informed by a 'set of values that defines not only a just legal order, but a caring civil society.'[188] Restorative justice, it is proposed, works best with a spectre of punishment in the background, but never in the foreground. It is claimed to deepen democracy as it moves away from being a coercive imposition of responsibility upon citizens to responsibility as something autonomous that citizens take after listening to a democratic conversation that includes concerns, harms and duties.[189]

---

187   Tony Freyer, *Antitrust and Global Capitalism 1930–2004* (2006), 361.

188   Braithwaite (2008) 91.

189   Braithwaite, *Restorative Justice* (2002) 10.

The democratic notions on which this is based come from the deliberative democracy discourse, summarised as 'inclusive, reasoned debate in public which creates decisive working agreements on any matters of collective concern, accountable to the people subject to those agreements, and conducted among equals'.[190] Parker has used deliberative democracy principles in developing a model that 'gives the state a role in *facilitating* the permeability of private organisational systems and social power directly to civil society and the public sphere'.[191] John Parkinson and Declan Roche point to a number of deliberative democratic features that should be considered in attempts at implementing restorative justice practices; these could include regulatory bodies. Their study examined restorative justice programs involving criminal offences, but which apply equally to other areas. The features they pointed to are: inclusiveness of all people affected by certain decisions; equality between participants; the transformative power of deliberative process which can create genuine bridges of understanding; scope and decisiveness, as individuals appreciate the scope for participation that democracy offers; and, decisiveness that such discretionary programs bring, as well as accountability which can be to a much wider population than is traditionally expected.[192]

Another group of scholars on regulatory capitalism are also relevant to this discussion.[193] They highlight the power exercised by global corporations in this field, as well as the lack of any coherent regulatory structure that can regulate such entities. In this arena, many states have little influence. Rather it is webs of influence operating in place of the regulatory structures, as we know them. These webs include webs of coercion and webs of dialogue, providing both a disparate and complex regulatory panorama. Corporate power today is more influential than the power of many states. This power has been clearly recognised by the increasing role of partnership approaches to governance, where both corporations and NGOs have been mobilised to participate in collective governance processes.[194] The importance of networked systems, where regulators can network with corporations to bring about compliance or monitoring or reform, is recognised by Peter Drahos.[195] This group of

---

190   John Parkinson and Declan Roche, 'Restorative Justice: Deliberative Democracy in Action?' (2004) 39(3) *Australian Journal of Political Science* 505, 507.

191   Christine Parker, *The Open Corporation: Effective Self-Regulation and Democracy* (2002) 40.

192   Parkinson and Roche (2004) 511–15.

193   See, for example, Braithwaite (2008); Michael Kempa, Clifford Shearing and Scott Burris, 'Changes in Governance: A Background Review' (Paper presented at the Global Governance of Health Seminar, Salzburg, 16 December 2005) <http://www.temple.edu/lawschool/phrhcs/salzburg/Global_Health_Governance_Review.pdf> at 18 December 2007; David Levi-Faur and Jacinta Jordana, 'The Global Diffusion of Regulatory Capitalism' (2005) 598(1) *The ANNALS of the American Academy of Political and Social Sciences (AAPSS)* 12.

194   Kempa, Shearing and Burris (2005). See David Vogel, *The Market for Virtue: The Potential and Limits of Corporate Social Responsibility* (2005) 3. See also Parker (2002).

195   Peter Drahos, 'Intellectual Property and Pharmaceutical Markets: A Nodal Governance Approach' (2004) 77(2) *Temple Law Review* 401; see also Michael Castels, *The Rise of the Network Society* (1996). Also see Parker, 'The "Compliance" Trap: The Moral Message in Responsive Regulatory Enforcement' (2006) 40(3) *Law and Society Review* 591.

scholars pointed to the inadequateness of national laws and advocated being more creative about responsiveness. This has been utilised by the ACCC in granting authorisations on conditions which often has the effect of increasingly compliance and providing appeal processes and complaints mechanisms.

To this scholarship has to be added the contributions of New Governance which sees the potential to nurture meaningful processes of cultural change within institutions that are decentred, experimental and founded on participation. These scholars see an expanded role for regulatory institutions.[196] Their proposal sees power as decentralised, to enable citizens as well as other actors to utilise their local knowledge to fit solutions to their individual circumstances. It also envisages coordinating bodies — including regulatory institutions — taking on new roles, such as assisting in benchmarking activities — the setting up of regulatory standards for market actors and requiring these actors to share their knowledge with others facing similar problems.

This new role is not a one-off regulatory strategy. Rather, under this proposal, the regulatory institution engages in continuous monitoring and cumulative self-scrutiny, leading to reviewing existing approaches and formulating new regulatory standards. These regulators must learn to contend with evasive and deceptive conduct, as well as other acts that prevent participation by those who may be affected. They must also learn to contend with those who use participation to frustrate, obstruct and paralyse. The description of the Bannerman style of chairmanship, discussed in Chapter 2, could be categorised as experimental — every technique from cajoling to public shaming (by being included in the annual reports) was utilised with the objective of bringing out the extent of cartel and collusive conduct prevalent in the Australian economy during the 1960s. Michael Dorf and Charles Sabel, scholars of the new governance vareity, proposed that such agencies engage in experimentalist regulation — which would connect rule-making to monitoring, followed by regulatory improvements.[197] The regulator's role would be an active one, responsible for scrutinising the effect of the rule and changing the rule as necessary. This is indeed a dramatically different role for regulatory agencies, which takes note of the shifting regulatory landscape and takes us beyond the familiar but flawed concepts of accountability to which we are accustomed.[198] Others who have contributed to new governance include commentators on management-based

---

196   Michael Dorf and Charles Sabel, 'A Constitution of Democratic Experimentalism' (1998) 98 *Columbia Law Review* 267.
197   ibid, 345.
198   See also Graine De Burca and Joanne Scott (eds), *Law and New Governance in the EU and the US* (2006); Vijaya Nagarajan, 'From "Command to Control" to "Open Method Coordination": Theorizing the Practice of Regulatory Agencies' (2008) 8 *Macquarie Law Journal* 63; David Trubek and Louise Trubek, 'New Governance & Legal Regulation' (2007) 13 *Columbia Journal of European Law* 540; Neil Gunningham, 'Environmental Law, Regulation and Governance: Shifting Architectures' (2009) 21(2) *Journal of Environmental Law* 179. Also see the discussion in Chapter 5.

regulation, meta regulation, principle-based regulation, hybrid regulation, decentered regulation, really responsive regulation, nodal governance and polycentric governance.[199]

Defining discretion is not an easy task and neither is it an easy task to show how discretion is perceived, used, constrained or limited. It is clear, however, that discretion exists within strict rules, broad principles and everything in between. The authorisation process is a complex one and, as this chapter illustrates through the empirical study, it represents an arbitrary exercise of discretion.

---

199   See See Parker, 'Meta Regulation: Legal Accountability for CSR' in Doreen McBarnet, Aurora Voiculescu and Tom Campbell (eds), *The New Corporate Accountability: Corporate Social Responsibility and the Law* (2007); Elinor Ostrom, 'A Polycentric Approach for Coping with Climate Change' (World Bank Policy Research Working Paper No 5095, World Bank, 2009; Drahos (2004); Cristie Ford and Natasha Affolder, Responsive Regulation in Context, Circa 2011 Preface' (2011) 44(3) *University of British Columbia Law Review* 463; Nagarajan, 'Regulating for Women on Corporate Boards: Polycentric Governance in Australia' (2011) 39 *Federal Law Review* 255.

6. Discretion, the ACCC and Authorisation Determinations

This chapter examines the use of discretion by the Australian Competition and Consumer Commission (ACCC), which, it argues, comes in many forms. Four types of discretion are conceptualised: epistemological, procedural, outcome weighting and immunity discretion. While epistemological discretion is related to the information considered, procedural discretion focuses on who is participating in these deliberations, outcome-weighting discretion looks at how discretion can be directed to specific results, and immunity discretion relates to the variety of ways to manage the issue at hand without necessarily making a specific decision. Although the ACCC has used all these forms of discretion to operate innovatively, it has at times silenced voices and views. To become a truly responsive regulator, the ACCC needs to show greater commitment to encouraging dialogue among the stakeholders and enhancing inclusivity.

Epistemological Discretion

There has been an ongoing cross-jurisdictional debate as to how to weigh public benefits, and whether they are quantifiable. The approaches taken vary, which illustrates the presence and exercise of discretion in deliberations. Different approaches have been adopted in different jurisdictions, also, thus illustrating the exercise of discretion.

Quantification of Public Benefits

Use of quantification, that is, statistical or econometric analysis and computer-simulated economic modelling, to estimate or quantify the outcome of strategic interactions between industry players in competition and antitrust cases, is increasing. This is partly because of the sophisticated economic-modelling packages that are available and because of the increase in economic experts who provide a seemingly objective, value-free basis for regulatory decision-making.[1]

Quantification provides three main benefits. First it provides clear guidelines for business. Business groups, when aware that possible benefits need to be expressed in dollar terms, are able to make their submissions on that basis. Second, it provides a platform for interested parties as well as regulators. Parties

---

1   Lewis Evans, 'Economic Measurement and the Authorisation Process: The Expanding Place of Quantitative Analysis' (1999) 13 *Competition and Consumer Law Journal* 99, 99.

seeking to make a submission are able to address specific matters and, where necessary, query specific benefits. Regulators find quantification useful to explain the process for exercising their discretion, interpreting the evidence and negotiating possible outcomes. Finally, quantification adds transparency to the decision-making process.

Four main problems commonly arise in requiring quantification of all benefits. First, there is no single quantification method and parties use this diversity in strategic ways. For example, in the Qantas Airways and Air New Zealand authorisation, economics experts submitted that the proposed arrangement between airlines would lead to a saving of A\$670 million in five years. Expert evidence by Professor Henry Ergas for the airlines claimed that this benefit would result in the form of cost savings, including removal of duplicative capacity, and from a projected increase in tourism. The applicants claimed some of the cost savings would be passed on to the consumer, while other benefits, such as increased tourism, would benefit a wider section of the market. Other competitors, particularly the Gulliver Group, did not accept this evidence and argued that it was an overestimate and queried the claimed 'pass-through effect'. The ACCC found that, rather than saving money, the proposed arrangement would lead to an increase in fares and decrease the capacity and quality of service of routes involving Australia where both airlines are present.[2] The ACCC also found co-operation between Qantas and Air New Zealand, without an authorisation, was possible and would yield some of the claimed benefits. The Australian Competition Tribunal (ACT) found it was unlikely that all the cost savings asserted would be passed on to travellers, although it accepted that a significant, albeit indeterminate, amount would be passed on.[3] The tribunal also accepted that not all the benefits claimed necessarily flowed from the authorisation and accordingly placed little weight on certain claimed benefits.[4] The tribunal noted that in the intervening eight months, the market had changed, as had the number of players in the market, and found that there were sufficient public benefits to warrant authorisation.[5] It is also relevant to note here that the New Zealand Commerce Commission considered the same arrangement and reached a different decision, accepting the econometric modelling evidence and granting authorisation.

Quantification of changing consumer demand is also a difficult area. Behavioural economists have suggested that the notion of the rational consumer is too simplistic and a more complex understanding of consumer behaviour is necessary. A consumer making a decision to take up an insurance policy will

---

2   *Qantas Airways and Air New Zealand* A30220–A30222, 9 September 2003, ii.
3   *Qantas Airways Limited* [2004] ACompT 9 (12 October 2004), paras 14, 211, 652.
4   ibid, 654.
5   ibid, 770.

decide the issue depending on the manner in which the terms are framed. Framing the product in terms of risks that may be incurred by not taking up an insurance policy will appeal to a different category of consumers than framing the production terms of the gains that may result in taking up an insurance policy.[6] Thus the forecasts of consumer demand and sales that are usually used in determining the future with/without the authorisation and the quantification used in this process would not be a straightforward task.

Second, adopting quantification in all cases will increase the expense incurred by applicants, who will have to avail themselves of econometric modelling in preparing their submissions. This would add to the concern expressed by non-profit organisations about the high costs of preparing such applications. It may also deter interested parties from making submissions because of the level of expertise that would be required. Third, the difficulties of quantifying certain benefits, particularly of a non-efficiency nature, cannot be ignored. Such problems have been discussed in other fields and are particularly evident in relation to environmental cases where the claims are hard to quantify because they require judgements to be made not only about the product, but also about hidden factors regarding its use, production and disposal.[7] Many non-efficiency benefits, such as product safety, promotion of ethical business practices or facilitating the right to justice and due process, may defy easy quantification and this could lead to them being discounted. In the Australian Association of Pathology Practices Incorporated, the tribunal acknowledged the difficulties in quantifying the impact of certain conduct.[8] Likewise, benefits that are likely to be delivered over a longer period may also be difficult to quantify.[9]

Finally, relying heavily on quantification would require ACCC staff to be skilled in handling such data. Use of consultants may be costly. One of the economists interviewed was critical of the level of skills of the ACCC staff, stating that they do not have a broad range of persons with expertise in economic matters.[10] Another economist compared the ACCC with its counterpart in the United States, stating that the Federal Trade Commission had dozens of staff with PhDs in econometrics.[11] Having staff capable of generating confidence is important and,

---

6   See Organisation for Economic Co-operation and Development, *Roundtable on Demand-side Economics for Consumer Policy: Summary Report 2006* (Report by Ian McAuley declassified by the Committee on Consumer Policy, 71st session, 29–30 March 2006) 11; see also Joshua Gans, '"Protecting Consumers by Protecting Competition": Does Behavioural Economics Support this Contention?' (2005) 13 *Competition and Consumer Law Journal* 3.

7   See Amanda Cornwall, 'Regulating Environmental Claims in Marketing' (1996) 3 Competition and Consumer Law Journal 1, 1.

8   *Australian Association of Pathology Practices Incorporated* [2004] ACompT 4 (8 April 2004).

9   See European Union (EU), 'Guidelines on the Application of Article 81(3) of the Treaty' (2004) *Official Journal of the European Union* C 101/08, 34 para 70.

10   Interview 10.

11   Interview 11.

in the absence of this, it may not serve the ACCC well to opt for quantification as a general rule for authorisation decisions. Such a strategy may be good in theory, but unrealistic given the world of public sector staffing.

In authorisation cases, public benefits and anti-competitive detriments can be quantified. This is commonly done in New Zealand in relation to authorisations. The New Zealand Commerce Commission has acknowledged that not all the elements that go to make up the judgement are equally capable of quantification. But quantification is the norm and the Commerce Commission has stated:

> The Commission encourages applicants to make submissions on, and to quantify as far as is possible, projected detriments because this ensures better-focussed submissions. This does not necessarily mean that the Commission itself will rely completely on quantification as a determinative measure of detriments, nor that it will accept any one party's estimation. The Commission will take each case on its own merits and use quantification to the extent that it is appropriate and not likely to distort the weighing process.[12]

Although the provision of quantified information has been acknowledged as useful by the ACCC, which has stated that 'the submission gives an indication of the likely costs to industry' and estimates the savings at 'over $100 million',[13] it has not sought to go down the path of the New Zealand regulator. A number non-efficiency-related benefits have been increasingly recognised in ACCC decisions (Figure 4.8). Michael Pusey's arguments that economic rationalism has led to an increasing emphasis on efficiency at the expense of many other values[14] can be directly contradicted by this evidence, which points to an early awareness on sustainability issues that have been given attention since 1976 and, particularly so, since 2003.

Measuring Public Benefits

As use of quantification has steadily increased in Australia there has been some pressure on the ACCC to adopt a uniform policy on the issue.[15] As discussed earlier, however, the claim that specific rules can constrain discretion is untrue[16] and discretion can simply move to another area. Rule ritualism may further

---

12   Government of New Zealand, Commerce Commission, *Guidelines to the Analysis of Public Benefits and Detriments* (revised ed, 1997) 11.

13   *Newcastle Port Corporation* A91072, A91073, A91074, 23 April 2008, 37. See also *CEMEX Australia Pty Limited* A91082, 2 July 2008.

14   See Michael Pusey, *The Experience of Middle Australia: The Dark Side of Economic Reform* (2003).

15   Interview 2; see also Department of Finance and Deregulation, Commonwealth of Australia, Office of Best Practice Regulation (OBPR) 'Cost Benefit Analysis', which emphasises cost benefit analysis. <http://www.finance.gov.au/obpr/cost-benefit-analysis.html > at 15 October 2008.

16   Julia Black, 'Managing Discretion', (Paper presented at Australian Law Reform Commission Conference, Penalties: Policy, Principles and Practice in Government Regulation, Sydney, June 2001), 2.

exacerbate the problem.[17] The main issue facing regulators is which test to adopt for the purpose of quantification in competition law cases. There have been four possible tests or standards mooted: the total welfare standard, the consumer welfare standard, the price standard and, the balancing weights standard.

Total Welfare Standard

The total welfare standard considers the economy-wide welfare effects, requiring that if/when one person is made better off, others are not made worse off. The focus is on efficiency.[18] The standard does not concern itself with wealth redistribution and does not require that benefits be passed on to the consumer.[19] Although not couched in these terms, the total welfare standard has been adopted in Australia in a few cases where the conduct is occurring at an intermediate level of production. One such example is the Port Waratah case, where the producers were the main beneficiaries of the authorisation. An ACCC staff member pointed to this decision as an example of the total welfare standard at work.[20] An economist, interviewed for this study, argued that the total welfare standard may result in making poorer shareholders better off, something which may be just as worthwhile as making consumers better off.[21] The same economist preferred the total welfare standard to any other and argued strongly that competition policy should not concern itself with wealth redistribution; wealth redistribution should be left to tax policy.[22] In the context of mergers, the ACT has stated it would adopt a total welfare standard subject to a caveat regarding the weight to be given to public benefits to the extent to which they are not shared generally among members of the community.[23] It has stated that there should be no difference in the weight attached to benefits or costs, irrespective of the beneficiaries or bearers of the detriments.[24]

17   John Braithwaite, Toni Makkai and Valerie Braithwaite, *Regulating Aged Care: Ritualism and the New Pyramid* (2007) 220.
18   Robert Officer and Philip Williams, 'The Public Benefit Test in an Authorisation Decision', in Megan Richardson and Philip Williams (eds), *The Law and the Market* (1995) 157–66. See also Suzanne Loomer, Stephen Cole and John Quinn, *Quantifying Efficiency Gains in a Competition Case: Sustaining a Section 96 Defence* (Paper presented at Canada's Changing Competition Regime, National Conference, Toronto, 26–27 February 2003) <http://www.coleandpartners.com/pdf/Quantifying_Monograph.pdf> at 30 February 2004.
19   The Canadian Competition Tribunal applied this standard in the *Superior Propane 1* case. The case dealt with a merger application and the tribunal found there were $29.21 million of efficiency gains that offset the deadweight loss of $3 million, which the commissioner of the Competition Bureau had established. The decision of the tribunal was rejected by the Court of Appeal in *Superior Propane 2*. The Federal Appellate Court in *Superior Propane 2* stated that it preferred the Balancing Weight approach and rejected the tribunal's decision.
20   Interview 2.
21   Interview 12.
22   Interview 12.
23   *Qantas Airways Limited* [2004] ACompT 9 (12 October 2004), paras 190–91.
24   *VFF Chicken Meat Growers* [2006] AComp Tribunal, para 75.

Consumer Welfare Standard

The second standard is the consumer welfare standard, which is the sum of the individual benefits derived from the consumption of goods and services.[25] This standard looks at the effect of a proposed authorisation on the consumer. It disregards the benefits experienced by producers or shareholders and requires the benefit to be passed on to consumers. The Canadian Competition Bureau preferred this approach in interpreting the efficiencies defence within section 90 of the Competition Act 1985 (Canada), although recent guidelines show it has now changed its approach.[26] In the context of mergers, Michal Gal pointed out that this standard requires substantial efficiency gains to ensure that there is no wealth transfer.[27] Michael Trebilcock argued that this standard is the most economically sound and tractable approach for small market economies.[28] A number of ACCC staff stated that they usually look at consumer welfare and are impliedly applying this standard.[29] It is evident that this is not always the case, as demonstrated by the discussion on collective bargaining, in which the main concern was to facilitate negotiations by small business.[30] Past ACCC staff members indicated that authorisation decisions made in the 1980s used the consumer welfare standard, albeit impliedly, and cited the examples of the Kuring-gai Building Society insurance cases.[31] The cost as well as the benefit that may reach the consumer has been considered in cases including the Refrigerant authorisation,[32] and the determinations appear to be paying greater attention to the issue of pass-through (Figure 3.2).

Price Standard

The third standard is the price standard, which examines the effect of the proposed authorisation on the price of the goods or service. If the likely result from the authorisation is that the downward pressure on price is greater than the upward pressure, the conduct should be allowed to proceed. The price standard

---

25 Rhonda Smith, 'Authorisation and the Trade Practices Act: More about Public Benefit' (2003) 11(1) *Competition and Consumer Law Journal* 21, 23.

26 Canadian Competition Bureau, *Merger Enforcement Guidelines*, (March 2001) <http://www.competitionbureau. gc.ca/internet/index.cfm?itemID=1673&Ig=e> at 15 May 2005. See also the recent Canadian Competition Bureau, *Merger Enforcement Guidelines* (September 2004) <http://www.competitionbureay.gc.ca/internet/index. cfm?itemID=1245&Ig=e> at 15 May 2005. For a fuller discussion of the total welfare standard see this paper, 69.

27 Michal Gal, *Competition Policy for Small Market Economies* (2003) 226.

28 Michael Trebilcock, 'The Great Efficiencies Debate in Canadian Merger Policy: A Challenge to the Economic Foundation of Canadian Competition Law or a Storm in a Teacup?' (Paper presented at the New Zealand Competition Law Conference, Auckland, 13–15 August 2004) 37. For an alternative view, see Gal (2003).

29 Interview 2; Interview 4; Interview 5; see also Smith (2003).

30 Konrad von Finckenstein, 'Remarks to the 2002 Competition Law Invitational Forum' (Speech delivered at the Competition Law Invitational Forum, Langdon Hall, Cambridge, Ontario, 9 May 2002) <http:// competition.ic.gc.ca/epic/internet/incb-bc.nsf/en/ct02361e.html> at 28 February 2004.

31 *Re Kuring-gai Building Society* (1978) 2 ATPR 40-094. See also *Royal Australasian College of Surgeons* A90765, 30 June 2003.

32 *Refrigerant Reclaim Australia Ltd* A91079, 14 May 2008.

examines the effect of the proposed conduct on the price paid by the consumer. Gains to producers, shareholders, employees or any other group is given little weight, whereas consumer gains are accorded a much larger weighting. It has been argued that there is no rationale to disregarding the benefits flowing to shareholders simply because they are shareholders.[33] Suzanne Loomer and Stephen Cole, and Treblicock have pointed out that this standard is harder to satisfy than the consumer welfare standard, since the proven efficiency gains must be so significant the post-authorisation price will be set at a level lower than the pre-authorisation price.[34] The European Commission's guidelines state that, although it requires the calculation of cost efficiencies, it does not require this for qualitative efficiencies.[35] It has also pointed out that qualitative efficiencies, such as improved products, may create sufficient value for consumers but may nevertheless be accompanied by a price increase,[36] illustrating the difficulties of relying on prices as a sole guide to determine efficiency or indeed public benefit. In Australian Association of Pathology Practices Incorporated, the tribunal recognised that, in certain circumstances, price may not necessarily reflect efficiencies. In this case, market failure was due to the principal–agent problem intrinsic to the asymmetry of information in the patient–doctor relationship,[37] in which the doctor, who does not pay for them, orders the necessary tests from a medical rather than consumer perspective.

Balancing Weights Standard

The balancing weights standard is sometimes used in Canadian merger cases. It gives a weighting for all effects, including the redistribution that may result from a merger. Applying this test to authorisations sees a weight attached to all benefits and detriments. Further, where a particular benefit results in regressive wealth transfers, for example, from poor consumers to wealthy producers, this net welfare loss is also measured.[38] In the context of mergers, Gal supported this standard because it is not limited to efficiencies but also looks at subsidiary issues such as market power.[39] The Federal Appellate Court in Superior Propane 2 suggested this would be the appropriate test to apply to the case, sending it back to the tribunal to do so. The tribunal was required to take into account all

---

33 See Trebilcock (2004).

34 Loomer, Cole and Quinn (2003) 7, discusses this standard in the context of mergers in Canada. See also Trebilcock (2004) 33, where the author rejects this standard on the basis that the requirements of the price standard are too demanding and would largely vitiate the rationale for an efficiencies defence in the context of Canadian merger law.

35 See EU (2004); EU, 'Commission Notice on Agreements of Minor Importance Which do not Appreciably Restrict Competition Under Article 81(1) of the Treaty Establishing the European Community (de minimis)', (2001) *Official Journal of the European Union* C 368/13. See also EU, 'White Paper on the Modernisation of the Rules Implementing Articles 85 and 86 of the EC Treaty', (1999) *Official Journal of the European Union* C 132/01, paras 56–57.

36 EU (1999) para 102.

37 *Australian Association of Pathology Practices Incorporated* [2004] ACompT (8 April 2004), para 34.

38 Loomer, Cole and Quinn (2003) 7.

39 Gal (2003) 224–28.

of the effects of the merger, including the negative effects on resource allocation. The tribunal found that it was difficult to quantify the net welfare loss. The approach of the European Commission also shares much in common with this approach. The European Commission adopts what it has termed the balancing test, which involves a careful consideration of the anti-competitive and pro-competitive effects of proposed undertakings or conduct.[40] The European Commission, however, has stated that efficiency gains may not necessarily affect the cost structure of the firm and has also acknowledged that qualitative efficiency gains may be hard to estimate.[41] Clearly, quantification of all the factors would be one of the drawbacks of this standard. To apply the standard, information must be available on the distribution of income between different consumer, shareholder and producer groups, which may easily be estimated incorrectly. One of the interviewed economists suggested that the ACCC's approach to authorisation determinations is best described as the balancing weights approach.[42] Another suggested that the approach of the ACT in the Qantas authorisation saw the application of a balancing weights standard rather than the total welfare standard because the tribunal did allocate weightings to the benefits. This argument is supported by the following statement in the decision:

> [W]e have also given due weighting to the fact that … benefits will accrue initially to Qantas, and its shareholders, and that not all the benefits will necessarily flow through to foreign shareholders in Qantas, we have not attributed any weight to those benefits …[43]

Given that there is no further clarification, however, it remains unclear as to whether this could definitely point to the balancing weights standard.

Trebilcock pointed out the main problems with this standard when he noted that, while it is more politically palatable than the total welfare standard, it is difficult to apply in practice and requires the competition authorities to make value judgements about who is more worthy of a dollar.[44] Such a standard may be much easier to justify politically than a total welfare standard, which permits conduct resulting in potentially regressive wealth transfers.[45] He criticised this standard on the basis that it does not take into account 'trickle down' effects and efficiency improvements introduced for private gains that will often have significant spill-over effects benefiting consumers. Further, this standard may not consider the manner in which certain conduct (in Trebilcock's case mergers)

---

40   See EU (2004) para 92.
41   ibid, paras 92, 100.
42   Interview 10.
43   *Qantas Airways Limited* [2004] ACompT 9 (12 October 2004), para 770.
44   Trebilcock (2004) 36.
45   ibid, 20.

speeds up innovation and induces technological diffusion. Thus, he argues, these gains cancel out some of the negative effects of the wealth transfers from consumers to producers.[46]

The Dawson Committee impliedly advocated the total welfare standard because of the emphasis it places on the importance of achieving efficiency gains.[47] The ACT appears to advocate a total welfare standard, although it has been suggested that there would be scope to give different weightings to different benefits. Interviews with ACCC staff indicated that one particular test is not used consistently. Two interviewees stated the consumer welfare standard was used in the College of Surgeons decision[48] and was commonly used in older decisions in the 1980s and 1990s. One staff member stated the total welfare standard was used in the Port Waratah decision,[49] while another staff member argued the Port Waratah decision illustrated the application of the balancing weights standard. One interviewed economist favoured the total welfare standard, while two other economists were equivocal about its application to all circumstances. In interviews with consumer groups, there was a general feeling that non-efficiency-based benefits would be harder to quantify than efficiency benefits and, accordingly, no standard may adequately reflect the non-efficiency benefits or detriments of proposed conduct. Another interviewee, however, pointed out that bad quantification could occur with both efficiency and non-efficiency data. Another lawyer interviewed contrasted the Australian approach with the New Zealand approach, saying the Australian approach was much more flexible and recognised a variety of benefits.

Until 2007 the ACCC did not publicly advocate any particular standard in non-merger authorisations.[50] It has been argued in the past that the commission favoured a consumer welfare standard, even though it also acknowledged private benefits in a number of its determinations.[51] Following the Qantas Airways application, however, the ACCC has been careful to point to this tribunal decision and refer to it as a public benefit standard,[52] stating:

> The term 'total welfare standard' has a variety of uses and meanings in economic and legal literature. To avoid any potential confusion, the

---

46   ibid, 30.

47   David Round, 'W(h)ither Efficiencies: What is in the Public Interest? A Commentary on "The Great Efficiencies Debate in Canadian Merger Policy: A Challenge to Economic Foundations of Canadian Competition Law or a Storm in a Teacup?" by Michael Trebilcock' (Paper presented at the Fifteenth Annual Workshop of the Competition and Policy Institute of New Zealand, Auckland, 13–15 August 2004) 12.

48   Royal College of Surgeons A90765, 30 June 2003.

49   *Port Waratah* A90650, 25 March 1998.

50   See ACCC, *Merger Guidelines* (June 1999) 69–71, paras 6.39–6.45. Here, the commission states that resource savings not passed on to the consumers in the form of lower prices can constitute a public benefit.

51   Smith (2003), 5; Alan Fels and Tim Grimwade, 'Authorisation: Is It Still Relevant to Australian Competition Law?' (2003) 11 *Competition and Consumer Law Journal* 187, 200–02.

52   ACCC, *Guide to Authorisation* (2007) 34.

ACCC proposes to refer to the approach taken by the tribunal in Qantas Airways as the application of a 'public benefit standard'. The ACCC will apply a public benefit standard when determining the weight to be given to productive efficiency savings in considering authorisation applications.[53]

This section illustrates the manner in which discretion can exist in giving effect to rules, reinforcing the concerns discussed in Chapter 5 that specific rules can increase discretion, rather than constrain it. It also illustrates the manner in which such exercise of discretion can vary over time within one regulatory agency, as well as the manner in which the exercise of discretion can be constrained by the tribunal. Methodologies can be much easier to apply in some contexts than others. I have attempted to show that choices of quantification methodologies can be fundamental drivers indeed of how discretion is exercised. Although outside the scope of this study, it is possible to apply a Foucauldian critique to these methodologies, that can see the use of quantification as a technology of control, which normalises certain practices while enabling new skills and capabilities. Certainly the use of quantification does just that while, at the same time, aligning itself to dominant neo-liberal discourses.

Procedural Discretion

The ACCC, in making authorisation determinations, has processes in place for collecting information and consulting with parties. This section looks at the main steps of the process before examining the ways in which participation is facilitated within the process and, by so doing, discretion is being exercised.

Steps in the Process

Information relevant to the authorisation application is obtained by the ACCC in a variety of ways. The authorisation application addresses in detail the proposed conduct, as well as the public benefits and possible detriments contended as likely to arise. This allows the ACCC to set the authorisation process in motion on the basis of significant information. After receiving the application, the ACCC invites interested parties to make submissions in response, and has stated that the nature of the authorisation will determine the parties it may seek to consult:

> The range of interested parties consulted by the Commission depends upon the nature of the conduct for which authorisation is sought and the types of persons likely to be affected. Typically, interested parties can

---

53   ibid, para 5.29.

include competitors, customers, suppliers and other persons affected by the conduct; relevant government bodies, including regulators; relevant industry associations, consumer groups and community associations; and industry experts. When appropriate, the Commission may also seek submissions from the community by advertising in newspapers and trade journals. As well as inviting submissions, the Commission conducts its own market inquiries and research.[54]

The first and most accessible information source is the formal submissions made to the ACCC by parties with an interest in the process. These can include other competitors in the market; other parties who may be affected by the conduct, be it upstream or downstream; industry groups; government bodies; and, independent bodies and non-industry groups. These submissions may either favour the application or refute the claims made in the application. Some of the submissions examined simply state that the party has no objection to the application. Others are lengthy, containing a significant degree of analysis. The majority of such submissions are briefer than the application itself, focusing on the viewpoint of the particular business. Most of this information, with the exception of submissions in which a confidentiality claim is accepted, is publicly available on the ACCC website.[55]

A draft determination is distributed to the applicant and all parties making submissions, and copies of the draft determination are placed in the public register on the ACCC website. Further formal submissions may also be made to the ACCC after the release of a draft determination. There are generally fewer submissions made at this stage. Here, the parties specifically address the ACCC's decision. In a number of cases, this stage provides the opportunity for a dialogue and, with the approval of the ACCC, the applicant may introduce changes to the application.[56] In other cases, the draft determination may be altered by the ACCC following consideration of the submissions made;[57] yet, in others, the draft determination remains unchanged.[58] Stakeholders rarely have the attitude that because the ACCC has taken a certain line in a draft determination, this sets the framework for the decision in concrete, because the commission has a track record of moving in response to critiques of its draft. The procedure of draft followed by revisions is at the heart of claims the ACCC can make to being genuinely responsive.

54 ACCC, 'Submission to the Commission of Inquiry: Review of the Competition Provisions of the *Trade Practices Act 1974* (Dawson Review)' (2002) 248.
55 Section 89 *Trade Practices Act*.
56 See *Port Waratah Coal Services Ltd* A90906–A90908, 9 July 2004; *Steggles Limited* A30183, 20 May 1998; *Showmen's Guild of Australasia* A90729, 25 February 2003.
57 *Federation of Australian Commercial Television Stations* A11909, 12 September 1984; *Medicines Australia Ltd* 90779, A90780, 14 November 2003.
58 *Port Waratah* A90906–A90908, 9 July 2004.

Information relevant to the deliberations is also collected informally. This may include telephone calls to lawyers, applicants or interested parties to discuss certain claims made in the application.[59] It can also include site visits and meetings to discuss the application. For example, in the Australian Dairy Farmers Association authorisation, ACCC officials met with members of the association in Adelaide to discuss the application further.[60] The process of recording such meetings has been finalised since 2006. File notes briefly stating the matters discussed, date and persons attending are now systemically used and placed on the website. Decisions prior to 2006 did not include such a systematic keeping of file notes with the materials publicly available.

Another step in this information-gathering process is the pre-decision conference. Following the draft determination, the ACCC invites applicants and interested parties to a pre-decision conference, which provides them with the opportunity to discuss the draft determination and to put their views directly to a commissioner.[61] Conferences are only called on matters involving diverse interests and, in some cases, these conferences can be perfunctory.[62] In certain complex cases, however, such as in the aviation industry where there are many counterfactuals proposed, the pre-decision conference may be an opportunity for an inclusive dialogue.[63] Such conferences are chaired by a commissioner and conducted informally, acting as a venue for all attendees to have a reasonable opportunity to express their views. The ACCC takes into account these views in making its decision. The record of the conference, which is on the public register, gives an outline of the issues raised and the persons in attendance. Following the pre-decision conference, it is usual practice for the ACCC to invite interested parties to lodge final written submissions. After this, a final determination is made and sent to the applicant as well as all interested parties and is also placed on the public register. The final determination usually mirrors the draft determination in its structure, although the substance will differ depending on the preceding consultative process. Applications for review of the authorisation may be lodged to the ACT by the applicant or a party with sufficient interest.[64]

---

59   *Australian Brick and Blocklaying Training Foundation* A90993, 26 April 2006.

60   *Australian Dairy Farmers Limited* A90966, 26 April 2006. Also see *Port Waratah* A90650, A90651, 25 March 1998; *BHP Billiton Iron Ore* A90981, A90982, A90983, 1 February 2006.

61   See section 90A; see also ACCC (2002) 249.

62   Interview 9.

63   See, for example, *Re International Air Transport Association — International Air Transport Association* A3485, A90408, 31 July 1984; *Re Qantas Airways Limited and British Airways Plc Applications for authorisation* A30226, A30227, 8 February 2005.

64   Sections 101, 102.

Participation in the Process

Section 90A requires the ACCC to consult, although it does not prescribe the process or the parties who should be consulted. The ACCC attempts to collate relevant information and consults widely. The authorisation process allows for a range of interested parties to be heard, including private parties, industry groups, governments, other independent bodies and non-industry bodies. Parties can be heard in both a formal and informal manner. It is easier to gauge the level of participation and its impact when examining formal submissions. The informal processes are harder to evaluate as they do not provide access to data or refer in detail to this process in the determinations. The ACCC is becoming more evidence-based on procedural fairness and undertakes survey research on business attitudes to their treatment by the ACCC.

Formal Submissions

The data are used to illustrate how the authorisation process has changed over the last 30 years by specifically examining the weight given by the ACCC to the submissions made to an authorisation application. Certain authorisation applications attract numerous submissions, often because a wide section of the community may be affected. For example, the Federation of Australian Wool Organisations authorisation attracted 25 submissions, with seven from industry associations and five from government departments.[65] In other cases, the ACCC seeks submissions from affected parties, as was the case in the EFTPOS authorisation, in which the ACCC sought public submissions from numerous bodies, including consumer organisations as well as other competitors in the market.[66] Although most submissions either favour or oppose the authorisation application, there are some that do not take any particular stance.[67] Formal submissions from five different groups — private parties, industry groups, governments, non-industry bodies and independent bodies — are examined below.

Submissions from Private Parties

Submissions by private parties provide the ACCC with important information about industry structure and practices. Robert Baldwin and Julia Black pointed to the importance of being responsive to the firm's operational and cognitive frameworks. Often this information is hard to obtain and such submissions

---

65 *Federation of Australian Wool Organisations* A90984–A90985, 11 January 2006.

66 *EFTPOS Interchange Fee Reform* A30224, A30225, 11 December 2003.

67 See, for example, *Association of Australian Bookmaking Companies* A30243, 30 March 2006, where 15 submissions prior to the draft decision were received. Here many of the parties simply indicated that they had no objection to the application or that they would not be making a submission and would simply like to be kept informed.

may present one opportunity to obtain such valuable information, allowing the regulator to facilitate competition and ethical practices in the industry. The participation by private actors making submissions has increased significantly since the Act's introduction. In 1976 business had little interest in engaging with the authorisation process and few submissions were made.[68] The commission was criticised for its adversarial approach by business.[69] This antagonism towards the commission's perceived intrusion into business was vividly expressed in the North Queensland Forest Products Association Ltd decision in which the parties were seeking authorisation of a recommended price list. Here the applicants refused to furnish the further information sought by the commission, saying that it did not have the time and finance to furnish the additional information sought and requesting that the commission rely on information previously supplied.[70] Business treated the law and the commission as restrictions on its freedoms. The practice was for the commission to make its own enquiry into the conduct rather than to rely on submissions by the applicant or other parties.[71]

The 1976 review committee commented on this and recommended increased dialogue between the commissioners and the regulatees.[72] The committee's advice was 'taken on board' and the picture changed with the ACCC seeking to harness business involvement in the authorisation process. By 1998 there was commonly more dialogue between interested businesses and the commission on such matters. This shift reflects the commission's use of a variety of regulatory practices and, as John Braithwaite stated, a 'willingness to broker a new kind of conciliation between the conflicting parties'.[73] There was also an attempt by the commission to reinforce the value of business involvement by clearly stating the influence such submissions had on its decisions. Such practices are important in gaining confidence and they are, perhaps, further evidence of the ACCC being responsive to the firms' own operating and cognitive frameworks.[74] In the Air New Zealand authorisation the airline sought authorisation to set up a joint agreement with all of its members to offer discounts on published fares to corporate customers.[75] Qantas made a submission staunchly opposing the application, arguing that it did not present a correct view of the market; the price-fixing conduct was unnecessary as multi-layered contractual relationships, which could be used to offer similar discounts already existed; the proposed conduct would lessen competition as the agreement would allow

---

68 *North Queensland Forest Products Association Ltd* A15536, A16527, A16528, 31 August 1976.
69 See Trade Practices Act Review Committee, Parliament of Australia, *Report to the Minister for Business and Consumer Affairs* (1976) 39, where this criticism is leveled in the context of public hearings.
70 *North Queensland Forest Products Association Ltd* A15536, A16527, A16528, 31 August 1976.
71 ibid, 101, where the process for making applications is discussed.
72 ibid, 103.
73 Braithwaite, *Restorative Justice and Responsive Regulation*, (2002) 231; see also Marshall Breger and Gary Edles, 'Established by Practice: The Theory and Operation of Independent Federal Agencies' (2000) 52 *Administrative Law Review* 1111, 1115.
74 Robert Baldwin and Julia Black, 'Really Responsive Regulation' (2008) 71(1) *Modern Law Review* 69–70.
75 *Air New Zealand on behalf of all members of the Star Alliance* A30209–A30213, 4 September 2003.

the participants to understand and utilise their competitor's pricing methods and strategies; and, the proposed arrangements were unlikely to give rise to public benefits.[76] The ACCC authorised the conduct subject to an undertaking that it negotiated with Air New Zealand to cease participation in the agreement and conventions program if it entered into an alliance with Qantas Airways.[77]

Submissions by Industry Groups

Industry groups have always been active in making formal submissions to the ACCC. After all, they have knowledge of the industry, their own interests to protect and the necessary skills to put together such submissions, and their participation is increasing. Many in the ACCC are aware of the allegation of being captured by industry groups, and many of the past and present officials interviewed pointed to the transparency and accountability mechanisms in place that would counter any such influence.[78]

Figure 6.1 collates the instances where submissions were made by industry bodies and categorises them on the basis of their success. In the 35 determinations studied for 1976, there were eight submissions made by industry bodies; authorisation was granted in six of these cases. By 1984 there were submissions made by industry bodies in 12 out of 35 cases. In 1998, 26 submissions from industry bodies were received and, of these, 20 were successful. This indicates that participation by industry groups in the authorisation process has been increasing steadily.

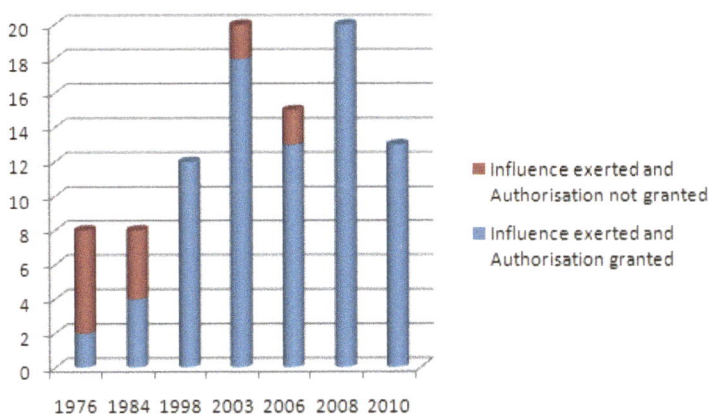

Figure 6.1: Influence and success of submissions by industry groups in authorisation determinations

Source: Author's research.

---

76 See submission by Qantas, *Air New Zealand* A30209, A30210, 4 September 2003, 15–16.

77 ibid, i.

78 Interview 2; Interview 3.

Groups such as the Australian Gas Users Group were able to exert an influence on the ACCC in the decision involving the North West Shelf Project. They raised concerns about the joint venture that prompted the ACCC to grant authorisation subject to conditions.[79]

The increasing participation by such groups is an example of the ascendency of New Public Management and consequent changes in public administration, including the deregulation of government businesses. As Michael Power pointed out, this is in part due to the creation of quasi-markets and the introduction of contracting between newly separated service providers and purchasers.[80] The empirical study shows that in 2003 and 2006, industry bodies made submissions in 26 out of 35 decisions. During these years, submissions by industry groups were made in authorisation applications involving section 45 including collective agreement,[81] industry groups seeking approval for a code of conduct,[82] as well as other agreements made within a professional or business association.[83]

Not all industry groups share the same view. This is illustrated by the Australian Brick and Blocklaying Training Foundation authorisation, where four industry bodies made submissions on an application that sought to impose a levy on the sale of bricks and concrete masonry products to fund a national program designed to alleviate the shortage of skilled bricklayers in the industry. Of these four industry bodies, two made brief but supportive submissions, whereas the other two were dubious of the benefits that such a scheme would bring, pointing to the duplication of resources as well as the existence of alternate training programs that may fulfil similar goals.[84] In 2008 and 2010, industry groups exerted influence in 20 and 13 cases respectively, with all being granted authorisation. Again, diverse industry bodies were represented and the industry groups related to the health industry that made submissions in 2008 included the Rural Dental Action Association,[85] Victorian Hospitals Industry Association, Victorian Health Care Association, Rural Doctors Association of Australia, Rural Doctors Association of Victoria,[86] Australian Medical Association Limited,[87]

---

79 See *North West Shelf Project* application by participants in relation to co-ordinated marketing, determined on 29 July 1998, 35.
80 Michael Power, *The Audit Society* (1997) 43.
81 See *Qantas Airlines* A90963, A 9 September 2003; *Air New Zealand* A30209, A30210, A30211, 4 September 2003; *Inghams* A90825, 22 January 2003; *Australian Dairy Farmers* A90961, A90962, 20 February 2006.
82 See *Re Medicines Australia Ltd* A90779, A90780, 14 November 2003; *Australian Direct Marketing* A90876, 29 June 2006.
83 See *NSW Health* A90754, A90755, 4 September 2003; *Refrigerant* A90854, 24 September 2003; *Agsafe* A90871, 18 September 2003; *Showmen's Guild* A90729, 25 February 2003; *College of Surgeons* A90765, 30 June 2003; *Australian Swimmers Association* (2006), *Federation of Wool Organisers* (2006).
84 *Australian Brick and Blocklaying Training Foundation Limited* A90993, 25.
85 *Australian Dental Association Inc* (2008).
86 *Australian Medical Association Limited & Ors* (2008).
87 *CALMS Ltd* (2008).

Australian Society of Anaesthetists, Rural Doctors Association of Victoria[88] and the Complementary Healthcare Association of Australia.[89] This reflects the the the complex and diverse interests that are present in the market and which have to be considered in decision-making by any regulator.

Submissions by Governments

In the Keynesian welfare state, the state played an important role in the provision of public services, such as telecommunications, electricity, gas and many forms of transport. These services were exempt from competition law and the worldwide competition commissions were focused on policing the activities of private corporations. Today the deregulation of government businesses has meant that these businesses are subject to competition law.[90] This has meant that both state and federal governments are now participating in the authorisation process by making submissions to the commission, attending pre-decision conferences and commenting on the final decision.

Many of these changes bring to the fore the significance of the historical, social and political context which shape the institution's response (in this case the regulatory agency's response). Fiona Haines referred to this as 'regulatory character', whereas Baldwin and Black called it the institutional environment.[91] Hubert Buch-Hansen and Angela Wigger have adopted a critical political economy perspective, linking the development of competition policy to the wider regulation of capitalism and the take up of competition principles in Europe as reflecting a shift to neoliberal discourses dominant in the 1980s.[92] In doing so they alert us to the political nature of competition law and policy which is undoubtedly also relevant to its development in Australia, where the notions of liberalism and state centric governance was displaced by the neoliberal discourse leading to the deregulation of government businesses and state enterprises in the mid nineties. This is demonstrated in the role played by government in making submissions on authorisation determinations where the state is now subject to market forces and the notions of economic efficiency take

---

88   *Rural Doctors Association of Australia Limited* (2008).
89   *ACT Health Food Co-Operative Limited* (2008).
90   See s 2A of the *Trade Practices Act 1974*, which opened Commonwealth Government businesses to the Act.
91   Fiona Haines, Globalisation and Regulatory Character: Regulatory Reform after the Kader Toy Factory Fire (2005) 36–37; Baldwin and Black (2008) 70–77; see also Julia Black, 'New Institutionalism and Naturalism in Socio-Legal Analysis: Institutionalist Approaches to Regulatory Decision Making' (2002) 19(1) Law and Policy 51–93; Michael Horn, The Political Economy of Public Administration: Institutional Choice in the Public Sector (1995) 42–43; Stephen Wilks and Ian Bartle, 'The Unanticipated Consequences of Creating Independent Competition Agencies' (2002) 25(1) *West European Politics* 148, 153–54.
92   See Hubert Buch-Hansen and Angela Wigger, The Politics of European Competition Regulation: A Critical Political Economy Perspective (2011), Hubert Buch-Hansen and Angela Wigger, 'Revisiting 50 years of market-making: The neoliberal transformation of European competition policy' (2010) 17(1) *Review of International Political Economy* 20 – 44.

prominence.[93] Figure 6.2 illustrates the changing role of the federal government and Figure 6.3 looks at the submissions made by the state governments in this process. The submissions by both federal and state governments have increased dramatically from 1984 to 1998 adding the Australian evidence to the bigger story told by Buch-Hansen and Wigger.

There were no submissions by either federal or state governments in 1976, as illustrated in Figure 6.2 and Figure 6.3. The period from 1998 onwards, however, saw a greater role for these governments. This is partly explained by the substantial degree of deregulatory activity and microeconomic reform taking place in Australia. For instance, in 1998 federal government departments made submissions in support of the deregulation of the electricity industry as well as the wool industry, while the state governments were involved in decisions about the restructuring of the egg and milk industries.[94]

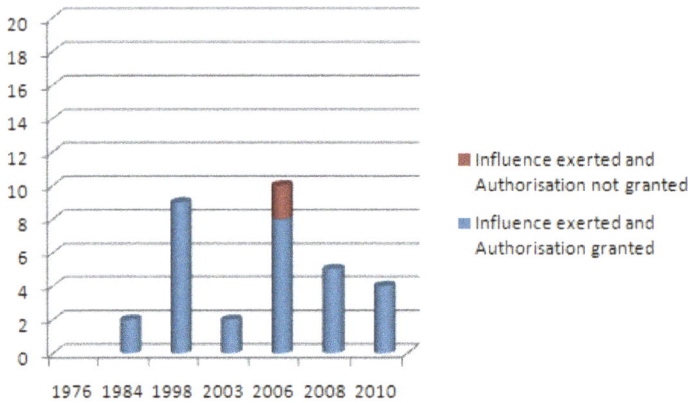

Figure 6.2: **Moderately and highly influential submissions by federal government in authorisation determinations**

Source: Author's research.

The Qantas authorisation is an interesting example of the different considerations involved in a highly regulated market for international travel. Here Qantas Airways Limited was applying for authorisation of a cooperation agreement with Orangestar Investments Holdings Pty Ltd to co-ordinate their flying operations in and out of Australia to predominantly Asian and Pacific locations and on routes in and out of Singapore to Asian locations. The Federal Department of Transport and Regional Services was strongly supportive of the application stating that the international aviation market has many barriers to entry, such

---

93   Buch-Hansen and Wigger (2010) 40. See Vijaya Nagarajan, 'The Paradox of Australian Competition Policy: Contextualizing the Coexistence of Economic Efficiency and Public Benefit' (2013) 36(1) *World Competition: Law and Economics Review* 133-164.
94   *National Electricity Code* A90652; *Australian Wool Exchange Limited* (1998); *Steggles Limited* (1998).

as the government imposed ownership restrictions that require carriers remain substantially owned and effectively controlled by their nationals. Such barriers restricted the access by airlines to certain markets. The Department noted: the 'proposed cooperation agreement will enable Qantas to take advantage of Orangestar's overseas networks that have been gained by Valuair and JA as Singaporean carriers'.[95] The Department suggested that the authorisation be granted for a period of 3–5 years. The ACCC granted authorisation for five years, stating that it retained the power to review the authorisation prior to expiry in case of any material change.[96] In the Tasmanian Forest Contractors authorisation in 2006 the applicants were not successful in their application. Figure 6.4 shows that there were two unsuccessful authorisations applications in 2006. Both of these were connected to Tasmanian Forest Contractors applications. Here the Department of Employment and Workplace Relations made a submission stating that it was generally supportive of collective bargaining arrangements that are in the public interest, but disputed a number of benefits claimed in this particular case. The queries raised by the Department were noted by the ACCC although it rejected the application.[97] This was also the case with the support shown by the Federal government for the application. It is interesting to note that the ACCC saw fit to clearly refuse to be persuaded by the position of both government departments illustrating the changing role of the regulatory agency in the regulatory state.

On the other hand, a good deal of influence was exerted on the ACCC in the 7-Eleven Stores Pty Ltd authorisation decision.[98] The ACCC was revoking an earlier authorisation under section 91(4) on the basis that several material changes had occurred. That decision had allowed for certain anti-competitive practices to continue in relation to the distribution system of newspapers. One of the material changes the ACCC cited for revoking the authorisation was that there had been far-reaching changes in competition policy, which required re-evaluation of the modes of newspaper distribution. Two Federal government submissions strongly argued that the maintenance of an efficient home delivery system for newspapers generated numerous public benefits. These benefits included the provision of business opportunities for small business; the distribution of information important for the functioning of a democratic society; assistance to vulnerable consumer groups such as the elderly and disabled; as well as the efficiency considerations arising from reduced wastage and better planning for publishers. The ACCC considered these submissions and concluded that the existence of an efficient home delivery service was in

---

95 *Qantas Airways Limited* A40107, A40108, A 40109, 26 April 2006, 19.
96 ibid, 40.
97 *Tasmanian Forest Contractors* A9073, A90974, 22 February 2006.
98 *Re 7-Eleven Stores Pty Ltd, Australian Association of Convenience Stores Incorporated; Queensland Newsagents Federation* (1994) ATPR 41-357, 42658.

the publishers' interests and that they were likely to ensure that it continued. The tribunal was sympathetic to the ACCC's position and stated that it 'is clear that the submissions of the government to the commission played a very large role in the deliberations of the commission in reaching its conclusions to grant authorisations'.[99]

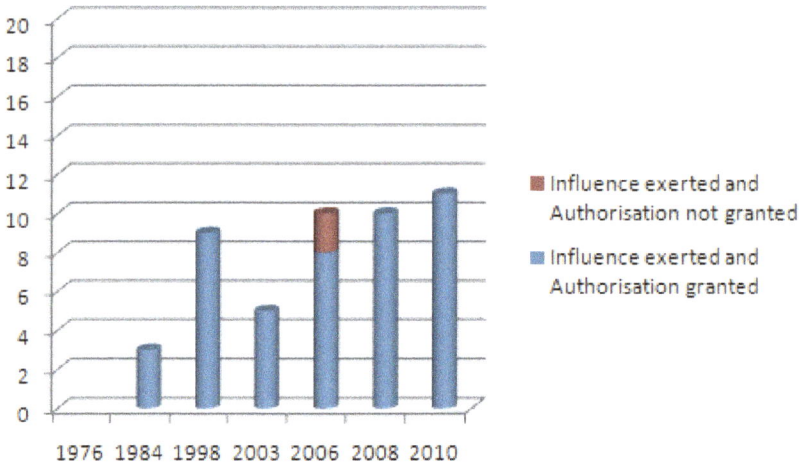

Figure 6.3: Moderately and highly influential submissions by state government and authorisation determinations in the sample studied

Source: Author's research.

The ACCC has received submissions from federal government departments where the authorisation involved deregulated industries. The detailed and considered submission made by the Commonwealth Department of Primary Industries and Energy in the Australian Wool Exchange Limited authorisation is a good example of these actors seeing their role as one of assisting the commission to reach its decision, rather than relying on the commission to cater to their interests.[100] This submission lists a number of reasons for supporting the self-regulating scheme the 'old' Australian Wool Corporation sought to implement.

State governments too are actively participating in this process. Issues involving benefits for the community, employment in industries based in the state, as well as maintaining professional standards aimed at protecting community rights

---

99   ibid; see also *Re 7-Eleven Stores Pty Ltd; Independent Newsagents Association; Australasian Association of Convenience Stores Incorporated* [1998] ACompT 3, 18 November 1998, in which the tribunal had the opportunity to consider the ACCC's revocation of an earlier authorisation. Here, the tribunal reiterated its earlier comments on the consideration given by the commission to the federal government's submissions in this matter. These submissions contained a detailed analysis of the public benefits derived through the newspaper distribution system.

100   *Australian Wool Exchange Limited* in relation to its business rules, 30 December 1998, 28.

attract such participation. At times the response of the state governments can be adversarial as the ACCC activities may directly impinge on their autonomy. In Re Australian Medical Association Limited the applicant sought approval for a fee agreement in rural South Australian public hospitals. This was a particularly controversial decision as it had the potential of directly impacting on the conduct of state public hospitals. The Queensland, Western Australian and Victorian governments all expressed concern about how the arrangement would affect costs and the operation of hospitals within their state.[101] In the Australian Dental Association authorisation[102] three state bodies and a federal body made submissions in favour of the application and in Refrigerant the importance of supporting industry initiatives was recognised by the Western Australian Department of Environmental Protection, which supported the application and stated that it believed it will result in a favourable environmental outcome.[103]

In the Ansett, however, the response from the two federal departments and six state departments was specifically directed at the proposed authorisation. Here a number of airlines sought to enter into an agreement to coordinate airline services and argued that increased tourism would be a resultant public benefit. The West Australian ministers for transport and tourism, the chief minister of the Northern Territory, the premier of Tasmania, as well as spokespersons for the Queensland Government, South Australia Government and Victorian Government all provided varying degrees of support for the authorisation.[104]

Submissions by Non-industry Bodies

The main criterion for belonging to this category is that the parties are not-for-profit bodies representing the interests of a societal sector. It does not include industry bodies that may be not-for-profit but which nevertheless pursue specific interests, for example, the Gas Users Group. Consumers Federation of Australia, Australian Council of Social Service, Victorian Council of Social Service and the Farmers Federation would fall into this category of non-industry bodies.

The short-lived effort to empower consumer groups at the inception of the Act resulted in a good deal of participation by these groups in the authorisation process.

---

101   See A90622, 18–19.
102   *Australian Dental Association Inc* A91094, A91095, 10 December 2008.
103   *Refrigerant* (2003) 13; for other 2003 decisions where such submissions were made see *EFTPOS interchange fees* A30224, A30225, 11 December 2003; *The Australian Self-Medication Industry* A30223, 8 January 2003; *College of Surgeons* A90765, 30 June 2003.
104   *Ansett Australia Limited and Others* A90649, A90655, 22 July 1998; for other 1998 decisions where such submissions were made see *National Electricity Code* A90652, A90553, A90654, 19 October 1998; *Association of Fluorocarbon Consumers and Manufacturers Inc* A90658 26 August 1998; *Port Waratah* A90650, A90651, 25 March 1998.

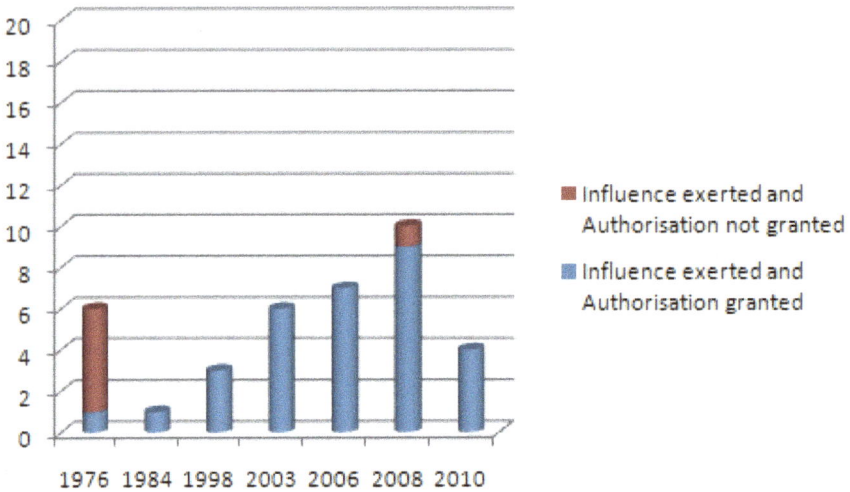

Figure 6.4: Moderately and highly influential submissions by non-industry groups and authorisation determinations

Source: Author's research.

This is reflected in Figure 6.4 which shows a relatively higher degree of participation by the not-for-profit sector in 1976. Out of the six authorisation decisions in which such submissions by non-industry bodies were made, however, only two were successful. In every year after 1976, participation was accompanied by a grant of authorisation. The manner in which the participation by non-industry groups has played out is not straightforward. In a minority of determinations studies, the non-industry groups supported the application and authorisation was granted.[105] In some other determinations studied, certain concerns were discussed in the draft determination and/or pre-decision conference and subsequent amendments were made to the authorisation application.[106] In the majority of the determinations studied, where concerns were raised by non-industry groups, some of these concerns were addressed through the imposition of conditions. This occurred in 12 out of a total of 17 determinations in which non-industry groups participated in the samples studied in 1984,[107] 1998,[108] 2003[109] and 2006.[110]

---

105   This only occurred in two determinations studied, both occurring in 2006: *Federation of Australian Wool Organisations* A90984 and A90985, 11 January 2006.

106   This occurred in the sample studied in the following determinations: in 2006 in *Australian Direct Marketing Association (ADMA)* A90984 and in 2003 in the *EFTPOS* A30224 and A30225, 11 December 2003.

107   *Federation of Australian Commercial Television Stations* A11709, A21265, 12 September 1984.

108   *Gas Services Business Pty Ltd: Service Performance Contracts* A90630, A90631, 19 August 1998.

109   *College of Surgeons* A90765, 30 June 2003; *Medicines Australia Ltd* A90779, A90780, 14 November 2003; *Australian Self-Medication Industry* A30223, 22 October 2003.

110   *Community Care Underwriting Agency* A90997 and A90998, 6 July 2006.

In the United Permanent Building Society authorisation, the applicants sought authorisation for an agreement to allow for property to be insured with a nominated insurer. The Canberra Consumers Incorporated and Australian Federation of Consumers Organisations made submissions opposing the application on the basis that it was a restraint of competition between insurance companies, it resulted in a denial of choice of insurers and policy benefits and, it also led to unsatisfactory premiums.[111] The ACCC took note and did not authorise the tying agreements, although it did authorise other proposed agreements in the application.[112] In Re Herald Weekly Times & Ors, the submissions of Canberra Consumers Incorporated did not have the same degree of sway. The commission noted that the demands by the consumer body for the codes of conduct to go beyond the legislative requirements and be more responsive to the needs of the public was 'a natural attitude for a consumer body and one that it is useful to have expressed publicly,' but the commission did not accept the arguments.[113]

This participation dwindled in 1984 primarily due to funding cuts for such groups. Another reason for the decreased participation was the enormous complexity of the authorisation decisions and the materials submitted by the applicant to such proceedings. Making sense of the data, undertaking independent research in order to verify or deny the claims of the applicants, and presenting a persuasive case involves a good deal of time and expertise, all of which involves high costs. There is limited participation by such groups in the determinations in 1984 and 1998, increasing again in 2003 and 2006. In 1984 only one case in the study had participation by non-industry bodies. This was in the FACTS authorisation, where the Federation of Australian Commercial Television stations sought authorisation for the rules, guidelines and procedures of the federation, which was charged with self-regulating advertising on commercial television. Three consumer groups, the Australian Federation of Consumers Organisation, the Australian Consumers Association (ACA) and Canberra Consumers Incorporated, made submissions critical of the guidelines, reflecting the public issues raised in the application. The main criticisms were that: the system being operated by the industry did not always interpret or apply laws and codes according to their purpose, the system was not open to external scrutiny and, there was insufficient public access to and knowledge of the system.[114] The ACA had undertaken a survey of 902 television commercials to support their arguments.[115] The commission stated of the ACA's submission:

> The importance of ACA's criticism is that it represents the perception
> of the largest consumer organisation in the country ... Even if the

---

111 *United Permanent Building Society* (1976) 16874.
112 It authorised the compulsory life insurance schemes, which was/were the content of A21059.
113 *Herald & Weekly Times & Ors* (1976) 16572.
114 *Re Federation of Australian Commercial Television Stations* A11709, A21265, 12 September 1984, ATPR 50-076, 55399.
115 ibid, (1984) ATPR 50-076, 55401.

perception is wrong, or partly wrong, that does not dispose of the matter, [I]t still seems evident that regulation of an industry so closely affecting consumers, when the regulation is done largely by the industry itself and purports to serve not primarily the industry itself but the community at large, needs community confidence rather than opposition. The criticisms, concerning [the]... way matters such as complaints are handled, represents a signal that the system is seen to be more industry-oriented than the industry itself perceives, or perhaps even deserves.[116]

In 1998 the role for non-industry groups to participate in decisions involving deregulation of essential services is demonstrated by the involvement of the Victorian Council of Social Services in Gas Services Pty Ltd.[117] This trend continued in later years with such groups becoming active in authorisations involving deregulated markets and professions, such Re College of Surgeons,[118] Re EFTPOS interchange fees,[119] and Re Federation of Australian Wool Organisations.[120] The non-industry groups that made submissions in successful authorisation decisions included:

- Australian Consumer Association (ACA)
- Australian Federation of Consumers Organisation
- Breast Cancer Action Group
- Canberra Consumers Incorporated
- Cancer Voices NSW
- Centre of Law and Genetics
- Consumer Credit Legal Centre NSW Incorporated
- Consumer Law Centre Victoria
- Consumers Federation of Australia
- Consumers Health Forum of Australia
- Council of Social Services of New South Wales
- Cyberspace Law and Policy Centre
- Financial Services Consumer Policy Centre, University of New South Wales
- Royal Institute for Deaf and Blind Children
- Volunteering Australia

---

116   ibid, 55405.
117   *Gas Services Business Pty Ltd* A90630, A90631, 19 August 1998, 8.
118   *Royal Australasian College of Surgeons* A90765, 30 June 2003.
119   *EFTPOS Interchange Fee Reform A30224 and A30225*, A30224, A30225, 11 December 2003.
120   Federation of Australian Wool Organisations A90984, A90985, A90984–A90985, 11 January 2006.

The ACA made the most submissions. The non-industry groups have been making more submissions since 1998 and the rate of success has been greater after 1976. The changes in this area should be viewed against the backdrop of a shift in the practice of government.[121] Power stated that the success of political discourses has demanded improved accountability from public services, not only in terms of their conformity to legally accepted process but also in terms of their performance.[122] So, citizens are now the consumers of public services and are entitled to monitor them. But it is difficult to reach a firm conclusion on the increasing emphasis given to 'the consumer' in all statements by the ACCC and the call by the ACCC for such not-for-profit groups to participate in its decision process.[123] It could be seen optimistically as an indication that the commission is ready to consider submissions if they are made or, more pessimistically, as an example of rhetoric by the ACCC.

Submissions from Independent Bodies

The influence of reports, directives, memoranda and general policy drives cannot be ignored. The recent past has seen a growing interdependency between government departments, all of whom may be actors within the regulatory space.[124] This interdependency is both implied and expressed. The most obvious example of implied interdependency will occur because the bodies share responsibility for the regulatory space. Express interdependency may be mandated by co-operative agreements or memoranda of understanding. For example, in September 1998 the ACCC and the Reserve Bank of Australia entered into a memorandum of understanding that set out an agreed basis for policy co-ordination and information sharing and, in 2001, the ACCC recommended that the Reserve Bank use its powers to regulate credit card schemes.[125] Many independent bodies make formal submissions to the ACCC where there is an overlap in responsibilities or where the decisions may affect the conduct of others associated with the same domain. Figure 6.5 shows that such involvement has changed over the past three decades and illustrates where the submission has either a moderate or high degree of influence on the ACCC's decision. From there

---

121   See Colin Scott, 'Accountability in a Regulatory State' (2000) 27(1) *Journal of Law and Society* 38, 44.

122   Power (1997) 44.

123   As was done in the *Vodaphone* A90681, 22 April 1998, where the ACCC called on the Australian telecommunications users group for comments.

124   Here I am restricting my discussion to the state actors. By doing so, I am not discounting the role of non-state actors, whose participation I have discussed above, under Submissions by Non-industry Bodies. See also Scott, 'Analysing Regulatory Space: Fragmented Resources and Institutional Design' (2001) (Summer) *Public Law* 329, 337.

125   ACCC, 'Australian Competition and Consumer Commission Recommends Reserve Banks Using Powers to Reform Credit Card Schemes' (Press Release, 21 March 2001).

being no submission made by another independent agency in 1976, the scene changed in 1984 when there were nine submissions, many involving capital and financial markets as well as approvals for codes of conduct.[126]

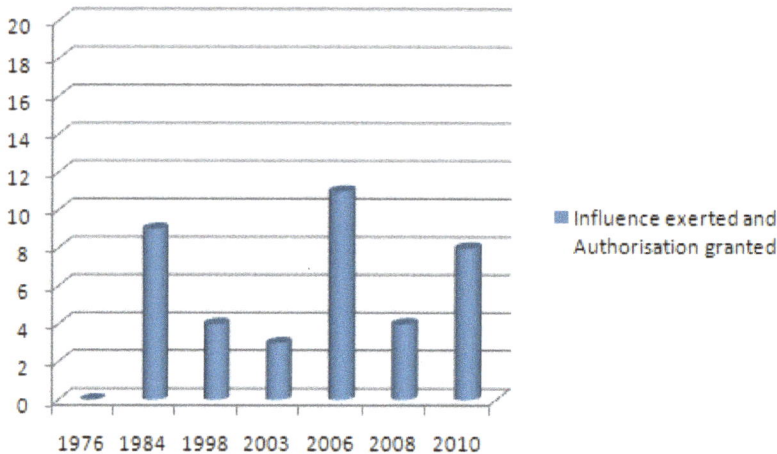

Figure 6.5: Moderately and highly influential submissions by independent groups and authorisation determinations

Source: Author's research.

In Re Australian Associated Stock Exchange — one of the ACCC decisions that engendered a transformation of an economically critical market — the authorisation was for an amendment of the Australian Stock Exchange rules, which resulted in placing restrictions on who could carry on the business of stockbroking. This arrangement had the effect of breaching section 45. The new membership rules had been scrutinised by the National Companies and Securities Commission while the business rules had been drawn up in consultation with the National Companies and Securities Commission. The role of this independent body was noted by the Trade Practices Commission in its determination.[127] Again in 1998, the Re Australian Stock Exchange authorisation was sought for business rules which governed the operation of the Stock Exchange Automated Trading system for the trading of securities in the stock market conducted by the Australian Stock Exchange. Here the Australian Securities Commission's views on the manner in which the facility would meet market efficiency and investor protection were accepted by the ACCC.[128] Likewise, it was the stability of the

---

126   The 1984 authorisation decisions, where independent bodies made submissions, included *Master Locksmiths Association of Australia Ltd* A90387, A90388, 15 March 1984; *International Air Transport Association*, A3485, A90408, 31 July 1984.

127   *Re Australian Associated Stock Exchange* (1984) 55468.

128   *Re Australian Stock Exchange* (1998) 26–27, 37.

financial market that was important in the EFTPOS authorisation in 2003,[129] the Investment & Financial Services authorisation in 2006,[130] and the Suncorp Metway[131] determination in which both the Reserve Bank and the Australian Securities and Investment Commission supported the application.

Informal Participation

In numerous authorisation cases it is clear that participation and influence can be indirect or informal. This section explores such participation under three headings: indirect influence of policies and past decisions, submissions and discussions following the draft determination, and public consultations and pre-decision conferences which can facilitate participation and influence outcomes.

Indirect Influence Evidenced by Reference to Policies and Past Decisions

Influence can be exerted in both a direct and indirect manner. General government policy is of concern to the ACCC which makes mention of it in its decisions. This has included reference to the Wallis Report,[132] national competition policy (Hilmer Report),[133] government ozone strategy,[134] and Council of Australian Governments (COAG) initiatives.[135] In the Australian Medical Association authorisation, the ACCC discussed the manner in which the medical profession came to be regulated by the Act and so was seeking authorisation here. It referred to the Hilmer Report and the COAG agreement to enact legislation to achieve universal application of competition laws to all businesses throughout Australia.[136] Government policy is clearly being given effect in this process. Another example is in Re Australian Communications Access Forum Inc, where the authorisation dealt with self-regulation via a constitution; the ACCC made reference to the second reading speech which accompanied the Trade Practices Amendment (Telecommunications) Bill 1996: 'It is a clear policy intention that ... both the determination of access rights and terms and conditions of access be the result of commercial processes and industry self-regulation.'[137]

In Re Investment and Financial Services Association the ACCC granted authorisation to the association for its draft policy on genetic testing for two

---

129 *EFPTOS* A30224, A30225, 11 December 2003.

130 *Investment and Financial Services Association Ltd* A90986, A90989, 8 March 2006.

131 Suncorp Metway Limited & Bendigo & Adelaide Bank Limited A91232, A91233, 13 September 2010.

132 *Australian Payments Clearing Association Limited* A90617; A90618, A90618.

133 *Inghams Enterprises Pty Limited* A90825, 22 January 2003.

134 *Refrigerant* A90829, 7 May 2003; *Agsafe Limited* A90871, 18 September 2003.

135 See *Vencorp* A90646, A90647, A90648, 19 August 1998.

136 *Australian Medical Association Limited and South Australian Branch of the Australian Medical Association Incorporated* A90622, 31 July 1998, 3.

137 *Australian Communications Access Forum Inc* A90613, 22 April 1998, 15.

years. This was to allow the issues surrounding testing to be debated and for the development of government and industry policy, including 'further development of self-regulatory and legislative safeguards'.[138]

While the ACCC also makes reference to its own decisions and investigations from time-to-time, it is worth noting that this has decreased over time, perhaps pointing to the growing sophistication of the decision-making process and the acute awareness of the scrutiny of its decisions by others, including the Dawson Review in 2003. Although the reference made by the ACCC to its own decisions looks particularly large in the 2008 and 2010 determinations, as seen in Figure 6.6, it can be explained by the fact that there were many repeat authorisation applications in which reference to earlier decisions would be expected; the Refrigerant determination in 2008 and the Agsafe determination in 2010 are examples of this.

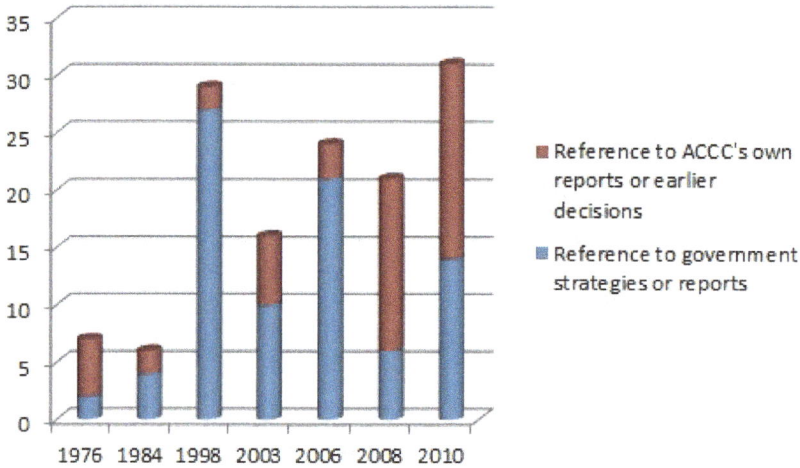

Figure 6.6: Moderately and highly influential reference by ACCC to its own decisions

Source: Author's research.

Submissions, Discussions and Reassessments after the Draft Determination

As discussed earlier, the draft determination is an important step in the authorisation process and the period after the draft determination is one where there can be a dialogue between the applicant, interested parties and the ACCC. This is a useful process for the ACCC, allowing it to discuss the issue with the applicant and other actors at greater length. The important role such

---

138   ACCC, *2000–2001 Annual Report* (June 2001) 84.

exchanges can have in developing new interpretative communities has been examined by Black in her work on regulatory conversations.[139] In a number of instances, interested parties have only sought to make submissions after the draft determination: Coalition of Major Professional Sports, 1984, FACTS, 1984, Golden Casket Agents' Association Ltd, 2003, Medicines, 2003 and Australian Self Medication, 2003. In the Australian Self-Medication authorisation, which involved gaining approval for a code of conduct, there were 12 submissions from interested parties before the draft decision and three submissions after the draft decision. All the submissions supported the application for authorisation.

In Re Medicines Australia Incorporated, the ACCC had imposed three conditions it had proposed in the draft application. Medicines Australia had accepted two of the conditions that had been proposed. The third condition required members of Medicines Australia to provide the association with various details about educational meetings that were organised or sponsored by these respective members prior to the event . Medicines Australia was required to make these details available to the public through its website.[140] Medicines Australia made a submission containing 10 points stating why this condition could not be accepted by its members.[141] They argued the condition would create a significant anti-competitive effect by requiring disclosure of confidential information. This would: inhibit pharmaceutical companies, reduce new membership, place an onerous administrative burden on Medicines Australia, and be largely irrelevant as most consumers were unaware of the name of the manufacturer of their medication and so unlikely to be able to assess whether their medical treatment may have been influenced by the provision of benefits.[142] The ACCC accepted these arguments and dropped the third condition in its final determination.

Public Consultation and Pre-decision Conferences

In certain complex cases, the ACCC has adopted a long public consultation and negotiation process. This was the case in the authorisations involving the dairy industry, which was being deregulated. Here, a year-long national consultation process was instituted to gain industry information and gauge measures that were likely to be effective. John Braithwaite would see this as developing a shared understanding, and Baldwin and Black would see this as one step toward really responsive regulation because it may constitute an attempt at increasing awareness and compliance and indicates a broader institutional awareness of the

139   Julia Black, *Rules and Regulators* (1997) 172; see also discussion in Chapter 5.
140   *Medicines*, A90779, A90780, 14 November 2003, 23.
141   ibid, 23.
142   ibid, 24.

regulatory regime.[143] Parker may well see this dialogue as nurturing compliance[144] and it may also be viewed as an attempt at developing a commitment to the regulatory agenda, that is, in this case the implementation of deregulatory policies.[145]

The pre-decision conferences are informal: a variety of groups contribute to the decision-making process by attending pre-decision hearings and making oral or written submissions. In the FACTS authorisation, many of the advantages of such a conference were brought to the fore. Here the consumer groups took the view that there were inadequate complaints mechanisms in place. The federation had responded to these objections by stating that complaints bodies were already established in the form of the Australian Broadcasting Tribunal and the Australian Securities Commission. These bodies responded to these comments and a consensus was reached between the parties; the commission altered its proposed conditions accordingly.[146] This highlights the very points made by the proponents of responsive and restorative regulation.[147]

In another such pre-decision conference, in 2004, that I attended, the Qantas Airways and British Airways joint venture,[148] there were representatives of the parties to the proposed agreement as well as representatives from other competitors and state government departments.[149] The meeting had been called by Virgin Airlines, a competitor of the applicants to the authorisation. It was presided over by a Commissioner John Martin who was assisted by two ACCC staff and an aviation consultant employed by the ACCC. The meeting ran for more than four hours, and provided the opportunity for written submissions and oral presentations. Legal representatives of the parties were present but did not make any presentations. Numerous suggestions were raised by Virgin Airlines on alternative approaches, including the possibility of including conditions to the grant of authorisation. Questions by the ACCC officials at the meeting on the different air routes and market share as well as hypothetical scenarios were addressed. Others at the meeting did not participate but did state that they would make written submissions prior to the final determination if they thought it necessary. A representative from South African Airlines commented to me that, although he had not made any submissions, he had found the conference and presentations by Virgin Airlines informative and would inform others in the industry on the developments.

---

143   Baldwin and Black (2008) 69.
144   See Christine Parker, 'Compliance Professionalism and Regulatory Community: The Australian Trade Practices Regime' (1999) 26(2) *Journal of Law and Society* 215.
145   Valerie Braithwaite, 'Responsive Regulation and Taxation' (2007) 29(1) Special Issue, *Law and Policy* 3.
146   *Federation of Australian Commercial Television Stations* A11709, A21265, 12 September 1984, ATPR 50-076, 55429.
147   See Baldwin and Black (2008); Black (1997).
148   See *Re Qantas Airways Limited and British Airways Plc* applications for authorisation, A30226, A30227 for pre-decision conference <http://www.accc.gov.au/content/index.phtml/itemId/744636/fromItemId/401858/display/preDecisionConference> at 30 December 2005.
149   The pre-decision conference was held on 1 November 2004.

Martin asked for further information to be provided in writing to the ACCC and agreed to the confidentiality claimed by Virgin Airlines. Overall, the conference was conducted in a semi-formal atmosphere where there was opportunity to ask questions and discuss issues as they arose, providing the right environment for restorative practices to be implemented.

There is a good deal of scholarship on the importance of allowing interested parties to come together to deal with an offence.[150] According to Tom Tyler, procedural justice is important in legitimising legal authority and process-based regulation results in greater compliance, co-operation and empowerment.[151] Tyler emphasises four significant elements of procedural justice: interpersonal respect, where parties are treated with dignity and respect and have their rights recognised and protected; neutrality, which requires decision-makers to be honest, impartial and base their decisions on fact; participation, whereby opportunity to express one's view to the decision-makers is provided; and trustworthiness, requiring decision-makers to treat people fairly.[152] This has been developed by Valerie Braithwaite in her work on motivational postures. These findings support the need for any regulator to consider how democratic principles of inclusion and participation can be incorporated into their processes.[153] In the trade practices area of enforceable undertakings, Parker argued that multi-party deliberation of well-facilitated restorative justice may be able to redress inequalities of bargaining power in a way that cannot be achieved otherwise.[154]

Interviews with ACCC staff suggested that, in certain cases, staff rely on consumer groups to bring specific issues to their attention.[155] Many consumer bodies, however, feel that they are at a disadvantage when faced with complex submissions and time constraints within which to respond. Further, the funding of such bodies is limited and the staff available to concentrate on such issues are few. One interviewee (14) representing a consumer group stated that some authorisation applications are unclear and rather than requiring the applicants to the authorisation to make sense of it, the consumer groups were required to respond.[156] There was a general consensus among consumer groups that the ACCC should provide more information in order to enable better participation. Currently, consumer groups are participating in certain public hearings but interviews with members indicate that there is a fear

---

150   Braithwaite (2002); Parker, 'Restorative Justice in Business Regulation? The Australian Competition and Consumer Commission's Use of Enforceable Undertakings,' (2004) 67(2), *The Modern Law Review* 209, 220.

151   Tom Tyler, 'Procedural Justice, Legitimacy, and the Effective Rule of Law' (2003) 30 *Crime and Justice* 283, 316.

152   Tyler, 'Public Trust and Confidence in Legal Authorities: What do Majority and Minority Group Members want from the Law and Legal Institutions' (2001) 19(1) *Behavioural Sciences and the Law* 215.

153   Valerie Braithwaite (2007).

154   Parker (2004); Christine Parker and Vibeke Nielsen, 'What Do Australian Businesses Think of the ACCC and Does It Matter?', (2007) 35(2), *Federal Law Review*, 187, 187.

155   Interview 4.

156   Interview 14.

that their concerns are dismissed as they 'do not speak the right language in order to get taken seriously'.[157] This is in contrast with consumer groups in the United Kingdom, which have adopted the necessary language only to find that important considerations are being left out of the deliberations.[158] Another interviewee (13) talked of the ACCC adopting a 'slow or stall process', whereby further information could be obtained and put in a digestible form which made it possible for consumer groups to participate in a meaningful way.[159]

Outcomes Weighting Discretion

The decision to grant or refuse an application is a straightforward exercise of power by the ACCC. In a number of cases, however, the ACCC grants the authorisation on certain terms that are incorporated as conditions and, on rare occasions, as undertakings. This section looks at the possible outcomes of an authorisation application that illustrates the exercise of discretion.[160]

Granting or Refusing the Authorisation Application

The ACCC can grant or refuse the authorisation. Authorisations are usually granted for a fixed period after which the parties have to reconsider their positions.

The percentage of successful applications has increased from 25 per cent in 1976 to 94 per cent in 1984, remaining reasonably constant after that, reaching the highest level in 2008 and 2010 at 97 per cent (Table 6.1). This is most likely because the ACCC has matured as an institution since its inception in 1976 and has a clear process in place with adequate staff to deal with enquiries at an early stage. This decreases the number of applications that are not likely to meet the public benefit test. This is evident from the Guide to Authorisation, which encourages people to contact and speak with staff prior to making an application. Further, the inclusion of a checklist in the guide, the payment of a reasonably large fee, as well as a trade practices community — including a legal fraternity well versed in the process — is likely to weed out unsuccessful applications at an early stage.[161]

---

157   ibid.

158   See Business in the Community, 'Response to the Conservative Party Commission on Waste and Voluntary Agreements', December 2008, in which the need for laws to accommodate voluntary agreements among business is discussed and the manner in which laws should be reformed to accommodate this is mooted.

159   Interview 13.

160   It should be noted that at times applications are withdrawn and do not proceed to determination. Such cases are not discussed here and the discussion is limited to those that reach final determination, although it is acknowledged that regulatory discretion is likely to have been exercised in all these instances.

161   See ACCC, *Guide to Authorisation* (2001); ACCC, *Guide to Authorisation* (2007).

Table 6.1: Success of authorisation applications, 1976 to 2006 (total of 35 authorisations studied in each year)

Year	Successful applications	Success rate (%)
1976	9 (out of 35)	25
1984	33 (out of 35)	94
1998	29 (out of 35)	82
2003	31 (out of 35)	88
2006	32 (out of 35)	91
2008	33 (out of 34)	97
2010	34 (out of 35)	97

Source: Author's research.

Granting Authorisations on the Basis of Undertakings

Section 87B gives the ACCC the power to accept a written undertaking in connection with a matter in which it has power, with the exception of Part X.[162] The ACCC has stated that this provision does not give it the power to demand an undertaking, but only to raise it as an option during negotiations with the parties to the conduct or proposed conduct.[163] Generally, this power has been used in the context of mergers and consumer protection offences.[164] The aim of such an undertaking is to reduce the likely public detriment or ensure that there is a net public benefit deriving from th e proposed action.

In the context of mergers, it has been argued that the ACCC's considerable discretionary powers are in practice only constrained by the bargaining power of the merging parties. Although the lack of a merits review and the absence of any obligation to publish clear and comprehensive reasons for accepting the enforceable undertakings could be understood on the basis of allowing a flexible and fast system, it has come at too high a cost, tending to reduce transparency, certainty and accountability in the decision-making process.[165] On the other hand, Parker examined the use of restorative justice in enforceable undertakings. She argued that this gives a place for participation within the formal accountability mechanisms as well as the informal mechanisms:

> Informal, deliberative accountability could include first, participation of, and consultation with, affected parties during and after the negotiation of the undertaking, second, internal decision making processes within

---

162 Section 87B, *Trade Practices Act*.
163 Section 87B of the *Trade Practices Act*: A guideline on the Australian Competition and Consumer Commission's use of enforceable undertakings, August 1999, 5.
164 See Parker (2004); Parker (1999); Karen Yeung, *Securing Compliance: A Principled Approach* (2004) Chapter 7.
165 Yeung (2004) 227, 228, 232; see also Dawson Report Committee of Inquiry, Commonwealth of Australia, *Review of the Competition Provisions of the Trade Practices Act* [Dawson Review] (2003).

the regulator that give the consumer and public interest an adequate voice in deciding whether to accept undertakings, third, making enforceable undertakings publicly available after they are agreed, and fourth, dialogic reviews or audits of compliance with the enforceable undertaking.[166]

In the Air New Zealand authorisation,[167] the members of the Star Alliance applied for authorisation to enter into a joint agreement and a conventions program that were in the form of guidelines, aimed at offering discounts on airfares for employees of the members as well as discount fares for certain convention delegates. Star Alliance had 20 airlines as members and was formed in 1997. Other such entities included One World (with Qantas Airlines as a member), Sky Team and Wings. The ACCC granted an authorisation subject to two undertakings to the effect that Star Alliance would cease entering into similar agreements with Qantas Airlines, which was not a member of this alliance and was a major competitor in the domestic market, with over 75 per cent of market share. These undertakings were proposed in the draft determination on 30 May 2003. The ACCC was of the view that the proposed agreement and conventions program generated a net benefit only if similar agreements were not made with Qantas, thereby ensuring that there was competition from Virgin Airlines and Qantas Airlines in the domestic market. In doing so, the ACCC was exercising its discretion in determining the manner in which to manage adequate competition in the market.

Granting Authorisations Subject to Conditions

Section 91(3) provides for the ACCC to grant authorisations subject to conditions. This power is used when there is uncertainty about whether the authorisation test is met. One example is the Surgeons authorisations, where the ACCC, although satisfied as to the significant public benefits generated, was concerned about the potential public detriments. Here a number of conditions were imposed, aimed at ensuring the public benefits were achieved. These conditions included increasing external involvement in the college's activities and increasing the transparency of the college's processes.[168] The ACT has stated that even in circumstances where a net public benefit results, authorisation can be granted on condition that changes are made to the arrangements so as to remove or lessen the potential for detriment, without impairing their essential

---

166   Parker (2004) 243.
167   *Air New Zealand* A30209, A30210, A30211, A30212, A30213, 4 September 2003.
168   ACCC, *Guide to Authorisation* (2007) 44.

components.[169] In the past, the ACCC has used the period following release of the draft determination as a period to negotiate amendments to the authorisation application, agree on undertakings, or consider the imposition of conditions.

The primary objective of conditions is to address anti-competitive detriment or to increase the likelihood of the public benefit claimed.[170] This remains the purpose for which the power under section 91(3) was granted. In the Application by Medicines Australia Inc appeal, the ACT stated that the purpose of the condition is to increase the likelihood that the public benefit claimed for the code is realised in respect of the provisions dealing with the conferral of such benefits to doctors.[171] Therefore, authorising a collective bargaining arrangement, on the condition that the parties can only make limited use of the shared information, is aimed at addressing potential anti-competitive practices, such as price-fixing.[172] Further, with respect to the limits on the discretion to impose conditions, the tribunal stated:

> There is no express limit upon the kinds of conditions that may be imposed. This does not mean that there is an unconfined discretion to impose whatever conditions the ACCC or the Tribunal on review, considers appropriate. The power to impose conditions is constrained, like the discretion discussed above, by the subject matter, scope and purpose of the statute.[173]

One of the persons interviewed expressed concern about the manner in which the ACCC has used conditions to manipulate the market, often only guessing at the effects that the conditions are likely to have on the market.[174] The North West Shelf Project authorisation was cited as an example where onerous conditions, which intruded into the market unnecessarily, were incorporated into the grant of authorisation.[175] These conditions included the price at which the product was to be marketed.[176] Dorf and Sabel may well see this as an example of democratic experimentalism where the regulator is setting standards for actors in the market, while others may be critical of the use of such powers on the grounds of certainty and accountability.[177]

---

169   *APRA* (1999) ATPR 41-701, 42997; See also ACCC, *Guide to Authorisation* (2007) 45.

170   See *Medicines* A90779, A90780, 14 November 2003.

171   Application by *Medicines Australian Inc* [2007] Australian Competition Tribunal 4 (27 June 2007) 7.

172   See *Australian Hotels Association* (2006) A90987; Inter-hospital agreement between *Friendly Society Private Hospital Bundaberg* etc. A50019, 1 September 1999.

173   *Medicines Australian Inc* [2007] 31.

174   Interview 9.

175   Interview 9.

176   See *North West Shelf Project* application by participants in relation to coordinated marketing, determined on 29 July 1998, 35.

177   Michael Dorf and Charles Sabel, 'A Constitution of Democratic Experimentalism' (1998) 98 *Columbia Law Review* 267.

At times, conditions fulfil other collateral objectives, such as setting up external and voluntary regulatory structures that allow appeal processes, complaints mechanisms, external monitoring and reviews of business practices or codes of conduct, and independent representation on industry committees. These types of conditions do more than address anti-competitive conduct. They are steps in managing markets, market conduct, and the actions of individual market actors. Below, I examine three collateral purposes served by conditions that go to managing the market.[178]

Enhancing Compliance

Compliance is addressed through increased monitoring, auditing and participation of conduct by business. Often this is in the context of codes of conduct and examples include: T imber and Building Materials Merchants Association,[179] FACTS,[180] Re Australian Self-Medication Industry,[181] Australian Performing Rights Association Limited (APRA)[182] and Re Australian Direct Marketing Association,[183] in which codes were authorised by the ACCC. In these cases, the ACCC considered whether the code of conduct is likely to provide a public benefit that might exist beyond authorisation.[184] The role of co-regulation and the manner in which voluntary codes regulate areas of conduct beyond the scope of law has been widely acknowledged by a variety of sources including the ACCC, which has published guidelines for the development of such codes.[185] In Re Australian Direct Marketing Association, the ACCC stated that it is appropriate for self-regulatory codes to replicate or exceed legislative requirements if they encourage better practice and behaviour from industry members.[186]

The adoption of a code does not, however, in itself guarantee effective compliance or enforcement and may require regular review and monitoring of how the codes operate. At times, the ACCC has been able to use conditions to improve compliance and incorporate review. In Re Australian Direct Marketing Association, the ACCC granted authorisation on the basis that the association

---

178 For further detailed discussion of this see Vijaya Nagarajan, 'Co-opting for Governance: The Use of the Conditions Power by the ACCC in Authorisations' (2011) 34 *University of New South Wales Law Journal* 785–810.

179 *Timber and Building Materials Merchants Association* A3483, 16 August 1976.

180 *FACTS* A11709, 1984.

181 *Re Australian Self-Medication Industry* (2003).

182 *Australian Performing Rights Association Limited (APRA)* (2006).

183 *Re Australian Direct Marketing Association* (2006).

184 *Re Australian Direct Marketing* A90876, 29 June 2006.

185 See ACCC, *Guidelines on Codes of Conduct* (2005); See also *Medicines* ACT 58–60; Australian Law Reform Commission (ALRC), Parliament of Australia, Compliance with the *Trade Practices Act 1974*, Report ALRC 68, (1994) at 3.7, Introduction of Part IVB of the *Trade Practices Act* in 1998.

186 *Australian Direct Marketing* A90876, 29 June 2006, 17–18.

conduct regular internal reviews of its code of practice. It also required the association to obtain an annual assessment of the findings of its internal reviews from an appropriately independent legal advisor.

In the Re Medicines Australia authorisation, the Australian Pharmaceutical Manufacturers Association sought authorisation of a code of conduct seeking to regulate the promotion of prescribed medicines by pharmaceutical companies, which was likely to breach section 45 of the Act. This code included the provision of information about prescribed medicines to health care professionals and the public by pharmaceutical companies and the regulation of the provision of financial and other benefits to health care professionals by pharmaceutical companies. The ACCC pointed out that for the code to work effectively and generate public benefits, appropriate enforcement would be required. It expressed concerns about how effectively the enforcement procedures were implemented, stating that seven relevant complaints over the past three years appeared very low.[187] It imposed a number of conditions on the grant of authorisation, including an expanded role for the association's monitoring committee. This condition required each member company of the association to provide full details of all educational symposia and meetings held by the company; the details of any hospitality or entertainment offered; the number, description and professional status of attendees; and, a copy of the material provided to attendees. It also provided for the monitoring committee to, in certain circumstances, make a complaint to the conduct committee, for example, where the code may have been breached. Further it required that details of this report, including the concerns raised and the manner in which there concerns were dealt with, be published on the Medicines website and in the association's annual report.[188] The ACT upheld the imposition of this condition and stated that it was designed to enhance compliance with and enforcement of the relevant provisions of the code consistent with the statutory scheme for authorisations, and with the objects of enhancing the welfare of Australians through the promotion of competition and fair trading and provisions for consumer protection within section 2 of the Trade Practices Act.[189]

Compliance can also be enhanced by the involvement of other interest groups and close analysis of the determinations show that the conditions incorporate different forms of external oversight: changing the composition of decision-making committees within the corporation to include parties outside the corporation, thereby increasing external oversight; mandating independent review and reporting on processes internal to the corporation; and, requiring the corporation to consider and implement the recommendations of the independent

---

187 *Medicines* A90779, A90780, 14 November 2003, 37.
188 ibid, 40.
189 ibid, 69.

review. Often the ACCC requires that it be informed of the outcome of the reviews. It is clear that each of these types of review is aimed at encouraging the participation of wider stakeholders while, at the same time, accompanied by a less direct involvement by the regulator. The regulator is choosing to regulate indirectly by co-opting others in regulation.

Altering the composition of committees by involving external stakeholders can bring about a cultural shift in decision-making, which was what was clearly articulated in an early decision of FACTS authorisation where the ACCC noted that the likelihood of achieving effective self-regulation by industry organisations is improved 'where consumer or consumer groups are drawn into the consultation process so that not only is the result better-tailored but there is less risk of resentment'.[190] In this authorisation the ACCC imposed a condition requiring annual consultations with consumer organisations and other relevant health and safety authorities in order to decide whether to extend or revise the guidelines.[191] In the Medicines authorisation, the ACCC noted that the members of the monitoring committee included industry, professional and consumer representatives, which added a level of independence to its decision-making.

Conditions have directed the corporation to conduct an independent review. In the Australian Associated Brewers authorisation, conditions imposed required an independent review to be conducted of the effectiveness of the Retailer Alert Scheme, which was a system for regulating the entry onto the market of inappropriately named or packaged alcohol products. The ACCC noted that this scheme was weak because it did not contain a mechanism to enforce compliance, and required the association to report on the findings of the review.[192] In Australasian College of Cosmetic Surgery, a condition required that the code be amended to allow for the appointment of an independent auditor to report findings of annual audit checks including the manner in which the complaints panel of the college dealt with complaints. The results of these audits are to be reported to the ACCC as well as the college's code administration committee.[193]

Some of the conditions go further by getting companies themselves to be reflexive about the way they consider and internalise compliance, and the manner in which they relate to both internal and external stakeholders. In a number of determinations, the reviews were directed at evaluating the level of compliance among the participants after consultation with stakeholders and making the results available to both corporation and the ACCC. In Grain Corp Operations, the corporation, in conjunction with an independent person, was required to develop and implement measures that ensured confidential information was not

---

190 *Federation of Australian Commercial Television Stations* (1984) A11709, 55427.
191 ibid.
192 *The Distilled Spirits Industry Council of Australia* A91054 & A91055, 31 October 2007, 34–35, 48.
193 *Australasian College of Cosmetic Surgery* A91106, 18 June 2009, 57, 79.

used improperly.[194] Similarly, in the International Air Transport Association authorisation, the independent consultant had to view the standard form contracts (that were the subject of authorisation) and consider whether these contracts could be improved in any way and the company was required to act on the recommendations of this review and report to the ACCC.[195]

Promoting Fairness and Justice

The ACCC has also used conditions to introduce independent and effective appeal processes or complaints mechanisms. These will have the effect of ensuring that anti-competitive practices will be scrutinised through the appeal or complaints process and these may also have the effect of introducing specific types of just practices and ethical conduct into specific sectors of the market.

In Re Allianz Australia Insurance Limited, the ACCC granted authorisation to three large insurance companies to set up a single co-insurance pool specifically for the provision of public liability insurance to not-for-profit organisations, which would otherwise contravene section 45. The conditions included a complaints-handling procedure consistent with the Australian standard AS4269-1995, as well as a requirement that all complaints and their outcome/s are reported to the ACCC on a quarterly basis.[196] In the Australian Payments Clearing Association authorisation, similar conditions were required for fair treatment of both members and non-members of the association, as well as providing equal access to facilities.[197]

Appeal mechanisms have been introduced via conditions since 1984, when there were numerous codes of conduct being authorised. For example, in Mercury Newsagency System,[198] NSW and ACT Newsagency System,[199] Master Locksmiths Association of Australia Ltd[200] and Royal Australian Institute of Architects,[201] the commission required the inclusion of an appeals process. In Re Australian Stock Exchange, the ACCC granted authorisation on the condition that the exchange provide an adequate appeal mechanism for individuals whose registration as a trading representative was refused, suspended or withdrawn by the exchange board. It required that the constitution be amended to make provisions for such a procedure.[202] In the Surgeons authorisation, the conditions addressed the composition of the appeal committee. The condition required that

---

194   *Grain Corp Operations*, AWB and Export Grain Logistics A30233, A30234, A30235, 15 April 2005, 80.

195   *International Air Transport Association* (2008) A91083, 28 August 2008, 20.

196   *Allianz Insurance Ltd, QBE Insurance (Australia) Ltd, NRMA Insurance Ltd* A30217, A30218, 24 March 2004, 55.

197   ibid; See also *Re Australian Payments Clearing Association* A30176, A30177, A90620, 24 March 2004; *Australian Direct Marketing* A90876, 29 June 2006.

198   *Mercury Newsagency System* 9 May 1984.

199   *NSW and ACT Newsagency System* 26 April 1984.

200   *Master Locksmiths Association of Australia Ltd* 15 March 1984.

201   *Royal Australian Institute of Architects* A58, 7 September 1984.

202   *Re Australian Stock Exchange* (1998) A90623, i–ii.

the appeal committee be comprised of a majority of members, including the chairman, be nominated by the Australian health minister, and only a minority of members be fellows of the college.[203] Likewise, in the Victorian Egg Industry Cooperative authorisation, the conditions provided an independent appeal mechanism for producers in addition to the procedures provided under the Commercial Arbitration Act 1984 (Vic).[204]

At times, these dispute-resolution processes are in addition to those that are available under the law. They offer, however, cheaper, quicker and less formal alternatives with more flexible remedies. In the Australian Amalgamated Terminals Pty Ltd authorisation, the ACCC required the incorporation of a dispute-resolution process, with provision for mediation and, ultimately, expert determination which can be accessed by end-users of AAT's terminals.[205] This process was in addition to the dispute resolution process that may be available to the parties to the contract, as well as those available to port authorities' dispute-resolution processes and were not intended to compromise the operation of these existing processes.[206] Likewise, in the Victorian Egg Industry Cooperative authorisation, the conditions provided an independent appeal mechanism for producers in addition to the procedures provided under the Commercial Arbitration Act 1984 (Vic).[207]

Another means of incorporating fair practices into an industry is by requiring independent review. In the Surgeons authorisation, the ACCC was concerned with the exclusive role of the college in setting the standards for accrediting hospitals and training positions within hospitals. The conditions imposed included a requirement that the college establish a public independent review of the criteria for accrediting hospitals for the provision of various surgical-training positions.[208] This condition was supplemented by others involving the participation of the state health ministers in the nomination of hospitals for accreditation.[209] Another condition required the college to establish an independently chaired committee to publicly review the tests that medical colleges use to assess overseas trained surgeons.[210]

Providing information to interested parties and increasing transparency of decision making is also a way of promoting ethical conduct. A number of conditions are directed at making information widely available. In Re Medicines

---

203   Surgeons A90765, 30 June 2003.
204   *The Victorian Egg Industry Co-operative* A40072, 13 September 1995, 29.
205   *Australian Amalgamated Terminals Pty Ltd* A91141, A91142, A91181, A91181, 3 December 2009.
206   ibid, 36–37.
207   *Victorian Egg Industry* (1995) A40072 29. This authorisation determination is not part of the empirical study.
208   *Royal Australasian College of Surgeons* A90765, 30 June 2003, 166.
209   ibid, 167–68.
210   ibid, 172.

the information was required to be posted on the association's website and, in Re Surgeons, the college was required to publish annually a range of information about its selection processes, training and examination processes.[211]

The information gathering process has been used to check on the rate and quality of compliance. In the Generic Medicines Industry Association, discussed above, the ACCC stated that it would seek further information from the association on how the code had been enforced and whether the association had been effective in encouraging compliance.[212] In Phonographic Performance Company, the ACCC required the company to monitor compliance with the guidelines it had developed, and to report to the ACCC the manner in which licensor's complied with the guidelines.[213] The ACCC is steering companies to enforce the law, sometimes with the help of independent consultation and staying informed about the process through the discretionary power granted under section 91(3). The threat that non-compliance may lead to litigation is always present in the grant of authorisation.[214]

Facilitating Deregulation

Conditions have been included in authorisation decisions involving both deregulated and other industries. Deregulatory policies took effect in Australia in the mid 1990s. In the 1998 authorisations, six applications from such groups were responded to with conditions. This was the highest number of authorisations in which conditions were imposed. This illustrates the important role of the regulator in giving effect to policies, which can be a difficult exercise where the outcomes may not be always predictable.

Four of the six applications were from previously government-owned and run service providers: National Electricity Code,[215] United Energy Limited,[216] Vencorp[217] and Gas Services Business Pty Ltd.[218] State-run businesses came under the jurisdiction of the Act in 1995.[219] There was one application from the Australian Medical Association, which became regulated by the Act as a result of amendments in 1995,[220] and another from the chicken industry, seeking authorisation for collective bargaining.[221]

---

211 Medicines A90779, A90780, 14 November 2003; Surgeons A90765, 30 June 2003, 177–80.
212 *Generic Medicines Industry Association Pty Ltd* (2010) A91218 & A 91219, iv.
213 *Phonographic Performance Company of Australia Ltd* (2007) A91041, A91042, 54-55.
214 For example see: *The State of Queensland Acting through the Office of Liquor and Gaming Regulation* (2010) A91224 and A91225.
215 *National Electricity Code* A90652, A90653, A90654, 19 October 1998.
216 *United Energy Limited* A90665, A90666, A90670, 25 November 1998.
217 *Vencorp* A90646, A90647, A90648, 19 August 1998.
218 *Gas Services Business Pty Ltd* A90630, A 90631, 19 August 1998.
219 See sections 13–15 of the *Competition Policy Reform Act 1995*.
220 See section 8 of the *Competition Policy Reform (New South Wales) Act 1995*.
221 *Steggles Limited and Others* A30183, 25 May 1998.

Immunity Discretion

Many enquiries about anti-competitive conduct never proceed to an authorisation application. They may be circumvented, with the parties satisfied that there is unlikely to be any prosecution should they follow the proposed course of action. Alternatively, discussions with the ACCC may present other pathways previously not considered. In other words, enquirers may receive a form of 'de facto' immunity, granted in an informal manner and demonstrating the exercise of discretion.

The Guide to Authorisation states that the ACCC encourages applicants to contact the ACCC for informal discussion and guidance before lodging an application. It also states that the ACCC will provide guidance on whether the proposed conduct is likely to raise concerns under the competition provisions of the Act, the type of public benefit claims that might be considered by the ACCC, the type of detriment, including anti-competitive detriment that might be taken into account, and the overall authorisation process.[222] This includes hypothetical scenarios, which companies may be considering, that the ACCC will discuss off the record. Clearly, this is cost effective and, further, it is acknowledged by the ACCC that these negotiations may themselves facilitate a commercially satisfactory outcome.[223] Further, the ACCC may ask the potential applicant to raise such issues in the relevant industry forum and gauge whether there may be any opposition to the proposed conduct before proceeding with the application. Alternatively, the ACCC may direct the organisation to consult non-industry bodies to ascertain their views on the proposed conduct. By doing so, the ACCC is doing what scholars have described as nodal governance or partnerships approaches to governance.[224]

In certain instances, the ACCC has held prolonged consultation in order to increase familiarity with the legislation and its effect on different sectors of industry. One such example was in relation to the medical profession, which became subject to the Act. Here, the ACCC undertook a long consultation process, which, while sharing many features with a pre-decision conference, was a distinctive strategy — not prescribed by the Act — and was aimed at encouraging awareness and compliance with the law. The advantages of nurturing compliance, increasing institutional awareness, and being responsive

---

222   ACCC, *Guide to Authorisation* (2007) 6; see also ACCC, *Guide to Authorisation* (1999) 2–3.

223   T Thomson and H Croft, 'Authorisations in Australia and New Zealand: Neighbours with Different Backyards' (2003) 19(4) *Australian and New Zealand Trade Practices Law Bulletin* 37, 38.

224   See Peter Drahos, 'Intellectual Property and Pharmaceutical Markets: A Nodal Governance Approach' (2004) 77(2) *Temple Law Review* 401; Michael Kempa, Clifford Shearing and Scott Burris, 'Changes in Governance: A Background Review' (Paper presented at the Global Governance of Health Seminar, Salzburg, 16 December 2005) <http://www.temple.edu/lawschool/phrhcs/salzburg/Global_Health_Governance_Review.pdf> at 18 December 2007.

are discussed earlier in the public consultation and pre-decision conference section and apply equally here. By so doing, the ACCC would be granting a period of grace or immunity from prosecution.

In summary …

This chapter has illustrated the complex task of the authorisation process and the manner in which discretion is used in practice. Discretion is like the tube of toothpaste — when squeezed it simply shifts to another place. This chapter has illustrated that the ACCC has exercised its discretion in many ways — by giving informal immunity guarantees to parties; by the choices of quantification methodologies it prefers; the parties it has consulted in the determination process and how much weight it has attached to their participation; and, the conditions under which authorisation has been granted. These bring to life the 'tube of toothpaste' analogy about discretion: discretion cannot be controlled — it simply is squeezed to another area in the tube.

Second, the chapter makes a link between current regulatory theories and how they can be used to explain the practice of this regulatory agency. The need to assure the applicants and members of the trade practices community and the officials within the regulator of the ways in which the regulator is both predictable and accountable, saw the description of public benefit in the form of a list. This was always viewed by the regulator, however, as a non-exhaustive list. The ACCC has used its discretion by operating at multiple levels of the regulatory pyramid (Figure 5.1). The draft determinations, public consultation processes and the use of pre-decision conferences aimed at facilitating wide participation can be termed restorative justice practices that fall within the base of the pyramid. Promising immunity from authorisation in certain circumstances, prosecuting those who continue with unlawful conduct without seeking authorisation, granting authorisation on the basis of undertakings not to engage in anti-competitive conduct, or the granting of authorisations on the basis of conditions that enhance self-regulation or incorporate procedural regulation of self-regulation can be classified as deterrence strategies that fall within the middle tier of the regulatory pyramid, as they are aimed at preventing future breaches of the Act. Finally the revocation of authorisation or the denial of authorisations fall into the top tier of the pyramid and can be considered as punitive because it is banning conduct that has either been taking place (in the case of revocation) or suspending plans for conduct which was the objective of the authorisation application.

In conclusion, the ACCC has been an innovative regulator from its inception, using its discretion in an experimental manner with an eye on the outcome, which has always been to create workable competition in the market. This is illustrated during the early days of the Act, where significant energies were expended in educating business, activating consumer advocacy and informing the wider public. More recently, it is illustrated by the manner in which the ACCC has used conditions to enhance compliance, promote fairness and facilitate deregulation. The ACCC itself has been reasonably responsive to the needs of industry, governments, independent bodies and non-government bodies. By not mandating quantification, it has been sensitive to the manner in which it has exercised epistemological discretion. It has used its discretion inclusively by having prolonged consultations to implement sensitive policies, such as those involving professional groups that came within the Act as well as effecting deregulatory policies in primary industries. The manner in which the ACCC has functioned can be best explained by the expanded model of accountability. This expanded model involves the ACCC being accountable to a wide trade practices community, including lawyers, economists, compliance officers, non-government organisations, other regulators, ministers, governments, the media and other networks, which makes for a diffused network of accountability.

As the regulatory scholarship on responsive regulation and restorative justice suggests, however, procedural justice requires that people are aware of their rights and given the opportunity to participate. The empirical study shows that participation by state governments and the federal government has increased significantly since 1984, demonstrating the changing nature of the market and regulation. The participation by independent groups, too, has increased, although not to the same extent as involvement by government. The participation by non-independent groups, however, has not increased in the same manner — Figure 6.6 shows that there were six submissions in 1976 and seven in 2006 in the sample studied for those yeas. Although the ACCC consistently refers to its consumer-oriented focus to regulation, this is not reflected in the authorisations arena. Although the ACCC has been experimental and outcome driven, it must give greater consideration to furthering procedural fairness by encouraging participation, to notions of restorative justice by enhancing inclusivity, and becoming really responsive by reflecting on its own performance.

7. Experiments in Discretion: How Effective is the Regulator?

This chapter acts as a conclusion by bringing together the earlier discussions on discretion and public benefit in the Australian Competition and Consumer Commission (ACCC) and directly addressing the central question of how effective the ACCC has been in exercising its discretion to determine public benefit. The data have been interpreted to reveal two areas where there have been limits to this effectiveness: first, the current ad hoc approach could be improved by developing a broader framework for determining public benefit; second, strategies to increase the participation of non-industry groups in the decision process could be refined and developed. This chapter addresses these two problem areas and proposes a set of nine principles toward a solution. These principles are aimed at thinking about how the ACCC might become a more responsive regulator. The discussion in this chapter is in five parts.

The first part consolidates earlier discussion on the use of discretion by the ACCC in determining public benefit over the last four decades. It concludes that these experiences demonstrate the regulator has been experimental in its use of discretion, often achieving desired outcomes. This is conceived as representing a triumph of practice over theory. The main criticism with the present approach is that there is no overarching set of principles to assist regulators, regulatees and other interested parties. The current ad hoc approach gives rise to numerous concerns. Three main ones are: What is the role of economic efficiency? Does the public benefit have to reach a small or wider group? What weighting is given to the different benefits? It is suggested that a less ad hoc approach to determining public benefit can be conceived from this experience. Currently, the ambit of public benefit remains unclear, with the ACCC relying primarily on a list of non-exhaustive categories that it has recognised.[1] It is proposed that it would be preferable to define public benefit in terms of a principle rather than a list of non-exhaustive categories. Such a principle is best founded on a discourse that is more universal than economic efficiency. It should also take into account the practice of the ACCC to date. The set of heuristics employed in this section aims to identify public benefits using human rights and ACCC practice. This is then articulated as one principle in a set of nine principles.

The second part of the chapter looks at the main challenges facing regulators, such as the ACCC, when making a decision: the regulator has to be responsive to the regulatee and anyone else who may be affected by its decision. This is a wider concept going beyond the confines of traditional or expanded accountability, as

---

1   See the discussions in Chapters 1 and 3.

discussed in Chapter 5. Here it is argued that the regulator should be responsive to the needs of all stakeholders and to the business community. Two methods for increasing the regulator's use of responsive strategies are explored: it could be mandated by legislative design; or, it could become part of the regulator's practice. It is acknowledged that, given Australia's history and regulatory architecture, legislation can be designed or redesigned to mandate such involvement. The focus of competition regulation in Australia has been the use of responsive practices demonstrated by the creation of a powerful independent agency. Accordingly, this section explores the manner in which the ACCC can become more responsive. A set of seven principles is developed, aimed at increasing the regulator's responsiveness. This is a contribution to grounding the theorising of responsiveness in regulatory scholarship.

The third part brings together the discussion in the first two sections to formulate nine principles, incorporating the eight developed earlier. These principles respond to the need for a less ad hoc approach to identifying public benefits and the need to facilitate greater participation by all stakeholders. The fourth part discusses the need for reflection by the regulator in implementing these principles. The upshot is a principle-based approach to reflective practice for increasing the responsiveness of the ACCC.

The fifth part proposes that a successful regulator has to move far away from lists and rule books to a storybook, which, like all good stories, contains morals that can be called upon time and again to underpin, inform and shape conduct. The nine principles form some of the morals of this storybook. Unlike a rule book, which sets itself up for failure, a supple storybook has wide applicability, where meaning can be extracted by new actors and wider networks, in known terrain and unforeseen crisis.

Experimental Governance

The ACCC was established in 1975 with the aim of linking consumer welfare and competition principles. The legislative design leaves a good deal to the discretion of the commission, allowing for different levels of consultations. These include formal and informal exchanges that are crafted to allow a range of interchanges. The formal exchanges include the submissions of authorisations by applicants, draft determinations by the regulator and pre-decision conferences prior to final determination. The informal discussions and exchanges with affected parties and requests by the regulator for interest groups to make submissions are also part of ACCC practice. This design was no accident. It was part of Australia's distinctive approach to regulating the entrenched, club-like environment in which cartels thrived in Australia's heavily concentrated and geographically distant market. This distinctive approach has given Australia a number of lasting legacies, one being the creation of a regulator, which, from its early days, has operated in an environment where business was oppositional, and where multiple strategies have been used, including soft and hard approaches such as education and enforcement. The ability to tread softly has been central to the determination of public benefit, where the regulator has demonstrated that it is aware of the need to be open to a range of discourses and interest groups. This pattern was laid down in the early days of the regulator under the leadership of Ron Bannerman, who founded and led the Australian competition regulation regime for 19 years — an unusually long time compared to other domains of Australian public administration and to competition enforcement in other nations.[2]

The ACCC has recognised diverse public benefits over the last four decades (Chapter 4). Efficiency benefits in the form of promotion of cost savings and industry rationalisation have always had a place, as have certain non-efficiency benefits, such as ensuring safety and improving the quality of products and services. The marketplace, however, is becoming more complex and regulation more open-textured. Many more benefits are being claimed by applicants. The role of non-efficiency benefits is increasing and newer benefits are popping up in determinations. These include improved environmental practices, better working conditions, superior information supply to targeted groups and promoting ethical conduct. The ACCC has recognised many of these diverse benefits, both in granting authorisations and in imposing conditions. There has always been a focus on achieving a reasonable outcome and of facilitating workable competition (Chapter 6).

Philosophically, the outsider could characterise the regulatory practice of Bannerman as in the tradition of American pragmatism in the vein of Philip Selznick's responsive law, though no claim to such theoretical terms was made. Integrity, political nuance[3] and being a slave to duty,[4] together with a conversational form of regulation being central to the authorisation process, characterised the practice of this commissioner. Even though subsequent chairmen were associated with different changes in emphasis and different pluralisations of the regulatory conversations, the regime remained fundamentally, conversationally and pragmatically path dependent. Many of the commissioners who followed emphasised different points. For example the Allan Fels and Allan Asher team have been labelled as 'Mr Inside' and 'Mr Outside' and, as chairman, Fels utilised his media skills to communicate

---

2   Ron Bannerman was commissioner of trade practices under the *Trade Practices Act 1965* from 1965 to 1974 and chairman of the Trade Practices Commission from 1974 to 1984.
3   David Merrett, Stephen Corones and David Round, 'The Introduction of Competition Policy in Australia: The Role of Ron Bannerman' (2007) 47(2) *Australian Economic History Review* 194–95.
4   ibid.

the consumer message, Asher as 'Mr Inside' tuned up the 'Commission's enforcement into an outcomes approach'.[5] Similarly, Graeme Samuel was seen as part of corporate Australia, able to talk to business, while Ron Sims is regarded as an experienced regulator, who will operate quietly and efficiently. All these leaders have their own pragmatic approaches that can operate at all levels of the regulatory pyramid and they have been successful in increasing their powers and budget.[6] The path pioneered by Bannerman persisted partly through the agency of many of his protégés, most notably the CEO Hank Spier, who was important in shaping the agency.[7] The agency was continuously shaped by the chairmen and officials that followed.[8]

Simultaneously, as the numbers of benefits claimed was becoming more and more varied, the ACCC was faced with enormous pressure to explain its decisions and account for its actions. Rules such as the total welfare standard or the consumer welfare standard have been mooted as appropriate tools for such accounts. At a time when regulators are facing increasing scrutiny from many sources, the temptation to adopt bright line rules such as the total welfare standard is high, as they are seen as offering answers that are easy to apply. The solution prescribed by the ACT, and closely adhered to by the ACCC, is the public benefit standard, which appears to be a hybrid between the more widely accepted total welfare standard and the balancing weights standard. The public benefit standard is not what can be termed a bright line rule. It calls for the weighing of different benefits, with little guidance about the actual weighing process. This weighing up is left to the commission. Using the definitions of rules and principles, the public benefit standard is best classified as a principle. Julia Black has described the difference between rules and principles: rules are detailed and prescriptive, while principles rely on more high-level, broadly stated standards.[9] I would argue that the public benefit standard is less like a rule and more like a principle, as the weighing-up process, which is central to any examination, is impossible to spell out with precision.

Black has argued that principles can be used to refer to general rules or to rules that are implicitly higher in the hierarchy of norms.[10] Using this definition, the public benefit standard, which involves determining the weight to be given to productive efficiency savings, is a principle or higher-level norm, rather than a rule.[11] John Braithwaite has discussed the circumstances in which principles

---

5   Fred Brenchley, *Allan Fels: A Portrait of Power* (2003) 119.

6   ibid.

7   Interview 5; see also the role of other ACCC officers and commissioners including Asher, Ross Jones and Sitesh Bhojani in Brenchley 2003 279.

8   See Anthony Giddens, *The Constitution of Society: Outline of the Theory of Structuration* (1984).

9   Julia Black, Martyn Hopper and Christa Band, 'Making Sense of Principles-based Regulation' (2007) *Law and Financial Markets Review* 191, 192.

10   ibid, 192.

11   ACCC, *Guide to Authorisation* (2007), para 5.29; see Chapter 6 discussion.

and rules may be appropriate. When the type of action to be regulated is simple, stable and does not involve huge economic interests, rules regulate with certainty.[12] But, when the type of actions that are being regulated are complex and occurring in changing environments, where large economic interests are at stake, principles are more likely to enable certainty than rules.[13] Braithwaite's proposals have immediate relevance here. These proposals explain the reason for the difficulties faced by current ACCC staff and the ACT in articulating simple, stable rules to regulate authorisations in a complex changing environment.

Principle-based Regulation

Black's contribution to principle-based regulation brings together much of the earlier debates in the area and is used here to assess whether principle-based regulation can be used to determine public benefit. Black, in her examination of financial services regulation, has pointed out there are eight key pre-conditions for making principle-based regulation work.[14] Many of these are relevant to the discussion on public benefit in ACCC authorisations, as discussed below:

1. *Developing criteria to identify the appropriate balance between principles and rules.* Black argues that there is a place for both rules and principles. Fixed points, which set out in more detailed form the conduct that is required, providing safe harbours from charges of non-compliance can often be just and effective.[15] These concrete fixed points are most likely to be served by rules. Applying this to the determination of public benefit may be appropriate for the ACCC to articulate the categories of public benefits as well as the weighing up of benefits and detriments as principles. Rules may be appropriate to describe the manner in which submissions may be called for, how draft determinations are made, when pre-decision conferences can be called, setting precise expiry dates for authorisations, as well as the manner in which an appeal can be mounted. As discussed in Chapter 3 the ACCC has included a non-exhaustive list of benefits in its guidance documents. The discussion in Chapter 4, however, illustrates that there are many more public benefits that have been recognised in the determinations. These are responses to changing political, global and economic contexts, supporting the notion that the ACCC's approach represents a triumph of practice over theory.

---

12   John Braithwaite, 'Rules and Principles: A Theory of Legal Certainty' (2002) 27, *Australian Journal of Legal Philosophy* 47, 52. For further discussion of the principles of responsive regulation see: John Braithwaite, 'The Essence of Responsive Regulation' (2011), 44, *University of British Columbia Law Review* 474–520.

13   ibid, 53.

14   Black, Hopper and Band (2007) 200–04.

15   ibid, 200–01.

2. *Discipline and restraint in provision of guidance documentation*. Here Black argues that there is a need to strike the right balance between providing useful information and bombarding firms with overly complex, prescriptive and inaccessible material.[16] For example, case studies to illustrate good or bad practice and guidance documentation, where kept concise, can be a useful resource. The ACCC guidance to authorisations does a helpful job of balancing such materials (discussed in Chapter 3).

3. *Meeting the needs of different firms*. This recognises that one size does not fit all. Any guidance should target firms of different sizes and with different needs.[17] As discussed in Chapter 6, outcome-based discretion demonstrates the ACCC understands the needs of different-sized firms operating in different, and distinctively Australian, contexts. The use of conditions in granting authorisations is a key example of how this has been done.

4. *Ensuring an appropriate style of supervision and enforcement and a balance between the two*. Black emphasises the importance of dialogue between the firms and the regulator, stating dialogue in turn is shaped by the enforcement context.[18] The authorisation process is strong on dialogue, with preliminary meetings being followed by formal and informal submissions by applicants and other interested parties. Certain informal participation can promote responsive regulatory practices and nurture compliance (discussed in Chapter 6: Procedural Discretion). At the front-end, informal enquiries are encouraged by the commission and, at the back-end pre-decision conferences can be the means of furthering such dialogue. This process of dialogue was initiated very early on, preceding the passing of the legislation. It stands as one of the legacies of the critical juncture (discussed in Chapter 2). In this case, the ACCC has been successful in adopting a balanced style.

5. *Redefining the role of decided cases*. Here Black recognises the important role that precedents can have and calls for greater consideration to be given by the regulator to the status of its own earlier decisions, both enforcements and settlements.[19] My empirical study of authorisation decisions illustrates that the ACCC does make reference to its past decisions, and is doing so increasingly (discussed in Chapter 6). Reference to the status of the tribunal's decisions is less clear, however, with the website recording that the appeal has been finalised and including a statement such as 'On 12 October 2004, the Australian Competition Tribunal granted authorisation for the arrangements between Qantas and Air New Zealand for a period of 5 years commencing on 12 October 2005'.[20] This does not provide further information as to the status

---

16   Black, Hopper and Band (2007) 202.
17   ibid, 202–03.
18   ibid, 202.
19   ibid, 203.
20   *Re Qantas and Air New Zealand* A90962, A90963, A30220, A30221, 9 September 2003; see also *Re Medicines Australia* A909894, A90995, A90996, 30 November 2005; *Re NSW Pathology* A90754, A90755, 1 November 2000.

of the ACCC decision, or the impact of the tribunal's decision on the ACCC's decision-making process.

6. *Ensuring accountability mechanisms in the regulatory rule-making process are not bypassed.* Here Black warns of the UK Financial Service Authority's intention of relying on industry to produce guidance to elaborate on principles, which could amount to outsourcing, raising concerns about how the guidance may be interpreted, the regulator's accountability and the status of such guidance documents.[21] In the authorisations area, public speeches are made by ACCC staff to industry groups[22] and the wider epistemic community, sometimes called the trade practices mafia,[23] and some guidance documents are prepared by industry bodies.[24] The ACCC acknowledges, however, that it must remain accountable.

7. *Changing the skills and mindset of regulators and firms.* Black has pointed out that the regulator has to change its supervisory and enforcement culture.[25] This includes the regulator adopting an educative role and encouraging firms to adopt a more strategic approach to regulation. Boards of directors have to encourage senior levels of management to develop the firms' business in line with regulatory requirements.[26] The ACCC has been adopting an educative role, focused on encouraging compliance. This is a continuous challenge, however, requiring the ACCC to be reflexive, and assessing its strategies constantly.

8. *Developing and maintaining a constructive dialogue.* Black builds on the contributions of scholars on the importance of trust, arguing it is critical to have an ongoing dialogue between the regulator and firms, which develops shared understandings of what is required by the principles.[27] An extensive study, carried out by Christine Parker and Vibeke Nielsen on the views of Australian businesses of the ACCC, found that the majority of the respondents to their questions 'were moderately positive about the ACCC's level of strategic

---

21 Black, Hopper and Band (2007) 203.

22 For example, see Michael Cosgrove 'Regulation and the Australian Broadband sector' (Paper presented at the 3rd Annual Broadband Australia Conference, 24 July 2008) <http://www.accc.gov.au/content/index. phtml/itemId/837276/fromItemId/8973>; see also Peter Clemes, 'The *Trade Practices Act* Implications for the seafood industry' <http://proceedings.com.au/seafood2007/presentations/thursday/Thur%201345%20 GB23%20Clemes.pdf> at 30 April 2009.

23 Christine Parker, Paul Ainsworth and Natalie Stepanenko, 'ACCC Compliance and Enforcement Project: The Impact of ACCC Enforcement Activity on Cartel Cases' (Working Paper, Centre of Competition and Consumer Policy, Australian National University, May 2004) 69.

24 See, for example, guidance documents prepared by the Construction Material Processors Association that provides guidance to the members on a variety of matters including standard form contracts: Construction Material Processors Association, 'Cartage Contractors in Extractive Industry' (2008) < http://www.cmpavic. asn.au/downloads/F-PAS-96.pdf> at 30 April 2009.

25 Black, Hopper and Band (2007) 203.

26 ibid.

27 ibid, 204–05; see Valerie Braithwaite, Kristina Murphy and Monika Reinhart, 'Taxation. Threat, Motivational Postures and Responsive Regulation' (2007) 29(1) *Law and Policy* 137.

sophistication and how accommodating the ACCC is.'[28] Business executives, however, were most negative about the ACCC's dogmatism, and many saw the ACCC as having an inflexible preference for taking organisations to court, a view that the ACCC did not have of itself.[29] Although this study is extremely useful in gaining an overview of the ACCC's regulatory strategies, it is of limited relevance here as it does not examine authorisations in detail. The authors found the ACCC performed poorly in relation to matters concerning mergers and acquisitions, where it was heavily criticised for lack of transparency and accountability and for adopting a commercially unrealistic application of the law.[30] For reasons that past commissioners would justify in terms of the commercial secrecy sensitivity of proposed mergers, the ACCC has indeed been less transparent and accountable in its mergers than its authorisations work. These complaints were addressed in the amendments made to the legislation via the introduction of a clearance process.[31]

From the above discussion, it is the first criterion that has to be addressed in deciding the applicability of principle-based regulation to determine public benefit within authorisations. This criterion points to the need to have a balance between rules and principles. Here, it is contended that public benefit defies encapsulation as a rule and is better explained as a principle or a set of principles. The ACCC performs poorly on this criterion because it has not developed a broader framework to articulate the concept of public benefits.

The ACCC currently states that both economic efficiency benefits and other general benefits will be considered in the process of granting an authorisation. This is a broad canvas and applicants would need further information before deciding whether the benefits they seek to claim would be accepted. The guidance documents incorporate a non-exhaustive list of public benefits that are important for parties seeking to make such an application. It may have the effect, however, of deterring or confusing parties who seek to claim benefits not included in this list. To date, the ACCC has seen public benefits as it finds them, rightly recognising health, environmental benefits, safety and equitable dealings. This process can best be described as both ad hoc and inclusive in the types of benefits it recognises. This does not provide sufficient guidance for applicants. Likewise, it poses a problem for those who may not be able to predict the kinds of benefits that may be acceptable to the ACCC. Developing a broader framework capable of accommodating the types of non-efficiency

---

28 Christine Parker and Vibeke Nielsen, 'What do Australian businesses think of the ACCC and does it matter?' (2007) 35(2) *Federal Law Review*, 187, 232.
29 ibid, 233.
30 ibid, 217.
31 See s 50(4) and (5).

benefits as they arise is the challenge. Human rights literature, together with the data collated on the ACCC deliberations, can be combined to develop this framework.

A Broader Framework for Public Benefits

Human rights discourse is being recognised as an important regulatory tool for global corporations.[32] Consumer law scholars, particularly in the European Union where the human rights discourse has always thrived, are emphasising the need for all public regulation undertaken in the consumer interest to be human rights proof.[33] This is a way of ensuring that it does not contravene the European Convention on Human Rights as well as any national legislation. It means that care should be taken in ensuring both business and consumer rights are not compromised, thus striking a balance between economic freedoms of traders and social rights of consumers, both of which are protected by the convention.[34] In Australia, the only relevant legislation is the *Human Rights Act (ACT) 2004*, which provides that, so far as it is possible to do so consistently with its purpose, a Territory law must be interpreted in a way that is compatible with human rights.[35] Although this does not have the same reach or impact as the convention, it does support the need to consider human rights discourse more widely.

As deputy chair of the ACCC, Asher signalled the important role of human rights. He proposed that the UN Consumer Protection Guidelines, an elaboration of the fundamental rights first articulated by US President John F Kennedy in 1962, which call on governments to develop, strengthen or maintain measures relating to the control of restrictive and other abusive business practices that may be harmful to consumers, be extended to include a specific elaboration of competition policy measures that governments can adopt in a way that enhances consumer welfare.[36] Although it may be more obvious to rely on consumer rights

---

32 See Amy Sinden, 'Power and Responsibility: Why Human Rights Should Address Corporate Environmental Wrongs', in Doreen McBarnet, Aurora Voiculescu and Tom Campbell (eds), *The New Corporate Accountability: Corporate Social Responsibility and the Law* (2007) 501; David Kinley, Justine Nolan, and Natalie Zerial, 'Reflections on the United Nations Human Rights Norms for Corporations' (2007) 25(1) *Company and Securities Law Journal* 30; David Kinley, 'Human Rights Fundamentalisms' (2007) 29(4) *Sydney Law Review* 545; Mary Dowell-Jones and David Kinley, 'Minding the Gap: Global Finance and Human Rights' (2011) 25(2) Ethics & International Affairs 183–210.

33 Geraint G Howells and Stephen Weatherill, *Consumer Protection Law* (2005) 94–97.

34 Article 10 of the European Convention on Human Rights, the fundamental right of the freedom of expression, is now being relied on by businesses to argue that certain advertising restrictions may be void. See Howells and Weatherill (2005) 97.

35 Section 30.

36 Allan Asher, 'Consumers 2000: Updating the UN Guidelines' (5 January 1997) <http://www.accc.gov.au/ content/index.phtml/itemId/96009> at 1 November 2004. The four consumer rights articulated by President John F Kennedy were the right to redress, the right to consumer education, the right to a healthy environment and the right to satisfaction of basic needs; see David Edward O'Connor, *The Basics of Economics* (2004) 146.

in dealing with competition issues, it is contended that, as consumer rights is a subset of human rights, the human rights framework is to be preferred. Whereas consumer rights may provide for the right to a safe product, they may not provide for a right to a safe workplace or a right for competitors to receive a fair hearing, or a right for freedom of expression for journalists, for example, in the media regulation cases.[37] The cases studied here have shown that these non-consumer rights issues come up regularly. Human rights would be the starting point, and conduct that enforces human rights would be viewed as a public benefit. Therefore, conduct that concerns the health of patients, the safety of goods, and the right to a healthy environment or the right to a fair trial can be couched in terms of human rights and can be viewed as public benefits. Alternatively, where conduct appears to adversely affect human rights, it should not be approved unless the effect could be remedied via the inclusion of conditions.

The use of human rights will shift the focus away from the current tensions between economic efficiency and non-efficiency factors. Rather than referring to issues of product safety and improved health services in negative terms by calling them non-efficiency factors or other factors, there is much to be gained in viewing them in the positive language of human rights. Asher has examined the types of rights that need to be examined when dealing with the deregulation of utilities to ensure the potential adverse impact of competition is minimised.[38] These include the facilitation of participation by consumers in decisions that affect them, inclusion of accountability measures that provide sufficient information and redress for consumers, and enhancing transparency in decision-making in the utilities sector.[39] This demonstrates the wider applicability of the human rights discourse.

Specifically, human rights can be used as a lens for authorising codes of conduct. When doing so, it is necessary to recognise the right to be heard and ensure consumer groups are represented in the authorisation process and their participation is facilitated in a meaningful way. Likewise, it is necessary to ensure the right to a fair hearing or procedural justice, which may mean appeal processes in the codes should be examined and, where necessary, any adverse effects reduced via the use of conditions. Further, it is necessary that the parties involved, be they consumers or other competitors, be informed on a regular basis; this may be effected by providing monitoring procedures within the codes. As the discussion on codes of conduct in Chapter 6 demonstrated,

---

37 See *Abbott Australasia Pty Ltd and Nestle Australia Limited* (1992) ATPR (Com) 50-123, *The Textile, Clothing and Footwear Union of Australia and the Council of Textile and Fashion Industries Limited* (2000) ATPR (Com) 50-282, *Steggles Limited and Others* A30183, 20 May 1998, all of which dealt with improved workplace, safer products and the right to appeal respectively.

38 Asher, 12.

39 ibid, 11–12.

the ACCC is currently considering such factors, either in the context of public benefit or via the imposition of conditions aimed at lessening the detriment that may flow from such proposed conduct.

Many organisations, such as the NSW Office of Fair Trading, adopt the human rights framework to explain their mandate. In this office, eight international consumer rights are used as a starting point: the right to safety, the right to be informed, the right to choose, the right to be heard, the right to satisfaction of basic needs, the right to redress, the right to consumer education, and the right to a healthy environment. Recently, a former deputy chair, Louise Sylvan, argued for a firmer connection between competition policy and consumer policy and has urged that consideration be given to the outcomes certain types of actions may have on both consumers and competition.[40] Thinking of the manner in which authorisations can benefit consumers may be one way of doing so. Many of the ACCC determinations can be cast in terms of such rights. In *Abbott Australasia Pty Ltd and Nestle Australia Limited*,[41] manufacturers and importers of infant formula applied for authorisation for its marketing obligations, which included exclusionary provisions. The commission granted authorisation and cited the Australian Government's commitment to the World Health Organisation International Code of Marketing of Breast Milk Substitutes, adopted by Australia in 1981. In 1983 Australian manufacturers and importers adopted a voluntary code based on this.

Not all issues involve human rights and this cannot be dismissed in developing an appropriate framework. The *Qantas and Air New Zealand*, the *Port Waratah* and the *Australian Payments Clearing Association* authorisations are three examples where the reasoning of the decisions did not involve human rights.[42] In such cases the benefits cannot easily be couched in terms of human rights, as enunciated in the international covenants. The *Qantas and Air New Zealand* authorisation concerned a proposed alliance between Qantas and Air New Zealand over specific routes as a response to competition from other airlines, in *Port Waratah* the authorisation involved an agreement between producers of coal to establish a distribution system for loading ships for export and, in *Australian Payments Clearing Association*, the authorisation dealt with membership of the body responsible for the implementation of effective payments clearing and settlement systems. Human rights are applicable, however, in the vast majority of cases and, here, the manner in which human rights are understood has to be

---

40   Louise Sylvan, 'Activating Competition: The Consumer–Competition Interface' (2004) 12(2) *Competition and Consumer Law Journal* 191. See also Jeremy Tustin and Rhonda Smith, 'Joined-up Consumer and Competition Policy: Some Comments' (2005) 12(3) *Competition and Consumer Law Journal* 305.

41   *Abbott Australasia Pty Ltd and Nestle Australia Limited* (1992) ATPR (Com) 50-123. See also Sitesh Bhojani, '"Public Benefits" under the *Trade Practices* Act' (Paper presented at the Joint Conference: Competition Law and the Professions, Perth, WA 11 April 1997) 4–5.

42   See *Qantas and Air New Zealand* A90862, A90863, A30220, A30221, 9 September 2003, *Port Waratah* A90650, 25 March 1998 and *Australian Payments Clearing Association Limited* A90617–A90619, 1 April 1998.

explored. It is widely accepted that human rights remain an incomplete idea because they are indeterminate and nearly criterion-less.[43] James Griffin points to the example of the right to health, which gives no indication of whether this refers to health or health care.[44] Does it mean it is a right to welfare that supports health, such as antibiotics, or education about medicines and disease-prevention measures. Could it mean, as some argue, every child living in the tropics has a right to a mosquito net to protect them from malaria? What it means will depend on the society in which it is being considered and the other priorities it is being considered alongside.[45] On the other hand, a right to health will universally mean more than a right to health care: for example, it will mean a right to clean air and clean water. Griffin proposes there are two ways to use philosophy to supply a more substantive account of human rights: the top-down and the bottom-up approach:

> There is the top down approach: one starts with an overarching principle, or principles or an authoritative decision procedure — say, the principle of utility or the Categorical Imperative or the model of parties to a contract reaching agreement — from which human rights can be derived. Most accounts of rights in philosophy these days are top-down. Then there is a bottom-up approach: one starts with human rights as used in our actual social life by politicians, lawyers, social campaigners, as well as theorists or various sorts, and then sees what higher principles one must resort to in order to explain their moral weight, when one thinks they have it, and to resolve conflicts between them.[46]

One clarification is required at this point — to distinguish between primary duties and secondary duties. Griffin points to this distinction and proposes that, while primary duties have the same content as the human right, secondary duties are those duties more loosely connected to the human right. The example used by Griffin is the duty to ensure compliance with human rights. Here it is clear that institutions populated by legislators, judges and police are necessary to create a just legal system to ensure compliance with human rights., The duty to create a just legal system, however, is not identical to a primary duty. Griffin calls this a secondary duty. Because this secondary duty is necessary for the primary duty to be given effect, the two duties are close enough to be treated for practical purposes as one. With the determination of public benefits, the duty to ensure that any person whose rights are violated shall have an effective remedy by virtue of Article 2 of the International Covenant on Civil and

---

43 James Griffin, *On Human Rights* (2008) 14.
44 ibid, 14, 99–101.
45 ibid, 99–100.
46 ibid, 29.

Political Rights (ICCPR) will be a primary duty. But setting up appeals systems within codes of conduct and prescribing the constituency of the appeals panels will be a secondary duty. The setting up of compliance systems to circumvent the breach of this duty is one further step removed from setting up appeals mechanisms. But, it too is linked to the human right and is called a called a controversial secondary duty. The discussion below examines both the primary and secondary (including controversial secondary) duties attached to the human right.

I explore both these approaches to evaluate their applicability to determining public benefits. In the following discussion I have first considered public benefits that have been acknowledged in practice (in Chapters 3, 4 and 6) and categorised them into a list of 22 separate public benefits (Table 7.1). Next, I have looked at how many would be accommodated by the top-down approach to human rights; 13 do not have a place. Then, I have applied the bottom-up approach to human rights, which is more accommodating, but still leaves out 11 public benefits. I then created a set of heuristics, which recognise ACCC practice, while also being faithful to human rights and can accommodate the 15 public benefits contained in the ACCC lists.

Using the Top-down and Bottom-up Approaches

All the public benefits (PB) discussed in Chapters 3, 4 and 6 have been collated and assessed to see if they can be accommodated by Griffin's top-down and bottom-up approach to human rights. Before doing so, I want to briefly refer to the public benefits to be considered. Chapters 1 and 3 noted 15 specific examples of public benefits that the ACCC considers as a non-exhaustive list (Table 7.1, column A).[47] Chapter 4 added seven further public benefits that have been recognised by the ACCC in practice to the non-exhaustive list (Table 7.1, column B). In the discussion on outcome-based discretion in Chapter 6, it was noted that the ACCC imposed conditions related to enhancing compliance; promoting fairness and justice (by requiring increased transparency and incorporating complaints mechanisms within codes of conduct); and related to facilitating deregulation. These were also public benefits recognised by the ACCC when it granted authorisations (Table 7.1, column C). There are three overlaps (indicated in Table 7.1 with data on same row): the right to due process and the right to justice overlaps with promoting fairness and justice, facilitating deregulation is in both columns B and C, and encouraging compliance and self-regulation overlaps with enhancing compliance. Of the 22 public benefits recognised in earlier chapters (Table 7.1), 15 are recognised by the ACCC in its lists (PB1–PB15) and seven are recognised by the ACCC in its practice (PB16–PB22).

---

47 Note that the category of 'Other' is not included here.

Table 7.1: Public benefits acknowledged in practice

Number of public benefits (PB) discussed	A. Public benefits recognised by the ACCC in its lists and discussed in chapters 1 and 3	B. Public benefits recognised by the ACCC in practice and discussed in chapter 4	C. Public benefits resulting from the imposition of conditions and discussed in chapter 6
PB1	Economic development		
PB2	Industry rationalisation		
PB3	Expansion of employment or prevention of unemployment in efficient industries		
PB4	Expansion of employment in particular areas		
PB5	Attainment of industry harmony		
PB6	Supply of better information to consumers and businesses		
PB7	Promotion of equitable dealings in the market		
PB8	Promotion of industry cost savings		
PB9	Development of import replacements		
PB10	Growth in export markets		
PB11	Steps to protect the environment		
PB12	Fostering business efficiency		
PB13	Assistance to efficient small business		
PB14	Enhancement of the quality and safety of goods and services		
PB15	Promotion of competition in the industry		
PB16		Regulation of illegal activity	
PB17		Health of patients, consumers and worker	

Number of public benefits (PB) discussed	A. Public benefits recognised by the ACCC in its lists and discussed in chapters 1 and 3	B. Public benefits recognised by the ACCC in practice and discussed in chapter 4	C. Public benefits resulting from the imposition of conditions and discussed in chapter 6
PB18		Right to due process and right to justice	Promoting fairness and justice (through complaints mechanisms and increased transparency)
PB19		Facilitation of deregulation of industries	Facilitating deregulation
PB20		Encouraging compliance and self-regulation	Enhancing compliance
PB21		Promotion of ethical conduct	
PB22		Protection of certain vulnerable sectors in society	

Source: Author's research.

Top-down Approach to Human Rights in Determining Public Benefits

Here I use the international bill of rights as constituted by the Universal Declaration of Human Rights 1948, ICCPR 1966 and the International Covenant on Economic Social and Cultural Rights 1966 (ICESCR), to derive the main human rights that can be linked to public benefits.[48] I begin with an explanation of the main instruments of international human rights, followed by an examination of how public benefits in practice may fit into the human rights enshrined in these instruments.

The Universal Declaration of Human Rights 1948 provides the starting point for any discussion of human rights. It defines human rights as basic rights that form the foundation for freedom, justice and peace and which apply equally and universally in all countries. The two major instruments of international human rights that derive from the declaration are the ICCPR and the ICESCR. Both have been ratified by Australia. The ICCPR is often referred to as the *first generation of human rights* — such as the right to life, the right to liberty and security, the right to a fair trial, the right to privacy, the right to freedom of thought, conscience and religion, opinion, expression, peaceful assembly and association. The ICESPR is referred to as the *second generation of human rights* and covers such rights as the right to work, the right to an adequate

---

48   Griffin (2008) 29. See also Tom Campbell, 'Introduction', in Tom Campbell and Seumas Miller (eds), *Human Rights and the Moral Responsibilities of Corporate and Public Sector Organisations* (2004) 12.

standard of living (food, clothing and housing) and the right to physical and mental health. The *third generation of human rights* that has emerged in recent years covers collective rights, such as the right to self-determination and the right to economic and social development. These rights have been championed primarily by developing nations within the United Nations, but have 'been only cautiously accepted by the mainstream international human rights community because of their challenge to the western, liberal model of individual rights invocable against the sovereign'.[49] While briefly touched on in the ICCPR, these rights have not yet been incorporated into any legally binding equivalent covenant or treaty.

These covenants do not deal with specifics but rather provide the framework for reform agendas within different nation states. They comprise non-exhaustive lists that are criterionless, leaving it to states and other bodies to fill in the details.[50] Some of these rights may not be considered as rights at all. Griffin argues that many statements in the international covenants are unlikely to be human rights and gives the example of Article 12 in the declaration, which deals with the rights to protection against attacks on one's honour and reputation, or Article 20, which states that any propaganda for war shall be prohibited by law.[51] Griffin proposes that practicalities need to inform the content of many human rights. By this he is referring to local conditions in the relevant country, as well as global considerations about human nature, which will inform the content of such rights.[52]

Often, national laws are not cast in terms of human rights even though it may be possible to do so, as illustrated by the development of industrial laws in Australia. Industrial laws could be hung on the human rights hook using articles 6 and 7 of the ICCPR, which are extremely general and provide for the right to work and the right to the enjoyment of just and favourable conditions of work. In many countries, however, including Australia, there has been a tendency to separate the developments in the workplace from the more recent developments of human rights jurisprudence.[53] More recently the focus has turned to the link between global finance and human rights and the need to 'close the gap' so as to ensure that global finance does not undermine human rights protections, but

49   Hilary Charlesworth, 'What are "Women's International Human Rights"?', in Rebecca J Cook (ed), *Human Rights of Women: National and International Perspectives* (1994) 58, 75.
50   Griffin (2008) 29–56.
51   ibid, 194–95.
52   ibid, 316.
53   For a discussion of some of the reasons for this in the area of industrial laws, see Peter Bailey, *Human Rights: Australia in an International Context* (1990) 360–62; see also Christine Williams, 'Sexual Harassment and Human Rights Law in New Zealand' (2003) 2(4) *Journal of Human Rights* 573, where it is argued that human rights may provide the appropriate vehicle to regulate sexual harassment.

rather can be used in ways to enhance human rights ends.[54] In support of this argument, it is possible to consider the ICESCR and other initiatives, such as the UN Environment Programme Finance Initiative.

Ratification of international instruments creates the basis for a legitimate expectation that administrative decision-makers will act in conformity with these instruments. Accordingly, the ACCC must take the international covenants into account in its decision-making. There remains, however, the problem of defining the kind of activities that are protected by the covenants.[55] In the past, the ACCC paid attention to what can be conceived of as human rights obligations in its authorisation decisions. In *Association of Fluorocarbon Consumers and Manufacturers Inc*,[56] it was recognised that the commission could consider not only state and national legislation but also international obligations and standards. Here there was no relevant and applicable national or state legislation, and the relevant international standards on emission of ozone-depleting substances had been established under international protocols. The control of hydrocholorofluorocarbon (HCFC) and hydrofluorocarbon (HFC) gases was dealt with by the Montreal Protocol 1987 and Kyoto Protocol 1997 respectively. The Association of Fluorocarbon Consumers and Manufacturers argued that one of the public benefits would be to encourage industrial activity consistent with Australia's domestic ozone protection policies and Australia's international obligations.[57] The commission accepted this proposition and stated: 'a scheme or arrangement which contributes to limiting the risk to human health and the improvement of the environment would benefit the Australian public'.[58] Further rights recognised in the ACCC's decision-making include the right to health and the right to ethical treatment by professionals.[59]

Table 7.2 links recognised human rights, as expressed in the international covenants that Australia has signed, to recognised public benefits detailed in Table 7.1. Public benefits are separated into three categories: public benefits that can be linked to a primary human right; public benefits that can be linked to a secondary human right or controversial secondary human right; and public benefits that cannot be linked to any human right.

---

54 Dowell Jones and Kinley (2011) 203–04.

55 See Ian Forrester, 'Modernization of EC Competition Law' (2000) 23 *Fordham International Law Review*, 1028, 1070, for a discussion on how human rights could be used in the European Union in cases of breaches of competition.

56 *Association of Fluorocarbon Consumers and Manufacturers Inc* A90658, 26 August 1998.

57 ibid, 4.

58 ibid, 10.

59 For a discussion of the right to health see the discussion on Health of Patients, Consumers and Workers in Chapter 4 of this book. For an example of professional ethics in codes see *ACT Law Society* authorisation A75 (1977) ATPR (Com) 16,615 where the society adopted a ruling that solicitors were prevented, except in certain circumstances, from acting for both the vendor and purchaser in the sale of land.

Table 7.2: Public benefits linked to human rights

	Human right (where relevant)	Public benefit
Public benefits that can be linked to recognised human rights	ICECSR, Article 7 — the right of everyone to the enjoyment of just and favourable conditions of work	Expansion of employment or the prevention of unemployment in efficient industries (PB3)
	ICECSR, Article 7 — the right of everyone to the enjoyment of just and favourable conditions of work	Expansion of employment in particular areas (PB4)
	ICECSR, Article 12 — the right of everyone to the enjoyment of the highest attainable standard of physical and mental health including the improvement of all aspects of environmental and industrial hygiene. Widely accepted as a third generation right	Steps to protect the environment (PB11)
	ICECSR, Article 12 — the right of everyone to the enjoyment of the highest attainable standard of physical and mental health, which can include increased consumer safety	Enhancement of the quality and safety of goods and services (PB14)
	ICECSR, Article 12 — the right of everyone to the enjoyment of the highest attainable standard of physical and mental health including provision of medical service and medical attention in the event of sickness and ICECSR, Article 7 — the right of everyone to the enjoyment of just and favourable conditions of work, including safe and healthy working conditions	Health of patients, consumers and workers (PB17)
Public benefits that can be linked to a secondary or controversial human right	ICCPR, Article 2 — ensure that any person whose rights are violated shall have an effective remedy and to ensure that any person claiming such a remedy shall have his right thereto determined by competent judicial, administrative or legislative authorities, or by any other competent authority provided for by the legal system of the state	Promotion of equitable dealings (PB7) (controversial secondary right)
	ICCPR, Article 2 — ensure that any person whose rights are violated shall have an effective remedy and to ensure that any person claiming such a remedy shall have his right thereto determined by competent judicial, administrative or legislative authorities, or by any other competent authority provided for by the legal system of the state	Assistance to efficient small businesses (controversial secondary right) (PB13)
	ICCPR, Article 2 — ensure that any person whose rights are violated shall have an effective remedy and to ensure that any person claiming such a remedy shall have his right thereto determined by competent judicial, administrative or legislative authorities, or by any other competent authority provided for by the legal system of the state	Rights to due process and justice/Promoting fairness and justice (secondary right) (PB18)
	ICECSR, Article 12 — the right of everyone to the enjoyment of the highest attainable standard of physical and mental health	Protection of certain vulnerable sectors in the society (secondary right) (PB22)

Human right (where relevant)	Public benefit
Public benefits that cannot be linked to a human right	Economic development (PB1)
	Industry rationalisation (PB2)
	Attainment of industry harmony (PB5)
	Supply of better information to consumers and business (PB6)
	Promotion of industry cost savings (PB8)
	Development of import substitution (PB9)
	Growth in export markets (PB10)
	Fostering business efficiency (PB12)
	Promotion of competition in the industry (PB15)
	Regulation of illegal activity (secondary right) (PB16)
	Facilitating deregulation (PB19)
	Encouraging compliance (PB20)
	Promotion of ethical conduct (PB21)

Source: Author's research.

As seen from Table 7.2, only five public benefits, four that have been included in the ACCC lists and one in ACCC practice, can be linked to recognised human rights, namely Article 7 and Article 12 of the ICESCR. There are seven public benefits that can be termed secondary or controversial secondary rights, all dealing with Article 2 of the ICCPR and Article 12 of the ICESCR. Of these, three can be found in the ACCC lists and four have been recognised by the ACCC in practice.

Of these four public benefits, two are secondary human rights, as they are creating mechanisms or pathways to give effect to the primary human right: right to due process and justice/promoting fairness and justice and the protection of vulnerable sectors of society. The former is creating pathways to the primary right enshrined in Article 2 of the ICCPR because they can be seen as creating a competent authority for ensuring that any person whose rights are violated has an effective remedy. The later public benefit of protecting vulnerable sectors of society is creating a pathway to the right enshrined in Article 12 of the ICESCR, as it is an attempt to provide for a reasonable standard of mental and physical health.

The two remaining public benefits are less clear-cut than the above four, and are classified as controversial secondary rights: promotion of equitable dealings and assistance to efficient small businesses. All these public benefits are linked to the right to freedom of association. We know restrictions on trade union activities will be clearly an infringement on the freedom of an association. It is not so easy, however, to make the same conclusions about competition law, which at its very core strikes at different types of associations such as cartels. These public benefits recognise that certain forms of association are appropriate — thus the promotion of equitable dealings, aimed at empowering smaller companies and not afforded to companies with market power, should be allowed. They are not constraints and they do not apply to all types of businesses or companies. They are means of facilitating associations by certain businesses or companies and, although controversial, they can be linked to the right to freedom of association. The same logic can be applied to the assistance to efficient small businesses that can engage in conduct that would not be countenanced by businesses with market share. Accordingly they are classified as controversial secondary human rights in Table 7.2.

There are 13 public benefits that cannot be linked to human rights (Table 7.2), nine of which are in the ACCC lists and four that come out of ACCC practice. An argument could be made to classify the regulation of illegal activity, supply of better information to consumers and business, and encouraging compliance, as secondary rights. This would be on the basis that, like the discussion on access to justice, providing countervailing power, enabling equitable dealing and empowering small business, these three above-mentioned rights may be viewed as secondary human rights, as they are necessary to give effect to a primary human right. I have not classified them in this manner, however, because they cannot be as directly linked to recognised human rights. Accordingly, I have placed them under the heading 'Public benefits that cannot be linked to a human right' (Table 7.2).

It is difficult, by any stretch of the imagination, to include benefits flowing from import substitution and the promotion of cost savings into any of the categories of human rights. Some of these may be, however, in specific circumstances, capable of being linked to a human right. For example, economic development in certain circumstances may be linked to the human right of the right to development.[60]

---

60 This right was proclaimed by the United Nations in 1986 in the Declaration on the Right to Development, which was adopted by the United Nations General Assembly resolution 41/128. The preamble states

It is difficult to see, however, these circumstances existing in Australia, which is generally regarded as a developed nation. Likewise, encouraging compliance, if it is aimed at the provision of an appeal process or improving the safety of goods produced, may be linked to a human right of access to a fair hearing or the attainment of the highest attainable standard of physical health. Compliance is usually encouraged for other purposes, however, such as the promotion of self-regulation or improving consumers access to information. Although, in some circumstances, some of these public benefits may be linked to a human right, this is unlikely to occur often and drawing such linkages is tenuous at best. In conclusion, although the top down approach to human rights can accommodate some public benefits, it does not easily accommodate the majority of public benefits that have been recognised.

Bottom-up Approach to Human Rights in Determining Public Benefit

Griffin's bottom up approach starts with human rights as used in our actual social life by politicians, lawyers and social campaigners and then sees what higher principle to resort to in order to explain their moral weight.[61] This approach may be better suited for the purpose of determining public benefit. It also comports with the real world of philosophical pragmatism in which authorisation evolved. It might be said in the same spirit that the case method of the common law is a device for discovering such benefits in a way that is philosophically bottom-up. The 22 public benefits collated in Table 7.1 are a combination of ACCC lists and practice and I have categorised these benefits under broad headings, which I have called immanent rights. Where relevant I have matched up the public benefit to an existing international covenant, as discussed in Table 7.2.

Of the 22 public benefits, 11 cannot be linked to an immanent right, related to either the functioning of the market or the promotion of ethical conduct (Table 7.3). There are nine dealing with the functioning of the market: economic development, industry rationalisation, attainment of industry harmony, promotion of industry cost savings, development of import replacements, growth of export markets, fostering business efficiency, promotion of competition in the industry, and facilitation of deregulation. There are two public benefits dealing with the promotion of ethical conduct: promotion of equitable dealings in the market and the promotion of ethical conduct. The remaining nine public benefits are linked to six immanent rights: right to quality of life; right to just treatment and just procedure; right to freedom of association; right to security; right to know; and right to securing rights.

'development is a comprehensive economic, social, cultural and political process, which aims at the constant improvement of the well-being of the entire population and of all individuals on the basis of their active, free and meaningful participation in development and in the fair distribution of benefits resulting there from.'
61   Griffin (2008) 29.

Table 7.3: Public benefits linked to immanent rights

Number of public benefits (PB) discussed	Public benefits recognised by ACCC	Relationship to human rights	Immanent right
PB1	Economic development	Cannot be linked to a human right	No clear immanent right (related to the functioning of the market)
PB2	Industry rationalisation	Cannot be linked to a human right	No clear immanent right (related to the functioning of the market)
PB3	Expansion of employment or prevention of unemployment in efficient industries	ICECSR, Article 7	Improve quality of life
PB4	Expansion of employment in particular areas	ICECSR, Article 7	Improve quality of life
PB5	Attainment of industry harmony	Cannot be linked to a human right	No clear immanent right (related to the functioning of the market)
PB6	Supply of better information to consumers and businesses	Cannot be linked to a human right	Right to know
PB7	Promotion of equitable dealings in the market	ICCPR, Article 2 (controversial secondary right)	No clear immanent right (related to the promotion of ethical conduct)
PB8	Promotion of industry cost savings	Cannot be linked to a human right	No clear immanent right (related to the functioning of the market)
PB9	Development of import replacements	Cannot be linked to a human right	No clear immanent right (related to the functioning of the market)
PB10	Growth in export markets	Cannot be linked to a human right	No clear immanent right (related to the functioning of the market)
PB11	Steps to protect the environment	ICECSR, Article 12	Improve quality of life
PB12	Fostering business efficiency	Cannot be linked to a human right	No clear immanent right (related to the functioning of the market)
PB13	Assistance to efficient small business	ICCPR, Article 2 (controversial secondary right)	Right to freedom of association
PB14	Enhancement of the quality and safety of goods and services	ICECSR, Article 12	Improve quality of life
PB15	Promotion of competition in the industry	Cannot be linked to a human right	No clear immanent right (related to the functioning of the market)
PB16	Regulation of illegal activity	Cannot be linked to a human right	Right to security
PB17	Health of patients, consumers and worker	ICECSR Article 12	Improve quality of life

Number of public benefits (PB) discussed	Public benefits recognised by ACCC	Relationship to human rights	Immanent right
PB18	Right to due process and right to justice/ promoting fairness and justice (eg through complaints mechanisms)	ICCPR, Article 2 (secondary right)	Right to just treatment and just procedure
PB19	Facilitation of deregulation	Cannot be linked to a human right	No clear immanent right (related to the functioning of the market)
PB20	Encouraging compliance	Cannot be linked to a human right	Right to securing rights
PB21	Promotion of ethical conduct	Cannot be linked to a human right	No clear immanent right (related to the promotion of ethical conduct)
PB22	Protection of certain vulnerable sectors in society	ICECSR, Article 12 (secondary right)	Improve quality of life

Source: Author's research.

This bottom-up approach (Table 7.3) works better than the top-down approach (Table 7.2) because it is able to link many more public benefits to human rights as they are widely understood in the broader community. Nevertheless, a total of 11 public benefits, related to the functioning of the market and the promotion of ethical conduct, do not have a natural home within an accepted immanent right. It is foreseeable that many more public benefits related to the promotion of ethical conduct are likely to arise in the future. Examples include voluntary agreements between corporations or associations reflecting climate change or environmental concerns, initiatives related to greater corporate social responsibility, increased disclosure of information to the public by corporations, and greater consideration given to specific sectors by corporations. It is possible that corporations decide to adopt a code of conduct that only allows them to deal with corporations that have the backing of the Organisation for Economic Co-operation and Development (OECD) or a non-government organisation (NGO) such as Amnesty International.[62] Likewise, corporations in the post-financial crisis market may wish to incorporate greater disclosure of financial information or make agreements among industry members on salary caps for senior executives. Other corporations, responding to the needs of the neighbouring Pacific states, may decide to give preferential treatment to workers from these states, to the

---

62 Doreen McBarret, 'Human Rights, Corporate Responsibility and the New Accountability' in Campbell and Miller (2004) 71.

exclusion of all others.[63] Such agreements could require authorisation and bring considerable public benefits. A framework that can accommodate all these benefits is necessary and is explored below.

Creating a Framework Based on Human Rights and Empirics

It is proposed that a set of heuristics can be developed to accommodate all the 22 public benefits. While recognising ACCC practice, these heuristics would be faithful to human rights principles, as generally accepted by the community. This set of heuristics consists of seven groupings: quality of life, market integrity, equitable dealings among market actors, economic efficiency and economic welfare, procedural fairness, increased enforceability and human security (Table 7.4).

Table 7.4: Locating public benefits based on rights and empirics

Public benefit (PB)	Immanent rights or recognised human rights	Heuristic
Enhancement of the quality and safety of goods and services (PB14)	Immanent right (improve quality of life) Also top down human right (Article 12 ICESR)	
Expansion of employment or prevention of unemployment in efficient industries (PB3)	Immanent right (improve quality of life) Also top down human right (Article 7 ICESR)	
Health of patients, consumers and worker (PB17)	Immanent right (improve quality of life) Also top down human right (Article 12 ICESR)	Improve quality of life
Steps to protect the environment (PB11)	Immanent right (improve quality of life) Also top down human right (Article 12 ICESR)	
Expansion of employment in particular areas (PB4)	Immanent right (improve quality of life) Also top down human right (Article 7ICESR)	

---

63 See Manjula Luthria, 'Guest Workers: A Pacific Solution that Benefits All', *Sydney Morning Herald*, 24 June 2008, 11; see also Allan Fels and Fred Brenchley, 'Black Jobs Gap Still a Chasm After Decades', *Sydney Morning Herald*, 13–14 December 2008, 39.

Public benefit (PB)	Immanent rights or recognised human rights	Heuristic
Promotion of equitable dealings in the market (PB7)	Immanent right (right to freedom of association) Also a secondary right	Provide for equitable dealings among market actors
Assistance to efficient small business (PB13)	Immanent right (right to freedom of association) Also a secondary right	
Attainment of industry harmony (PB5)	No clear immanent right	
Supply of better information to consumers and businesses (PB6)	Immanent right (right to know)	Increase market integrity
Promotion of ethical conduct (PB21)		
Protection of certain vulnerable sectors in society (PB22)		
Economic development (PB1)	No clear immanent right	Encourage economic efficiency and welfare
Industry rationalisation (PB2)	No clear immanent right	
Promotion of industry cost savings (PB8)	No clear immanent right	
Development of import replacements (PB9)	No clear immanent right	
Development of import replacements (PB9)	No clear immanent right	
Growth in export markets (PB10)	No clear immanent right	
Fostering business efficiency (PB12)	No clear immanent right	
Facilitating competition (PB15)	No clear immanent right	
Regulation of illegal activity (PB16)	Immanent right (right to security) Also a secondary right	Provide human security
Right to due process and right to justice/promoting fairness and justice (eg through complaints mechanisms) (PB18)	Immanent right (rights to just treatment and just procedure) Also a top down right (Article 2 ICCPR)	Enhance procedural fairness
Encouraging compliance (PB20)	Means of securing rights ACCC practice	Increasing enforceability

Source: Author's research.

These groupings make it possible to express public benefit as a principle in the following terms:

> *Principle: A public benefit can fall into one of the following categories: secure a basic human right, improve quality of life, provide for equitable dealings among market actors, increase market integrity, encourage economic efficiency and economic welfare, provide for human security, enhance procedural fairness and increase enforceability.*

It is proposed that this framework for public benefits, based on both the empirical data as well as the recognised human rights, will work more effectively than the present ad hoc approach, which has been described as a triumph of practice over theory. This framework is grounded on a widely accepted discourse as well as reflecting practice; it is inclusive while providing greater guidance to applicants and all stakeholders; it will allow both efficiency-based benefits as well as non-efficiency benefits; it will be flexible enough to accommodate new public benefits as they arise without adding to the existing list of public benefits; and it will reflect an approach which is universally understood both by applicants as well as all other interested parties.

Promoting Responsiveness

The manner in which regulatory agencies have changed the way in which they function reflects the changes in the wider society including the role of governments and the increasing importance of local and global networks. Chapter 6 examines the manner in which regulatory agencies today do the complex business of regulating. It also discusses the strategies available to these agencies and ties them to the theory underlying the strategies. The ACCC has been an innovative regulator, using a great variety of strategies from its inception, as demonstrated in the discussion in Chapter 2 on the distinctive trajectory that is the authorisation process. The ACCC has been quick to adapt to the changes in the wider society, as demonstrated in Chapter 6 by the manner in which it has used its discretion to facilitate desired outcomes. As one of Australia's main corporate regulators, the ACCC has faced considerable scrutiny (discussed in Chapter 5). It has been conscious of the scrutiny and has addressed it, sometimes with military precision, illustrated by the format closely followed in the determinations,[64] the consistent references to accountability[65] and the websites which have been redesigned to provide minutes of all meetings.[66] This

---

64   See the section on Causal Link — The Benefit Must Flow from the Conduct, in Chapter 3.
65   See the discussion on Accountability in Chapter 5.
66   See the discussion on Procedural Discretion in Chapter 6.

is further supported by a recent study that points to overall business satisfaction with the ACCC's strategic sophistication and how procedural and substantive justice is accommodated.[67]

As discussed in Chapter 6, however, there remains at least one important criticism — the participation by certain non-industry groups has fallen. This issue becomes more important in a deregulated market and a decentred regulatory environment, where there is an important role for non-industry groups to bring relevant information to the regulator and to contest settlements that are 'cosy' for the regulator and regulatee but not for civil society. It is connected to the notion of procedural justice and how the regulator is perceived (discussed in Chapter 6).

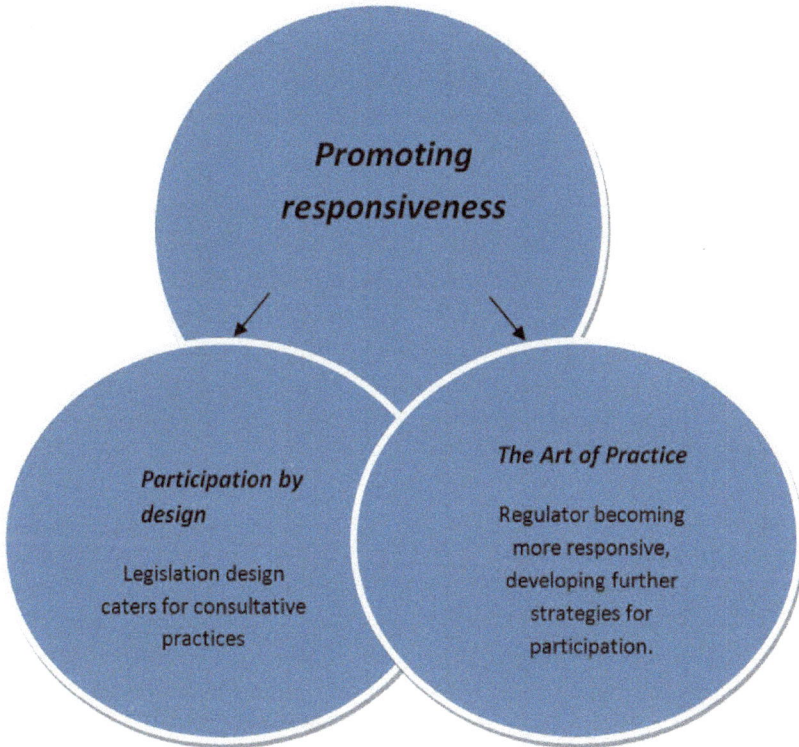

Figure 7.1: Two methods for promoting institutional responsibility

Source: Author's research.

Advocates of responsive regulation and restorative justice would see the importance of welcoming the voice of dissidents, engaging in an ongoing dialogue and incorporating mechanisms for facilitating participation, all of

---

67   Parker and Nielsen (2007).

which foster principles of democracy.[68] Here, I want to canvas two methods to improve responsiveness of the regulator in increasing participation: participation by design and the art of practice (Figure 7.1). These methods are not mutually exclusive; rather they work together and the catalytic mix will depend on the conduct and the context, as discussed below.

Participation by Design

One way to increase the regulator's responsiveness is through legislative design. This is a top-down process where the legislature allows for a new and more consultative process of administration. Law that enables consultative process, as does the *Trade Practices Act*, will provide a sound foundation for the institution to develop channels of communication with the groups it seeks to regulate. Law that relies more on broad principles rather than concise rules, providing the regulatory institution with the fiat for formulating specific policy in consultation with regulated groups, may be more successful in allowing the institution to assume responsibility for its actions.

Design alone is not sufficient to allow for participation. Discretion exercised in interpreting the provision is also necessary. For example, lodging authorisation applications previously incurred a standard fee of $7500, which was particularly onerous for not-for-profit organisations.[69] Following an amendment to the Act, the ACCC is now provided with the power to waive the lodgment fee if it is satisfied that its imposition would impose an undue burden on the applicant.[70] Schedule 1B of the regulations lists the concessional fee for these non-merger applications at $1500, and the ACCC *Guide to Authorisations 2007* provides that the fee for such groups will be $2500, illustrating the effect of practice within a minor rule.

Designing specific pathways for non-industry groups to participate is one way of creating a level playing field where all the parties affected by a decision are heard. The main pathways are represented in Figure 7.2. While the first and second pathways are relevant to ACCC determinations of authorisations, the third pathway is less so. It has been included to provide a complete picture of how participation can be incorporated via legislative design.

---

68   Valerie Braithwaite (ed), 'Responsive Regulation and Taxation: Introduction' (2007) 29 (1) special issue *Law and Policy* 5; see also Parker, *The Open Corporation: Effective Self-Regulation and Democracy* (2002) 40; John Braithwaite, *Restorative Justice and Responsive Regulation* (2002) 10; Robert Baldwin and Julia Black, 'Really Responsive Regulation' (2008) 71(1) *Modern Law Review* 59.
69   See Committee of Inquiry, Commonwealth of Australia, *Review of the Competition Provisions of the Trade Practices Act* [Dawson Review] (2003) 113, for discussion on waiver of such fees for particular types of applicants.
70   Regulation 75, Trade Practices Regulations 1974.

The first pathway is to equip the general regulator with the power to take the interests of different parties into account. The main interest considered is the consumer or the public. As discussed in Chapter 2, the design of the *Trade Practices Act* provides for consultation and participation. It requires the commission to take into account submissions made by the applicant, Commonwealth, state or any other person.[71] The legislation also prescribes that a draft determination has to be issued,[72] that an interested party may call a pre-determination conference,[73] and the procedure for such conferences.[74] The legislation also provides a place for the National Competition Council, which is required to promote competition in the public interest, thereby giving effect to the Competition Principles Agreement.[75] As discussed in Chapter 5, the paradox of discretion is that it can exist within strict rules as well as vague phrases. The interpretation of the vague phrase 'public benefit' has given the ACCC considerable scope to exercise its discretion. This reiterates the point made above, that design alone may not be sufficient to ensure participation. The regulator has to use the discretion well.

Creating specific regulators for certain areas and empowering them to consider the interests of other groups that may be poorly represented is also an option. Such regulators gain an understanding of the industry and its participants, which is important in decision-making. As discussed in Chapter 6, such bodies make submissions and are part of the expanded accountability model that is recognised by the ACCC. For example the Australia Energy Regulator, which was created in 2005, is responsible for the regulation of the wholesale energy market. It prepares market reports and analysis on energy issues which informs the ACCC in its decisions. Likewise, the Australian Communications and Media Authority, a regulator of the Australian communications industry, also formed in 2005, performs a similar role informing debate. Through its Consumer Consultative Forum, the authority gains understanding of the manner in which consumers are affected by its functions. It consults with the ACCC about the possible impact new technology may have on its determinations. Such bodies are able to participate by making a formal submission (discussed in Chapter 6), or more informally, particularly when the ACCC gives effect to broader government objectives.

Legislation can be focused on a specific group. One example of legislation that provides such a direct legislative mandate to consider the wider interest is the UK

71 Section 90A(2).
72 Section 90A(1).
73 Section 90A(2).
74 Sections 90A(7) and 90A(8).
75 See National Competition Commission mission statement <http://www.ncc.gov.au/> For a discussion on the interpretation of the phrase 'public interest' in the context of this commission see John McDonald, 'Legitimating Private Interests: Hegemonic Control Over "the Public Interest" in National Competition Polity' (2007) 43(4) *Journal of Sociology* 349.

Communications Act 2003. Ofcom, the telecommunications regulator established by this Act, is mandated to represent consumers. This legislation provides that it shall be the principal duty of Ofcom, in carrying out their functions, to further the interests of citizens in relation to communications matters; and to further the interests of consumers in relevant markets, where appropriate by promoting competition.[76] In 2006 after an assessment of the manner in which consumer interests were addressed, Ofcom established a consumer policy team to address the manner in which it can improve its performance, illustrating the recognition given to the consumer voice.[77] This English regulator has a more specific mandate than its Australian counterparts.

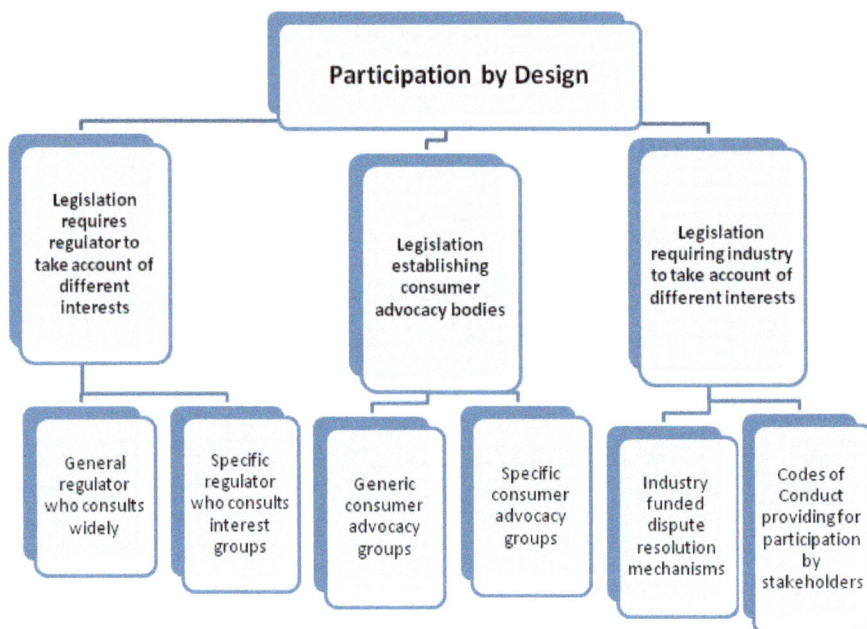

Figure 7.2: Participation by design

Source: Author's research.

The second pathway in Figure 7.2 is for legislation to create consumer advocacy bodies. Consumer advocacy groups historically have given voice for underrepresented and disadvantaged groups, enabling their interests to be considered as part of the consultative process. The Productivity Commission has recognised that consumer advocates have a role in providing a counterbalance to producer groups seeking to maintain anti-competitive arrangements that lead to

---

76   Section 3(1) Communications Act 2003 (UK).
77   Ofcom, 'Taking Account of Consumer and Citizen Interests' <http://www.ofcom.org.uk/about/accoun/interests.pdf> at 28 February 2007.

higher prices, reduced service quality or less market innovation.[78] Establishing consumer advocacy bodies to actively participate in decision-making requires political commitment and funding. The *Trade Practices Act* made a conscious link between consumer protection and competition issues (discussed in Chapter 2). Although the Australian Consumers Association (Choice) was started in 1963, many other groups originated later, in the 1970s. The government of the day solicited consumer involvement, giving impetus to the consumer movement, which continued to play an important role until the mid 1990s. Funding for such groups dried up and their role has diminished over the last decade. This is in contrast, however, to the numerous interest groups representing large consumers, such as the *Business Council of Australia* and small businesses, such as the Energy Users of Australia, that have been started. Such groups feel that their interests are ignored and have been actively participating in the authorisation process (discussed in Chapter 6).

The diminishing role of consumers has been acknowledged in the energy industry where user participation is much lower than supplier participation.[79] Currently, the chief consumer advocacy group is the Consumers Federation of Australia, which consists of more than 100 member groups, including: community legal centres, health rights groups, local consumer organisations and public interest bodies.[80] Although previously funded by government, it now relies on donations and voluntary work , hence its role has decreased. Its participation is restricted to making submissions in relation to key authorisation determinations.[81] Another body that is considered a leader in national consumer debate is the NGO Choice, which is funded by its membership. It too has made a number of submissions to the ACCC on authorisation determinations. It is second to the Australian Consumers Federation in making submissions on authorisation determinations included in the empirical study.[82] Other bodies exist at state level and include: the Public Interest Advocacy Centre in New South Wales, Consumer Utilities Advocacy Centre Ltd in Victoria and the Consumer Law Centre in Victoria. Some states, such as Victoria, have increased funding for advocacy bodies, including the Consumer Law Centre, the Consumer Credit Legal Service and the Financial

---

78 Productivity Commission, Commonwealth of Australia, Review of National Competition Policy Reforms — Discussion Draft (2004) 301.
79 Ministerial Council on Energy, (Department of Resources, Energy and Tourism), Commonwealth of Australia, *Reform of Energy Markets* (Report to the Councils on Australian Governments, 11 December 2003) 11.
80 See Consumer Federation of Australia <http://www.consumersfederation.org.au/> at 1 November 2008.
81 See Chapter 6 for a discussion of the instances where submissions were made by Consumers Federation of Australia or its predecessor. They include *United Permanent Building Society* (1976); *Re Surgeons* A90785, *Re EFTPOS* interchange fees A30224, A30225. Also see *Cash Convertors Pty Ltd* N70435 for a detailed submission to the ACCC <http://www.consumersfederation.org.au/documents/CLCV-FAsub171105reACCCauthorisation. pdf> at 30 April 2009.
82 See the discussion on Submissions by Non-industry bodies in Chapter 6.

and Consumer Rights Council. Smaller bodies dealing with specific issues, such as the Communications Law Centre, Consumers Health Forum of Australia and the Breast Cancer Action Group, have made submissions in their areas.

Unlike Australia, consumer advocacy groups have had a resurgence in the United Kingdom and the European Union. Specific bodies include energywatch, Postwatch and the National Consumer Council. These bodies were all merged, however, to form one, well-funded, national consumer council with extensive legislative powers called Consumer Focus.[83] The concern that the expertise that industry specific regulators have built up may be lost in this unified body has been voiced by energywatch.[84] The powers it has been given include the right to investigate any consumer complaint if they are of wider interest, the right to publish information from providers, the power to conduct research and the ability to make an official super-complaint about failing services.[85] Perhaps the strongest power of this body, which was also possessed by its predecessors, is the power to make a super-complaint. This power is given to specific consumer bodies via the *Enterprise Act 2002* (UK) and it is intended to provide a fast track process of resolution.[86] To date, six such complaints have been filed, demonstrating the role of such organisations in participating in enforcement and monitoring the market. The European approach has also been to provide financial support for the activities of consumer organisations.[87] It is important to acknowledge the advantages of having well-funded consumer bodies that can participate in consumer policy debates and advocacy and have a research facility with the expertise to make submissions on highly technical issues. To streamline such participation, the European Union has started a register of lobby groups.[88] Unlike the United Kingdom and the European Union, consumer and citizen representation is left in the hands of regulators in Australia. This places greater responsibility on the regulator to be responsive to the needs of such groups, and to be facilitative.

The third pathway in Figure 7.2 is a legislative requirement to incorporate participation by industry. This is usually via a variety of mechanisms, such as dispute resolution or complaints systems being included in codes of conduct.

---

83   This body is created by virtue of the *Consumers, Estate Agents and Redress Act 2007* (UK).

84   Asher, 'The National Consumer Congress; In Pursuit of World-class Consumer Policy', paper presented to Third Annual Consumer Congress, Consumer Affairs Victoria, Melbourne, 15–17 March 2006.

85   See Consumer Focus website <http://www.consumerfocus.org.uk/en/content/cms/About_Us/About_Us.aspx> at 1 December 2008.

86   Section 11 of the *Enterprise Act 2002* (UK).

87   See Article 2(b) Decision 283/1999/EC and 2003/C 132/04. Also see the *Enterprise Act 2002* (UK). The Dawson Committee looked at the possibility of introducing a super complaints procedure designed to enable consumer bodies to make complaints about conduct that may be significantly harming consumers; see [Dawson Review] (2003) 175. A super complaints body is looking at the role of consumer groups in enforcement rather than participating in the process of decision making on authorisation.

88   Leigh Phillips, 'Major Lobby Firms set to join EU register', *EUobserver* <http://euobserver.com/9/26744> at 30 October 2008.

Such measures are usually funded by a levy on industry members and it has been important in Australia, with examples including the Energy and Water Ombudsman of New South Wales[89] and the Banking and Financial Ombudsman. The main issue here is that such bodies can have difficulty balancing the competing interests of the industry that appoints its members and the consumers that make the complaint. Although this pathway is important to understanding the regulatory picture, it does not directly affect participation within the authorisation process and is not discussed further. It can, however, indirectly create accountability networks, which take better care of consumer and public interests.

In conclusion, there are numerous ways of designing legislation to provide for participation. The two main options relevant to this study are to design legislation mandating the regulator to consider the interests of all stakeholders or, alternatively, to give this power to government-funded consumer advocacy groups. The former is preferred in Australia, whereas both have a role in the European Union and the United Kingdom. There have been numerous calls for a national consumer council in Australia. Such a council would be expected to be funded by government but remain independent from it, while being a centre for a network of consumer advocacy and service agencies to connect in initiating debate, carrying out research and advocating policies.[90] These calls have not received any support from government to date in Australia. Thus, it is the Art of Practice, discussed below, that offers greater scope for increasing responsiveness in the current Australian socio-political environment.

The Art of Practice

As concluded in Chapter 6, the ACCC has exercised its discretion in an experimental manner, accommodating a variety of interests and giving effect to changing objectives at different times. This is perhaps best demonstrated by the manner in which it has used the conditions power in granting authorisations, and developing networks of governance structures among the private actors in the market. It has also been reasonably inclusive in its decision–making, demonstrated by its use of formal and informal mechanisms for participation. The major query raised in Chapter 6 is whether it has been responsive enough to non-industry groups. Three main tactics for becoming more responsive were canvassed in earlier chapters. First, interpreting the term 'public' to include the interests of a variety of constituencies, including consumers and community, will increase inclusivity. Second, processes that encourage participation by all groups should be facilitated. Third, a variety of benefits going beyond

---

89   See <http://www.ewon.com.au/> at 30 March 2008.
90   David Tennant, 'Australia's Desperate Need for a National Consumer Council' <http://www.consumersfederation.org.au/documents/NCCPaperbyDavidTennantMarch05.doc> 15 October 2008.

efficiency-based benefits have to be recognised. Another strategy that should be added to the above three is that the ACCC should set in motion a reflective process whereby it examines its own performance, makes an assessment and revises its approach as a result.

Chapter 4 discussed the meanings that can be attached to the term 'public' and the manner in which the ACT and ACCC had tackled this issue. It has a direct impact on the type of public benefits that will be accepted. The ACCC has made it clear that it will accept benefits accruing to a sectoral group, or to a wider group. This approach could be articulated as three principles in the following manner:

Principle: Anticompetitive conduct may be authorised if it results in a benefit to a specific group.

Principle: Anticompetitive conduct may be authorised if there is some consumer benefit.

Principle: These benefits will be weighed by the ACCC, bearing in mind the size of the benefits and the parties who are likely to benefit.

The empirical findings demonstrate that the manner in which the state and federal governments influence ACCC decisions has changed over the last four decades. Rather than directing the institution, these governments now participate in a more reserved manner, making written submissions like any other private actor, indicating their views on the matter under consideration. State and federal governments also send representatives to attend pre-decision conferences, and ministers have frequently commented on draft decisions. Particularly extensive submissions were made in relation to deregulated industries and the *Australian Wool Exchange Limited* authorisation. The Commonwealth Department of Primary Industries and Energy supported the self-regulating scheme that the deregulated industry was seeking to implement. In many of these cases, government departments and ministers see their role as one of assisting the ACCC to reach its decision rather than relying on it to cater to their interests.[91]

The empirical findings also illustrate that business groups and industry bodies have harnessed this consultative process most effectively. Formal written submissions by such groups to the ACCC have increased considerably from 1976 to 1998 when deregulatory policies were given effect. They have remained stable since. The ACCC had been able to facilitate business involvement in the authorisation process. There has been an attempt by the commission to reinforce the value of business involvement by clearly stating the influence such

---

91   *Australian Wool Exchange Limited* in relation to its business rules, determined on 30 December 1998, 28.

submissions had on its decisions. Such practices became important in gaining business confidence and support. As has been noted, lore can be as important as law and often agency practice becomes embodied in law.[92] The ACCC must, however, attend to accusations of capture and safeguard its independence. The following principle would have such an effect:

> *Principle: Assessing public benefits in authorisations involves assessing total welfare, while being mindful of the risk of concentrated business interests capturing debate to undervalue consumer welfare.*

The empirical study demonstrates that participation by business groups, industry bodies as well as state and federal governments has risen steadily. It also demonstrates, however, that participation by the not-for-profit groups has not been similarly and consistently increasing. Here, participation varies significantly. Whereas the participation by some not-for-profits, such as those representing specific interest groups, has increased, this has not been the case across the board. For example, representatives of consumer interests or the economically disadvantaged have not increased. Many of the NGOs that were funded during the 1970s and early 1980s have not retained government funding and their participation has dwindled. Furthermore, the discourse has become more technical, relying significantly on econometrics and expert views. Even though the ACCC has not mandated quantification of public benefits, parties are regularly making use of such methods. This has increased the need to participate using the same language, thereby increasing the cost of participation. This technocratic factor has adversely affected participation by such groups, which find written submissions take too much time and quantification of benefits that rely on expert reports are too expensive to compile. These groups feel that many important benefits are not adequately considered because they either cannot be measured or have not been measured. While acknowledging the need to incorporate efficient processes, the ACCC must ensure that it considers the position of all interested parties and allows them the chance to put their views forward. The following two principles provide a proper place for quantification, while asserting the commitment of the ACCC to consider all benefits, including those that can be measured and those that cannot. These two principles could be phrased as follows:

> *Principle: Benefits should be quantified where this can be done validly and cost-effectively.*

> *Principle: The more measurable should never be allowed to drive out the more important in assessing public benefit.*

---

92 Marshall J Breger and Gary J Edles, 'Established by Practice: The Theory and Operation of Independent Federal Agencies' (2000) 52 *Administrative Law Review* 1111, 1115.

Scholarship on procedural fairness and restorative justice point to the importance of incorporating mechanisms allowing for participation by affected groups. Without the presence of well-funded, active advocacy groups to bring the views of consumers and citizens to the attention of the regulator, the task lies with the ACCC to become responsive to the broader institutional environment of the regulatory regime.[93] The call is for the ACCC to be 'really responsive' to the need of all the stakeholders in the market, including consumers. Becoming a responsive regulator can be both a top-down and a bottom-up process. The top-down strategy would call for the ACCC to incorporate more responsive measures into its existing practices, by instigating the changes necessary to nurture greater participation and involvement. Alternately, it can also be a bottom-up process: the ACCC can be more responsive to criticisms and protest from other sources including the media, the public and advocacy groups, re-evaluating its practices as it opens its doors to critics.

One domain in which the ACCC incorporates top-down responsive practice is the pre-decision conference. These multi-party deliberations facilitate a limited form of restorative justice, redressing inequalities of bargaining power and allowing for a more inclusive decision-making framework. Within the authorisation process, the inability of disadvantaged groups, such as consumer groups, to participate could also be addressed by changing the process and language of the discourse which currently constrains participation. Rather than relying exclusively on quantification of benefits as a matter of course, it may be fruitful to include more general notions that introduce factors, such as increased product safety, improved access to justice, enhanced environmental policies or enhancing ethical practices, into the equation when they are relevant. The seven public benefit principles based on rights and empirics, discussed earlier in the chapter, encompass this proposition. Using universally accepted language, by its very nature, changes the rules of the game, creating a more inviting playing field. As discussed earlier this could be phrased as follows:

> *Principle: A public benefit can fall into one of the following categories: secure a basic human right, improve quality of life, provide for equitable dealings among market actors, increase market integrity, encourage economic efficiency and economic welfare, provide for human security, enhance procedural fairness and increase enforceability.*

Further, it is crucial to nurture meaningful participation. This may be achieved by accepting informal submissions from consumer groups rather than requiring written submissions in all cases. It may also be achieved by allowing such groups to have discussions with corporations and other interested bodies in a process of consensus-building. The current Consumer Consultative Committee

---

93   Baldwin and Black (2008) 59, 61. See also John Braithwaite (2011) 476.

is one step along the road towards such consensus-building.[94] Another example of such top down practices is the UK Office of Fair Trade, which has stated that all its actions are guided by whether consumer welfare will be optimised. While there is the possibility that such statements are bald assertions with little follow through, there is also the possibility of them being much more.[95] By doing so, it can also be placing the consumer interest at the centre of any decision, including all enforcement activities.

As discussed earlier, the bottom-up process, where change is called for by outsiders, requiring the regulator to really respond by listening to different points of view, reflecting upon them and re-evaluating its own practices, is also relevant here. Braithwaite calls for the regulator in such circumstances to engage those who resist with fairness; show them respect by construing their resistance as an opportunity to learn how to improve regulatory design.[96] Such calls from outsiders can be either suppressed by the regulator or can lead to a shift in the regulator's position.[97] The *Medicines* authorisation was one in which there was such a shift in position.[98] Here, authorisation was sought for a code of conduct, developed by Medicines Australia, the industry's national association which governs the activities of pharmaceutical companies when they promote prescription medicines to doctors. This code regulates matters such as drug company sponsorship of medical conferences, the payment of travel and accommodation expenses of doctors attending such conferences, and the provision of other forms of hospitality. The code had been subject to considerable media scrutiny and criticism on the basis that it did not provide sufficient safeguards against potential abuse.[99] The ACCC gave due consideration to these complaints and granted authorisation on the basis of a number of conditions. The aim of the conditions was to assist scrutiny of sponsorship activities of pharmaceutical companies by the general public. The ACCC was responding to concerns and enlisting others to its regulatory project. This bottom-up process requires the regulator to be humble and open. It expands on the current notions of procedural justice and accountability and it demands a regulator that has been reasonably responsive to be even more responsive. It has

---

94 The Consumer Consultative Committee was established in 2001 by the ACCC as way of providing an opportunity to comment on issues affecting consumers that fall within the scope of the ACCC administration. See <http://www.accc.gov.au/content/index.phtml/itemId/800732> at 30 May 2008.

95 Office of Fair Trade, 27.

96 Braithwaite (2011) 476.

97 For an example of such a call to shift position see *Choice*, 'Choice opposes CBA's move on Bank West', 3 November 2008 <http://www.choice.com.au/viewArticle.aspx?id=106593&catId=100570&tid=100008&p=1&title=Calling+for+BankWest+buyers> at 3 November 2008.

98 <http://www.accc.gov.au/content/index.phtml/itemId/744908/fromItemId/278039> at 4 January 2008; also see Elisabeth Sexton, 'Papers Must Be Released, ACCC Told', *Sydney Morning Herald*, 1 April 2008, 2.

99 David A Newby and David A Henry, 'Drug Advertising: Truths, Half-truths and Few Statistics' (2002) 177(6) *The Medical Journal of Australia* 285; Viola Korczak, 'The Pharmaceutical Industry's Code of Conduct is Not Working', July 2006, Edmund Rice Centre, *Newsletter*, <http://www.erc.org.au/goodbusiness/page.php?pg=0607inprofile0> at 4 January 2008.

suggested that this can be done by the regulator improving existing practices to be more inclusive, and being more receptive to criticism as an opportunity for reflexivity. The commitment to responsiveness can be expressed as follows:

Principle: Openness to all public benefits, even where they are complex public benefits that have not been considered in previous authorisations, should be assured by an ACCC culture of dialogue with stakeholders.

The Nine Principles for Determining Public Benefit in Authorisation Determinations

The two main concerns expressed about the public benefit test within the authorisation process are that the approach is ad hoc and does not facilitate sufficient participation by non-industry groups. This chapter has proposed that principle-based regulation might be useful in addressing these criticisms. It goes about addressing the first concern on the current ad hoc approach, proposing a principle of immanent rights, which is based on an amalgam of recognised top-down human rights, accepted bottom-up human rights and ACCC practice. It proposed that this principle could be framed as follows:

Principle: A public benefit can fall into one of the following categories: securing a basic human right, improving quality of life, provide for equitable dealings among market actors, increase market integrity, encourage economic efficiency and economic welfare, provide for human security, enhance procedural fairness and increase enforceability.

Then the chapter addressed the second criticism on the need to facilitate participation by non-industry groups. Here it assessed the manner in which this could be done: by design or by practice. It is concluded that the design is unlikely in the Australian regulatory climate and context. The preferred and more pragmatic option is the art of practice whereby the regulator becomes more responsive to the needs of such groups and adopts strategies for inclusion. Such strategies will deal with the types of people consulted, the variety of information considered, the manner in which the dialogue that may start at the beginning of an authorisation determination can continue, and the stakeholders who can be co-opted into the regulatory game. Earlier chapters have discussed the different ways in which discretion can be exercised for inclusivity. This includes the need to look beyond measurable public benefits to consider all types of public benefits using a widely accepted language. It also includes the incorporation of practices that encourage participation by stakeholders: both formal and informal submissions and pre-decision conferences. Further, it points to the need to clearly acknowledge the expanded accountability model which sees the ACCC being accountable to a variety of stakeholders and give effect to it by including their views in deliberations. And it acknowledges that there may be a variety of experimental ways in which such stakeholders can become part of the process. Accordingly a set of nine principles that can be put into practice by the ACCC has been developed as discussed. These principles take on board current ACCC practice, the need for providing fixed points to the applicants and the importance of developing and maintaining a constructive dialogue. They also increase the participation of all stakeholders in decision-making. These principles are aimed at making the ACCC more effective in exercising its discretion to determine public benefit within the authorisation process.

These are broad principles that have to be brought to life by concrete examples by way of authorisation determinations by the ACCC, which can then become part of the shared understanding among the members of the trade practices community.[100] The use of public speeches; guidance documents; the public registers on authorisation applications, submissions and determinations; informal meetings; the pre-decision conferences; and, the soliciting of views from NGOs are all examples of how the ACCC has nurtured the trade practices community. But, as demonstrated in this study, the regulator could become even more responsive by adopting an inclusive language to define public benefit that can accommodate a range of future potential benefits; by providing access to past decisions going back before 1999 online, and by giving greater direction on the status of the Australian Trade Practices Tribunal's decisions.

The Place for Reflection in the Art of Practice

As discussed in Chapter 5, the manner in which rules are interpreted or discretion is exercised is constrained and influenced by multiple factors that come from both within and outside the regulator. A list of nine principles can be nothing more than a list of rules that can be read either up or down, producing radically distinct outcomes. They can become either bald assertions without substance, or they can do what they are intended to — they can make the regulator more responsive. We can consider this in the context of Principle 4, which requires the ACCC to weigh benefits, bearing in mind the size of the benefits and the parties likely to benefit. This principle means nothing unless the regulator adequately explains the weighting used. The explanation will articulate how the weighing-up practice works, making the regulator accountable to all stakeholders for its actions. The explanation has to be clear, simple and, most importantly, understood by all those to whom it matters. It cannot simply be

---

100 See Parker, Ainsworth and Stepanenko (2004) for a discussion on the understandings of the trade practices community on the cartel leniency policy and the cartel cooperation policy, 69–70.

speaking to some with the technical knowledge to interpret the information, and it cannot be obscured by professional mystique.[101] Likewise Principle 8, which states that the more measurable should never drive out the more important, means little unless there is commitment by the regulator to the values this principle embodies, namely that all types of public benefits will be considered, irrespective of whether they have been measured or not. It embodies inclusivity both by considering all types of public benefits and by being open to different types of exchanges and communication. Similarly, Principle 9, which promises a culture of dialogue with stakeholders, is pointless if it is interpreted to be no more than talking to all the parties that are routinely consulted. What is required of the ACCC is that it should become a reflective regulator that examines its own performance and learns from it. This type of reflective regulator will be able to engage in single loop, double loop and triple loop learning.

'Single loop' learning is the act of giving effect to the written word rather than the underlying values inherent in the principles.[102] It is an operationalised act rather than one that is thought about, questioned and then undertaken. As discussed earlier, giving effect to rules, without a commitment to the underlying values, may introduce new processes without having any effect on the end result. For example, making available all the submissions in an authorisation determination on the ACCC website may make it clear that the views of different stakeholders have been considered. A commitment to the underlying values means that the ACCC will take on the responsibility of determining whether there are other stakeholders who should be considered and actively pursuing them prior to making a decision. Thus, where the institutional values and norms haven't changed, the end result won't either.

Double loop learning requires a further commitment by the regulator to the principles and its underlying values. Double loop learning occurs when an error is detected and then corrected in ways that involve modification of the organisation's underlying norms, policies and objectives.[103] It requires a regulator to consider the success of the strategies it has employed and evaluate its performance and failures. As Parker has stated, it involves 'being able to detect and correct errors in policies, procedures, cultures and traditions of the whole organisation'.[104] Here, the regulator commits to the values embodied in the principles and will take it on itself to consider how the principles are applied. If required it may have to re-evaluate the strategies used and reconsider the best processes to adopt in order to give effect to these values. Consequently, the institutional values and norms are changing, leading to a change in outcomes.[105]

---

101   Donald Schon, *The Reflective Practitioner; How Professionals Think in Action* (1995) 301.
102   Chris Argyris and Donald Schon, *Organizational Learning II* (1996) 20.
103   Argyris and Schon, *Organizational Learning: A Theory of Action in Perspective* (1978) 2–3.
104   Parker (2002) 239.
105   ibid, 21; see also Braithwaite (2011) 514.

In authorisation determinations, the ACCC may seek to check whether the conditions it attached to a grant of authorisation are delivering the outcomes sought. If such conditions are successful, the ACCC may seek to use them as a standard clause in similar determinations. Conditions are a flexible and useful tool, as discussed in Chapter 6. They can be used to manage markets by providing information and processes to stakeholders who can then use them to hold corporations to account. Currently, however, conditions are rarely monitored by the ACCC.[106] By doing so, the ACCC will be evaluating its own performance.

Where submissions in relation to an authorisation application are scant, the ACCC may seek to investigate the reasons for this further. It may then seek to consider how the policies could be varied: Should officials be given the responsibility to speak with representatives of all stakeholders? Should telephone conversations be substituted for written submissions in certain circumstances? Should non-industry groups be consulted as a matter of course? If there were systematic performance evaluation, the ACCC would be bound to consider whether pre-decision conferences are effective and why? Such evaluations would tell us if, as discussed in Chapter 6, such conferences present the possibility of encouraging the development of a shared ethos and opens channels of communicating between stakeholders.

Triple loop learning goes even further, requiring the regulator to be able to assess the manner in which it functions and change as necessary; this is likely to include the creation of new structures and strategies. Parker's examination of triple loop learning and the regulator in the context of self-regulation is also relevant here. She has proposed that regulators must collect information on the problems they are supposed to solve and evaluate their performance by reference to impacts on those problems; they must report the data to all stakeholders including government and industry; and use the information and feedback to adjust regulatory strategies and objectives.[107] There is much in common between triple loop learning and really responsive regulation, which sees the need for performance sensitivity through assessment procedures and fostering the capacity of regimes to change regulatory direction.[108] All this is possible only where the regulator has an on-going dialogue with stakeholders and a shared understanding of what is required. Trust is the essential ingredient for any such dialogue and understanding to flourish. Using the universally accepted language of human rights to determine the meaning of public benefit is one step in developing such a dialogue. Developing this trust involves the

---

106   See ibid, 251 for a discussion of similar issues in the context of undertakings under section 87B of the *Trade Practices Act 1974*.

107   Parker (2002) 290, Also see: Braithwaite (2011) 514.

108   Baldwin and Black (2008) 75.

accommodation of all stakeholders and being accountable to all interested parties. Accommodating such diverse interests leads to more complex deliberations, such as consultation with consumers and community groups, on how public benefits can flow through to them, including the kinds of conditions that may be needed to ensure such flow through.

Once there is this trust, the regulator can be innovative in how it regulates, engaging in democratic experimentalism.[109] For example, the regulator may see a greater role for the presence of civil society on the boards of industry associations, acting as scrutineers on how codes of conduct, which have been authorised, are working in practice. The regulator may also be experimental enough to set up benchmarking by making one industry association's practices a benchmark for all other industry associations to compare against, with the aim of improving governance practices in the market generally. This benchmarking may be aimed at increasing accountability and self-reporting and could include the use of websites for greater disclosure to all interested parties, inclusion of consumer and NGO representatives on boards of the association, regular monitoring and annual reporting to the ACCC of the resulting public benefit and the parties whom it reached. These strategies would continue changing, co-opting all the stakeholders in regulating through changing times.

Conclusion

The ACCC has, in general, been a responsive regulator. It has performed reasonably well in determining public benefit within the authorisation process. There are, however, two main areas that require re-evaluation: first, the current approach of the ACCC lacks a theoretical foundation; and, second, as this study over three decades reveals, there has been an increasing inclusivity deficit.

This study has addressed these criticisms in proposing that the ACCC should develop a set of overarching principles founded on a combination of human rights and immanent rights recognised by the regulator in practice, which is immediately more universal than the language of economic efficiency. This book addresses the manner in which the principles, informed by responsive regulation and restorative justice, addresses the inclusivity deficit.

This approach relies on creating a shared understanding, founded on these principles among the trade practices regulatory community, which will continue to shape and reshape these principles. The regulator will need to nurture these understandings, bringing on board as many members of the community as it

---

109   Michael Dorf and Charles Sabel, 'A Constitution of Democratic Experimentalism' (1998) 98 *Columbia Law Review* 267, 345; also see the discussion on Regulatory Theories and Regulators in Chapter 6.

can. These principles will not be a rule book, but, rather, valued objectives that all commit to. These principles will not be fixed, but, rather, flexible, being able to bend and reshape themselves while always loyal to the core objectives. When faced with a new type of challenge, whether a global financial crisis or a new environmental dilemma, these members of the regulatory community will be able to break from the past and engage their community in a new solution to the problem, while still being committed to these principles. They will know that the regulator will be predictably responsible when faced with a fresh challenge in terms of the principles. The regulator will be accountable to all these members with shared sensibilities on human rights, competition policy and the meaning of public benefit as they all collaborate within this shared space.

Appendix

Selecting the Determinations for the Empirical Study

The determinations were selected from a pool in order to allow a general picture to emerge of how determinations are made from year to year. Each of the authorisation determinations was read and information from them coded systematically using the same method. A total of 244 authorisation determinations were used.

Weights Attached to the Benefits and Detriments

Each public benefit and public detriment was weighed and the following table explains the weights used in analysing the determination.

Table 1: Weights attached to public benefit and public detriment

Weight	Public benefit	Public detriment
1	Not important. The commission has accepted such a benefit can be classified as a public benefit, however, the commission did not accept the applicant's assessment of the benefit in this case or that the benefit is likely to be of such a small magnitude that it will be given minimal weight in the determination or because it was unlikely to result in this case. Either this is explicitly stated by the commission or the author has decided that, given the context, it should be considered not important.	Not important. Although this public detriment was acknowledged, the commission did not regard it is as important. Either this was explicitly stated by the commission or the reader decided that, given the context, it is not an important public detriment.
2	Minor importance. The commission acknowledged that this public benefit may result from the conduct claimed. The commission, however, only regards it of minor importance. Either this is explicitly stated by the commission, or the reader has decided that, given the context, it has only warranted minor importance status.	Minor importance. The commission acknowledged that such a public detriment may result from the proposed conduct, but only regards it to be of minor importance. Either this is stated by the commission, or the reader has decided that given the context it has really only warranted minor importance status.

Weight	Public benefit	Public detriment
3	Important. The commission accepted that this claimed public benefit is important in making its determination and this is usually expressly stated in the authorisation determination.	Important. The commission accepted that this is an important public detriment and it is usually expressly stated in the authorisation determination.
4	Very important. This public benefit is critical in the determination. It is generally expressly recognised as such by the commission in the determination.	Very important. This detriment is of critical importance in the determination. It is generally expressly recognised as such by the commission in the determination.

Other Factors that were Collated

A number of factors that impacted on the commission's decision-making were collated. There were seven such factors as follows:

1. The section that the conduct or proposed conduct was likely to breach — the conduct could potentially breach the price-fixing provisions (s 45A), substantial lessening of competition provisions (s 45), exclusionary conduct provisions (s 45) and exclusive dealing provisions (s 47).

2. The type of industry that the applicant belongs to.

3. Whether conditions were imposed by the ACCC in granting authorisation.

4. The type of conditions imposed — for example, conditions could be imposed requiring that codes of conduct include an appeals process, or to safeguard against the misuse of market power, or to encourage the participation of external bodies in decision-making.

5. Whether any evidence of pass-through of public benefit was discussed in the application, submissions or determination — pass-through refers to evidence of whether the benefits flow on to the consumer.

6. Whether there was discussion of particular tests or standards to determine public benefit — there are four such tests/standards that have been used to quantify public benefits: total welfare standard, consumer welfare standard, price standard, and the balancing weights standard.

7. Whether there was reliance on the quantification methods to substantiate public benefits.

Because different types of information about each of these factors were collated, a different code to the one used above was used. The details of the factors and the manner in which the factors were coded are contained in the following table.

Table 2: Participation in the authorisation process

Identity of the participants	Other information
Individuals	Reference to government policies
Industry group	Reference to ACCC documents/decisions
Non-industry group	Reference to other reports or strategies
State government	
Federal government	
Independent agency	

Table 3: Weights used to assess the importance attached to the participation

Weight	Public benefit
1	There is minor influence exerted. Either this is explicitly stated by the commission or the reader has decided this on the basis of the context after examining the determination, draft determination, submissions and other available information.
2	There is major influence exerted. Important. Either this is explicitly stated by the commission or the reader has decided this on the basis of the context after examining the determination, draft determination, submissions and other available information.
3	Very important. This public benefit is critical in the determination. It is generally expressly recognised as such by the commission in the determination.
0	Cannot gauge influence from examining the determination, draft determination, submissions and other available information; or No participation; or No influence.

Other relevant qualitative factors were also collated as described in Table 4.

Table 4: Other related qualitative factors

Qualitative factor	Example of data collected
Was this a single determination or did it involve multiple determinations?	*Qantas Airways Ltd* involved four determinations made on 9 September 2003 (A90862, A90963, A30220, A30221).
Was notification also sought?	In *Australian Wool Exchange Limited* (A30185) decided on 30 December 1998, both authorisation and notification was sought.
Number of industry groups that made submissions.	In *Australian Brick and Blocklaying Training Foundation* (A90993) authorisation determination made on 26 April 2006, four industry bodies made submissions to the ACCC.
Other factors considered?	Importance of globalisation.

References

Articles/Books/Reports

Adler, M and Asquith, S, (eds), *Discretion and Welfare* (1981)

Administrative Review Council, Parliament of Australia, *Automated Assistance in Administrative Decision Making*, Report No 46 (2004) <http://www.ag.gov.au/agd/www/archome.nsf/Page/Publications_Reports_> at 24 November 2008

Allars, Margaret, *Introduction to Australian Administrative Law* (1990)

——, 'The Rights of Citizens and the Limits of Administration Discretion: The Contribution of Sir Anthony Mason to Administrative Law' (2000) 28 *Federal Law Review* 197

——, 'Public Administration in Private Hands' (2005) 12 *Australian Journal of Administrative Law* 126

Argyris, Chris and Schon, Donald, *Organizational Learning: A Theory of Action in Perspective* (1978)

——,——, *Organizational Learning II* (1996)

Aronson, Mark, 'A Public Lawyer's Responses to Privatisation and Outsourcing', in Taggart (1997) 40

Australian Law Reform Commission (ALRC), Parliament of Australia, *Compliance with the* Trade Practices Act 1974, Report ALRC 68 (1994)

Ayres, Ian and Braithwaite, John, *Responsive Regulation: Transcending the Deregulation Debate* (1992)

Bailey, Peter, *Human Rights: Australia in an International Context* (1990)

Baldwin, Robert, 'Why Rules Don't Work' (1990) 53(3) *Modern Law Review* 321

——, *Rules and Government* (1995)

—— and Black, Julia 'Really Responsive Regulation' (2008) 71(1) *Modern Law Review* 59

—— and McCrudden, C (eds), *Regulation and Public Law* (1987)

Bannerman, Ron, 'Points from Experience 1967–84', in Trade Practices Commission (1984)

Barwick, Garfield, *A Radical Tory. Garfield Barwick's Reflections & Recollections* (1995)

Baxt, Robert, 'Consumer and Business Protection', in Frances Hanks and Philip Williams (eds), Trade Practices Act: *A Twenty Five Year Stocktake* (2001)

—— and Brunt, Maureen, 'The Murphy Trade Practices Bill: Admirable Objectives, Inadequate Means (1974) 2 *Australian Business Law Review* 3

——,——, 'A Guide to the Act', in John Nieuwenhuysen (ed), *Australian Trade Practices: Readings* (2nd edn, 1976) 88

Bernstein, Marver, *Regulating Business by Independent Commission* (1955)

Birch, Alan, and Blaxland, JF, 'The Historical Background', in AG Lowndes (ed), *South Pacific Enterprise: The Colonial Sugar Refinery Company Limited* (1956) 51

Black, Julia, 'New Institutionalism and Naturalism in Socio-Legal Analysis: Institutionalist Approaches to Regulatory Decision Making' (2002) 19(1) *Law and Policy* 51

——, *Rules and Regulators* (1997)

——, Hopper, Martyn and Band, Christa, ' Making a Success of Principles-based Regulation' (2007) 1(3) *Law and Financial Markets Review* 191

Blainey, Geoffrey, *The Steel Master: A Life of Essington Lewis* (1981)

Braithwaite, John, *Restorative Justice and Responsive Regulation* (2002)

——, 'Rules and Principles: A Theory of Legal Certainty' (2002) 27 *Australian Journal of Legal Philosophy* 47

——, *Regulatory Capitalism: How it Works, Ideas for Making it Work Better* (2008)

——, 'The Essence of Responsive Regulation' (2011) 44 *University of British Columbia Law Review* 475

—— and Drahos, Peter, *Global Business Regulation* (2000)

——, Grabovsky, Peter and Walker, John, 'An Enforcement Taxonomy of Regulatory Agencies' (1987) 9 *Law and Policy* 323

——, Makkai, Toni and Braithwaite, Valerie, *Regulating Aged Care: Ritualism and the New Pyramid* (2007)

—— and Parker, Christine, 'Conclusion', in Christine Parker, Colin Scott, Nicola Lacey and John Braithwaite (eds), *Regulating Law* (2004)

Braithwaite, Valerie (ed), 'Responsive Regulation and Taxation' (2007) 29(1) Special Issue, *Law and Policy* 3

——, Murphy, Kristina and Reinhart, Monika, 'Taxation. Threat, Motivational Postures and Responsive Regulation' (2007) 29(1) *Law and Policy* 137

Breger, Marshall and Edles, Gary, 'Established by Practice: The Theory and Operation of Independent Federal Agencies' (2000) 52 *Administrative Law Review* 1111

Brenchley, Fred, *Allan Fels:A Portrait of Power* (2003)

Brunt, Maureen, 'The Trade Practices Bill II: Legislation in Search of an Objective' (1965) 41 *The Economic Record* 357

——, 'Legislation in Search of an Objective', in John Nieuwenhuysen (ed), *Australian Trade Practices: Readings* (2nd edn, 1976) 240

——, 'The Australian Antitrust Law After 20 Years — A Stocktake' (1994) 9 *Review of Industrial Organization* 483

——, *Economic Essays on Australian and New Zealand Competition Law* (2003)

Buch-Hansen and Angela Wigger, The Politics of European Competition Regulation: A Critical Political Economy Perspective (2011).

____, 'Revisiting 50 years of market-making: The neoliberal transformation of European competition policy' (2010) 17(1) *Review of International Political Economy* 20 – 44.

Caldor, Kent and Ye, Min, 'Regionalism and Critical Junctures: Explaining the "Organization Gap" in Northeast Asia' (2004) *Journal of East Asian Studies* 191

Campbell, Elaine, 'Towards a Sociological Theory of Discretion' (1999) 27 *International Journal of the Sociology of Law* 79

Campbell, Tom, 'Introduction', in Tom Campbell and Seumas Miller (eds), *Human Rights and the Moral Responsibilities of Corporate and Public Sector Organisations* (2004) 12

Carter, Neil, Klien, Rudolf and Day, Patricia, *How Organisations Measure Success: The Use of Performance in Government* (1995)

Castels, Michael, *The Rise of the Network Society* (1996)

Caves, Richard, 'Scale, Openness and Productivity in Manufacturing Industries', in Richard Caves and Lawrence Krause (eds), *The AustralianEconomy: A View from the North* (1984) 313

Charlesworth, Hilary, 'What are "Women's International Human Rights"?', in Rebecca J Cook (ed), *Human Rights of Women: National and International Perspectives* (1994) 58

Collier, Ruth Berins, and Collier, David, *Shaping the Political Arena: Critical Junctures, the Labor Movement, and Regime Dynamics in Latin America* (1991)

Cornwall, Amanda, 'Regulating Environmental Claims in Marketing' (1996) 3 *Competition and Consumer Law Journal* 1

Corones, Stephen, *Competition Law in Australia* (3rd ed, 2004)

Craig, Paul 'The Monopolies and Mergers Commission: Competition and Administrative Rationality', in Baldwin and McCrudden (1987)

Cutt, James and Murray, Victor, *Accountability and Effectiveness Evaluation in Non Profit Organizations* (2000)

Davis, Kenneth Culp, *Discretionary Justice: A Preliminary Inquiry* (1969)

Dawson Report Committee of Inquiry, Commonwealth of Australia, *Review of the Competition Provisions of the* Trade Practices Act [Dawson Review] (2003)

De Burca, Graine, and Scott, Joanne (eds), *Law and New Governance in the EU and the US* (2006)

Donald, Bruce and Heydon, John Dyson, *Trade Practices Law* Vol 1 (1978)

Dorf, Michael and Sabel, Charles, 'A Constitution of Democratic Experimentalism' (1998) 98 *Columbia Law Review* 267

Drahos, Peter, 'Intellectual Property and Pharmaceutical Markets: A Nodal Governance Approach' (2004) 77(2) *Temple Law Review* 401

Dowell-Jones, Mary and Kinley, David, 'Minding the Gap: Global Finance and Human Rights' (2011) 25(2) *Ethics & International Affairs* 183–210

Dunlavy, Colleen, 'Political Structure, State Policy, and Industrial Change: Early Railroad Policy in the United States and Prussia', in Steinmo, Thelen and Longstreth (1992)

Duns, John, 'Competition Law and Public Benefits' (1994) 16 *Adelaide Law Review* 245

Dworkin, Ronald, *Taking Rights Seriously* (2005)

Evans, Lewis, 'Economic Measurement and the Authorisation Process: The Expanding Place of Quantitative Analysis' (1999) 13 *Competition and Consumer Law Journal* 99

Feintuck, Mike, *'The Public Interest' in Regulation* (2004)

Fels, Allan, ACCC Update, 13 June 2003, <http://www.accc.gov.au/content/item.phtml?itemId=349239&nodeId=34326161a1928dde07b97cf4878b8390&fn=Update_13.doc> at 10 December 2007

——, 'Distinguished Fellow of the Economic Society of Australia 2006: Maureen Brunt' (2006) 83 *Economic Record* 204

—— and Grimwade, Tim, 'Authorisation: Is it Still Relevant to Australian Competition Law?' (2003) 11(1) *Competition and Consumer Law Journal* 187

Cristie Ford and Natasha Affolder, Responsive Regulation in Context, Circa 2011 Preface' (2011) 44(3) *University of British Columbia Law Review* 463

Forrester, Ian, 'Modernization of EC Competition Law' (2000) 23 *Fordham International Law Review* 1028

Fox, Eleanor, 'The Modernization of Antitrust: A New Equilibrium' (1981) 66 *Cornell Law Review* 1141

—— and Sullivan, Lawrence, 'Antitrust — Retrospective and Prospective: Where Are We Coming From? Where Are We Going?' (1987) 62 *New York University Law Review* 936

Freeman, Jody, 'Private Parties, Public Functions and the New Administrative State' (2000) 52 *Administrative Law Review* 813

——, 'The Private Role in Public Governance' (2000) 75(3) *New York University Law Review* 543

Freigang, Jan, 'Is Responsive Regulation Compatible with the Rule of Law' (2002) 8(4) *European Public Law* 463

Freyer, Tony, *Regulating Big Business: Antitrust in Great Britain and America: 1890–1990* (1992)

——, *Antitrust and Global Capitalism 1930–2004* (2006)

Gal, Michal, *Competition Policy for Small Market Economies* (2003)

Galbraith, John Kenneth, 'The Development of Monopoly Theory', in Alex Hunter (ed), *Monopoly and Competition: Selected Readings* (1969)

Galligan, DJ, *Discretionary Powers: A Legal Study of Official Discretion* (1986)

Gans, Joshua, '"Protecting Consumers by Protecting Competition": Does Behavioural Economics Support this Contention?' (2005) 13 *Competition and Consumer Law Journal* 3

Gelsthorpe, Lorraine and Padfield, Nicola (eds), *Exercising Discretion: Decision-making in the Criminal Justice System and Beyond* (2003)

Gentle, Geraldine, 'Economic Welfare, the Public Interest and the Trade Practices Tribunal', in John Nieuwenhuysen (ed), *Australian Trade Practices: Readings* (2nd ed, 1976)

Giddens, Anthony, *Profiles and Critiques in Legal Theory* (1982)

——, *The Constitution of Society: Outline of the Theory of Structuration* (1984)

Gilardi, Fabrizio, 'Institutional Change in Regulatory Policies: Regulation Through Independent Agencies and the Three New Institutionalisms', in Jacinta Jordana and David Levi-Faur (eds), *The Politics of Regulation: Institutions and Regulatory Reforms for the Age of Governance* (2004)

Goodin, Robert, 'Welfare Rights and Discretion' (1986) 6 *Oxford Journal of Legal Studies* 232

Gorges, Michael J, 'The New Institutionalism and the Study of the European Union: The Case of the Social Dialogue' (2001) 24(4) *West European Politics* 152

Graham, Cosmo, 'Is There a Crisis in Regulatory Accountability?', in Robert Baldwin, Colin Scott and Christopher Hood (eds), *A Reader onRegulation* (1998)

Grant, Richard, Politics and Public Administration Section, Department of Parliament Services, *Australia's Corporate Regulators — the ACCC, ASIC and APRA* (Research Brief No 16, 14 June 2005)

Griffin, Joseph and Sharp, Leeanne, 'Efficiency Issues in Competition Analysis in Australia, the European Union and the United States' (1996) 64 *AntitrustLaw Journal* 649

Gunningham, Neil, 'Environmental Law, Regulation and Governance: Shifting Architectures' (2009) 21(2) *Journal of Environmental Law* 179

Haas, Peter M, 'Epistemic Communities and International Policy Coordination' (1992) 46(1) *International Organization* 1

Haines, Fiona, *Corporate Regulation: Beyond 'Punish or Persuade'* (1997)

——, *Globalisation and Regulatory Character: Regulatory Reform after the Kader Toy Factory Fire* (2005)

Hall, Peter and Taylor, Rosemary 'Political Science and the Three New Institutionalisms' (1996) 44 *Political Studies* 936

—— and Soskice, David, 'An Introduction to Varieties of Capitalism', in Hall and Soskice (eds), *Varieties ofCapitalism: The International Foundations of ComparativeAdvantage* (2001)

Hanks, Frances and Williams, Philip, 'The Treatment of Vertical Restraints Under the Australian Trade Practices Act' (1987 15 *Australian Business Law Review* 147

Harlow, Carol, 'Law and Public Administration: Convergence and Symbiosis' (2005) 79(2) *International Review of Administrative Sciences* 279

—— and Rawlings, Richard, *Law and Administration* (1984)

Hatch, John, 'The Implications of the Frozen Case for Australian Trade Practices Legislation' (1972) 48(121) *Economic Record* 374

Hawkins, Keith (ed), *The Uses of Discretion* (1992)

Hay, Colin and Wilcott, Daniel, 'Structure, Agency and Historical Institutionalism' (1998) 44 *Political Studies* 951

Hogan, James, 'Remoulding the Critical Junctures Approach' (2006) 39(3) *Canadian Journal of Political Science* 657

Hood, A, 'The Confused Case of Countervailing Power in Australian Competition Law' (2000) 8(1) *Competition and Consumer Law Journal* 1

Hood, Christopher, 'A Public Management for all Seasons' (1991) 69 *Public Administration* 3

Hopkins, Andrew, *Crime, Law and Business: The Sociological Sources of Australian Monopoly Law* (1978)

Horn, Michael, *The Political Economy of Public Administration: Institutional Choice in the Public Sector* (1995)

Howells, Geraint G and Weatherill, Stephen, *Consumer Protection Law* (2005) 94–97

Hunter, Alex, 'Restrictive Practices and Monopolies in Australia' (1961) 37 *Economic Record* 25

—— (ed), *Monopoly and Competition: Selected Readings* (1969)

Hutton, J and Nieuwenhuysen, JP, 'The Tribunal and Australian Economic Policy' (1965) 41 *Economic Record* 2387

Ikenberry, John, *Institutions, Strategic Restraint and the Rebuilding of Order after Major Wars* (2001)

Independent Committee of Inquiry, Commonwealth of Australia, *National Competition Policy* (1993) [Hilmer Report]

Jacobs, Michael S, 'An Outsiders Perspective of Australian Competition Law', in Ray Steinwall (ed), *25 Years of Australian Competition Law* (2000) 144

Karmel, Peter and Brunt, Maureen, *The Structure of the Australian Economy* (1963)

Jowell, Jeffrey, 'The Legal Control of Administrative Discretion' (1973) *Public Law* 178

Kinley, David, 'Human Rights Fundamentalisms' (2007) 29(4) *Sydney Law Review* 545

——, Nolan, Justine and Zerial, Natalie, 'Reflections on the United Nations Human Rights Norms for Corporations' (2007) 25(1) *Company and Securities Law Journal* 30

Lacey, Nicola, 'The Jurisprudence of Discretion: Escaping the Legal Paradigm', in Hawkins (1992)

Laffan, Brigid, 'Becoming a "Living Institution": The Evolution of the European Court of Auditors' (1999) 37(2) *Journal of Common Market Studies* 251

Lempert, Richard 'Discretion in a Behavioural Perspective', in DJ Galligan (ed), A *Reader* on *Administrative Law* (1996)

Levi-Faur, David, 'Comparative Research Designs in the Study of Regulation: How to Increase the Number of Cases Without Compromising the Strength of Case-oriented Analysis', in Jacinta Jordana and David Levi-Faur (eds), *The Politics of Regulation: Institutions and Regulatory Reforms for the Age of Governance* (2004)

—— and Jordana, Jacinta, 'The Global Diffusion of Regulatory Capitalism' (2005) 598(1) *The ANNALS of the American Academy of Political and Social Sciences (AAPSS)* 12

Levy, Brian and Spiller, Pablo (eds), *Regulation, Institutions and Commitment: Comparative Studies of Telecommunications* (1996)

Lloyd, Christopher, 'Regime Change in Australian Capitalism: Towards a Historical Political Economy of Regulation' (2002) 42(3) *Australian Economic History Review* 238

Maher, Imelda, 'Competition Law in the International Domain: Networks as a New Form of Governance' (2002) 29(1) *Journal of Law and Society* 112

——, 'Networking Competition Authorities in the European Union: Diversity and Change', in Claus Dieter Ehlermann and Isabela Atanasiu (eds), *European Competition Law Annual 2002: Constructing the EU Network of Competition Authorities 2002* (2005) 223

Mahoney, James, 'Path Dependency in Historical Sociology' (2000) 29(4) *Theory and Society* 507

March, James G, and Olsen, Johan P, 'The New Institutionalism: Organizational Factors in Political Life' (1984) 78(3) *The American Political Science Review*, 734

Marr, David, *Barwick* (2005)

McBarret, Doreen, 'Human Rights, Corporate Responsibility and the New Accountability', in Tom Campbell and Seumas Miller (eds), *Human Rights and the Moral Responsibilities of Corporate and Public Sector Organisations* (2004)

McCallum, D, 'Informal Powers and the Removal of Aboriginal Children: Consequences for Health and Social Order' (2007) 35 *International Journal of the Sociology of Law* 29

McDonald, John, 'Legitimating Private Interests: Hegemonic Control Over "the Public Interest" in National Competition Polity' (2007) 43(4) *Journal of Sociology* 349

McGlew, T and Robertson, A, 'Social Change and the Shifting Boundaries of Discretion in Medicine', in Adler and Asquith (1981)

Meltz, Daniel, 'Happy Birthday Mr Nordenfelt! – The Centenary of the Nordenfelt Case' (1994) 2 *Trade Practices Law Journal* 149

Mercer, Helen, *Constructing a Competitive Order: The Hidden History of British Antitrust Policies* (1995)

Merrett, David, Corones, Stephen and Round, David, 'The Introduction of Competition Policy in Australia: The Role of Ron Bannerman' (2007) 47(2) *Australian Economic History Review* 178

Miller, Russell V, *Miller's Annotated Trade Practices Act* (2002)

Ministerial Council on Energy (Department of Resources, Energy and Tourism), Commonwealth of Australia, *Reform of Energy Markets* (Report to the Councils on Australian Governments, 11 December 2003)

Morgan, Bronwen, *Social Citizenship in the Shadow of Competition: The Bureaucratic Politics of Regulatory Justification* (2003)

_____, Bronwen Morgan, 'The Economization of Politics: Meta-Regulation as a Form of Nonjudicial Legality' (2003) 12(4) *Social & Legal Studies* 489

—— (ed), *The Intersection of Rights and Regulation — New Directions in Sociolegal Scholarship* (2007)

Moran, Michael, 'Understanding the Regulatory State' (2002) 32(1) *British Journal of Political Science* 431

Moses, Jonathan, 'Legal Spin Control: Ethics and Advocacy in the Court of Public Opinion' m(1995) 95(7) *Columbia Law Review*, 1811

Mulgan, Richard, '"Accountability": An Ever-expanding Concept?' (2000) 78 *Public Administration* 555

Nagarajan, Vijaya, 'Reform of Public Utilities: What About Consumers?' (1994) *Competition & Consumer Law Journal* 155

——, 'The Accommodating Act: Reflections on Competition Policy and the Trade Practices Act' (2002) 20(1) *Law in Context* 34

——, '"From Command to Control" to "Open Method Coordination": Theorizing the Practice of Regulatory Agencies' (2008) 8 *Macquarie Law Journal* 63

——, 'Co-Opting for Governance: The Use of the Conditions Power by the ACCC in Authorisations' (2011) 34 University of New South Wales Law Journal 785

——, 'Regulating for Women on Corporate Boards: Polycentric Governance in Australia' (2011) 39 *Federal Law Review* 255

———, "The Paradox of Australian Competition Policy: Contextualizing the Coexistence of Economic Efficiency and Public Benefit' (2013) 36(1) *World Competition: Law and Economics Review* 133-164.

Nielsen, Vibeke, 'Are Regulators Responsive?' (2006) 28(3) *Law and Policy* 396

Newby, David A, and Henry, David A, 'Drug Advertising: Truths, Half-truths and Few Statistics' (2002) 177(6) *The Medical Journal of Australia* 285

Nieuwenhuysen, John, 'The Nature of Trade Practices and the Impact of the 1965 Act', in John Nieuwenhuysen (ed), *Australian Trade Practices: Readings* (2nd ed, 1976)

—— and Norman, Neville, *Australian Competition and Prices Policy* (1976)

Norman, Neville, 'Progress Under Pressure: The Evolution of Antitrust in Australia' (1994) 9 *Review of Industrial Organization* 527

North, Douglass C, 'Institutions', in *Institutional Change and Economic Performance* (1990)

O'Connor, David Edward, *The Basics of Economics* (2004)

Ogus, Anthony, *Regulation: Legal Form and Economic Theory* (1994)

Officer, Robert and Williams, Philip, 'The Public Benefit Test in an Authorisation Decision', in Megan Richardson and Philip Williams (eds), *The Law and the Market* (1995)

Organisation for Economic Co-operation and Development (OECD), *Economic Surveys: Australia* (August 2001)

——, 'The Goal of Competition Law and Policy and the Design of Competition Law and Policy Institutions' (2004) 6 (1 & 2) *Organisation for Economic Co-operation and Development Journal of Competition Law and Policy* 78

——, *Roundtableon Demand-side Economics for Consumer Policy: Summary Report 2006* (Report by Ian McAuley, declassified by the Committee on Consumer Policy, 71st session, 29–30 March 2006)

Parker, Christine, 'Compliance Professionalism and Regulatory Community: The Australian Trade Practices Regime' (1999) 26(2) *Journal of Law and Society* 215

——, *The Open Corporation: Effective Self-Regulation and Democracy* (2002)

——, 'Restorative Justice in Business Regulation? The Australian Competition and Consumer Commission's Use of Enforceable Undertakings' (2004) 67(2) *The Modern Law Review* 209

——, 'The "Compliance" Trap: The Moral Message in Responsive Regulatory Enforcement',(2006) 40(3) *Law and Society Review* 591

—— and Nielsen, Vibeke, 'Do Businesses take Compliance Systems Seriously? An Empirical Study of the Implementation of Trade Practices Compliance Systems in Australia' (2006) 30(2) *Melbourne University Law Review* 441

——, and ——, 'What do Australian Businesses Think of the ACCC and Does It Matter?'(2007) 35(2) *Federal Law Review*, 187

Parkinson, John and Roche, Declan, 'Restorative Justice: Deliberative Democracy in Action?' (2004) 39(3) *Australian Journal of Political Science* 505

Porter, Michael, *The Competitive Advantage of Nations* (1990)

——, Takeuchi, Hirotaka and Sakakibara, Mariko, *Can JapanCompete?* (2000)

Pierson, Paul, 'The Path to European Integration: A Historical Institutionalist Analysis' (1996) 29(2) *Comparative Political Studies* 123

Power, Michael, *The Audit Society* (1997)

Productivity Commission, Commonwealth of Australia, *The Growth and Revenue Implications of Hilmer and Related Reforms: A Report of the Industry Commission to the Council of Australian Governments* (1995) 385 <http://www.pc.gov.au/ic/research/independent/hilmer/finalreport> at 1 November 2007

——, —— *Setting the Scene: Monitoring Micro Reform*, Report 95/1 (1996) <http://www.pc.gov.au/bie/report/96-01> at 20 March 2008

——, ——, *Review of National Competition Policy Reforms — Discussion Draft*, Canberra (2004)

Prosser, Tony, 'The Politics of Discretion: Aspects of Discretionary Power in the Supplementary Benefits Service', in Adler and Asquith (1981)

Pusey, Michael, *The Experience of Middle Australia: The Dark Side of Economic Reform* (2003)

Redmond, Paul, *Companies and Securities Law* (2004)

Report from the Joint Committee, Parliament of Australia, *Constitutional Review* (1959)

Richardson JE, 'The 1965 Bill: The Legal Framework', in John Nieuwenhuysen (ed), *Australian Trade Practices Readings* (2nd ed, 1976)

Royal Commission on Prices and Restrictive Trade Practices in Tasmania, Parliament of Tasmania, *Report of the Royal Commissioner on Prices and Restrictive Trade Practices in Tasmania* (1965)

Robertson, Donald, 'Comment on "The Evolution of Antitrust Law in the United States"', in Frances Hanks and Philip Williams (eds), *Trade Practices Act: A Twenty Five Year Stocktake* (2001)

Rostow, Eugene V, 'British and American Experience with Legislation against Restraints of Competition' (1960) 23(4) *Modern Law Review* 477

Sainsbury, R, 'Administrative Justice: Discretion and Procedure in Social Security Decision-Making', in Hawkins (1992)

Schneider, Carl, 'Discretion and Rules: A Lawyers' View', in Hawkins (1992)

Schon, Donald, *The Reflective Practitioner; How Professionals Think in Action* (1995)

Schudson, Michael, 'The News Media as Political Institutions' (2002) 5 *Annual Review of Political Science* 249

Scott, Colin, 'Accountability in a Regulatory State' (2000) 27(1) *Journal of Law and Society* 38

——, 'Analysing Regulatory Space: Fragmented Resources and Institutional Design' (2001) *Public Law* 329

Senate Economics References Committee, Parliament of Australia, *The Effectiveness of the* Trade Practices Act 1974 *in Protecting Small Business* (2004)

Sinden, Amy, 'Power and Responsibility: Why Human Rights Should Address Corporate Environmental Wrongs', in Doreen McBarnet, Aurora Voiculescu and Tom Campbell (eds), *The New Corporate Accountability: Corporate Social Responsibility and the Law* (2007)

Smith, G, 'Discretionary Decision-making in Social Work', in Adler and Asquith (1981)

Smith, Rhonda, 'Authorisation and the *Trade Practices Act*: More about Public Benefit' (2003) 11(1) *Competition and Consumer Law Journal* 21

Stalley, DJ, 'The Commonwealth Government's Scheme for the Control of Monopoly and Restrictive Practices — A Commentary' (1963) 37 *Australian Law Journal Reports* 85

Steinmo, Sven, Thelen, Kathleen, and Longstreth, Frank (eds), *Structuring Politics: Historical Institutionalism in Comparative Analysis* (1992)

Steinwall, Ray, 'Tensions in the Development of Australian Competition Law', in Ray Steinwall (ed), *25 Years of Australian Competition Law* (2000)

——, 'The Dawson Committee on Competition, Economic Efficiency, Universality and Public Policy' (2003) *University of New South Wales Law Journal* 12.

Stiglitz, Joseph, *Globalization and its Discontents* (2000)

Sylvan, Louise, 'Activating Competition: The Consumer–Competition Interface' (2004) 12(2) *Competition and Consumer Law Journal* 191

Taggart, Michael (ed), *The Province of Administrative Law* (1997)

Tennant, David, 'Australia's Desperate Need for a National Consumer Council' <http://www.consumersfederation.org.au/documents/NCCPaperbyDavidTennantMarch05.doc> 15 October 2008

Thelen, Kathleen, 'Historical Institutionalism in Comparative Politics' (1999) 2 *Annual Review of Political Science* 369

——, and Steinmo, Sven, 'Historical Institutionalism in Comparative Politics', in Steinmo, Thelen and Longstreth (1992)

Thomson, T and Croft, H, 'Authorisations in Australia and New Zealand: Neighbours with Different Backyards' (2003) 19(4) *Australian and New Zealand Trade Practices Law Bulletin*, 37

Trade Practices Commission, Commonwealth of Australia, *Annual Report 1982–83* (1983)

Trade Practices Act Review Committee, Parliament of Australia, *Report to the Minister for Business and Consumer Affairs* (1976)

Trubek, David and Trubek, Louise, 'New Governance & Legal Regulation' (2007) 13 *Columbia Journal of European Law* 540

Tustin, Jeremy and Smith, Rhonda, 'Joined-up Consumer and Competition Policy: Some Comments' (2005) 12(3) *Competition and Consumer Law Journal* 305

Tyler, Tom, 'Public Trust and Confidence in Legal Authorities: What do Majority and Minority Group Members want from the Law and Legal Institutions' (2001) 19(1) *Behavioural Sciences and the Law* 215

——, 'Procedural Justice, Legitimacy, and the Effective Rule of Law' (2003) 30 *Crime and Justice* 283

Vogel, David, *The Market for Virtue: The Potential and Limits of Corporate Social Responsibility* (2005) 3

Walker, Geoffrey de Q, *Australian Monopoly Law: Issues of Law, Fact and Policy* (1967)

——, 'The *Trade Practices Act* at Work', in John Nieuwenhuysen (ed), *Australian Trade Practices: Readings* (2nd ed, 1976)

Warhurst, John, 'Exercising Control over Statutory Authorities: Study in Government Technique', in Patrick Weller and Dean Jaensch (eds), *Responsible Government in Australia* (1980)

Wilks, Stephen, *In the Public Interest: Competition Policy and the Monopolies and Mergers Commission* (1999)

—— and Bartle, Ian, 'The Unanticipated Consequences of Creating Independent Competition Agencies' (2002) 25(1) *West European Politics* 148

Williams, C, 'Sexual Harassment and Human Rights Law' (2003) 2(4) *Journal of Human Rights* 573

Wilson, JL, 'Legislating for Restrictive Trade Practices' (1963) 32(2) *Current Affairs Bulletin* 19

Yeung, Karen, *Securing Compliance: A Principled Approach* (2004)

——, 'Does the ACCC Engage in "Trial By Media"?' (2005) 27(4) *Law and Policy* 549

Zeleznikow, John, 'Building Judicial Decision Support Systems in Discretionary Legal Domains' (2000) 14(3) *International Review of Law, Computers & Technology* 342

Legislation

Australia

Australian Industry Preservation Act 1906 (Cth)

Trade Practices Act 1965 (Cth)

Trade Practices Act 1974 (Cth)

Competition Policy Reform Act 1995 (Cth)

Monopolies Act 1923 (NSW)

Profiteering Prevention Act 1948 (Qld)

Fair Prices Act 1924 (SA)

Prices Act 1963 (SA)

Unfair Trading and Profit Control Act 1956 (WA)

Trade Associations Registration Act 1959 (WA)

International

Combines Investigations Act 1951 (Canada)

Trade Practices Act 1958 (New Zealand)

Monopolies and Restrictive Practices (Inquiry and Control) Act 1948 (UK)

Restrictive Trade Practices Act 1956 (UK)

Enterprise Act 2002 (UK)

Communications Act 2003 (UK)

Consumers, Estate Agents and Redress Act 2007 (UK)

Sherman Act 1890 (US)

Clayton Act 1914 (US)

Treaties

Treaty of Rome, Treaty Establishing the European Economic Community (25 March 1957)

United Nations, Universal Declaration of Human Rights (1948)

United Nations, International Covenant on Civil and Political Rights (1966) (ICCPR)

United Nations, International Covenant on Economic Social and Cultural Rights (1966) (ICESCR)

Other Sources

ABC Radio, 'States block ACCC appointment', *The World Today* 13 November 2002

<http://www.abc.net.au/worldtoday/stories/s726027.htm> at 8 February 2008

ABC News, 'Qantas fined $20 million for price fixing' 28 October 2008 <http://www.abc.net.au/news/stories/2008/10/28/2403687.htm> at 28 October 2008

ABC Television, 'Controversy surrounds ACCC appointment', *The 7.30 Report* 29 May 2003 <http://www.abc.net.au/7.30/content/2003/s867709.htm> at 6 January 2008

Ackland, Richard, 'Gov't gets Tough with New Trade Practices Laws' *The Australian Financial Review*, 1 June 1973, 5

——, 'Trade Practices Bill Cracks Down on Business', *Australian Financial Review*, 18 September 1973, 1, 18

——, 'Administration in public is a very fine discipline to have' *Australian Financial Review*, 8 October 1975, 5

Asher, Allan 'Consumers 2000: Updating the UN Guidelines' (Speech delivered at the Consumers International New Delhi Conference 5 January 1997) <http://www.accc.gov.au/content/index.phtml/itemId/96009> at 1 November 2004 ch6 f260

——, 'Sustainable Economic Growth for Regional Australia' (Speech delivered at the Competition Issues and the Regions, National Conference, Beaudesert, 3 November 1998) <http://www.accc.gov.au/content/index.phtml/itemId/96907> at 1 November 2004

——, 'Regulatory Risks' (Committee for Economic Development of Australia — Infrastructure Deficiencies: The Strategic Imperatives Conference, 3 December 1998)

——, 'The National Consumer Congress; In Pursuit of World-class Consumer Policy' (Paper presented to Third National Consumer Congress, Consumer Affairs Victoria, Melbourne, 15–17 March 2006)

Australian Bankers Association, 'Submission to the Review of the *Trade Practices Act* (Dawson Review)' (July 2002)

Australian Competition and Consumer Commission, 'Submission to the Financial System Inquiry (Wallis Inquiry)' (September 1986).

——, *Guide to Authorisation* (1999)

——, *Authorisations and Notifications, Guidelines* (May 1999)

——, *Merger Guidelines* (June 1999)

——, *Guide to Authorisation* (2001)

——, *2000–2001 Annual Report* (June 2001)

——, 'Australian Competition and Consumer Commission, Recommends Reserve Banks Using Powers To Reform Credit Card Schemes' (Press Release, 21 March 2001)

——, 'Submission to the Commission of Inquiry: Review of the Competition Provisions of the *Trade Practices Act 1974* (Dawson Review)' (2002)

——, 'ACCC Authorises Agvet Chemical Safety Program' (Press Release MR 131/02, 28 May 2002), <http://www.accc.gov.au/content/index.phtml/itemId/88082/fromItemId/378014> at 20 May 2004

——, 'ACCC Proposes to Allow Inghams to Continue Collective Negotiations with S.A. Chicken Growers' (Press Release MR 312/02, 9 December 2002)

——, 'ACCC Proposes Surgical College Reform to Help Address Surgeons Shortage' (Press Release MR 016/03, 6 February 2003)

——, 'ACCC Draft Decision Proposes to Allow Greenhouse Gas, Ozone Recovery Program' (Press Release MR 042/03, 27 February 2003)

——, 'ACCC to Endorse High Standard Voluntary Industry Codes of Conduct' (Press Release MR 168/03, 11 August 2003)

——, 'ACCC Authorises Industry Code to Restrict Manufacture of Illegal Amphetamines' (Press Release MR 229/03, 27 October 2003)

——, 'Authorising and Notifying Collective Bargaining and Collective Boycott: Issues Paper' (July 2004)

——, 'ACCC Allows Tasmanian Vegetable Growers to Collectively Bargain' (Press Release MR 257/04, 18 November 2004)

——, *Cracking Cartels: International and Australian Developments* (Law Enforcement Conference, Sydney, 24 November 2004)

——, *Guidelines on Codes of Conduct* (2005)

——, *Annual Report 2004–2005* (2005)

——, 'Guidelines for Excluding Information from the Public Register for Authorisation, Merger Clearance and Notification Processes' (2007) <http://www.accc.gov.au/content/index.phtml/itemId/776053> at 23 August 2007

——, *Authorisations and Notifications: A Summary* (2007)

——, *Guide to Authorisation* (2007)

——, *Guide to Collective Bargaining Notifications* (March 2008)

——, 'ACCC Proposes to Authorise Employment Services Collective Tendering Arrangements' (Press Release MR 183/08 26 June 2008) <http://www.accc.gov.au/content/index.phtml/itemId/833255> at 30 September 2008

Australian Development Industries Commission, 'The Trade Practices Bill 1973 — An Analysis, with Proposals for Amendment' (February 1974)

Barwick, Garfield, 'Some Aspects of Australian Proposals for Legislation for the Control of Restrictive Trade Practices and Monopolies' (Paper presented at 13th Legal Convention, Law Council of Australia, Canberra, January 1963)

——, 'Administrative Features of the Legislation on Restrictive Trade Practices' (The Robert Garran Memorial Oration, speech delivered at the Australian Regional Groups Royal Institute of Public Administration, Canberra, 3 November, 1963)

Bhojani, Sitesh, '"Public Benefits" under the *Trade Practices Act*' (Paper presented at the Joint Conference: Competition Law and the Professions, Perth, 11 April 1997)

Black, Julia, 'Managing Discretion' (Paper presented at the Australian Law Reform Commission Conference, Penalties: Policy, Principles and Practice in Government Regulation, Sydney, June 2001)

Braithwaite, John, 'Thinking Laterally: Restorative and Responsive Regulation of OHS' (Working Paper No. 13, Regulatory Institutions Network (RegNet), ANU, August 2003)

—— and Makkai, Toni, 'Trust and Compliance Administration' (Working Paper No. 9, Compliance and Governability Program, February 1993)

'Brewery Keen to Protect Interests' *Australian Financial Review*, 22 November 1963, 4

Brunt, Maureen, 'Practical Aspects of Conducting a Hearing Before the Australian Competition Tribunal' (Paper presented at The New Era of Competition Law in Australia Conference, Perth, July 1995, in Stephen Corones *Competition Law in Australia* (2006)

Business in the Community, 'Response to the Conservative Party Commission on Waste and Voluntary Agreements', December 2008 <http://www.bitc.org.uk/document.rm?id=8579 at July 2009

Business Council of Australia, 'Submission to the Committee of Inquiry: Review of the Competition Provisions of the *Trade Practices Act 1974*' (9 July 2002)

Canadian Competition Bureau, *Merger Enforcement Guidelines* (March 2001) <http://www.competitionbureau.gc.ca/internet/index.cfm?itemID=1673&Ig=e> at 15 May 2005

——, *Merger Enforcement Guidelines* (September 2004) <http://www.competitionbureay.gc.ca/internet/index.cfm?itemID=1245&Ig=e> at 15 May 2005

'Changing the ACCC Guard', *Australian Financial Review* (Sydney), 2 April 2003, 62

'Choice opposes CBA's move on Bank West', *Choice*, 3 November 2008 <http://www.choice.com.au/viewArticle.aspx?id=106593&catId=100570&tid=100008&p=1&title=Calling+for+BankWest+buyers> at 3 November 2008

Clemes, Peter, 'The Trade Practices Act Implications for the Seafood Industry' <http://proceedings.com.au/seafood2007/presentations/thursday/Thur%201345%20GB23%20Clemes.pdf> at 30 April 2009

Consumer Federation of Australia <http://www.consumersfederation.org.au/> at 1 November 2008

'Container Makers Defend Price Fixing — "We Must Co-operate"', *Australian Financial Review*, 27 February 1973, 18

Cosgrove, Michael, 'Regulation and the Australian Broadband Sector' (Paper presented at the 3rd Annual Broadband Australia Conference, 24 July 2008) <http://www.accc.gov.au/content/index.phtml/itemId/837276/fromItemId/8973>

Department of Consumer and Employment Protection (WA), 'Submission to the Productivity Commission: Review of Australia's Consumer Policy Framework' (July 2007) <http://www.pc.gov.au/__data/assets/pdf_file/0020/65810/sub099.pdf> at 30 May 2008

Department of Finance and Deregulation, Commonwealth of Australia, Office of Best Practice Regulation (OBPR) (Cost Benefit Analysis' updated <http://www.finance.gov.au/obpr/cost-benefit-analysis.html>) at 15 October 2008

European Union, 'White Paper on the Modernisation of the Rules Implementing Articles 85 and 86 of the EC Treaty', [1999] *Official Journal of the European Union* C 132/01, paras 56–57

——, 'Commission Notice on Agreements of Minor Importance Which do not Appreciably Restrict Competition Under Article 81(1) of the Treaty Establishing the European Community (de minimis)' (2001) *Official Journal of the European Union* C 368/13 para 70

——, 'Introduction', Council Regulation (EC)' No 1/2003 (16 December 2002) para 3

——, 'Guidelines on the Application of Article 81(3) of the Treaty' (2004) *Official Journal of the European Union* C 101/08

Fels, Allan, Chairman, Trade Practices Commission, 'The Future of Competition Policy' (Address to The National Press Club, Canberra, 10 October 1991)

——, 'The Public Benefit Test in the *Trade Practices Act 1974*' (Paper presented at the National Competition Policy Workshop, Melbourne, 12 July 2001)

——, 'Regulation, Competition and the Professions' (Paper presented at the Industry Economics Conference, Melbourne, 13 July 2001)

—— and Brenchley, Fred, 'Black Jobs Gap Still a Chasm After Decades', *Sydney Morning Herald* (Sydney), 13–14 December 2008, 39

Fingleton, John and Nikpay, Ali, 'Stimulating or Chilling Competition' Office of Fair Trading (United Kingdom) (Paper presented at Competition Enforcement Conference, 25 September 2008) <http://www.oft.gov.uk/news/speeches/2008/0808> at 25 October 2008

French, Robert 'Authorisation and Public Benefit — Playing with Categories of Meaningless Reference?' (Paper presented at 4th Annual University of South Australia Trade Practices Workshop, 20–21 October 2006) <http://www.fedcourt.gov.au/aboutct/judges_papers/speeches_frenchj21.rtf > at 1 September 2007

Hyden, Goran, 'Institutions Power and Policy Outcomes in Africa' (Discussion Paper No 2, Richard Crook (ed) APPP Discussion Paper Series, *The Africa Power and Politics Programme* (APPP), Overseas Development Institute, June 2008), <http://www.institutions-africa.org/filestream/20080623-discussion-paper-2-institutions-power-and-policy-outcomes-in-africa-goran-hyden-june-2008> at 25 July 2008

Kempa, Michael, Shearing, Clifford and Burris, Scott, 'Changes in Governance: A Background Review' (Paper presented at the Global Governance of Health Seminar, Salzburg, 16 December 2005) <http://www.temple.edu/lawschool/phrhcs/salzburg/Global_Health_Governance_Review.pdf> at 18 December 2007

Korczak, Viola, 'The Pharmaceutical Industry's Code of Conduct is Not Working', July 2006, Edmund Rice Centre, Newsletter, <http://www.erc.org.au/goodbusiness/page.php?pg=0607inprofile0> at 4 January 2008

Lieberman, David, Commissioner, ACCC, 'Aspects of National Competition Policy' (Speech presented at the Real Estate Institute of Australia, Annual Policy Conference, Canberra, 15 October 1998) 9

Loomer, Suzanne, Cole, Stephen and Quinn, John, 'Quantifying Efficiency Gains in a Competition Case: Sustaining a Section 96 Defence' (Paper presented at Canada's Changing Competition Regime National Conference, Toronto, 26–27 February 2003) <http://www.coleandpartners.com/pdf/Quantifying_Monograph.pdf>

Luthria, M, 'Guest Workers: A Pacific Solution that Benefits All', *Sydney Morning Herald*, 24 June 2008, 11

McCran, Terry, 'Rap Over Fels' Knuckles — Trade Practices Review Gives Him a Sole Goodbye Gift', *Daily Telegraph*, 17 April 2004, 59

Macintyre, Laura 'ACCC Considers Criminal Penalties for Cartels' *Lawyers Weekly Online* <http://www.lawyersweekly.com.au/articles/ACCC-considers-criminal-penalties-for-cartels_z165897.htm> at 10 November 2008

Maher, Imelda, 'Networking Competition Authorities in the European Union: Diversity and Change' (Paper presented at the 2002 EU Competition Law and Policy Workshop/Proceedings, 2002) 2

——, 'Regulating Competition' (Paper presented at the Regulating Law Conference, Canberra, 21 March 2003)

——, 'The Rule of Law and Agency: The Case for Competition Policy' (Working Paper No 06/01, International Economics Program 2006)

Martin, John, 'The ACCC & Small Business' (Speech delivered at the Swan Chamber of Commerce Conference, Perth, 27 October 2005) <http://www.accc.gov.au/content/index.phtml/itemId/713033> at 31 October 2008

——, 'Trade Practices Issues for Small and Medium Enterprises' (Speech delivered at the Law Institute of Victoria Commercial Law Conference, Melbourne, 18th November 2005) <http://www.accc.gov.au/content/index.phtml/itemId/715317> at 31 October 2008

——, 'Racing, Sports Betting and the ACCC' (Speech delivered at the Racing and Sports Betting Forum, Sydney, 12 December 2006) <http://www.accc.gov.au/content/item.phtml?itemId=776979&nodeId=a8da0e38e9e32a4aabae7582da16ae9a&fn=Racing,%20sports%20betting%20and%20the%20ACCC.pdf> at 31 October 2008

Nagarajan, Vijaya, 'Evaluating the Public Benefit Test' (Paper presented to the ACCC and stakeholders, Canberra, 8 April 2005) 87–9, <http://ccc.anu.edu.au/projects/project3.html> at 4 January 2008

Government of New Zealand, Commerce Commission, *Guidelines to the Analysis of Public Benefits and Detriments* (revised ed, 1997)

Ofcom, 'Taking Account of Consumer and Citizen Interests' <http://www.ofcom.org.uk/about/accoun/interests.pdf> at 28 February 2007

Papadatos, Andrew, 'Fels at Front in Fight for Fair Play', *The Daily Telegraph* (Sydney), April 24 2004, 4

Parker, Christine, Ainsworth, Paul and Stepanenko, Natalie, 'ACCC Compliance and Enforcement Project: The Impact of ACCC Enforcement Activity on Cartel Cases' (Working Paper, Centre of Competition and Consumer Policy, Australian National University, May 2004)

——and Nielsen, Vibeke, 'Do Businesses take Compliance Seriously?' (Research Paper No. 197, University of Melbourne Legal Studies, 2006)

Phillips, Leigh, 'Major Lobby Firms set to join EU register' <http://euobserver.com/9/26744> at 30 October 2008

Reserve Bank of Australia, 'Reforms of Australia's Payment Systems: Conclusions of the 2007/08 Review' (September 2008)

Robinson, Peter, 'The Man with the Plan', *Wheels Magazine*, 15 April 2008 <http://www.wheelsmag.com.au/wheels/site/articleIDs/9C2C51C8E6517AC DCA25742D0018FE70> at 20 April 2008

Round, David, 'W(h)ither Efficiencies: What is in the Public Interest? A Commentary on "The Great Efficiencies Debate in Canadian Merger Policy: A Challenge to Economic Foundations of Canadian Competition Law or a Storm in a Teacup?" by Trebilcock, Michael, 'The Great Efficiencies Debate in Canadian Merger Policy: A Challenge to the Economic Foundation of Canadian Competition Law or a Storm in a Teacup?' (Paper presented at the Fifteenth Annual Workshop of the Competition and Policy Institute of New Zealand, Auckland, 13–15 August 2004)

Samuel, Graeme, 'Big Business v Small Business' (Speech delivered at the Australian Graduate Management School Dinner, Sydney, 4 November 2004)

——, 'Taking a Holistic Approach to Assisting Small Business' (Speech delivered to the National Small Business Summit, 11 June 2008)

Scott, Colin, 'Spontaneous Accountability', in Tony Prosser et al (eds), 'Law, Economic Incentives and Public Service Culture' (Working Paper Series No 05/129, Centre for Market and Public Organisation, University of Bristol 2005)

Sexton, Elisabeth, 'Papers Must Be Released, ACCC Told' *Sydney Morning Herald* April 1 2008, 2

Spigelman AC, Honourable JJ 'Are Lawyers Lemons? Competition Principles and Professional Regulation' (The 2002 Lawyers Lecture, St James Ethics Centre, 29 October 2002)

Trade Practices Commission, Commonwealth of Australia, *Authorisation* [pamphlet] (March 1990)

Trebilcock, Michael, 'The Great Efficiencies Debate in Canadian Merger Policy: A Challenge to the Economic Foundation of Canadian Competition Law or a Storm in a Teacup?' (Paper presented at the New Zealand Competition Law Conference, Auckland, 13–15 August 2004) von Finckenstein, Konrad, 'Remarks to the 2002 Competition Law Invitational Forum' (Speech delivered at the Competition Law Invitational Forum, Cambridge, Ontario, 9 May 2002) <http://competition.ic.gc.ca/epic/internet/incb-bc.nsf/en/ct02361e.html> at 28 February 2004

www.ingramcontent.com/pod-product-compliance
Lightning Source LLC
Chambersburg PA
CBHW061243270326

41928CB00041B/3388